Anthology of Armageddon

Anthology of Armageddon

Edited and compiled by
Bernard Newman and I.O. Evans

Greenhill Books, London
Presidio Press, California

Greenhill
Books

This edition of the *Anthology of Armageddon*
first published in 1989 by Greenhill Books,
Lionel Leventhal Limited, Park House,
1 Russell Gardens, London NW11 9NN
and
Presidio Press
31 Pamaron Way, Novato, Ca.94947, U.S.A.

Copyright Denis Archer, 1935

All rights reserved. No part of this publication
may be reproduced, stored in a retrieval system
or transmitted in any form by any means electrical,
mechanical or otherwise without first seeking the
written permission of the copyright owner and
of the publisher.

British Library Cataloguing in Publication Data
Anthology of Armageddon
1. English literature, 1900 – 1945.
Special Subjects: World War 1 – Anthologies
I. Newman, Bernard, *1897 – 1968*
II. Evans, I.O (Idrisyn Oliver), *1894 –*
820.8'0358
ISBN 1–85367–047–2

Publishing History
Anthology of Armageddon was first published in 1935
(Denis Archer) and is reproduced now exactly as the
original edition, complete and unabridged.

Printed by Bookcraft (Bath) Ltd.

CONTENTS

	PAGE
INTRODUCTION	15
DEATH AT SARAJEVO. By Stephen Graham. From *St. Vitus' Day*	21
FRANCS-TIREURS. By Ludwig Renn. From *War* . .	24
REFUGEES. By Marthe McKenna. From *I Was a Spy* .	28
THE RETREAT FROM MONS. By Arthur Osburn. From *Unwilling Passenger*	29
FATIGUE. By George W. Crile. From *A Mechanistic View of War and Peace*	33
KITCHENER'S ARMY. By Donald Hankey. From *A Student in Arms*	36
IN TRAINING. By Ian Hay. From *The First Hundred Thousand*	37
RUMOUR! By The Rt. Hon. Arthur Ponsonby. From *Falsehood in War-time*	39
ANTWERP. By The Rt. Hon. Winston S. Churchill, C.H. From *The World Crisis, 1911–1914*	40
FIRST YPRES. By H. M. Tomlinson. From *All Our Yesterdays*	42
BAPTISM OF BLOOD. By Donald Hankey. From *A Student in Arms*	45
BEHIND THE LINES. By Captain W. H. L. Watson. From *Adventures of a Despatch Rider*	47
CORONEL. By The Rt. Hon. Winston S. Churchill, C.H. From *The World Crisis, 1911–1914*	50
THE RUSSIAN "STEAM-ROLLER." By John Morse. From *An Englishman in the Russian Ranks* . . .	52

CONTENTS

	PAGE
PRISONERS AND CAPTIVES. By Duncan Grinnell-Milne. From *Fortune of War*	55
TRENCH WARFARE. By Ian Hay. From *The First Hundred Thousand*	58
THE CHRISTMAS TRUCE. By Wilfrid Ewart. From *When Armageddon Came*	59
DRAFTS. By General A. A. Brussilov. From *A Soldier's Notebook*, 1914–1918	62
GAS. By Arthur Conan Doyle. From *The British Campaign in France and Flanders*, 1915	64
ON THE HOME FRONT. By H. G. Wells. From *Mr. Britling*	65
SUBMARINE AND ANTI-SUBMARINE. By "Taffrail." From *A Little Ship*	67
GALLIPOLI—THE LANDING. By John Masefield. From *Gallipoli*	70
GALLIPOLI—THE BASE AT LEMNOS. By Ernest Raymond. From *The Jesting Army*	72
GALLIPOLI—TRENCH WARFARE. By A. P. Herbert. From *The Secret Battle*	75
GALLIPOLI—THE LIGHTER SIDE. By Compton Mackenzie. From *Gallipoli Memories*	77
GALLIPOLI—THE END. By John Masefield. From *Gallipoli*	80
THE RAIDERS. By Freiherr Treusch von Buttlar Branderfels. From *Zeppelins over England*	81
THE RAIDED. By Mrs. C. S. Peel, O.B.E. From *How We Lived Then*, 1914–1918	84
HUN BAITING. By E. Sylvia Pankhurst. From *The Home Front*	86
OVER THE TOP. By H. S. Clapham. From *Mud and Khaki*	88
GENTLEMEN—TEMPORARY AND PERMANENT. By Robert Graves. From *Good-bye to All That*	92
ITALY COMES IN. By Lord Northcliffe. From *At the War*	94
GUNS AT LOOS. By Gilbert Frankau. From *Peter Jackson, Cigar Merchant*	96
INFANTRY AT LOOS. By Carroll Carstairs. From *A Generation Missing*	99

CONTENTS

	PAGE
BLOOD BATH IN CHAMPAGNE. By Henri Barbusse. (Translated from the French by Fitzwater Wray.) From *Under Fire*	100
FRONT LINE SUPREMACY. By Robert Graves. From *Goodbye to All That*	104
YPRES, 1915. By J. H. Morgan. From *Leaves from a Field Note-book*	106
AIR SKIRMISH. By Gilbert Frankau. From *Peter Jackson, Cigar Merchant*	108
ESPIONAGE. By Colonel W. Nicolai. From *The German Secret Service*	110
COUNTER-ESPIONAGE. By Basil Thomson. From *Queer People*	112
NURSE CAVELL. By Arnold Zweig. From *Young Woman of 1914*	114
CONDEMNED AS A SPY. By Sir Harry Johnston. From *Mrs. Warren's Daughter*	118
INTELLIGENCE. By Ferdinand Tuohy. From *The Crater of Mars*	121
METAL SOLDIERS. By H. G. Wells. From *Mr. Britling*	123
THE BANGALORE TORPEDO. By Private Frank Richards. From *Old Soldiers Never Die*	125
BALKAN FRONT. By Jan and Cora Gordon. From *The Luck of Thirteen*	127
THE AGONY OF SERBIA. By Dr. I. Emslie Hutton. From *With a Woman's Unit in Serbia, Salonika and Sebastopol*	129
THE RUSSIAN RETREAT. By Sophie Botcharsky and Florida Pier. From *They Knew How to Die*	131
CANNON FODDER. By John Reed. From *The War in Eastern Europe*	134
BILLETS. By R. H. Mottram. From *The Spanish Farm Triology*	136
CRYING IN THE WILDERNESS. By His Holiness Pope Benedict XV. From *The Pope on Peace and War*	139
CHRISTMAS, 1915. By Ll. Wyn Griffith. From *Up to Mametz*	141
THE WAR OF PAPER. By Mark Severn. From *The Gambardier*	143

CONTENTS

VERDUN: THE DECISION. By General Erich von Falkenhayn. From *General Headquarters, 1914–1916, and Its Critical Decisions* 145

VERDUN: THE ONSLAUGHT. By Marshal Pétain. From *Verdun* 148

VERDUN: THEY SHALL NOT PASS! By Marshal Pétain. From *Verdun* 151

GUESTS OF THE UNSPEAKABLE. By Francis Yeats-Brown. From *Golden Horn* 154

THE BATTLE OF DUBLIN. By Eimar O'Duffy. From *The Wasted Island* 157

THE LAST GRIP OF THE BEAR. By Rodion Markovits. From *Siberian Garrison* 164

RUSSIAN PRISONERS. By Erich Maria Remarque. (Translated from the German by A. W. Wheen.) From *All Quiet on the Western Front* 168

MOUNTAIN WARFARE! By Ernest Hemingway. From *A Farewell to Arms* 170

JUTLAND—NIGHT ONSLAUGHT. By the Navigating Officer of H.M.S. *Broke*. From *The Fighting at Jutland* . . 173

JUTLAND—HUMAN FLOTSAM. By the Commanding Officer of H.M.S. *Ardent*. From *The Fighting at Jutland* . . 175

JUTLAND—RETROSPECT. By The Rt. Hon. Winston S. Churchill, C.H., M.P. From *The World Crisis, 1916–1918*. Part I 177

KITCHENER. By The Rt. Hon. Lord Beaverbrook. From *Politicians and the War, 1914–1916* 178

THE SOMME—MAMETZ WOOD. By Ll. Wyn Griffith. From *Up to Mametz* 182

THE SOMME—RED BATTLE. By Private 19022. From *Her Privates We* 185

THE SOMME—A "PREMATURE." By Richard Blaker. From *Medal Without Bar* 189

THE SOMME—ENEMY PRISONERS. By Sidney Rogerson. From *Twelve Days* 192

THE SOMME—THE O.P. By Richard Blaker. From *Medal Without Bar* 193

CONTENTS

	PAGE
THE SOMME—KNIGHTS OF THE AIR. By Frederick Sleath. From *The Seventh Vial*	196
THE SOMME—THE BLOOD BATH OF THE NEW ARMIES. By The Rt. Hon. Winston S. Churchill, C.H., M.P. From *The World Crisis, 1916–1918*	199
THE NEW WARFARE. By F. Britten Austin. From *A Saga of the Sword*	200
BREAKING THE NEWS. By H. M. Tomlinson. From *All Our Yesterdays*	203
HIGH COMMAND—THE IDEAL. By Commandant Bugnet. From *Foch Talks*	206
HIGH COMMAND—THE REAL. By Sir Philip Gibbs. From *Realities of War*	206
END OF AN EPOCH. By The Rt. Hon. Winston S. Churchill, C.H., M.P. From *The World Crisis, The Eastern Front*	209
IN THE TRENCHES. By Henry Williamson. From *A Soldier's Diary of the Great War*	212
MINNIES. By James Lansdale Hodson. From *Grey Dawn—Red Night*	214
SNIPERS. By Patrick MacGill. From *The Red Horizon*	216
LICE. By Hans Carossa. From *A Roumanian Diary*	218
P.B.I. By Rowland Feilding. From *War Letters to a Wife*	219
A "BLIGHTY." By W. V. Tilsley. From *Other Ranks*	221
TRENCH BREAKFAST. By Sidney Rogerson. From *Twelve Days*	226
WINTER QUARTERS. By Edmund Blunden. From *Undertones of War*	227
BATTLE IN ROUMANIA. By Hans Carossa. From *A Roumanian Diary*	231
CONSCRIPTS. By C. E. Montague. From *Disenchantment*	234
DISCIPLINE. By Stephan Graham. From *A Private in the Guards*	237
"CONCHIES." By John W. Graham, M.A. From *Conscription and Conscience—a History, 1916–1919*	240
THE LABOUR CORPS. By Roger Pocock. From *Chorus to Adventurers*	242

CONTENTS

ACCORDING TO PLAN. By Rudolf Binding. (Translated from the German by Ian F. D. Morrow.) From *A Fatalist at War*	245
THE BASE CAMP. By Ex-Private X. From *War is War*	247
HORSES. By Erich Maria Remarque. (Translated from the German by A. W. Wheen.) From *All Quiet on the Western Front*	249
ARRAS. By Lord Dunsany. From *Unhappy Far-off Things*	250
ATTRITION. By Richard Aldington. From *Death of a Hero*	253
RUSSIA IN REVOLUTION—THE GERMAN REASONING. By Colonel W. Nicolai. From *The German Secret Service*	256
RUSSIA IN REVOLUTION—THE JOURNEY OF LENIN. By Nadezhda K. Krupskaya. From *Memories of Lenin*	257
RUSSIA IN REVOLUTION—MUTINY. By General A. A. Brussilov. From *A Soldier's Note-book, 1914–1918*	260
THE CRATER. By Patrick MacGill. From *The Brown Brethren*	262
OCCUPIED FLANDERS. By Rudolf Binding. (Translated from the German by Ian F. D. Morrow.) From *A Fatalist at War*	265
PASSCHENDAELE—THE MUD BATH. By General Sir Hubert Gough, G.C.M.G., K.C.B., K.C.V.O., etc. From *The Fifth Army*	268
PASSCHENDAELE—THE PILL-BOX. By Carroll Carstairs. From *A Generation Missing*	270
PASSCHENDAELE—GAS. By Lt.-Col. A. A. Hanbury-Sparrow. From *The Land-locked Lake*	272
PASSCHENDAELE—SHELL-FIRE. By Charles Edmonds. From *A Subaltern's War*	275
PASSCHENDAELE—WAR FROM THE AIR. By Captain Norman MacMillan, M.C., A.F.C. From *Into the Blue*	279
TANKS AT CAMBRAI. By Major W. H. L. Watson, D.S.O., D.C.M. From *A Company of Tanks*	281
THE FALL OF JERUSALEM. By W. T. Massey. From *How Jerusalem was Won*	284
CAMPAIGNING IN PALESTINE. By Donald Black. From *Red Dust*	287

CONTENTS

	PAGE
THE CORPSE FACTORY. By Arthur Ponsonby, M.P. From *Falsehood in War-time*	289
TOMMY'S SONGS. By Ex-Private X. From *War is War* .	292
TRENCH NEWSPAPERS. By Ferdinand Tuohy. From *The Crater of Mars*	295
LEAVE. By James Lansdale Hodson. From *Grey Dawn—Red Night*	299
FIELD PUNISHMENT. By Donald Black. From *Red Dust* .	300
CONDEMNED TO DEATH. By A. P. Herbert. From *The Secret Battle*	301
SHOT AT DAWN. By Brig.-Gen. F. P. Crozier, C.B., C.M.G., D.S.O. From *A Brass Hat in No Man's Land* .	303
SHELL SHOCK. By Arthur Osburn. From *Unwilling Passenger*	304
BARBED WIRE SICKNESS. By Paul Cohen-Portheim. From *Time Stood Still*	307
TUNNELLING TO FREEDOM. By Hugh Durnford. From *Escapers All*	310
EXPLOITS OF THE ESCAPING CLUB. By A. J. Evans. From *Escapers All*	311
INVETERATE ESCAPERS. By Duncan Grinnell-Milne. From *Escapers All*	315
LIMBLESS. By Paul Alverdes. From *The Whistlers' Room* .	317
THE GREAT FIRE OF SALONIKA. By Dr. I. Emslie Hutton. From *With a Woman's Unit in Serbia, Salonika and Sebastopol*	318
SUBMARINES IN THE BALTIC. By Sir Henry Newbolt. From *Submarine and Anti-Submarine*	321
THE HUNTER HUNTED. By William Guy Carr. From *By Guess and By God*	324
U-BOATS. By "Etienne." From *The Diary of a U-Boat Commander*	328
Q-BOATS. By Rear-Admiral Gordon Campbell, V.C., D.S.O. From *My Mystery Ships*	329
SUBMARINE SURGERY. By "Etienne." From *The Diary of a U-Boat Commander*	333

CONTENTS

PAGE

SHELLED CITY. By Mary Borden. From *The Forbidden Zone* . 335

GUERRILLA WARFARE. By General von Lettow-Vorbeck. From *My Reminiscences of East Africa* 338

FIFTH ARMY—RETREAT. By General Sir Hubert Gough, G.C.M.G., K.C.B., K.C.V.O., etc. From *The Fifth Army* 341

FIFTH ARMY—THE ONSLAUGHT. By Richard Aldington. From *Roads to Glory* 345

FIFTH ARMY—SAVING THE GUNS. By Charles R. Benstead. From *Retreat* 349

FIFTH ARMY—THE FLAME-THROWER. By Charles Yale Harrison. From *Generals Die in Bed* 353

FIFTH ARMY—TANK FIGHTS TANK. By F. Mitchell, M.C. From *Everyman at War* 357

FIFTH ARMY—RUNNERS. By Rowland Feilding. From *War Letters to a Wife* 359

FIFTH ARMY—NOT "ACCORDING TO PLAN." By Rudolf Binding. (Translated by I. F. D. Morrow.) From *A Fatalist at War* 360

ALBERT, 1918. By Stephen Graham. From *The Challenge of the Dead* 362

TORPEDOED. By Upton Sinclair. From *Jimmie Higgins* . 364

ST. GEORGE AND THE DRAGON. By Percival Hislam. From *How we twisted the Dragon's Tail* 367

UNITY OF COMMAND. By Commandant Bugnet. From *Foch Talks* 369

BACKS TO THE WALL. By Brigadier-General John Charteris, G.M.C., D.S.O. From *At G.H.Q.* . . . 371

THE CREEPING BARRAGE. By Edlef Köppen. From *Higher Command* 375

CHÂTEAU THIERRY. By Upton Sinclair. From *Jimmie Higgins* 376

'FLU. By Michel Corday. From *The Paris Front* . . 378

OVER THERE! By "The Diary of an Unknown Aviator." From *War Birds* 379

CONTENTS

Thought in War-Time. By I. O. Evans. From *A Junior Outline of History* 381

No Quarter! By Company-Sergeant-Major ——, M.C. From *A Suppressed Speech* 382

Protest of Conscience. By Siegfried Sassoon. From *Memoirs of an Infantry Officer* 386

The Turn of the Tide. By Theodor Plivier. From *The Kaisers Go: The Generals Remain* 390

Yanks and Limeys. By William T. Scanlon. From *God have Mercy on Us!* 392

Death in the Forest. By Edlef Köppen. From *Higher Command* 393

The Black Day of the German Army. By General Ludendorff. From *My War Memories, 1914–1918* . 396

The Last Hundred Days. By "Saml. Pepys, Junr." From *A Last Diary of the Great Warr* . . 400

Advance! By Carroll Carstairs. From *A Generation Missing* 404

Break Through. By Bernard Newman. From *The Cavalry Went Through* 406

Doughboys in Action. By William T. Scanlon. From *God have Mercy on Us!* 410

Armageddon. By Antony Bluett. From *With Our Army in Palestine* 412

Mutiny. By Theodor Plivier. From *The Kaiser's Coolies* . 416

Surrender. By B. H. Liddell Hart. From *A History of the World War* 420

Armistice. (Translated by Colonel T. Bentley Mott.) From *The Memoirs of Marshal Foch* 425

Armistice Night. By Ferdinand Tuohy. From *The Crater of Mars* 428

The Fourteen Points. By President Wilson . . . 432

The Peace Terms. By I. O. Evans. From *A Junior Outline of History* 434

Personalities of the Peace Conference. By Georges Clemenceau. From *Grandeur and Misery of Victory* . 436

Demobilisation. By Rowland Feilding. From *War Letters to a Wife* 440

CONTENTS

	PAGE
THE HERO'S HOME-COMING. By Guy Chapman. From *A Passionate Prodigality*	441
RECOVERY. By André Maurois. From *The Silence of Colonel Bramble*	444
MEMORIES. By Henry Williamson. From *The Wet Flanders Plain*	446
THE COST OF ARMAGEDDON. From *The World's Almanac for 1933*	449
TWENTY YEARS AFTER. By S. F. Hatton. From *The Yarn of a Yeoman*	450

Anthology of Armageddon

INTRODUCTION

To date some twenty thousand books have been written about the War. Yet no critic will deny that the *classic* war book has yet to be published. It can scarcely be expected so soon: the War is too near to be viewed dispassionately, its panorama too vast to be seen in adequate perspective. The world had to wait forty years for Tolstoi's *War and Peace*, and a hundred years for Hardy's *The Dynasts*. Maybe the epic of our own conflict will not appear in our own time.

This does not mean that the existing books are without quality—far from it. There is at least one admirable history of the War; there are hundreds of first-rate and sincere sketches of its details—particularly of its horrors; many books of reminiscences continue its atmosphere right up to our own day, since in them politicians and generals wage an internecine strife which would be amusing were it not so tragic.

But no *one* of these books gives anything like a complete picture of the War. A history is necessarily concerned with important facts, and spares no space for the mental and bodily torment of men; books by fighting men, on the contrary—and understandably—reflect the individual viewpoint, ignoring general causes in the overwhelming horror of blood and mud; and leaders are more anxious to justify themselves than to contribute to the true story of the War.

If, therefore, a man could read the whole or even representative samples of all these books, he would get a far truer picture of the War than a single book could possibly give. To men of limited leisure this is impossible, and herein lies our excuse for presenting this Anthology. From over one hundred and fifty books, well-known or unknown, short extracts have been taken. Linking up the extracts is a connecting narrative which should not only be of use to the general reader, but should also make this book unique among Anthologies, enabling it to be read straight through without effort, and not to depend for its value upon mere isolated extracts to be read casually and at random.

This, then, is an account of the Great War, written by those who took part in it. Front-line soldiers, sailors, airmen, high commanders directing the operations from afar, statesmen seeking to steer their nations through these perilous times, war-resisters suffering imprisonment and torture, revolutionaries hoping to use the conflict for the furtherance of their own ideals, politicians and publicists, civilians watching the decaying *morale* of their people—all have contributed to this record of battle, murder and sudden death.

The object of the compilers has been to show the War as it really was, its honour as well as its horror, its humours no less than its hatreds. They did not aim to produce an "anti-war" book, to set out merely the evils of competitive nationalism, to force a foregone conclusion on the minds of their readers. They seek to act as sociological investigators, studying and setting out the process of an experiment in human relationships. Such and such are the facts; thus and thus the War happened; and now it is for the reader to use his own judgment, to decide whether war is tolerable in the modern world, or whether it is worth while making an effort to abolish it forever.

The editors have two qualifications for their task: both took part in the War, and can describe it from the personal point of view; both have studied the directional side of the War for many years. Nevertheless, they realise full well the imperfections of their Anthology. No Anthology ever pleased everyone, since individual tastes are so divergent, and even like tastes so individual. Much excellent material has perforce been omitted through sheer lack of space. If, therefore, the reader seeks in vain for some author whose descriptions he has found especially impressive, let him remember that the number of books written on the War is legion, that the mere list of titles of war-books up to 1920 alone fills a special catalogue of two hundred pages in the British Museum, and that to quote from every such work would mean the unsatisfactory course of restricting each extract to an isolated sentence!

INTRODUCTION 17

Further—although authors and publishers have been extraordinarily helpful—some of our original selections had to be abandoned for lack of the necessary permission to reproduce. This explains one or two obvious omissions—T. E. Laurence's *Revolt in the Desert*, for example. Thus the neglect of what may be your own favourite War book is not necessarily the fault of the editors.

Wherever possible, extracts have been chosen typical of the angle on the War for which each writer is famed. Remarque is the prototype of " horror " war books, and hence has been chosen to illustrate the morbid dreariness of war psychology. H. G. Wells, in spite of his spirited narrations of battle in the air, is above all the historian of the social aspects of the conflict, and hence has been used to show the realities of life on the " home front." Ian Hay's humorous descriptions of the training of Kitchener's Army have been used to develop the lighter side of army life.

It has been no part of the compilers' task to apportion praise or guilt among individuals, and hence the whole class of literature in which generals, admirals and politicians endeavour, in the most dignified of English, to pass the blame for various ineptitudes on to one another has been largely excluded, entertaining reading though it makes. The quiet determination of the common man in the line of battle is the keynote of the Anthology, as it was of the War.

Actually, the ordinary man has been most neglected in War literature: he is, as usual, almost inarticulate. Not one per cent of the books on the War have been written by ordinary men. Look at the names of the best-known British authors of War books—Blunden, Sassoon, Graves and the rest. These men are *poets*; their reactions to the filth and horror of war are profoundly interesting and exquisitely phrased; but they are not the reactions of the miners, navvies and clerks who made up the vast bulk of the British Army.

The editors have naturally aimed at such a construction as to make the Anthology attractive to widely spread classes of readers; to ex-service men, for the memories it will revive; to women, whose judgment of their men was warped by the spate of war books some years ago, in which the soldier was generally represented as a lecherous and drunken brute; to general adult readers, confused by the apparently conflicting pictures of the War; and particularly to the new generation which never knew the War, and whose view has not yet been formed. We do seriously suggest that—failing the appearance of the War classic—a story which gives very many points of view is essential.

The editors offer their sincerest thanks to all the authors and publishers whose willing co-operation has made this Anthology possible. A full list of authors will be found in the index at the end of the book. The publishers by whose courtesy extracts are included are:

G. Allen & Unwin, Ltd.; E. Arnold & Co.; J. W. Arrowsmith (London) Ltd.; Arthur Barker, Ltd.; Ernest Benn, Ltd.; W. Blackwood & Sons; Jonathan Cape, Ltd.; Cassell & Co., Ltd.; W. & R. Chambers, Ltd.; Chatto & Windus; R. Cobden-Sanderson, Ltd.; W. Collins, Sons & Co., Ltd.; Constable & Co.; Peter Davies, Ltd.; J. M. Dent & Sons; Dial Press, Inc.; Doubleday, Doran & Co., Inc.; Gerald Duckworth & Co., Ltd.; Elkin Mathews & Marrot, Ltd.; Faber and Faber, Ltd.; Victor Gollancz, Ltd.; Grayson & Grayson, Ltd.; John Hamilton, Ltd.; G. G. Harrap & Co., Ltd.; William Heinemann, Ltd.; Hodder & Stoughton, Ltd.; Hurst & Blackett, Ltd.; Hutchinson & Co. (Publishers) Ltd.; Jarrolds, Publishers (London) Ltd.; Herbert Jenkins, Ltd.; John Lane, the Bodley Head, Ltd.; T. Werner Laurie, Ltd.; Martin Lawrence, Ltd.; Longmans Green & Co., Ltd.; Macmillan & Co., Ltd.; The Medici Society; Andrew Melrose, Ltd.; Methuen & Co., Ltd.; John Murray; Ivor Nicholson & Watson, Ltd.; Stanley Paul & Co., Ltd.; Putnam & Co., Ltd.; Rich & Cowan, Ltd.; Charles Scribner's Sons; Martin Secker, Ltd.; Williams & Norgate, Ltd.

The thanks of the editors are gratefully extended to authors and publishers alike. In addition, special thanks are due to Major Deedes, for permission to use the extract from Sir Harry Johnston's *Mrs. Warren's Daughter*; to Mr. C. B. Purdom in respect of the extract from *Everyman at War*; to Sir George Sutton and Sir Campbell Stuart for the extract from Lord Northcliffe's *At the War*; to Mr. John Gawsworth and Mr. Herbert Ewart for the selection from Wilfrid Ewart's *When Armageddon Came*; to Mrs. W. H. L. Watson for the extracts from her late husband's books *Adventures of a Despatch Rider* and *A Company of Tanks*. We would also like to express our great appreciation of the friendly assistance of several of the leading literary agents, including Messrs. Christy & Moore, Ltd.; Messrs. Curtis Brown, Ltd.; Messrs. Hughes Massie & Co.; Messrs. A. P. Watt & Son; Messrs. Raymond Savage, Ltd.; Messrs. J. B. Pinker & Sons; Mr. W. A. Bradley; and the Incorporated Society of Authors, Playwrights and Composers.

For some years prior to 1914, Europe had been an armed camp—an arsenal of guns waiting to go off. The necessary spark was struck by Gavro Princip, one of a band of revolutionary Slavs, when on June 28th, 1914, he assassinated at Sarajevo the Archduke Franz Ferdinand, heir to the Austro-Hungarian Empire.

DEATH AT SARAJEVO
From *St. Vitus' Day*.[1]
By Stephen Graham

They walked leisurely down the street toward the quay. Princip felt he had plenty of time. The Archduke must pass him if he followed the scheduled route which had been printed in the papers. The car with the Deputy Mayor and the representative and two police officials came shooting along at a great pace, sounding its klaxon and clearing the roadway. Princip still sauntered on with Semes alighting behind him, holding on as it were to his coat tails.

Suddenly the Archduke's car came round the corner, taking the curve at a great pace with Count Harrach hanging on to the opposite side to that on which Princip was walking. That was wrong. That was not the way to the hospital. Potiorek at once saw the mistake and shouted to the chauffeur.

" Stop, stop ; turn about ! You're going wrong," he called. Ferdinand remained quite impassive ; he did not know the geography of Sarajevo, but the chauffeur was scared by the shout, and, used to obeying orders peremptorily, put on all the force of his brakes at once. The automobile came to a sudden halt with a great jerk which caused the august personages to lean forward. And it came to a halt opposite

[1] Published by Ernest Benn, Ltd.

the only one of the conspirators who had a deep unchanging will to kill. Suddenly by a miraculous chance Princip was face to face with the man he had determined to kill. He mechanically lifted his hand and shot him near to the heart. Princip was terribly calm. He knew that his bullet had done its work; he saw the massive Ferdinand fall forward. He saw the revengeful brutal face of Potiorek and slightly shifted his aim to kill him also.

It was quiet and sudden. The chauffeur did not start the car; he was not sure where to go. He was in such a daze he did not even realise that the Archduke was killed. Von Harrach was spellbound and did not know what to do. An amateur photographer calmly took a snapshot. Semes had seen enough; he bolted back to his café thoroughly sobered by murder. Sophie herself did not realise for a moment that her husband had been shot. She could not understand why Potiorek had stopped the car there. Someone had fired a shot. Surely! She looked round, and suddenly saw her husband's collapsed figure and screamed. She stood up to clasp him to herself and she stood up just at the moment when Princip fired his second shot, and as she swayed in agony toward her Ferdinand her body crossed the path of the bullet and she fell back in her seat in an immediate death struggle. The dying Ferdinand did not know that she was dying also. He had recognised her loving anxiety for him; he turned to her feebly as if to caress her.

"Sophie, Sophie, live for our children," he moaned.

But Sophie did not answer. She was already unconscious. They loved one another, this Archduke Ferdinand and poor unrecognised Archduchess Sophie. That was the finest thing in their lives, and in the thought of them personally that love causes all else to be forgiven. . . . And they died together!

There was a moment of awe, and then hubbub indescribable. Gendarmes and officers sprang at Princip with drawn swords. A Mohametan police agent dashed in and seized him by the wrist, but at the same moment a sympathiser with Princip dealt the spy a terrible blow in the stomach; he relaxed his hold and Princip cracked him on the head with the

DEATH AT SARAJEVO

butt end of his revolver. But there was now a clash of swords and sabres about his shoulders. Staggering back toward a shop entrance he got the phial of prussic acid out of his pocket, but he was being so roughly handled he could not get it properly to his lips. The poison went half into his open mouth and half over his face and clothes. Still he might have died then, but he at once vomited, and almost choked. He could not have retained a drop of cyanide in his body—for he survived. Sabres were slashing at him; someone dealt him a blow that broke one of his ribs. There were only hostile cries about him now, though a few yards away another Slav was being mistaken for him, and was defending himself against the police.

A gendarme struck a blow at Princip's stomach and withdrew an injured hand. Something heavy and metallic fell with a crash upon the pavement. It was the bomb which the gendarme had struck out of its fastening at Princip's middle.

" Bomb, bomb, look out ! " cried someone in the crowd. " Bomb, bomb, bomb. . . . ! "

Princip gave it a kick and the wild men with swords and sabres jumped back in fear. The poison had failed. There was only one thing left. Princip turned his revolver against his own head. His hand was on the trigger when someone dashed out of a barber's shop on the corner, he had been having a shave during the affair, and he snatched the revolver away and quixotically saved Princip's life. Then someone struck him with a sword on the nape of the neck and he became unconscious, and was hauled away to the Town Hall. The car with the dead Archduke and Archduchess was slowly backed from Franz Joseph Strasse to the bridge over the river, their bridge from this world to the next, the bridge that led from peace to war. For four years afterwards it was known as the Bridge of Ferdinand and Sophie, and their figures in stone were wrought at the entrance, one on each side of it and looking up the fatal strasse where Austria met her first defeat. But when liberation came the figures were carted away and the bridge became the bridge of the hero of the liberation movement, the Bridge of Princip.

* * *

With such pretext, the nations were not long in disclosing their long-smouldering enmities. Within five weeks the greater part of Europe was at war, and the German masses were pouring through Belgium.

Apprehensive of irregular acts of warfare on the part of the civilian inhabitants, the invaders displayed a certain severity, which to the inhabitants appeared as merciless cruelty.

FRANCS-TIREURS

From *War*.[1]

By Ludwig Renn

After a while I gathered myself together. I must do something. I went below to see how the wounded were getting on. Lehmann's head had sunk forward. He was pale and snoring with his mouth open. Sander was still gazing motionlessly into the air. He is dying, I thought, and wanted to pray. But I could not.

I went into the yard and looked round the corner of the house. There the dead lay on the road. What if there were wounded among them? One could bring them help now. But I hadn't any more spirit left. The sunshine and the roaring of the guns made me feel ill.

I crept upstairs again and sat down on the chair. Lamm was standing in the window looking out. How horribly long this day was!

"Some men coming!" said Lamm suddenly. "Sergeant Ernst with some men."

I got up. They were alive still! But they had better not go on too far! Curious that they hadn't stopped a bullet or two yet.

I ran down. Ernst came straight into the yard with two sections.

"Where is the house occupied by the *franc-tireurs*?"

He liked to show off his education a bit.

I pointed it out to him.

[1] Published by Martin Secker.

"We'll take the factory. You lead us."

I fetched my rifle and the hatchet. "It would be better, sergeant, to go in single file behind that next house."

I ran behind the waggon and a little kitchen garden into the narrow passage between the quarry wall and the house. I saw the back wing of the factory only about a hundred yards before me. I rattled the door. It was barred. I set my rifle against the wall and banged at the iron lock with the blunt head of the hatchet. While I was doing this Ernst came running with his first few men.

"Look out!" I shouted, for I was drawing back for my second blow, and there was very little room in the passage. I brought the hatchet down with both hands. The door groaned. The latch fell on the stones.

I drew back for another blow. A shot rang out sharply. It must have hit just behind me.

"You damned dogs!" shouted Ernst.

Another shot. Some kind of noise behind me. I struck again, but with less force this time.

"Smash the door in!" someone called.

I turned the hatchet round the other way. Several shots crackled. One went off at my ear, deafening me. I struck again. The hatchet bit all right, but the door was very strong. I tugged the hatchet out of the wood. More shots.

"Over here!" cried Ernst, and he ran with several of his men out of the passage towards the factory. I paid no attention but struck again. The rifle-shots came still hotter. It seemed to me as if shrapnel was coming over, too.

"Give it here," cried someone behind me. I gave him the hatchet. The bullets were not coming our way. I could see no sign of Ernst.

"Push!" shouted the other man. We put our shoulders against the door, which was already cracked. It snapped and gave way. I seized my rifle and ran in. In the lobby stood a man and a woman with their hands raised above their heads, barring my way.

"Get out!" I shouted, pushed the man aside with my elbow and ran up the stairs. I tore open a door. Two children were standing there trembling. I had no time for them. Several of our men came running behind me. I rushed to the window. There lay the factory. But fruit trees partly concealed it. To its left behind a grass-grown wall a few men were lying and firing across at it. That must be Ernst.

"Occupy all the windows!" I cried. "These cursed trees!"

I ran out. In their fear the children ran right between my legs. I tore open the next door.

"Here!" I shouted to two men who were still coming upstairs. "Shoot at everybody you can see in the factory!" These men were all so slow!

I ran downstairs. The man and woman were still standing with their hands up, and they looked at me expressionlessly. I rushed to the lower windows which faced towards the factory. Here the trees did not cut off so much of the view. Men were firing from the windows upstairs.

Over by the wall I saw Ernst standing up; he began to run across to us. Two men followed him. But there were some men still lying there; how many I could not make out. I ran to the door.

"The cursed pack!" cried Ernst. "If we once get them there will be no quarter!" He was out of breath and panting with rage.

The other two came running in, one of them with his helmet shot through. He took it off. Blood ran out, over his forehead and down the right side of his nose to his mouth. He stuck out his tongue and licked it up. "Have a look and see what it is." He bent his head forward. A short strip of his hair was matted with blood.

"It has only grazed your scalp," said Ernst.

"I didn't think it was much," he laughed.

"There seems to be a door to a cellar here, sergeant," said someone, pointing to a square trap-door in the floor. The man and the woman looked at him, still holding their hands up.

I pulled at a little ring, and the trap-door opened. There was a narrow little stair.

Ernst shouted a command to the man. He went out and came back with a candle. Ernst went down the stair with one of his men. I was thinking again of the wounded beside the wall. I ground my teeth with helpless rage.

Then out of the trap-door rose a civilian smiling evilly. He roused a horrible feeling in me.

He turned round and looked contemptuously at the man and the woman with their hands raised. Oh, how horrible it all was! Why had nobody told them yet that they could let their arms down again?

Ernst came out and held out a packet of cartridges to the man who was smiling. The man shrugged his shoulders and said something. Ernst spoke to both the men. The one who had been in the cellar answered only with a mocking grin. The other crossed himself over his brow and his heart and between times always raised his arms again. My anxiety rose.

"There's no help for it," said Ernst suddenly in German. "They must be shot according to military law."

I had been afraid of that, but now all at once I felt cool.

"Excuse me, sergeant," I said, and I was surprised at my own coolness, "that's military law, perhaps, but wouldn't it be better to say to them: 'If you'll fetch in the wounded out there, then the matter's settled.'? Perhaps there are wounded men in the road, too. And the Belgians surely won't shoot at their own people."

Ernst looked at me thoughtfully. "Well, they don't deserve it!" He turned to the men, who had been following our conversation intently without apparently understanding any of it.

Ernst sent them out and posted a man at the door with orders to shoot at once if they attempted to escape.

I went across to the woman and signed to her to take her hands down. She obeyed. But someone came out of a door, and she lifted her arms again, trembling.

"The swine!" growled the soldier at the door. "Be careful there!" he bellowed across, and raised his rifle. I looked over his shoulder. "The dirty lot," he cursed, "they're letting the legs of the wounded men drag on the ground. But now they're paying better attention!"

* * *

REFUGEES

From *I was a Spy*.[1]

By Marthe McKenna

Day by day rumour swept through the country towns of Flanders. Then there came that distant roll of gun-fire, and sudden flashes would flicker across the skyline of nights. Our troops were falling back. Liège had fallen, its dozen forts pounded to dust beneath the ruthless iron heel of Ludendorff. Namur, held by our men till the last, had also crumbled to a heap of jagged stone and scrap-iron. Every morning we learned that the relentless grey wave had come closer, and there we remained, stunned, unable to believe that one day we should see men in spiked helmets in the village street.

One day a little donkey-cart piled high with mattresses and bundles, accompanied by a tall young peasant woman, with two little children who trotted at her heels, halted in the roadway outside our house.

Her lips were tightly set and she held a far-away look in her eyes as she leaned over the gate.

" Have you any food you can spare for the children, please ? Perhaps I could do some work for you in payment for the food."

I brought the little family into the kitchen, where my mother attended to them. The young mother had heard nothing of her husband since the day he hurried to join his regiment. Their village had been shelled out of existence, she and her children had walked for three days, she had no more money to buy food. They had heard they would find shelter and rations at Ypres. There were thousands more like them, and even now they were pouring through the village street. Later when I went shopping the entire roadway was blocked with creaking carts, sweating animals and weary dust-smothered human beings. Animals were eating the hedges and the grass in the front gardens unchecked. One horse lay dead in the shafts, and the owner, a young well-dressed woman, sat on the step sobbing bitterly. Her husband was dead, her home

---

[1] Published by Jarrolds (Publishers), Ltd.

razed to the ground, she had lost her little son in the mêlée, and was penniless. The children hopped in and out cheerfully nothing daunted by their plight, but bravest were the old white-haired men and women, many of them lying sick on their bundles. Vituperatively they cursed the invaders, but they looked upon all that happened with philosophical eyes.

The stream of refugees seemed never-ending. Westroosebeke became a huge temporary camp. As can be understood many were starving, but the houses in the village were rarely broken into. Our house, barns and outhouses were packed with unfortunates, as were all the other houses. Old people died and were hastily buried and their relations passed on. Small children were making their way across country by themselves. One day three stragglers, cut off from the Army, limped into Westroosebeke. It was our first sight of men who had emerged from the flaming furnace. In their eyes was the look of wild beasts, filthy, unshaven, their tattered uniforms streaked with blood and dirt, their blistered feet bursting through their boots, fatigue had turned their speech to an incoherent babble. Then the sky darkened, and the rain hissed down on the turmoil, but the long procession walked on doggedly through the mire, often at nights sleeping in the sticky, saturated pastures.

* * *

THE RETREAT FROM MONS
From *Unwilling Passenger*.[1]
By Arthur Osburn

We entered the little town of Thulin in darkness and silence; indeed, I was rather surprised how silent everything had suddenly become. There was but one building that had any light in it. As we passed it I was besieged by a party of Belgian priests and nuns.

"M'sieur is a doctor? Please come in at once—in here! There are many English wounded! There are no doctors! We do not know what to do!"

[1] Published by Faber & Faber, Ltd.

I dismounted and entered what was evidently the Mairie or Town Hall. The steps were thronged with a jostling crowd of wounded. Many excited Belgian peasants and Sisters of Mercy were carrying in mattresses, straw, jugs of water and old sheets of bandages.

The scene inside was one with which I was soon to be only too familiar. It was packed with wounded, lying down, crouching or standing; the stairs were blocked with sitting cases, the passages with loaded stretchers. There were several whose hastily applied tourniquets had evidently slipped, lying in a dead faint from loss of blood. Everywhere lights and confusion and a babel of tongues—Cockney "French," Flemish and broken English. I spoke only a little French, and getting hold of the most responsible looking of the priests and the older of the Catholic Sisters, I urged them to keep the badly wounded cases on the ground floor, and send all the slightly wounded cases up to the rooms on the upper floors of the building; they had started doing the very reverse!

"But why, m'sieur?"

"Because in case of fire, you will never get the stretcher cases down again in time, if you carry them up those narrow stairs."

"Fire! But why should there be a fire? The bad cases will be more comfortable upstairs. Besides, there are far too many slight cases to put up in the small rooms above. And some of the upper rooms are locked—half-full of the town records."

"Never mind," I said. "Burst the door open. Let all the wounded who can walk go up and leave the stairs and passages free. They can sit down on the floor in the upstairs rooms."

We began gradually to get the place in some sort of order. The palliasses and mattresses which were being brought in we arranged in rows. Straw had been put down where there were no mattresses; much too much straw—the harvest was just beginning.

The Sisters were giving the men cigarettes. I tried to dissuade them. "Don't encourage them to smoke here, or you will soon have all this straw on fire."

"Soldiers! Poor English soldiers! Not smoke! After such a brave battle!" They gazed at me, astonished. I might as well have ordered them to stop the men breathing.

Soon I was terribly busy with the worst cases. Only two can I remember in all that confusion. One badly wounded in the head, yet conscious enough to point to the man lying next to him.

"Sir, that man alongside blew off his own right hand recharging a fuse to blow up a bridge across that canal which the Germans had captured. He went back alone of his own accord to do it himself—the first charge wouldn't go off. If he hadn't stopped the Germans, they would have enfiladed our whole line."

The men were, I think, both Royal Engineers. I dressed the stump of the hero of the bridge and hastily scribbled his name and number in my notebook.

"You won't be forgotten," I said; "you deserve a V.C. I'll see that the General hears about it."

I was in the midst of giving instructions as to each wounded man not injured in the stomach having at least a litre of milk a day when an excited Sister seized me by the arm.

"M'sieur! Go at once! The Germans are here!"

"Here!"

"Yes, m'sieur, in the street outside! No! Not that way! By the side door—to the right! Quick! Quick!"

I dashed to the side door to find my groom and orderly, looking pale and excited. They, too, had just seen the Germans, indeed had actually rubbed shoulders with them in the darkness outside. We all three flung ourselves on our horses and dashed away from the Mairie, not knowing in the least which direction to take.

A light rain had begun to fall and the cobblestones were greasy. Shots behind added wings to our speed. Galloping madly in the darkness, slithering and skidding through those silent streets, we were nearly down half a dozen times.

Where was everybody? What had become of the British Army? Why had nobody told me? Where were we galloping to?

"*Où sont lès Chasseurs Anglais? Où sont les Dragons de*

la Garde?" I shouted through the echoing streets, the excitement playing havoc with my scanty French. There was no answer to my ill-judged questions, only shots and the echoes of our clattering hoofs.

Suddenly we were fired at point-blank from in front; the flash showed a group of dismounted cavalry on the left of the road. Someone shouted in French: "*Qui va là?*"

The voice had an unmistakable English accent.

"Who's that?" I shouted. "I'm 4th Dragoon Guards."

"Ninth Lancers," answered the voice. "Where the hell have you come from?"

. . . . . .

Presently a bright light flared up on the sky behind us; some of the refugees turned, their white faces lit by the glare.

"What's that?" I asked.

"It must be the Town Hall, m'sieur. It is the only building of that size in Thulin!"

So the expected had happened! I have always had a horror of fire, especially in hospitals; I thought of that crowded building with so many nearly helpless men and confused and frightened priests and Sisters—of the suffocating blaze and smoke from damp straw, khaki clothing and mattresses. How ghastly! But with all that straw and all those men smoking it needed no prophet to foresee what was almost a certainty.

And my V.C. hero—too weak from loss of blood from that jagged stump to walk! Poor devil! He had looked as white as a sheet—was he at that moment being burnt alive?

I fumbled for my notebook. At least this gallant soldier should have posthumous honour—his mother and his relations, his corps and his country should know of his self-sacrifice. My notebook was gone! I had had it in my hand when the Sister warned me. That panic-stricken dash from the Town Hall, the mad ride over those greasy cobblestones, accounted only too easily for the loss. Should any Royal Engineer who fought near Thulin that night read these lines, possibly even now the man's name might be discovered. Perhaps he has already been posthumously honoured, or best of all, possibly he escaped from that blazing hospital and was cared for by the enemy. As I learnt afterwards, the Germans—all things considered—devoted great care and skill, sometimes were even very kind, to our wounded.

* * *

FATIGUE

From *A Mechanistic View of War and Peace*.[1]

By George W. Crile

Perhaps one of the greatest retreats in history was that of the allied armies from Mons to the Marne. Again and again I listened to the story from men who participated in that retreat and their personal experiences varied but little.

After a sustained and heavy action at Mons, being overpowered by the enemy, the allied armies began the retirement which continued for nine days and nights. One hundred and eighty miles of marching without making camp is the story of that great retreat in which the pace was set by the enemy. Only rarely were sufficiently long halts made for the men to catch a few moments of rest. Food and water were scarce and were irregularly supplied.

The point of paramount interest in that retreat is found in the sleep phenomena experienced by these men. It has been shown that animals subjected to the most favourable conditions, kept from exertion or worry, supplied with plenty of food, and in good hygienic surroundings, do not survive longer than from five to eight days without sleep. The mere maintenance of the conscious state is at the expense of the brain, the adrenals, and the liver, and these changes are identical with the changes in these organs wrought by exertion, infection and emotion. The changes wrought by these activators *can be repaired only during sleep. Sleep, therefore, is as essential as food and air*. In this retreat from Mons to the Marne we have an extraordinary human experiment, in which several hundred thousand men secured little sleep during nine days, and in addition made forced marches and fought one of the greatest battles in history.

[1] Published by T. Werner Laurie, Ltd.

How then did these men survive nine days apparently without opportunity for sleep? They did an extraordinary thing—they slept while they marched! Sheer fatigue slowed down their pace to a rate that would permit them to sleep while walking. When they halted they fell asleep. They slept in water, and on rough ground, when suffering the pangs of hunger and of thirst, and even when severely wounded. They cared not for capture, not even for death, if only they could sleep.

The unvaried testimony of the soldiers was that every one at times slept on the march. They passed through villages asleep. When sleep deepened and they began to reel, they were wakened by comrades. They slept in water, on stones, in brush, or in the middle of the road as if they had suddenly fallen in death. With the ever on-coming lines of the enemy, no man was safe who dropped out of the ranks, for no matter on what pretext he fell out, sleep conquered him. Asleep, many were captured. That the artillery men slept on horseback was evidenced by the fact that *every man lost his cap*.

The complete exhaustion of the men in this retreat from Mons to the Marne is vividly told by Dr. Gros of the American Ambulance, who with others went to the battlefield of the Marne to collect the wounded. On their way to Meaux they met many troops fleeing, all hurriedly glancing back, looking more like hunted animals than men, intent only on reaching a haven of safety.

When the ambulances arrived at Meaux at midnight they found the town in utter darkness. Not a sound was heard in the street, not a light was seen. The only living things were hundreds of cats. They called, they shouted, in vain they tried to arouse someone. At last they succeeded in awakening the mayor, to whom they said: " Can you tell us in what village we will find the wounded? We were told there were many here." The mayor replied: " My village is full of wounded. I will show you." With the aid of a flickering lamp, they threaded their way through dark streets to a dilapidated school building. Not a light! Not a sound! There was the stillness of death! They rapped louder, there was no response! Pushing open the door, they found the building packed with wounded—over five hundred—with all kinds of wounds. Some were dying, some dead, but every one was in deep sleep. Bleeding, yet asleep; legs shattered, yet asleep; abdomen and chest torn wide open, yet asleep. They were lying on the hard floor or on bits of straw. Not a groan, not a motion, not a complaint—only sleep!

Surgical aid, the prospect of being taken to a good hospital, the thought of food and drink, of being removed from the range of the enemies' guns, awakened no interest. There was a sleepy indifference to everything in life. They had reached the stage of unconditional exhaustion, and desired only to be left alone.

Dr. Gros' ambulance corps took the worst cases first. These were soldiers with shattered legs and arms, some with compound fractures, some with penetrating wounds of the abdomen and chest. They made little or no complaint on being picked up, placed in ambulances and transported. The only sound they uttered was when the torn flesh, glued to the floor by dried blood, was pulled loose.

Thus these men, goaded by shot and shell, and the ever-advancing army; for nine days without adequate sleep or food; in constant fear of capture, and finally wounded—thus these men, more dead than alive, came to the hospital: and thus they slept on while their wounds were dressed.

After deep sleep for two or three days, during which they wanted neither food nor drink, they began to be conscious of their surroundings: they asked questions; they experienced pain; they had discomforts and wants; they had returned from the abysmal oblivion of sleep.

That these men had conquered the overwhelming impulse to sleep sufficiently to continue marching and fighting during that nine days' retreat testifies to the dominating power of battle. That a soldier falls asleep during the dressing of severe wounds tells a trenchant story of the intensity of the stimulus that kept him awake. The exhausted, half-dead appearance of these soldiers was usually transformed by one long seance of sleep during which the brain, the adrenals, and the liver had in some measure overcome their physical exhaustion.

* * *

To support the Regular Army, Kitchener appealed for recruits, and the flower of British youth rushed to the Colours.

KITCHENER'S ARMY
From *A Student in Arms*.[1]
By Donald Hankey

"The New Army," "Kitchener's Army," we go by many names. The older sergeants—men who have served in regular battalions—sometimes call us "Kitchener's Mob," and swear that to take us to war would be another "Massacre of the Innocents." At other times they affirm that we are a credit to our instructors (themselves); but such affirmations have become rarer since beer went up to three-pence a pint.

We are a mixed lot—a triumph of democracy, like the Tubes. Some of us have fifty years to our credit, and only own to thirty; others are sixteen and claim to be eighteen. Some of us enlisted for glory and some for fun, and a few for fear of starvation. Some of us began by being stout, and have lost weight; others were seedy, and are filling out. Some of us grumble, and go sick to escape parades; but for the most part we are aggressively cheerful, and were never fitter in our lives. Some miss their glass of claret, others their fish-and-chips; but as we all sleep on the floor, and have only one suit, which is rapidly becoming very disreputable, you would never tell t'other from which.

We sing as we march. Such songs we sing! All about coons and girls, parodies about Kaiser Bill, and sheer unadulterated nonsense. We shall sing:

> "Where's yer girl?
> Ain't yer got none?"

as we march into battle.

Battle! Battle, murder and sudden death! Maiming, slaughter, blood, extremities of fear and discomfort and pain! How incredibly remote all that seems! We don't believe in it

[1] Published by Andrew Melrose, Ltd.

really. It is just a great game we are learning. It is part of the game to make little short rushes in extended order, to lie on our bellies and keep our heads down, snap our rifles and fix our bayonets. Just a game, that's all, and then home to tea.

Some of us think that these young officers take the game a jolly sight too seriously. Twice this week we have been late for dinner, and once they routed us out to play it at night. That was a bit too thick! The canteen was shut when we got back and we missed our pint.

Anyhow, we are Kitchener's Army, and we are quite sure it will be all right. Just send us to Flanders, and see if it ain't. We're Kitchener's Army, and we don't care if it snows ink!

* * *

So farm-hand, clerk, mechanic, miner, were absorbed into the military machine. Scattered in improvised training camps in all quarters of the British Isles, Territorials and Kitchener's Army alike applied themselves with cheerful vigour to the task of becoming soldiers.

IN TRAINING

From *The First Hundred Thousand*.[1]

By IAN HAY

Considered all round, Divisional Training is the pleasantest form of soldiering that we have yet encountered. We parade bright and early, at full battalion strength, accompanied by our scouts, signallers, machine-guns and transport, and march off at the appointed minute to the starting-point. Here we slip into our place in an already moving column, with three thousand troops in front of us and another two thousand behind, and tramp to our point of deployment. We feel pleasantly thrilled. We are no longer a battalion out on a route march: we are members of a White Army, or a Brown Army, hastening to frustrate the designs of a Blue Army, or a Pink Army, which has landed (according to the General Idea issued from headquarters) at Portsmouth, and is reported to

[1] Published by William Blackwood & Sons, Ltd.

have slept at Great Snoreham, only ten miles away, last night.

Meanwhile our Headquarters Staff is engaged in the not always easy task of " getting into touch " with the enemy—*anglice*, finding him. It is extraordinary how elusive a force of several thousand troops can be, especially when you are picking your way across a defective half-inch map, and the commanders of the opposing forces cherish dissimilar views as to where the point of encounter is supposed to be. However, contact is at length established; and if it is not time to go home, we have a battle.

Various things may now happen to you. You may find yourself detailed for the firing-line. In that case your battalion will take open order; and you will advance, principally upon your stomach, over hill and dale until you encounter the enemy, doing likewise. Both sides then proceed to discharge blank ammunition into one another's faces at a range, if possible, of about five yards, until the " cease fire " sounds.

Or you may find yourself in Support. In that case you are held back until the battle has progressed a stage or two, when you advance with fixed bayonets to prod your own firing-line into a further display of valour and agility.

Or you may be detailed as Reserve. Membership of Brigade Reserve should be avoided. You are liable to be called upon at any moment to forsake the sheltered wood or lee of a barn under which you are huddling, and double madly up a hill or along a side-road, tripping heavily over ingenious entanglements composed of the telephone wires of your own signallers, to enfilade some unwary detachment of the enemy or repel a flank attack. On the other hand, if you are ordered to act as Divisional Reserve, you may select the softest spot on the hillside behind which you are sheltering, get out your haversack ration, and prepare to spend an extremely peaceful (or extremely dull) day. Mimic warfare enjoys one enormous advantage over the genuine article: battles—provided you are not out for the night—*must always* end in time for the men to get back to their dinners at five o'clock. Under this inexorable law it follows that, by the time the General has got into touch with the enemy and brought his firing-line, supports and local reserves into action, it is time to go home. So about three o'clock the bugles sound, and the combatants, hot and grimy, fall back into close order at the point of deployment, where they are presently joined by the Divisional Reserve, blue-faced and watery-eyed with cold. This done, principals and understudies, casting envious glances at one another, form one long column of route and set out for home, in charge of the subalterns. The senior officers trot off to the " pow-wow," there, with the utmost humility and deference, to extol their own tactical dispositions, belittle the achievements of the enemy, and impugn the veracity of one another.

* * *

RUMOUR is always rife in war-time. The 1914 conflict was not long in producing its own particular crop of legends, ranging from the Angels of Mons to gory atrocities. While many of these were repulsive, some were merely amusing.

RUMOUR!

From *Falsehood in War-time*.[1]

By THE RT. HON. ARTHUR PONSONBY

No obsession was more widespread through the War than the belief in the last months of 1914 that Russian troops were passing through Great Britain to the Western Front. Nothing illustrates better the credulity of the public mind in war-time and what favourable soil it becomes for the cultivation of falsehood.

How the rumour actually originated it is difficult to say. There were subsequently several more or less humorous suggestions made: of a telegram announcing the arrival of a large number of Russian eggs, referred to as " Russians "; of the tall, bearded individual who declared from the window of a train that he came from " Ross-shire "; and of the excited French officer with imperfect English pronunciation who went about near the Front, exclaiming: " Where are de rations." But General Sukhomlinoff, in his memoirs, states that Sir

[1] Published by George Allen & Unwin, Ltd.

George Buchanan, the British Ambassador in Russia, actually requested the dispatch of " a complete Russian army corps " to England, and English ships were to be brought to Archangel for the transport of these troops. The Russian General Staff, he adds, came to the conclusion that " Buchanan had lost his reason."

Whatever the origin may have been, the rumour spread like wild-fire, and testimony came from every part of the country from people who had seen the Russians. They were in trains with the blinds down, on platforms stamping the snow off their boots; they called hoarsely for " vodka " at Carlisle and Berwick-on-Tweed, and they jammed the penny-in-the-slot machine with a rouble at Durham. The number of troops varied according to the imaginative powers of the witness.

As the rumour had undoubted military value, the authorities took no steps to deny it. A telegram from Rome appeared giving " the official news of the concentration of 250,000 Russian troops in France." With regard to this telegram, the official Press Bureau stated : " That there was no confirmation of the statements contained in it, but that there was no objection to them being published." As there was a strict censorship of news, the release of this telegram served to confirm the rumour and kept the false witnesses busy.

* * *

WITH the exception of Antwerp, the Belgian fortresses had now fallen. To the relief of the city rushed the British Naval Division, delaying its capitulation for five invaluable days.

ANTWERP

From *The World Crisis*, 1911–1914.[1]

By THE RT. HON. WINSTON S. CHURCHILL, C.H.

Although the artillery fire of the Germans at Antwerp was at no time comparable to the great bombardments afterwards endured on the Western Front, it was certainly severe. The Belgian trenches were broad and shallow, and gave hardly any

[1] Published by Thornton Butterworth, Ltd.

ANTWERP

protection to their worn-out and in many cases inexperienced troops. As we walked back from the edge of these inundations along a stone-paved high-road, it was a formidable sight to see on either hand the heavy shells bursting in salvoes of threes and fours with dense black smoke near or actually inside these scanty shelters in which the supporting troops were kneeling in fairly close order. Every prominent building—château, tower or windmill—was constantly under fire; shrapnel burst along the roadway, and half a mile to the left a wooded enclosure was speckled with white puffs. Two or three days at least would be required to make sound breastworks or properly constructed and drained trenches or rifle pits. Till then it must be mainly an affair of hedges and of houses; and the ineffective trenches were merely shell traps.

Antwerp presented a case, till the Great War unknown, of an attacking force marching methodically without regular siege operations through a permanent fortress line behind advancing curtains of artillery fire. Fort after fort was wrecked by the two or three monster howitzers; and line after line of shallow trenches was cleared by the fire of field-guns. And following gingerly upon these iron foot-prints, German infantry, weak in numbers, raw in training, inferior in quality, wormed and waddled their way forward into " the second strongest fortress in Europe."

As the fire of the German guns drew ever nearer to the city, and the shells began to fall each day upon new areas, the streams of country folk escaping from their ruined homes trickled pitifully along the roads, interspersed with stragglers and wounded. Antwerp itself preserved a singular calm. The sunlit streets were filled with people listening moodily to the distant firing. The famous spires and galleries of this ancient seat of wealth and culture, the spacious warehouses along the Scheldt, the splendid hotels " with every modern convenience," the general air of life, prosperity and civilisation created an impression of serene security wholly contradicted by the underlying facts. It was a city in a trance.

The Marines did not arrive until the morning of the 4th, and went immediately into the line. When I visited them the same evening they were already engaged with the Germans in the outskirts of Lierre. Here, for the first time, I saw German soldiers creeping forward from house to house or darting across the street. The Marines fired with machine-guns from a balcony. The flashes of the rifles and the streams of flame pulsating from the mouth of the machine-guns, lit up a warlike scene amid crashing reverberations and the whistle of bullets.

Twenty minutes in a motor-car, and we were back in the warmth and light of one of the best hotels in Europe, with its perfectly appointed tables and attentive servants all proceeding as usual !

* * *

THE remnants of the British Expeditionary Force, hurried from the Aisne in a vain attempt to outflank the German thrust, found itself involved in the grimmest struggle of the War. " First Ypres " was the Inkerman of the Great War —a soldier's battle.

FIRST YPRES

From *All Our Yesterdays*.[1]

By H. M. TOMLINSON

And for such a reason it happened that along the line of Belgium's River Yser, in the first October of the War, young German volunteers were hurriedly assembled. They had come from school to war because their Emperor and famous soldiers had failed to take Paris, and had not abolished the French Armies ; winter was at hand, and the confident theory of a rapid overthrow of Germany's enemies somehow had disclosed a fault in its calculations. There was no longer a French centre to pierce, but there was still one flank that could be turned, and so along the Yser German youth mustered to do it. The German High Command, compelled to the next thing, knew it should send its men across the river, take the Channel ports as a threat to England—which Berlin, in all the popular cartoons, knew as the obdurate foe of good Teutons—and strike at the communications and the rear of the Allied forces in the north.

[1] Published by William Heinemann, Ltd.

FIRST YPRES

The young levies were marshalled for that emergency; they were ordered forward, they clasped hands, and advanced chanting national songs. But the land was a swamp, and their masters did not know it. A flood was rising; the sluice-gates had been opened by the sea. Belgian machine-guns stopped the singing; and the lads moved towards the Channel, in their threat to London, only as flotsam on the drift of sluggish waters.

Yet men who have staked much in a gamble always see it would be wrong to confess failure because dice are inconsiderate. They must double the stakes. The flooded country of the Yser, though men, guns and stores had sunk in it, was an advantage after all, for the German generals saw well enough that if it defended the left flank of the Allies, it also defended their own right flank. It freed their men to make elsewhere a successful spearhead. The German forces therefore gathered more to the east and the south, and struck at the approaches to Ypres. Germany would reach the sea along the Menin Road.

It was in that pass that the remnants of the British Army stood. Upon it, desperate through loss of time, with winter at hand, Germany hammered. Thin companies of men in khaki, the rags of battalions, haggard with weeks of battle, and none there yet to relieve them, numbed by continuous shell-fire, sheltering among ruins and beet fields while existing on rum and biscuits, resisted the renewed attacks, and melted fast. The survivors did not retire. No orders had been given to them. They dragged their wounded behind hedges and broken walls, if they could find any, and left them there to wait for water and aid which could not always reach them; they tightened their harness for the next bout, not knowing that they were all that remained between Germany and Calais. They knew nothing except that their enemy would give them no rest, and that soon none of them would be left; most of them did not know where they were. They kept free the bolts of their rifles, and looked for the signs of the next attack.

And the German commanders were perplexed, when their next attack, fashioned hard and heavily with new men, awakened steady volleys from ground where they thought all must be dead under renewed bombardments, and when their new troops were met in the open by scarecrows in khaki whose desperation to have done with this was all that flickered their bayonets. The German commanders considered so unreasonable an obstinacy in the light of military science, and the solution was plain to them. They had no doubt that the British must have heavy reserves. There must be a trap prepared in the woods to the west, for otherwise odd and ragged groups of men would not resist properly constituted brigades. They hesitated. They reformed, and planned anew. Yet nothing was between the German Army and the sea except tired men who guessed that life for them was over, and the wounded and the dead, and the staffs of headquarters; and the last indeed were puzzled themselves, while waiting for the signs of the approach of the foe, to hear British rifle-fire break out once more on the road ahead. Some men were left?

In mid-November, in the morning mists of the first of winter, the Kaiser himself announced his presence, and brought up his Prussian guardsmen; and this time there should be no doubt. Those stout soldiers suffered, but they broke the thin barrier, and advanced into the woods beyond. There they paused. They did not know what next to do. Nobody was there to direct them along the road to Calais. And there they were found by casual detachments of the British, who learned, when they tried, that they could butcher these formidable Prussians among the trees like pheasants, for they were leaderless. The road to the Channel was closed because the Germans did not know it was open.

That evening of November 11th, 1914, when the gun-fire of Germany's last attempt to break through had died down, storms of rain swept the battle-ground. The British lay in the mud, listening to the voices of the wounded, knowing no help was near, and waited for light. That would end it. The next lot would finish it. They could not know the last serious effort of the enemy upon Ypres had been made. They would have to face it at daylight. Their sentries, too weary to feel hunger, watched the fear of the battle-ground after dark, the sudden threats of odd shapes in rain and quick gleams, the fitful lights from nowhere, and the desultory explosions. Their shallow trenches dissolved in the runnels and drainage.

They were abandoned to rain in the dark. The only reality

for them was a night of ill-omened phantoms and the cries of men dying in the mire. There it was. The many inventions of years of Downing Street and Whitehall had come to mud and havoc. The road paved with the good intentions of sage ministers was the Menin Road. But those soldiers who lay in the filth, expecting to be on the morrow what their mates were whose groaning grew less towards daybreak, who were of no importance, Tom, Dick and Jim, without knowing what it was they did, had stopped with their bodies on that road the coming of retribution to others far from it who had devised elaborate evil, sure that in its patriotism and cleverness it was good.

* * *

To replace the tremendous casualties of the old professional army, the first reinforcements from Kitchener's Army and the Territorials were now arriving in France.

BAPTISM OF BLOOD
From *A Student in Arms*.[1]
By DONALD HANKEY

A whistle blew. The first platoon scrambled to their feet and advanced at the double. What happened no one could see. They disappeared. The second line followed, and the third and fourth. Surely no one could live in that hell. No one hesitated. They went forward mechanically, as men in a dream. It was so mad, so unreal. Soon they would awake....

It appeared that there was a trench at the edge of the wood. It had been unoccupied. A couple of hundred yards in front, across the open ground, was the trench which they were attacking. Half a dozen men found themselves alone in the open ground before the German wire. They lay down. No one was coming on. Where was every one? They crawled cautiously back to the trench at the edge of the wood, and climbed in. One or two were there already. Two or three wounded men limped in from the rear, and sank on the floor

[1] Published by Andrew Melrose, Ltd.

of the trench. The storm raged on; but the attack was over. These were what was left of two companies. All stain on the honour of the brigade had been wiped out—in blood.

There were three men in a bay of the trench. One was hit in the leg, and sat on the floor cutting away his trousers so as to apply a field-dressing. One knelt down behind the parapet with a look of dumb stupor on his face. The third, a boy of about seventeen from a London slum, peered over the parapet at intervals. Suddenly he disappeared over the top. He had discovered two wounded men in a shell-hole just in front, and was hoisting them into the shelter of the trench. By a miracle not one of the three was hit. A message was passed up the trench: " Hold on at all costs till relieved." A council of war was held. Should they fire or lie low? Better lie low, and only fire in case of attack. They were safe from attack as long as the Bosches kept on firing. Someone produced a tin of meat, some biscuits and a full water-bottle. The food was divided up, and a shell bursting just in rear covered everything with dirt and made it uneatable. The water was reserved for the wounded. The rest sucked their pebbles in stoical silence.

Supports began to trickle in, and the wounded who could not stand were laboriously removed from the narrow trench to some dug-outs in the rear. Two of them were badly hit, and crying out incessantly for water, or to shift their position. One was unconscious and groaning. From the wood came frenzied shouts from a man in delirium. The more slightly wounded tried to look after the others; but soon the water was exhausted, and all they could do was to promise that as soon as darkness fell help would come.

Darkness fell. The battalion had been relieved; but the better part of it lay out in the wood, or in the open before the wood, dead or dying. The wood was full of groaning. Four stretcher-bearers came and took away one man, an officer. The rest waited in vain. An hour passed, and no one else came. Two were mortally hit, and began to despair. For Christ's sake get some water. There was none to be had.

A man wounded in the leg found that he could crawl on all fours. He started to look for help. He crawled laboriously along the path through the wood. It was choked with corpses.

He crawled over them as best he could. Once he found a full water-bottle, which he gave to a sentry to send back to his mates. At last he was picked up, and taken to the doctor, while others went to look for his mates.

The doctor was in a field. Rows of wounded lay there waiting for stretcher-bearers to come and take them to the ambulances. As many as could went on, those wounded in the leg with their arms on the shoulders of those whose legs were whole. They limped painfully along the interminable road till they came to the ambulance. Then their troubles were over. A rapid drive brought them to the dressing station. There they were given cocoa, inoculated for tetanus, their wounds washed and bound up. Another drive took them to the camp by the railway. Next morning they were put in the train, and at length reached the hospital. There at last they got the longed-for bath and the clean clothes and—joy of joys— were put to sleep, unlimited sleep, in a real bed with clean white sheets. They were at peace. But out in the open space between the trenches lay some they had known and loved, unburied. And others lay beneath wooden crosses behind the wood. Yet it was well. The brigade was saved. Its honour was vindicated. Though its men might be fresh from home and untried in war, they would not fail. The brigade had had its baptism in blood, and its self-confidence was established for all time.

* * *

BEHIND THE LINES

From *Adventures of a Despatch Rider*.[1]

By Captain W. H. L. Watson

When first the corps came to Hinges, the inhabitants were exalted. The small boys came out in puttees and the women put ribbons in their hair. Now, if you pronounce Hinges in the French fashion, you give forth an exclamation of distressful pain. The name cannot be shouted from a motor-cycle. It has its difficulties even for the student of French. So we all called it, plainly and bluntly, Hinges, as though it were

[1] Published by William Blackwood & Sons.

connected to a door. The inhabitants noticed this. Thinking that they and their forefathers had been wrong—for surely these fine men with red hats knew better than they—the English pronounciation spread. The village became 'Ingees, and now only some unfashionable dotards in Béthune preserved the tradition of the old pronunciation. It is not only Hinges that has been thus decently attired in British garb. Le Cateau is Lee Catòo. Boescheppe is Bo-peep. Ouderdon is Eiderdown.

Béthune was full of simple pleasures. First there were the public baths, cheap and good, and sundry coiffeurs who were much in demand, for they made you smell sweetly. Then there was a little blue and white café. The daughter of the house was well-favoured and played the piano with some skill. One of us spent all his spare time at this café, in silent adoration—of the piano, for his French was exiguous in the extreme. There was a *patisserie* crammed full of the most delicious cream cakes. The despatch rider who went to Hinges about 3.30 p.m. and did not return with cakes and tea, found life unpleasant. Near the station three damsels ruled a tavern. They were friendly and eager to teach us French. We might have left them with a sigh of regret if we had not once arrived as they were eating their midday meal.

At one time the Germans dropped a few shells into Béthune, but did little damage. Bombs fell, too. One nearly ended the existence of " Sadders "—also known as " Boo." It dropped on the other side of the street; doing our despatch rider no damage, it slightly wounded Sergeant Croucher of the Cyclists in a portion of his body that made him swear when he was classed as a " sitting-up case."

. . . .

Very content, we rode on to Caestre, arriving there ten minutes before the advance-party of the Signal Company. Divisional Headquarters were established at the House of the Spy. The owner of the house had been well treated by the Germans when they had passed through a month before. Upon his door had been written this damning legend:

HIER SIND GUETIGE LEUTE[1]

[1] Here are kindly people.

and, when on the departure of the Germans the house had been searched by an indignant populace, German newspapers had been discovered in his bedroom.

It is the custom of the Germans to spare certain houses in every village by chalking up some laudatory notice. We despatch riders had a theory that the inhabitants of these marked houses, far from being spies, were those against whom the Germans had some particular grievance. Imagine the wretched family doing everything in its power to avoid the effusive affection of the Teuton, breaking all its own crockery, and stealing all its own silver, defiling its beds and tearing its clothing. For the man whose goods have been spared by the German becomes an outcast. He lives in a state worse than death. He is hounded from his property, and driven across France with a character attached to him, like a kettle to a cat's tail. Genuine spies, on the other hand—so we thought— were worse treated than any and secretly recompensed. Such a man became a hero. All his neighbours brought their little offerings.

· · · · · · ·

A battalion that has come many miles is nearly silent. The strong men stride tirelessly without a word. Little weak men, marching on their nerves, hobble restlessly along. The men with bad feet limp and curse, wilting under the burden of their kit, and behind all come those who have fallen out by the way—men dragging themselves along behind a waggon, white-faced men with uneasy smiles on top of the waggons. A little farther back those who are trying to catch up: these are tragic figures, breaking into breathless little runs, but with a fine wavering attempt at striding out, as though they might be connecting files, when they march through a town or past an officer of high rank.

A battalion that has just come out of action I cannot describe to you in these letters, but let me tell you now about Princess Pat's. I ran into them just as they were coming into Bailleul for the first time and were hearing the sound of the guns. They were the finest lot of men I have ever seen on the march. Gusts of great laughter were running through them,

In the eyes of one or two were tears. And I told those civilians I passed that the Canadians, the fiercest of all soldiers, were come. Bailleul looked on them with more fright than admiration. The women whispered fearfully to each other—" Les Canadiens, les Canadiens ! ..."

* * *

MEANTIME, the British Navy was not idle. Immediately on the declaration of War a Blockade of Germany was instituted, never to be relaxed until the War was won. The German High Seas Fleet was pinned to its base; only its submarines and commerce-destroyers were active.

At the outbreak of War, however, a German squadron was cruising in the Pacific. This chanced to encounter a British squadron of considerably inferior armament.

CORONEL

From *The World Crisis*, 1911–1914[1]

By THE RT. HON. WINSTON S. CHURCHILL, C.H.

But nothing was farther from the mind of Admiral Cradock. He instantly decided to attack. As soon as the *Glasgow* had sighted the enemy, she had turned back towards the flagship, preceded by the *Monmouth* and the *Otranto*, all returning at full speed. But Admiral Cradock, at 5.10, ordered the squadron to concentrate, not on his flagship the *Good Hope*, the farthest ship from the enemy, but on the *Glasgow*, which, though retreating rapidly, was still the nearest. At 6.18 he signalled to the distant *Canopus* : " I am now going to attack enemy." The decision to fight sealed his fate, and more than that, the fate of the squadron.

To quote the log of the *Glasgow* : " The British squadron turned to port four points together towards the enemy with a view to closing them and forcing them to action before sunset, which if successful, would have put them at a great

[1] Published by Thornton Butterworth, Ltd.

disadvantage owing to the British squadron being between the enemy and the sun." The German Admiral easily evaded this manœuvre by turning away towards the land and keeping at a range of at least 18,000 yards. Both squadrons were now steaming southward on slightly converging courses—the British to seaward with the setting sun behind them, and the Germans nearer the land. And now began the saddest naval action in the War. Of the officers and men in both the squadrons that faced each other in these stormy seas so far from home, nine out of ten were doomed to perish. The British were to die that night: the Germans a month later. At 7 o'clock the sun sank beneath the horizon, and the German Admiral, no longer dazzled by its rays, opened fire. The British ships were silhouetted against the after-glow, while the Germans were hardly visible against the dark background of the Chilean coast. A complete reversal of advantage had taken place. The sea was high, and the main deck 6-inch guns both of the *Monmouth* and of the *Good Hope* must have been much affected by the dashing spray. The German batteries, all mounted in modern fashion on the upper deck, suffered no corresponding disadvantage from the rough weather. The unequal contest lasted less than an hour. One of the earliest German salvos probably disabled the *Good Hope's* forward 9·2-inch gun, which was not fired throughout the action. Both she and the *Monmouth* were soon on fire. Darkness came on and the sea increased in violence, till the *Good Hope*, after a great explosion, became only a glowing speck which was presently extinguished; and the *Monmouth*, absolutely helpless, but refusing to surrender, was destroyed by the *Nürnberg* and foundered, like her consort, with her flag still flying. The *Otranto*, an unarmoured merchantman, quite incapable of taking part in the action, rightly held her distance and disappeared into the gloom. Only the little *Glasgow*, which miraculously escaped fatal damage among the heavy salvos, continued the action until she was left alone in darkness on the stormy seas. There were no survivors from the two British ships: all perished, from Admiral to seaman. The Germans had no loss of life.

Quoth the *Glasgow* in her subsequent report :

" . . . Throughout the engagement the conduct of officers and men was entirely admirable. Perfect discipline and coolness prevailed under trying circumstances of receiving considerable volume of fire without being able to make adequate return. The men behaved exactly as though at battle practice ; there were no signs of wild fire, and when the target was invisible the gunlayers ceased firing of their own accord. Spirit of officers and ship's company of *Glasgow* is entirely unimpaired by serious reverse in which they took part, and that the ship may be quickly restored to a condition in which she can take part in further operations against the same enemy is the unanimous wish of us all."

* * *

In these early days, the English people were calculating the time likely to be taken to reach Berlin by the " Russian Steam-roller." Unfortunately, it is a property of steam-rollers to move both forward and backward. Within a few weeks, the Russians were in wholesale retreat. On this front the character of the warfare was more open, retaining its individual and barbaric characteristics.

THE RUSSIAN " STEAM-ROLLER "

From *An Englishman in the Russian Ranks*.[1]

By John Morse

Much of the scene of the operations I have been describing was very beautiful country, studded with homesteads and farms that, in normal times, must have been quiet and peaceful places, occupied by well-to-do yeomanry and peasantry, living happy and contented lives. Orchards were numerous, but the fruit had entirely disappeared, either prematurely removed by its owners to make what they could of it, or plundered by the passing troops. Frequently we rode by

[1] Published by Duckworth & Company.

cornfields that had been burned; and potato fields had been dug up and wasted, thousands of potatoes the size of marbles lying on the ground. Our raiders got hold of many fowls and pigs; and for a week or two pork was always to be had at two or three meals per day.

Most of the people had fled from this country; those that remained seemed to fear their own countrymen as much as they did our Cossacks, and remained in hiding while we were passing. Generally speaking they were not ill-used when our men discovered them; but scant respect was shown to the rights of womanhood by the Germans themselves, who had become brutal. No doubt many of the German officers made great efforts to maintain order; but the licence of war is notorious, and many opportunities for wrong-doing must necessarily arise in countries under its influence.

Houses and whole villages were wrecked and burned. We were constantly passing through smouldering ruins, and at night the land resembled our "Black Country" for blazing fires, and reflections of fires. We saw bodies of civilians who appeared to have been executed by shooting; and in one wrecked and smoke-blackened street, a couple of our own Cossacks, and another Russian soldier, were seen hanging to lamp-posts—probably marauders who had wandered away from their ranks, and fallen amongst the Philistines—a fate such people often meet.

Acting on orders, the cavalry spread out into a vast screen, covering the movements of the infantry, and gradually fell back before the enemy. The movement was described as being strategical, for the purpose of drawing the Germans into a favourable position for attack; but this assertion was probably made to keep up the spirits of our troops.

The enemy fired at us a good deal; but as they could not bring their guns to bear on a group of men, very little execution was done. There were some charges between small parties, always much less than a squadron in strength: and in all these that I saw or heard of the Germans got the worst of the fight; and besides those cut down, in three or four days, our men captured more than two hundred prisoners, half a dozen of whom were officers. I believe that the Germans claimed to have captured some of our soldiers, but I much doubt if they secured as many as a score.

The Cossack has a strong disinclination to be taken prisoner; and I knew of several of them sacrificing their lives rather than fall into the hands of the Germans, who heartily detest these men, and usually murdered such as they succeeded in catching —and murdered them after preliminary tortures, according to reports which reached us. The country people certainly showed no mercy to stragglers falling into their hands. They usually pitch-forked them to death; and this lethal weapon was a favourite with the ladies on both sides of the border, many a fine Teuton meeting his end by thrusts from this implement. For in some of the fights the peasantry, including women of all ages, took part, and showed that farm instruments are as deadly as any kind of *arme blanche*. (*Arme blanche* is the term used by military scientists to include bayonets, lances and swords of all descriptions. Perhaps the nearest English equivalent is " cold steel.")

Riding through a burnt village near Neidenburg, half a *sotnia* of our fellows fell into a Prussian trap and had a third of their saddles emptied in a few seconds. The survivors were equal to the occasion; and charged so vigorously that they completely routed their opponents—about one hundred of a reservist corps with the figures 239 on their shoulder-straps.

Two of these men were impaled on the same Cossack lance, an almost incredible circumstance. The Cossacks are in the habit of lowering their lances as they charge without removing them from the buckets. Holding them loosely by the lanyards, they kick them into their enemies with such irresistible force, aided by the speed of the charging horse, that to parry the weapons is impossible. In the case mentioned, the men must have been standing one close behind the other, and the lance was driven right through bodies, packs and all. It was some time before one of the men died: in fact, not before the Cossack drew his sword and finished him off by a sabre cut. The soldier could not withdraw his lance, so firmly was it embedded in the bodies, a circumstance which much aroused his ire, for all Cossacks are much attached to their weapons.

* * *

It is never pleasant to be taken prisoner, and in the early days of the War, the feelings of civilian populations relieved themselves in acts of hostility towards the helpless captives. It is only fair to the Germans to point out that this attitude was not unknown in certain of the Allied countries.

PRISONERS AND CAPTIVES
From *Fortune of War*.[1]
By Duncan Grinnell-Milne

The doors of the cars were being rattled and slid back; some of them hinged at the bottom and let down to the ground to allow animals to be loaded and unloaded easily. The interiors of such trucks, when open, could plainly be seen. They were filthy. The old whitewash had long since worn from their walls or was hidden beneath a coating of dung. The floors were littered inches deep with dirty straw, refuse of all kinds, manure. Men lay there, crouched, leaned against the walls. The crowd gaped.

Orders were shouted; the guards yelled, waved their arms fiercely, unslung their rifles, took a few steps up the lowered planking to grab an arm or a leg; or, standing by the door of a freight wagon, jabbed about in the inner darkness with the butt of a rifle. And slowly from the foul and shameful train there crept, staggered, stumbled, a weary band of most unfortunate men.

There was a sudden, sharp silence. The crowd was moved. But in what direction? Was it a feeling of shame at witnessing such a spectacle? Or, was it pity; or was it some remnant of the days when men took pleasure in baiting captured wild beasts? Perhaps for that instant of silence it was none of these, but merely the sensation of surprise, to be followed by quick-growing rage.

Who were these men? They were fair—mostly—slim; young, too, in spite of their ragged, unkempt appearance.

[1] Published by John Lane, The Bodley Head, Ltd.

What were these uniforms? Brown, sand-coloured—what was it called?—" Khaki."

" *Engländer!* " The word, pronounced clearly by a young voice, was taken up as by a chorus and passed round. The murmur of the crowd rose in five seconds to a shout, to a roar, increasing in volume till the din was deafening, breaking here and there into excited screams and yells.

" *Engländer!* God in Heaven! *Here?* How did they get here? Where were they taken? "—" *Engländer!* the cursed dogs! The swine! " " They have fought against our people—perhaps they have killed some of them! "—" Look at the pigs! They can scarcely walk! They must have been taught a few sound lessons by our incomparable troops."—" May they rot in hell for fighting against us! "—" Look, some of them are wounded! I'd like to tear the bandages off them—why are they bandaged, anyway? "—" Spit at them, the beasts! Throw something in their impudent faces! Hey, you damned English pigs, wait till I get near you! "

A fat, red-faced woman in black alpaca, with a mass of purple velvet ribbon round a brim of yellow straw perched high on her head, was seized with unusual fury and aimed an awkward, lunging blow with her parasol at a khaki-clad figure standing next to a guard just in front of her. Twice she struck, her blows doing little or no harm; but the man put up his arm to ward off the blows, the parasol struck the German guard. Doubtless the guard thought he was being attacked—by an unarmed man—for he raised the butt of his rifle and struck him—a wounded man at that—hard on the chest. The man fell back, coughing.

Some of the prisoners glanced astonished at the crowd. They talked into each other's ears, trying to look unconcerned, but so startled by the strange outburst that they felt positively ashamed for the human beings who could make such a display of their feelings. One of them faced the crowd with a certain hauteur in his bearing, disdain shaped his lips; he struck something of an attitude—foolish, perhaps, but his nerves were overstrung. His gesture was scarcely noticeable, slightly ridiculous at the most. The Lieutenant of Reserve strutting proudly down the line stopped as he caught sight of him.

He paused a moment, encouraged by yells of hate; then in full view of the crowd, swung his arm and struck the Englishman in the face. The crowd screamed in approval and derision as the prisoner was held back by his own comrades. Young women and children worked themselves into a frenzy, trying to spit in spluttering imitation of grown men, whose accuracy and Oriental fluency must have been the result of many years' careful practice.

The patient, unsmiling group of exhausted men was at length lined up two deep. They had nothing to carry, no kit or equipment—only here and there a wounded comrade to assist. They stood there endeavouring not to notice the crowd; they bore the insults with courage, with dignity, with the superb stoicism of their race.

An order to " turn left " and " march " was snapped in the peculiar, irritating, high-pitched yap of the German word-of-command from which Pomeranian dogs must have copied their bark. Not understanding much of what was said to them, the prisoners marched off, pushed roughly into place by the guards.

There was a rough-and-tumble in the crowd as people scrambled for the exits so as to have a better view of the prisoners from the street. From those whose view had hitherto been obstructed by the packed mass in the station—and they were in the majority—there now burst a new shout as the head of the column of captives came into the open.

" *Offiziere! Es sind Offiziere!* "—" Dear God! so they are—look at their badges! I know the English uniforms."—" But it seems impossible! What! those men so dirty and with their coats torn—unshaven, too—those are officers? "—" No wonder they were captured! They must be cowards—*our* officers would never be taken like that."—" Our officers? Don't compare that lousy gang to our fine, smart officers! These men are of a lower type; I doubt if they can even read or write."—" Well, then, if they stay here a long time it may do them some good—they will learn a little of our *Kultur*, of our wonderful civilization! "—" They don't deserve it. They ought to have been killed at the Front—why weren't they killed? "—" Too quick at putting their hands up. But—*pfui!* they smell bad—let me get through. I want to spit!"—"Well, spit in the face of that lanky, insolent dog there.... Bravo! A good shot—full in the face!"—"But it's not enough! Give me something to throw."—"Here you are—a pile of rubbish—and some stones. Don't let the guard see you!"—"Now then! Ready?"—"Good shot again! More! That will teach the pigs to fight against Germany!"

* * *

AFTER the First Battle of Ypres both sides settled down in a double line of entrenchments, stretching from Switzerland to the sea; these lines were scarcely disturbed until the mammoth conflicts of 1918.

TRENCH WARFARE
From *The First Hundred Thousand*.[1]
By IAN HAY

The trench system has one thing to recommend it. It tidies things up a bit.

For the first few months after the War broke out confusion reigned supreme. Belgium and the north of France were one huge jumbled battlefield, rather like a public park on a Saturday afternoon—one of those parks where promiscuous football is permitted. Friend and foe were inextricably mingled and the direction of the goal was uncertain. If you rode into a village, you might find it occupied by a Highland regiment or a squadron of Uhlans. If you dimly discerned troops marching side by side with you in the dawning, it was by no means certain that they would prove to be your friends. On the other hand, it was never safe to assume that a battalion which you saw hastily entrenching itself against your approach was German. It might belong to your own brigade. There was no front and no rear, so direction counted for nothing. The country swarmed with troops which had been left "in the air," owing to their own too rapid advance, or the equally rapid retirement of their supporters; with scattered details

[1] Published by William Blackwood & Sons, Ltd.

trying to rejoin their units; or with despatch riders hunting for a peripatetic Divisional Headquarters. Snipers shot both sides impartially. It was all most upsetting.

Well, as already indicated, the trench system has put all that right. The trenches now run continuously—a long, irregular, but perfectly definite line of cleavage—from the North Sea to the Vosges. Everybody has been carefully sorted out—human beings on one side, Germans on the other. ("Like the Zoo," observes Captain Wagstaffe.) Nothing could be more suitable. *You're there, and I'm here, so what do we care?* in fact.

* * *

THE hatred of the civilians formed a strange contrast to the attitude of the actual combatants. Beneath their professional hostility, there was a very real respect—even a sympathy—towards their opponents.

THE CHRISTMAS TRUCE
From *When Armageddon Came*[1]
By WILFRID EWART

Less than a week later, the first Christmas morning of the War dawned.

After weeks of rain and mud, we are told, it broke keen and clear, with white frost powdering everything. The flat Flanders landscape was strangely silent and still. No guns fired, and few rifles. Birds usually so rare in winter trenches appeared in numbers, as many as fifty sparrows being fed around a dug-out.

At 8.30 a.m., a British officer, looking over his parapet, saw four unarmed Germans leave their trenches, which at this point were some three hundred and fifty to four hundred paces distant. This officer and one from another company immediately went out and met the enemy outside our barbed wire. The latter consisted of three private soldiers and a stretcher-bearer, and stated that they thought it only right to come over and wish us a happy Christmas, trusting us implicitly to keep the peace.

[1] Published by Rich & Cowan, Ltd.

The spokesman of the party, who spoke excellent English, asked that a postcard—which he wrote forthwith—might be sent to a young woman whom, together with a motor-bicycle, he had left in Suffolk. This request was carried out by one of the British officers.

These four Germans were Jaegers and Saxons of the 158th Infantry Regiment—the troops which had successfully defended their trenches on the night of December 18th–19th. They protested that they had come over out of good-will; that they had no feeling of enmity towards the English; that everything lay with their authorities, and, being soldiers, they had to obey. There had come into their possession a copy of the *Daily Telegraph* of December 10th of that year which, they averred, had caused no end of amusement. "You English are being hoodwinked!" France was "done," they said, Russia had received a series of very heavy blows and would shortly give in. England alone carried on the War! There was more conversation of the same sort in the middle of No Man's Land. The Germans protested that the English Press was to blame for working up feeling against them by publishing atrocity reports. There was a discussion about soft-nosed bullets (which the Germans claimed to have seen in possession of English prisoners), dum-dum bullets, and the high-velocity, sharp-nosed bullet. Finally, the truce was formally ratified, a ditch being appointed as a half-way meeting-place. The interview terminated with an exchange of English cigarettes and German cigars.

A short while later there floated down between the two lines of trenches the strains of the well-known marching song, "Tipperary," followed by those, taken up all along the German line, of "Deutschland, Deutschland über Alles." Out in the middle of No Man's Land stood six or seven large groups of mingled Germans and English. And, although it must be said that the fraternisation was of the most genuine character, considerable suspicion prevailed on the part of the English, and no precautions against possible treachery had been neglected. Not so soon could the lessons of Zonnebeke, of Krusseik be forgotten! Every sort of souvenir was exchanged, and many strange presents given. Addresses were taken down and the photographs of families handed round among those who, six nights before, had been locked in a life-and-death struggle. One German, on being offered a Virginian cigarette, said smilingly: " No, thanks, I only smoke Turkish ! "

Next, a Saxon non-commissioned officer, wearing the Iron Cross and the badge of an expert sniper, started his men on a marching song, the British meanwhile chanting national airs and Christmas carols such as " Good King Wenceslas." Finally, the frosty, keen Christmas air of this desolate spot in Artois was awakened to the loud singing of " Auld Lang Syne," in which all, English, Prussians, Scots, Saxons, Irish and Würtembergers alike joined. For the groups of Jaegers and Saxons of the 158th Regiment had been swollen by men of the 37th and 15th Infantry Regiments.

After the singing of " Auld Lang Syne," it is related, and not surprisingly startled by so unwonted a sound, a hare rose from between the trenches, and across the frozen plough, through the soaking cabbage-patches, over the ditches and over two lines of disused trenches, British and Germans gave chase until all of a heap, they killed in the open.

It was at this juncture that the commanding officer of the British battalion appeared and, wishing everyone present a " Merry Christmas," produced from his pocket a bottle of rum, at which a shout of joy went up exceeding all that had gone before. A German soldier uncorked it and proceeded ceremoniously to drink his opponents' health in behalf of his *Kamaraden*. All then retired to their respective trench-lines for the Christmas dinner.

During the afternoon similar scenes were enacted. There was another coursing meeting. Of four more hares pursued, one was killed; this by right went to the Germans. There was much conversation. A German said that he hoped to get back to London soon; a British soldier remarked: " So do I ! " A number of English newspapers were handed to the Germans who, with few exceptions, agreed that the War would be over within three weeks. Blind, incomprehensible delusion ! Judging by the censored letters of that and a later time, it was one entirely shared by the British private soldier. The enemy expressed admiration for the charge of the English on the night of the 18th–19th, and announced that they also had suffered many casualties. They further expressed their intention of not renewing hostilities unless our side did: there would be no more shooting until they were relieved.

Nor had the hours of this day been, nor were those of the succeeding days, wasted. A great deal of work had been done —work which could not be done in ordinary times without mortal danger from snipers. Masses of timber, wire and trench-material were carried up in full view; parties were hard at work at drainage and on the parapets and on the roofs of dug-outs. At night, wiring went forward at speed and without risk. And there were not lacking among the British officers eyes to espy something of the siting, something of the conditions and wiring of the German defences.

* * *

ON the South-Eastern Front, in the region of Przemysl, Russia and Austria were held in mortal conflict. In the early stages, despite a woeful lack of material and trained men, the Russians more than held their own.

DRAFTS

From *A Soldier's Note-Book*, 1914–1918.[1]

By GENERAL A. A. BRUSSILOV

This battle of Przemysl, which had continued incessantly for a whole month, was the last one in which I can say that I had an army that had been properly taught and trained before the War. After hardly three months of war the greater part of our regular, professional officers and trained men had vanished, leaving only skeleton forces which had to be hastily filled with men wretchedly instructed who were sent to me from the depots; while the strength of the officers was kept up by promoting subalterns, who likewise were inadequately trained. From this period onwards the professional character of our

[1] Published by Macmillan & Co., Ltd.

forces disappeared, and the Army became more and more like a sort of badly trained militia. The question of N.C.O.'s became a particularly acute one; we had to institute training squads so as to provide, hastily and anyhow, N.C.O.'s who assuredly could not take the place of their well-trained predecessors. On this point also one is bound to blame the War Ministry for not foreseeing these difficulties in their preparations for war. I repeat, the new officers came to us absolutely unqualified and in insufficient numbers; the N.C.O.'s, of whom there were great numbers in the Reserve, had not been put specially through a fresh course of training as a valuable body of subordinate officers with a view to their ultimate use in that capacity. Many of them were put into the ranks as privates during mobilisation, and at the beginning of the campaign we had far too many N.C.O.'s, while later on we had none at all. We who were in charge of operations were obliged to have instructional squads behind the line for each regiment. Last of all, the men sent to replace casualties generally knew nothing except how to march; none of them knew anything of open order, and many could not even load their rifles; as for their shooting, the less said about it the better.

In every regiment, then, we had to have the new drafts put through a course behind the lines before they could go into the ranks. But even so, our losses in the bigger battles were so enormous that very often we had to dump men into the line who had had absolutely no training whatever. Such people could not really be considered soldiers at all; they did not always show the necessary steadiness during the fighting, and they had no proper discipline. On top of this, the standard of training of the drafts sent up to us got worse and worse, despite all the protests, complaints and recriminations of those in command. True, very many of these officers, N.C.O.'s, and privates, trained at express speed, afterwards turned out skilful fighting-men and filled their respective posts with distinction; but what an amount of useless waste, disorder, and delay was caused as a result of these second-rate, unorganised drafts!

* * *

The Great War was notable for the introduction of several military novelties. The use of lethal gas was specifically forbidden by Hague Conventions, and its adoption by the Germans aroused indignation which recalls the wrath of Bayard against " the sooty cannonier."

GAS

From *The British Campaign in France and Flanders*, 1915.[1]
By Arthur Conan Doyle

About 5 p.m., on Thursday, April 22nd, a furious artillery bombardment from Bixschoote to Langemarck began along the French lines, including the left of the Canadians, and it was reported that the 45th French Division was being heavily attacked. At the same time a phenomenon was observed which would seem to be more in place in the pages of a romance than in the record of an historian. From the base of the German trenches, over a considerable length, there appeared jets of whitish vapour, which gathered and swirled until they settled into a definite low cloud-bank, greenish-brown below and yellow above, where it reflected the rays of the sinking sun. This ominous bank of vapour, impelled by a northern breeze, drifted swiftly across the space which separated the two lines. The French troops, staring over the top of their parapet at this curious screen which ensured them a temporary relief from fire, were observed suddenly to throw up their hands, to clutch at their throats, and to fall to the ground in the agonies of asphyxiation. Many lay where they had fallen, while their comrades, absolutely helpless against this diabolical agency, rushed madly out of the mephitic mist and made for the rear, overrunning the lines of trenches behind them. Many of them never halted until they had reached Ypres, while others rushed westwards and put the canal between themselves and the enemy. The Germans, meanwhile, advanced, and took possession of the successive lines of trenches, tenanted only by the dead garrisons, whose blackened faces, contorted figures, and lips fringed with the blood and

[1] Published by Hodder and Stoughton.

foam from their bursting lungs, showed the agonies in which they had died. Some thousands of stupefied prisoners, eight batteries of French field-guns, and four British 4·7's, which had been placed in a wood behind the French position, were the trophies won by this disgraceful victory. The British heavy guns belonged to the 2nd London Division, and were not deserted by their gunners until the enemy's infantry were close upon them, when the strikers were removed from the breech-blocks and the pieces abandoned. It should be added that both the young officers present, Lieutenants Sandeman and Hamilton Field, died beside their guns after the tradition of their corps.

By seven o'clock the French had left the Langemarck district, had passed over the higher ground about Pilken, and had crossed the canal towards Brielen. Under the shattering blow which they had received, a blow particularly demoralising to African troops, with their fears of magic and the unknown, it was impossible to rally them effectually until the next day. It is to be remembered in explanation of this disorganisation that it was the first experience of these poison tactics, and that the troops engaged received the gas in a very much more severe form than our own men on the right of Langemarck. For a time there was a gap five miles broad in the front of the position of the Allies, and there were many hours during which there was no substantial force between the Germans and Ypres. They wasted their time, however, in consolidating their ground, and the chance of a great *coup* passed for ever. They had sold their souls as soldiers, but the Devil's price was a poor one. Had they had a corps of cavalry ready, and pushed them through the gap, it would have been the most dangerous moment of the War.

* * *

ON THE HOME FRONT
From *Mr. Britling*.[1]
By H. G. WELLS

Tormenting the thought of Mr. Britling almost more acutely than this growing tale of stupidly inflicted suffering and

[1] Published by W. Collins, Sons & Co., Ltd.

waste and sheer destruction was the collapse of the British mind from its first fine phase of braced-up effort into a state of bickering futility.

Too long had British life been corrupted by the fictions of loyalty to an uninspiring and alien Court, of national piety in an official Church, of freedom in a politician-rigged State, of justice in an economic system where the advertiser, the sweater and usurer had a hundred advantages over the producer and artisan, to maintain itself now steadily at any high pitch of heroic endeavour. It had bought its comfort with the demoralisation of its servants. It had no completely honest organs; its spirit was clogged by its accumulated insincerities. Brought at last face to face with a bitter hostility and a powerful and unscrupulous enemy, an enemy socialistic, scientific and efficient to an unexampled degree, it seemed indeed to be inspired for a time by an unwonted energy and unanimity. Youth and the common people shone. The sons of every class went out to fight and die, full of a splendid dream of this war. Easy-going vanished from the foreground of the picture. But only to creep back again as the first inspiration passed. Presently the older men, the seasoned politicians, the owners and hucksters, the charming women and the habitual consumers, began to recover from this blaze of moral exaltation. Old habits of mind and procedure reasserted themselves. The War which had begun so dramatically missed its climax; there was neither heroic swift defeat nor heroic swift victory. There was indecision; the most trying test of all for an undisciplined people. There were great spaces of uneventful fatigue. Before the Battle of the Yser had fully developed the dramatic quality had gone out of the War. It had ceased to be either a tragedy or a triumph; for both sides it became a monstrous strain and wasting. It had become a wearisome thrusting against a pressure of evils. . . .

Under that strain the dignity of England broke, and revealed a malignity less focused and intense than the German, but perhaps even more distressing. No paternal government ha organised the British spirit for patriotic ends; it became now peevish and impatient, like some ill-trained man who is sick, it directed itself no longer against the enemy alone, but fitfully against imagined traitors and shirkers; it wasted its energies in a deepening and spreading net of internal squabbles and accusations. Now it was the wily indolence of the Prime Minister, now it was the German culture of the Lord Chancellor, now the imaginative enterprise of the First Lord of the Admiralty that focused a vindictive campaign. There began a hunt for spies and for suspects of German origin in every quarter except the highest; a denunciation now of "traitors," now of people with imaginations, now of scientific men, now of the personal friends of the Commander-in-Chief, now of this group, then of that group. . . . Every day Mr. Britling read his three or four newspapers with a deepening disappointment.

When he turned from the newspaper to his post, we would find the anonymous letter-writer had been busy. . . .

Perhaps Mr. Britling had remarked that Germans were after all human beings or that if England had listened to Matthew Arnold in the 'eighties, our officers by this time might have added efficiency to their courage and good temper. Perhaps he had himself put a touch of irritant acid into his comment. Back flared the hate. "Who are *you*, sir? What are *you*, sir? What right have *you*, sir? What claim have *you*, sir?" . . .

* * *

DEADLOCK having been reached on the Western Front, the Germans were striking at their island foe not merely in the air, but under the sea. The smaller craft of the Navy accomplished titanic tasks in their guardianship of the narrow seas.

SUBMARINE AND ANTI-SUBMARINE
From *A Little Ship*.[1]
By "TAFFRAIL" (CAPTAIN TAPRELL DORLING, D.S.O., R.N.)

"Something on the port bow, sir!" howled the look-out man in the bows, galvanised into sudden activity.

[1] Published by W. & R. Chambers, Ltd.

The commanding officer leapt to the fore side of the bridge, to see a vague, blurred-looking object looming up through the mist broad on the port bow. It was a bare eighty yards distant. It might be a buoy. But who ever saw a buoy like that? It was much too big.

The ship was travelling at eighteen knots, and in the drawing of a couple of breaths the thing was level with the bows. It was disappearing fast beneath the surface in a swirl of whitened water. It was an elongated grey mass, with hand-rails along its upper surface and a couple of upstanding things like spars. It had indistinct white figures on it. Bundy, trembling with excitement and his heart thumping like a sledge-hammer, knew!

In the brief moment vouchsafed to him in which to act he never lost his head. His mind worked quite clearly, and almost instantaneously he checked the first natural impulse to give the *Cyclone* full starboard helm in an effort to get home by ramming. Had he done so, the final result might have been very different, for the submarine was well inside the destroyer's turning circle, and the *Cyclone* would never have swung round in time to deliver the blow.

Instead of that he did the very opposite, and shouting: " Hard aport! " to the astonished quartermaster, who luckily had the presence of mind to obey the order without hesitation, swung the stern of his little ship towards the spot where the enemy was fast disappearing.

In another moment she had vanished; but the captain, bending down, had his hands on something on the floor of the bridge. He craned his neck to keep his eyes fixed on that whitened patch in the water. . . . He waited breathlessly. The *Cyclone's* stern was slewing fast.

" Good old girl! " he murmured beneath his breath. He pulled something hard, waited a moment, and pulled again.

He stood up with the sweat pouring off his face as the ship continued to swing. He darted round to the opposite side of the bridge to keep the spot under observation, jostling the astonished brigadier most rudely as he did so.

" Lord! " he murmured wildly. " Don't say they're duds! "

They weren't. Hardly were the words out of his mouth

when there came the muffled thudding roar of an underwater explosion. The ship danced and trembled as if she had struck a rock, and some distance away, on the starboard quarter, a huge mushroom-shaped dome of snowy water came to the surface and broke like a bursting bubble into a sparkling column of upflung spray. Another deep concussion, and then the scene beggared description. The sea seemed literally to burst asunder with a rumbling crash like the eruption of a volcano. Then came a whistling roar like the sound of escaping steam, and a great fan-shaped mass of greyish white water, stained with streaks of some denser, brownish liquid, went spouting skywards. And in the midst of the awful waterspout they saw the bodies of men, their arms and legs flung out at impossible angles, revolving grotesquely through the air; fragments of splintered wreckage and debris whirled round and round, up and down, like leaves in an autumn gale.

The submarine had been blown in two, divided like an egg, and the air from her interior, rushing to the surface, had carried in its stupendous blast every loose fitting and nearly every man.

It was a ghastly spectacle, and Bundy, sick at heart, felt his knees trembling beneath him. Even the brigadier, seasoned warrior though he was, seemed appalled, for his face was white under its tan as he clutched the bridge-rail and gazed at the eruption.

Then the scene became suddenly blotted out in a mist of spray as the torrent fell pattering down on the water with a hiss like heavy rain. The air was filled with the pungent reek of oil-fuel. Great oily waves came rippling across the surface, and heavy, ominous splashes told of bodies and debris falling into the sea.

The *Cyclone* stopped her engines and went astern to check her way, and the atmosphere started to clear; but when they could see again there was nothing but a huge circular patch of oil-fuel floating on a thick black scum on the surface, with here and there fragments of wood and a lifebelt or two. And there also were the remains of what, thirty seconds before, had been hale and hearty men. Their faces were bleeding, their bodies broken, mangled and torn. They cried piteously for help—help which so often they themselves had denied to their victims.

" Oh-a-a-ah! " came their drawn-out howls of agony. " Ah-a-a-a-a-h! "

An arm waved hopelessly in the air, and then disappeared slowly beneath the surface. A boat had been lowered from the *Cyclone* to save life. She was in the water in record time, her crew pulling lustily towards the spot on their errand of mercy as if they were rescuing their own countrymen. But one by one the poor fellows sank, and their agonised crying was for ever stilled. At last only one was left. He floated motionless, making no effort to save himself, and him the *Cyclone's* whaler rescued. He was an officer, the U-boat's commander, and still breathed when they brought him on board and laid him out on the steel deck. But the flickering spark of life in the battered body was nearly extinct, and he died a minute later without even opening his eyes.

It was all over.

Less than an hour afterwards a very chastened-looking little destroyer crept apologetically alongside a jetty in a certain French port.

"Report why you are so late in arriving," signalled the senior naval officer.

"Submit," the *Cyclone* replied, "we were delayed through stopping to sink a hostile submarine. Request an officer may be sent to examine evidence."

* * *

SUBSIDIARY to the main struggle on the Western and Eastern Fronts were the "side shows." Not least important of these was the attempt to capture Constantinople. The fleet having failed to force the passage of the Dardanelles, Sir Ian Hamilton hurried to the scene with a gallant army of home troops, Australians and New Zealanders, and French. In the face of almost incredible obstacles, he gained a foothold on the tip of the Gallipoli peninsula.

GALLIPOLI—THE LANDING

From *Gallipoli*.[1]

By JOHN MASEFIELD

The 29th Division went forward under these conditions on May 6th. They dashed on, or crawled, for a few yards at a

[1] Published by William Heinemann, Ltd.

time, then dropped for a few instants before squirming on again. In such an advance men do not see the battlefield. They see the world as the rabbit sees it, crouching on the ground, just their own little patch. On broken ground like that, full of dips and rises, men may be able to see nothing but perhaps the ridge of a bank ten feet ahead, with the dust flying in spouts all along it, as bullets hit it, some thousand a minute, and looking back or to their flanks they may see no one but perhaps a few men of their own platoon lying tense but expectant, ready for the sign to advance, while the bullets pipe over them in a never-ending bird-like croon. They may be shut off by some all-important foot of ground from seeing how they are fronting, and from all knowledge of what the next platoon is doing or suffering. It may be quite certain death to peep over that foot of ground in order to find out, and while they wait for a few instants, shells may burst in their midst and destroy a half of them. Then the rest, nerving themselves, rush up the ridge, and fall in a line dead under machine-gun fire. The supports come up, creeping over their corpses, get past the ridge, into scrub which some shell has set on fire. Men fall wounded in the fire, and the cartridges in their bandoliers explode and slowly kill them. The survivors crawl through the scrub half choked, and come out on a field full of flowers tangled three feet high with strong barbed wire. They wait for a while, to try to make out where the enemy is. They may see nothing but the slope of the field running up to a sky-line, and a flash of distant sea on a flank, but no sign of any enemy, only the crash of guns and the pipe and croon and spurt of bullets. Gathering themselves together, these brave men dash out to cut the wire, and are killed; others take their places, and are killed; others step out with too great a pride even to stoop, and pull up the supports of the wires and fling them down, and fall dead on top of them, having perhaps cleared a couple of yards. Then a couple of machine-guns open on the survivors, and kill them all in thirty seconds, with the concentrated fire of a battalion.

The supports come up, and hear about the wire from some wounded man who has crawled back through the scrub. They send back word: "Held up by wire," and in time the message comes to the telephone which has just been blown to pieces by a shell. Presently, when the telephone is repaired, the message reaches the gunners, who fire high-explosive shells on to the wire, and on to the slopes where the machine-guns may be hidden. Then the supports go on over the flowers, and are met midway by a concentrated fire of shells, shrapnel, machine-guns, and rifles. Those who are not killed lie down among the flowers, and begin to scrape little heaps of earth with their hands to give protection to their heads. In the light sandy marl this does not take long, though many are blown to pieces or hit in the back as they scrape. As before, they cannot see how the rest of the attack is faring, nor even where the other platoons of the battalion are; they lie scraping in the roots of daffodils and lilies, while bullets sing and shriek a foot or two over their heads. A man peering from his place in the flowers may make out that the man next to him, some three yards away, is dead, and that the man beyond is praying, the man beyond him cursing, and the man beyond him out of his mind from nerves or thirst.

Long hours pass, but the air above them never ceases to cry like a live thing with bullets flying. Men are killed or maimed, and the wounded cry for water. Men get up to give them water, and are killed. Shells fall at regular intervals along the field. The waiting men count the seconds between the shells to check the precision of the battery's fire. Some of the bursts fling the blossoms and bulbs of flowers into the bodies of men, where they are found long afterwards by the X-rays. Bursts and roars of fire on either flank tell of some intense moment in other parts of the line. Every feeling of terror and mental anguish and anxiety goes through the mind of each man there, and is put down by resolve.

* * *

GALLIPOLI—THE BASE AT LEMNOS
From *The Jesting Army*.[1]
By ERNEST RAYMOND

In the days of the Dardanelles fight, if anyone had wanted to obtain in a single glance a conception of the vast and varied

[1] Published by Cassell & Co., Ltd.

demands of the campaign, he should have shipped himself to Mudros Harbour. For the whole Merchant Service of Britain and half the Navy seemed to be anchored in the gulf, to say nothing of French warships, Italian warships, Greek vessels and tank-boats bringing water from Alexandria; and on all the hills around, like browsing sheep, were the white tents of rest camps and hospitals and stores, British, Australian, Indian and French. So full was the harbour of shipping that the water was fouled for bathers, unless they were game to swim through the off-scourings of the ships : sodden loaves, joints of meat, garbage and floating films of grease and oil that presented prismatic colours to the sky; but generally, in the summer heat, the tommies were more than game for this experience and added to the objects that littered the harbour their shouting shoals of naked men.

This Lemnos was a happy hunting-ground for insects. Flies battened on the sick men in the wards, centipedes climbed up the sides of the bell-tents, locusts leaped about the world outside, and the praying mantis prayed upon his bush and caught flies between his devotions. And ants : you could sit in your tent and watch a pair of ants with great bullet-heads and legs as long as spiders' contesting a point at issue, first by a round of fisticuffs and then by a wrestling bout, while others of the tribe were shoplifting portions of the floor-matting and carrying them to their homes. And perky little lizards stared up at you and hoped you thought they were crocodiles.

But that was in the dusty summer months. When Tony O'Grogan came to Lemnos its inhabitants were fighting the rain; deep trenches were dug all round the tents to draw off the water, metalled roads were being laid by Turkish prisoners and imported Egyptian coolies, and daily the hills echoed to the blasting of the Engineers, who were finding the stone for the roads.

In Lemnos the hills were the seats of the audience, and the water was the theatre of events. By the rapidity with which the tidings, "The *Mauretania*'s coming in," or "The *Aquitania*'s anchored," overspread the camps and drew all men to their tent doors, you could plumb the monotony of the land. Little else was discussed; we knew all about the submarines which had threatened this particular vessel, and the skilful way she had evaded them; the number of troops aboard her and her final destination. And by our envy of those high officers who would go aboard her to-night and dine in her lavish saloon, you could plumb our weariness of the dusty Mudros meats. You should have been there that day when a murmur of admiration and amazement arose from the Mudros hills as the *Mauretania*, no longer a black transport, entered the harbour in the white paint and the green sash of a hospital ship. Oh, how lovely she was, and what—*what* did this change portend? Or you should have been there that evening when the old *Southland*, with a jagged hole in her bows, came limping into harbour at the pace of an old man's walk.

The news of her nearness had been conveyed to the hills by a racing rumour: "The *Southland* with twelve hundred Australians aboard has been torpedoed and is going down twenty miles from Lemnos." This ugly story was confirmed by a snort from a French destroyer which lit out of the harbour at thirty-odd knots. The snort was a "halloo" to the other sea-hounds, who slipped their leashes and sped away on the scent sniffed up by the destroyer. They had gone to pick up the survivors. The harbour, you can be sure, waited to witness their return. Small rowing-boats and gay Greek yachts were in big demand by the military, who desired to drift about the boom and give a cheer, when the time should come, to rescuers and rescued. First home and first to draw the cheers was the French destroyer, whose tiny decks were massed with Australian infantry. Then to the harbour and the hills was given the story of what had happened twenty miles out at sea. The torpedo, striking the *Southland*, blew a hole in her bows thirty foot long, killing in the explosion a small tale of men. She began to settle rapidly. The Australians, usually the most unruly army of dare-devils that ever enjoyed a war, this time tried perfect discipline for a change; and in the absence of all panic they were easily distributed into the lifeboats, which, taking to the sea, lay by to watch the *Southland* sink. But the Captain and the others who remained aboard decided that with a big effort they might yet force the old ship into harbour and beach her somewhere and save her. Exulting in the decision, for a ship is a lovable thing, they called to the boats for volunteers who would accept the risks of her stokeholds and see about getting her safely into port. Among the Australians hearing this there was a fight for precedence; and now at the time these details were being told to Lemnos the selected volunteers were stoking up below the waterline and forcing the vessel onwards at three miles an hour. Now the harbour was more excited to welcome the *Southland* herself than to watch the coming of the rescue ships. They waited and they waited—for three miles an hour is slow going. But the moment came when she rounded the islands at the mouth of the harbour, moving more slowly than the moon as it rises behind the hill; and she came on, dragging herself into safety; and there were some men watching who said afterwards that, although they had intended to cheer with the loudest, their throats were too full to do it, as they saw this splendid laggard, with a jagged wound in her bows, creeping into harbour at the pace of an old man's walk.

* * *

GALLIPOLI—TRENCH WARFARE

From *The Secret Battle*.[1]

By A. P. Herbert

So many men have written descriptions of trench life in France; there have been so many poems, plays and speeches about it that the majority of our nation must have a much clearer mental picture of life on the Western Front than they have of life at the Savoy, or life in East Ham. But the Gallipoli Peninsula was never part of the Western Front, and no man came back from that place on leave; lucky, indeed, if he came back at all. The campaign was never, for obvious reasons, an important item in official propaganda, and the various non-official agencies which now bring home the War to Streatham had not begun to articulate when the campaign came to an end. And so neither Streatham nor anyone else knew anything about it. And though for a soldier to speak,

[1] Published by Methuen & Co., Ltd.

however distantly, of the details of trench life in France, is now in some circles considered a solecism equivalent to the talking of " shop," I hope I may still without offence make some brief reference to the trenches of the Peninsula. For, in truth, it was all very different. Above all, from dawn to dawn it was genuine infantry warfare. In France, apart from full-dress attacks, an infantryman may live for many months without once firing his rifle, or running the remotest risk of death by a rifle bullet. Patiently he tramps, and watches, and digs, and is shelled, clinging fondly to his rifle night and day, but seldom or never in a position to use it; so that in the stagnant days of the past he came to look upon it as a mere part of his equipment, like his water-bottle, only heavier and less comforting; and in real emergencies fumbled stupidly with the unfamiliar mechanism. This was true for a long time of the normal, or " peace-time," sectors of France.

But in those hill-trenches of Gallipoli the Turk and the Gentile fought with each other all day with rifle and bomb, and in the evenings crept out and stabbed each other in the dark. There was no release from the strain of watching and listening and taking thought. The Turk was always on higher ground; he knew every inch of all those valleys and vineyards and scrub-strewn slopes; and he had an uncanny accuracy of aim. Moreover, many of his men had the devotion of fanatics, which inspired them to lie out behind our lines, with stores of food enough to last out their ammunition, certain only of their ultimate destruction, but content to lie there and pick off the infidels till they, too, died. They were very brave men. But the Turkish snipers were not confined to the madmen who were caught disguised as trees in the broad daylight and found their way into the picture papers. Every trench was full of snipers, less theatrical but no less effective. And in the night they crept out with inimitable stealth and lay close in to our lines, killing our sentries, and chipping away our crumbling parapets.

So the sniping was terrible. In that first week we lost twelve men each day; they fell without a sound in the early morning as they stood up from their cooking at the brazier, fell shot through the head, and lay snoring horribly in the dust; they were sniped as they came up the communication trench with water, or carelessly raised their heads to look back at the ships in the bay; and in the night there were sudden screams where a sentry had moved his head too often against the moon. If a periscope were raised, however furtively, it was shivered in an instant; if a man peered over himself, he was dead. Far back in the Reserve Lines or at the wells, where a man thought himself hidden from view, the sniper saw and killed him. All along the line were danger-posts where many had been hit; these places became invested with a peculiar awe, and as you drew near to them the men said: " Keep low here, sir," in a reverential whisper, as though the Turk could hear them. Indeed, so uncanny were many of the deaths, that some men said the Turk could see impossibly through the walls of the trench, and crouched nervously in the bottom. All the communication trenches were watched, and wherever a head or a moving rifle showed at a gap a bullet came with automatic regularity. Going down a communication trench alone a man would hear the tap of these bullets on the parapet following him along, and break into a half-hysterical run in the bright sunlight to get away from this unnatural pursuit; for such it seemed to him to be.

The fire seemed to come from all angles; and units bitterly accused their neighbours of killing their men when it seemed impossible that any Turk could have fired the shot.

For a little, then, this sniping was thoroughly on the men's nerves. Nothing in their training had prepared them for it. They hated the "blinded" feeling it produced; it was demoralizing always to be wondering if one's head was low enough, always to walk with a stoop; it was tiring to be always taking care; and it was very dangerous to relax that care for a moment.

* * *

GALLIPOLI—THE LIGHTER SIDE
From *Gallipoli Memories*.[1]
By Compton MacKenzie

On June 9th George Brodrick,[2] who was A.D.C. to Sir Ian Hamilton, brought me the good news that a large package in

[1] Published by Cassel & Co., Ltd. [2] Viscount Dunsford.

brown paper of the most promising shape, covered with Egyptian stamps, and addressed to me was waiting in one of the Q tents.

"It must be your uniform at last," he said encouragingly.

We hurried over to the Q tent, and there, sure enough, was the parcel covered with Egyptian stamps. It was grabbed up, and my keenness to know what kind of a job Mr. Phillips had made of it led me to stop at George Brodrick's tent and cut the string. Appeared a service-jacket of almost as exquisite a shade of *eau de nil* as George Lloyd's; but when it was unfolded rapture was succeeded by dismay at the tailor's mistake in having affixed the red tabs of a Staff Officer, to which, of course, I was not entitled, being merely attached to G.H.Q.

"I say, look what the ass has done!"

"Never mind," said George Brodrick, "we can soon rip them off."

It took us some time, however, before we managed with a pair of sand-blunted scissors to rip the tabs from a pair of jackets, for the thread was tough and the sewing was close. However, we managed at last to pluck the uniforms of their borrowed plumes, and divesting myself of that Tommy's jacket which had been fretting my vanity for nearly a month, I donned the new arrival.

"It bags a bit behind," said Brodrick in those accents of carefully considered and sage gloom which were always so unanswerable.

"And it's about a couple of inches too big round the waist," I groaned. "What the deuce has the damn fellow been playing at? There isn't a tailor among the Guard, is there?" I asked hopefully, for the Guard consisted of West Surrey Yeomanry, of which George Brodrick was a Lieutenant.

"I doubt it," he said, shaking his head, for he would never surrender to an easy optimism.

All my peacock hopes vanished. I might have exclaimed with the wretched Moor:

> Pride, pomp, and circumstance of glorious war,
> Farewell! Othello's occupation's gone.

I saw myself doomed for the rest of the campaign to pace the sandy cape of Kephalo with an accordion-pleated back, the mere anatomy of a Royal Marine. And then an idea struck me.

" I suppose these *are* my things ? "

George Brodrick looked at the brown paper.

" My God," he exclaimed, " it's the wrong parcel! This is addressed to Colonel Beynon ! "

The first emotion of relief faded rapidly in the murk of a new problem.

" I don't know where on earth he'll find anyone here to sew his tabs on again," Brodrick muttered hopelessly as he stooped to pick up from the sandy bottom of the tent those little scarlet tabs disfigured by loose ends of thread which belonged to the mutilated uniform of the Assistant Adjutant-General.

At this moment Pollen put his head round the flap of the tent.

" Hullo ! The new uniform at last ? " he asked with quick and courteous sympathy.

" Well, not exactly, Pollen," I replied, and I think I must have given the kind of smile that is called sickly.

" We made a little mistake," George Brodrick put in. " There were several parcels in the Q tent, and as a matter of fact in a hurry we opened the wrong parcel. This is Colonel Beynon's uniform. I don't quite know what we'd better do about it."

" Why, you'd better take it round to his tent and explain the mistake," Pollen advised.

" Yes, but we've cut off his tabs," said Brodrick.

Even Pollen's urbanity was not proof against the shock of this announcement.

" Well, I wouldn't be in your shoes for something," he declared fervidly.

" Yes, I'm afraid he may be rather annoyed," I suggested in a vague hope that Pollen would laugh at such a preposterous notion.

" I should think he'll be absolutely furious," said Pollen, with an accent as near to brutality as it was possible for that soft, somewhat ecclesiastical voice to achieve.

I am glad to take this opportunity of paying a tribute to George Brodrick's conspicuous gallantry by setting it on record that he actually volunteered to come with me to Colonel Beynon's tent and help me to explain how the mistake had occurred.

It was like a nightmare walking through the Lines with these violated uniforms over our arms, for everybody we passed greeted us with "Hullo, the new uniform at last? How splendid!" And we had to call back cheerfully: "Yes, isn't it topping?"

Outside Colonel Beynon's tent we paused and looked at one another.

"I wonder if I could get Eddie Keeling to take them back. He's had a diplomatic training and he has no reverence for..."

"Come on," Brodrick interrupted firmly, "we'd better get it over."

The Assistant Adjutant-General was writing letters at a camp table when we entered, and he gave that day one of the noblest exhibitions of self-restraint I have beheld. The only thing he could not quite manage was a smile.

"Shall I put the things down here, sir?" I asked with an exaggerated solicitude as if by laying them down gently enough on the camp bed the wounded uniforms might recover.

"Anywhere," said the Colonel coldly.

I do not recall that to express our penitence we actually went out backward from the tent; but I am sure that we retired on tiptoe as one retired from an invalid's room, and I can still see the expression of Colonel Beynon's face and, deposited by George Brodrick in a neat little packet on his pillow, those outraged scarlet tabs.

* * *

THERE are some difficulties which no gallantry can overcome. The successive attempts to force the Peninsula were failures. Though in the light of later knowledge it is clear that the Turks were at the end of their tether, the British forces were withdrawn after eight months of battle.

GALLIPOLI—THE END

From *Gallipoli*.[1]

By JOHN MASEFIELD

"Still," our enemies say, "you did not win the Peninsula." We did not; and some day, when truth will walk clear-eyed,

[1] Published by William Heinemann, Ltd.

it will be known why we did not. Until then, let our enemies say this : " They did not win, but they came across three thousand miles of sea, a little army without reserves and short of munitions, a band of brothers, not half of them half-trained, and nearly all of them new to war. They came to what we said was an impregnable fort, on which our veterans of war and massacre had laboured for two months, and by sheer naked manhood they beat us, and drove us out of it. Then rallying, but without reserves, they beat us again, and drove us farther. Then rallying once more, but still without reserves, they beat us again, this time to our knees. Then, had they had reserves, they would have conquered, but by God's pity they had none. Then, after a lapse of time, when we were men again, they had reserves, and they hit us a staggering blow, which needed but a push to end us, but God again had pity. After that our God was indeed pitiful, for England made no further thrust, and they went away."

* * *

Towards the middle of 1915 began the air raids on England. At first carried out by Zeppelin airships, improved methods of defence eventually made this form of attack expensive ; subsequent raids were invariably made by airplanes.

THE RAIDERS
From *Zeppelins over England*.[1]
By Freiherr Treusch von Buttlar Brandenfels

We were flying at a height of 15,000 feet. Suddenly the steersman called out to me : " Searchlights on our starboard bow ! " Then the whole car became alive, and with our binoculars to our eyes we leant out of the control car down to our waists.

What a magnificent sight ! How wonderful to see the beams of the searchlights exploring the heavens inch by inch, intersecting one another, then collecting into groups of three, four and five from different directions, and cutting each other again, and at last, at the point where they intersected, possibly

[1] Published by George G. Harrap & Co., Ltd.

finding a Zeppelin hanging like a huge incandescent cigar in the sky!

In a moment red lights were scattered through the blackness. They were the shrapnel-bursts.

Soon corresponding red lights appeared below on the ground. They were our own bombs.

There could not be the slightest doubt that our ship, too, was now quite close to the English coast.

Suddenly I staggered and was enveloped in blackness. In the heat of the fight I had lost my liquid-air pipe. It had dropped off the mouthpiece. It grew darker and darker. I felt I was going to be sick. I groped madly about the floor and seized hold of legs, cables, machine-gun belts. At last, just as I felt I should faint from the leaden weight on my head, I found the pipe!

It was marvellous. The moment I was able to breathe in the liquid air again I felt I could have knocked down whole barricades of brick walls, or lifted our tender with my little finger, or juggled with the machine-gun as though it were a billiard-cue, so elemental and powerful is the sudden fresh breath of life that is breathed into one!

"Climb to 18,000 feet!"

Minus twenty-one degrees, thirty degrees, thirty-five degrees Centigrade! Splendid! We met with no inversion. On the contrary, the temperature decreased appreciably the higher we rose.

A quarter of an hour later we had made the coast. We could see the lights of towns and villages, and of railways with their red and green signals, quite plainly. Suddenly everything below went black again. The district was certainly very skilful at putting out or concealing lights. It knew all about airship raids!

Ahead of us, I should say about ten miles away, one of our ships was attacking, and it immediately occurred to me that I ought to keep a more southerly course. So I changed my direction, intending, as soon as I had the attacking ship on my starboard beam, to course about and, flying north-east, to attack the same objective.

Everything depended on our reaching our objective

unobserved. We were lucky. It was not long before we located the brightly illumined ship four points abaft the starboard beam, and I gave the order to steer north-east with rudder hard aport. The attack could begin.

The trap-doors for the bombs, which were in the catwalk, could be opened by the *Wachoffizier* by simply pressing a button. We were on the western edge of our objective. I gave the order for action!

Schiller pressed the first button and the first ten-pounder bomb whistled down to the depths. In spite of the buzz of the engines we could hear it whizzing through the air. The whole thing happened in a flash; the next bomb followed, then the third and fourth.

The bombs were plainly visible. A tiny blob of light appeared 18,000 feet below us, a few seconds later we heard the dull thud above the hum of the engines.

There could be no doubt that we were well over our objective, so the heavier fellows, the one-hundredweight and two-hundredweight bombs, were also dropped. They were released at regular intervals and crashed down below with a loud whine, followed quite rhythmically by a heavy thud as they reached the ground. The last three bombs were released simultaneously, and a heavy roll of thunder resounded below.

The crew knew what to do. Out with the ammunition!

It was so light that my eyes began to smart. Immediately after the first burst the searchlights had found us. One, two, three, four! We were flying through a cloud of glaring light. I could read the smallest print on the map before me.

How magnificent the huge, dazzlingly bright form of the ship must have looked 18,000 feet up in the sky, as she steered her way across the heavens!

The shrapnel salvoes drew nearer and nearer. At first they burst 3000 feet below us. Oh, so the man in front of us had been flying at 15,000 feet!

But they corrected their range damnably quickly. Now they were getting very close indeed. We could hear the shells bursting all round and the whine of the splinters as they hurtled through space—high-explosive shells.

Should we climb higher, exhaust our last reserve strength,

and, for the sake of 300 feet, risk being brought down by a hit, in which case all would be lost?

Suddenly on our port bow we saw a brilliant light, but no searchlight beam. It was deep and broad, a regular bank of light. The searchlight was penetrating a cloud.

"All engines full throttle." We were saved! Up we climbed into the cloud. The next salvo would certainly have hit the ship if we had not been able to hide.

* * *

THE RAIDED
From *How We Lived Then*, 1914–1918.[1]
By Mrs. C. S. Peel, O.B.E.

It was estimated that 396 bombs were dropped and 343 shells fired in this district alone, and so frequent were the raids that the whole system of living was altered and subterranean refuge cities were evolved in caverns and other underground places. In Ramsgate it would have been almost impossible to throw a stone in any direction without nearing a spot where a bomb or shell had fallen. Hospitals, hotels and schools were hit, but mercifully the bombs did not do as much damage as might have been expected. On one occasion, though 10,000 sheets of glass were smashed and 660 houses damaged, the total casualties in that town were only 24 killed and 51 injured. It was during that raid that a man and a woman were buried in the ruins of the Bull and George Inn, and the barmaid had a wonderful escape, for she had just left her bed when a bomb passed through the centre of it. A fancy bazaar was wrecked, a bomb falling close to the bed of a man, who suffered nothing worse than to be temporarily smothered by an avalanche of children's spades. Crowds of sightseers hurried into the towns and an enterprising trader whose premises had been damaged announced to them: "The glass has gone but the goods are here."

At Broadstairs, although schools in which children were then in class were hit, only three people lost their lives—a mother and two children. A bomb struck the roof of a well-

[1] Published by John Lane, The Bodley Head, Ltd., London.

known girls' school, and when it exploded, a room on the top floor in which fourteen children were at lessons was smothered in dust and debris. In this building, filled with children and directly hit, only two people were injured, and these slightly. They were a child of nine and a housemaid. The children behaved splendidly, and before many hours had passed, one of them was busy making sketches of the air raid, showing the scene in the classroom before and after the advent of the bombs. A sad occurrence at Ramsgate was the falling of a bomb which killed or injured twelve children who were on their way to Sunday School. On another occasion a girl was standing at the garden gate waiting for her parents to arrive from London when a bomb exploded at her feet. She died a few days later. The horse of a cabman driving along a street was blown up, but he and his fare escaped with light injuries, and two farm labourers who were having an argument about the nationality of the machines as they came over the sea had just concluded a bet on the matter when a bomb fell fifteen yards from them. They at once went to a tavern to settle up their wager.

Dover suffered terribly. It became necessary to prepare shelters capable of holding a large number of people. The first to be made was in Connaught Park, and was designed to shelter the children playing there. Later it was occupied at night by the residents of that quarter. Some great caves were used for the same purpose and were furnished with seating accommodation and electric light. Other caves at the eastern end of the town also were arranged as shelters, and by the end of 1917 it was calculated that 25,000 people could be protected from attack. These shelters were brightly illuminated, and in them one might see beds in which people slept, or endeavoured to sleep, for there would be near by a party of children at play, a little further a tea and coffee stall, a concert party and a group of card-players. Special Constables kept order, and in the larger caves arrangements were made to deal with cases of sickness. At one time, on thirteen consecutive nights the sirens sounded the alarm, and large numbers of men, women and children spent their nights underground.

* * *

The impotent rage and fear aroused by these raids sought expression in attacks on inoffensive enemy (or suspected enemy) civilians. From these achievements the element of loot was not altogether wanting.

HUN BAITING
From *The Home Front*.[1]
By E. Sylvia Pankhurst

Crowds, mostly made up of women, gathered before each ruined home. One, where a child had been killed, was still inhabited. A soldier in khaki stood at the door striving in vain to keep back the press of human bodies surging against it. The people who lived there were scarcely able to force a way to their own door. A bomb had descended upon a brewery; from the roof to the cellar all had fallen, only the outer walls remained, and a mass of charred wood in the basement. Many dwellings were thus completely gutted. In the ashes left by the fires which had ravaged them nothing save the twisted ironwork of the bedsteads could be identified. A chorus of wailing stirred amongst the women: " Oh, my God! Look at the home! Oh, my God! "

Rumour raced hot-foot: " There were little lights signalling, telling them where to drop the bombs! " . . . " Germans! " . . . " Beasts." . . . " Germans! " . . . " I saw taxi-cabs driving up and down signalling! " . . . " Germans! " . . . " They should all have been cleared out at the beginning of the War! " . . . " The Government has nowhere to put them! " . . . " They go and give themselves up to the police and they tell them to go home. . . . Everywhere a bomb is dropped you'll find one of their shops was wrecked near! "

Alas, where in the East End would one fail to find a German shop which had been wrecked in the anti-German riots? Near to the brewery was a baker's shop with a German name on the fascia; the door, the shutters, the very window-frames had been torn off. It was boarded up now with new, unpainted wood. The crowds as they passed it growled imprecations; wild stories grew there. . . .

[1] Published by Hutchinson & Co. (Publishers), Ltd.

In Hoxton Street was a rush of excitement. A German baker's, one of the few still remaining, had just been raided. "They were serving bread there an hour ago!" a surprised voice uttered. "They go in to buy bread from them, and they wreck the shop," another answered. The windows were smashed, only a few jagged bits of glass still attached to the framework. The pavement was littered with glass and flour. The shop had been cleared of everything portable. A policeman stood at the door. Two soldiers came out, laughing. "There is plenty of new bread downstairs if you want it; it will only be wasted there!" they called as they went off, seeking new quarry.

Down the street police whistles sounded vociferously: a babel of shouting, tremendous outcry. A crowd was advancing at a run, a couple of lads on bicycles leading, a swarm of children on the fringes, screaming like gulls. Missiles were flying. In the centre of the turmoil men dragged a big, stout man, stumbling and resisting in their grasp, his clothes whitened by flour, his mouth dripping blood. They rushed him on. New throngs closed round him. . . .

From another direction arose more shouting. A woman's scream. The tail of the crowd dashed off towards the sound. Crowds raced to it from all directions . . . fierce, angry shouts and yells. . . . A woman was in the midst of a struggling mob; her blouse half torn off, her fair hair fallen, her face contorted with pain and terror, blood running down her bare white arm. A big, drunken man flung her to the ground. She was lost to sight. . . . "Oh, my God! Oh! They are kicking her!" a woman screamed.

"Do help her!" I pleaded with a soldier who stood watching. He shrugged his shoulders. "I can't do anything." "You are a soldier; they will respect you!" "Why should I?" he asked with a curl of the lip. "Look, there's another soldier: can't you get on to *him*?"

"She is covered with blood!" a woman's voice cried again. I struggled to reach her, but the closely packed onlookers would not make way for me. An Army motor drove up and was halted by the press. An officer, hawk-eyed, aquiline, sat in the front; there were vacant seats behind. I sprang to the step: "A woman is being hurt here. Will you take her away from the crowd?" "I don't think we can; we are on military business," he answered curtly. The horn was sounded, the people made way, the car drove on. . . .

The woman on the ground was unconscious. Those who a moment before had shrieked imprecations, were seized with pity. The nearest raised her and rested her on a fruiterer's upturned barrel. A couple of women supported her with their arms; another was fastening up her hair. She drooped, still nerveless, her colour gone, her eyes closed. They chafed her hands, the crowd about them silent and awed. Passion was spent. "I believe in all things being done in a proper manner." "Killing the woman won't do any good!" Two voices were heard. . . .

"Make a way there! Make a way there! Move on! Move on!" The police came shouting and pushing through the throng, hustling away with equal roughness the onlookers, the fainting woman and those who bore her.

Another mob swept round the corner, hot in fury, baiting a man in flour-covered clothing, wrenched and jerked by the collar, thumped on the back, kicked from the rear. "All right, Gov'ner; all right," he articulated between the blows, in humble and reasoning Cockney-tones fully typic as that of his assailants. Alas, poor Patriotism, what foolish cruelties are committed in thy name!

* * *

THE spring and summer of 1915 were chiefly devoted—so far as the British Front in the west was concerned—to a series of small attacks. Though these achieved no tactical result, they were of value educationally, in accustoming men and commanders to the needs of modern warfare.

OVER THE TOP
From *Mud and Khaki*.[1]
By H. S. CLAPHAM

We started again at dusk and passed down the railway cutting, but, instead of turning off into the fields, we went on

[1] Published by Hutchinson & Co. (Publishers), Ltd.

as far as the Menin Road, at what is known as "Hell Fire Corner." A few hundred yards down the road we turned into the fields on the left, and found a resting-place for the night in some shallow "jumping-off" trenches, a few yards back from the front line. It was very dark, and the trench was small, and sitting in a huddle I got cramp and felt miserable.

The Huns started by putting over big crumps all around us. They seemed to aim for the relics of a building a hundred yards in the rear, and there the bricks were flying, but otherwise they did no damage. Still, they kept us guessing, and, knowing what was in front of us, I found sleep impossible.

Then at 2.50 a.m. our own guns started and kept up a heavy bombardment of the trenches in front until 4.15, by which time it was quite light. I don't know whether the Huns kept it up, too. In any case, one couldn't have heard them or their explosions: there was such a devil of a row going on.

At 4.15 a whistle blew. The men in the front line went over the top, and we scrambled out and took their places in the front trench. In front of us was a small field, with grass knee-high, split diagonally by an old footpath. On the other side of the field was a belt of trees, known as Y Wood, in which lay the first Hun trench.

In a few moments flags went up there, to show that it had been captured and that the troops were going on. Another whistle, and we ourselves scrambled over the parapet and sprinted across the field. Personally, I was so overweighted that I could only amble, and I remember being intensely amused at the sight of a little chap in front of me who seemed in even worse case than myself. Without thinking much about it, I took the diagonal path, as the line of least resistance, and most of my section did the same.

When I dropped into the Hun trench I found it a great place, only three feet wide, and at least eight deep, and beautifully made of white sandbags, back and front. At that spot there was no sign of any damage by our shells, but a number of dead Huns lay in the bottom. There was a sniper's post just where I fell in, a comfortable little square hole, fitted with seats and shelves, bottles of beer, tinned meats, and a fine helmet hanging on a hook.

Our first duty was to change the wire, so, after annexing the helmet, I slipped off my pack, and, clambering out again, started to move the wire from what was now the rear to the new front of the trench. It was rotten stuff, most of it loose coils, and the only knife-rests were not more than a couple of feet high. What there was movable of it we got across without much difficulty, and we had just finished when we were ordered to move down the trench as our diagonal advance had brought us too far to the right.

We moved down along the belt of woodland, which was only a few yards broad, to a spot where one of our companies was already hard at work digging a communication trench back to our old front line. Here there was really no trench at all. One or more of our own big shells had burst in the middle, filling it up for a distance of ten yards and practically destroying both parapet and parados. Some of us started building up the parapet with sandbags, and I saw the twins merrily at work hauling out dead Huns at least twice their own size.

There was a hedge along the back of the trench, so I scrambled through a hole in it, piled my pack, rifle and other things, including the helmet, on the farther side, and started again on the wire. Hereabouts it was much better stuff, and it took us some time to get it across and pegged down. We had just got the last knife-rest across when I saw a man who was placing sandbags on the parapet from the farther side swivel round, throw his legs into the trench and collapse in a heap in the bottom. Several others were already lying there, and for the first time I realised that a regular hail of machine-gun bullets was sweeping over the trench.

I made a dive for my pack, but though I found that, my pet helmet had disappeared. Quite a string of wounded and masterless men had passed down the back of the hedge while I was working, and one of them must have thought it a good souvenir to take into hospital.

We all started work at a feverish pace, digging out the trench and building up some sort of shelter in front. One chap, a very nice kid, was bowled over almost at once with a bullet in the groin, and lay in the trench, kicking and shrieking, while we worked.

The attacking battalions had carried several more trenches, and we were told that two at least had been held, but our own orders were to consolidate and hold on to the trench we were in at all costs. We could see very little in front. There was a wide field of long grass, stretching gently upward to a low mound of earth several hundred yards away. This was the next line. Away on the right front was Belleward Wood and Hooge Château, both above us, but the latter was partly hidden by the corner of Y Wood.

I had just filled a sandbag and placed it on the top of the parapet when I happened to glance down and saw a slight movement in the earth between my feet. I stooped and scraped away the soil with my fingers and I found what seemed like palpitating flesh. It proved to be a man's cheek, and a few minutes' work uncovered his head. I poured a little water down his throat and two or three of us dug out the rest of him. He was undamaged except for his feet and ankles, which were a mass of pulp, and he recovered consciousness as we worked. The first thing he said was in English: "What corps are you?" He was a big man, and told us he was forty-five and had only been a soldier for a fortnight.

We dragged him out and laid him under the hedge. There was nothing else we could do for him. He had another drink later, but he must have died in the course of the day. I am afraid we forgot all about him, but nothing could have lived there until evening.

The captain was the next to go. He insisted on standing on the parados, directing operations, and got a bullet in the lungs. He could walk, and two men were detailed to take him down to the dressing-station. One came back, to be killed later in the day, but the other stopped a bullet *en route*, and followed the captain.

When we had got our big Hun out, he left a big hole in the ground, and we found a dead arm and hand projecting from the bottom. We dug about, but did not seem to be able to find the body, and when I seized the sleeve and pulled, the arm came out of the ground by itself. We had to dig deeper for our own sake, but there was nothing else left, except messy earth, which seemed to have been driven into the side of the trench. The man helping me turned sick, for it wasn't pretty work, but I claimed a substitute, and between us we carted out a barrowful in wetter sheets and dumped it under the hedge. After that I had had enough myself.

* * *

At this stage in the conflict the civilian soldiers were playing an active part. The welcome extended to them by the more " exclusive " of the professional officers was not always one of unmixed enthusiasm.

GENTLEMEN—TEMPORARY AND PERMANENT
From *Good-bye to All That*.[1]
By Robert Graves

About fifteen officers of various ranks were sitting in chairs reading the week's illustrated papers or (the seniors at least) talking quietly. At the door I said : " Good morning, gentlemen," the new officer's customary greeting to the mess. There was no answer. Everybody looked at me curiously. The silence that my entry had caused was soon broken by the gramophone, which began singing happily :

> We've been married just one year,
> And oh, we've got the sweetest,
> And oh, we've got the neatest,
> And oh, we've got the cutest
> Little oil stove.

I found a chair in the background and picked up *The Field*. The door burst open suddenly and a senior officer, with a red face and angry eye, burst in. " Who the blazes put that record on ? " he shouted to the room. " One of the bloody warts, I expect. Take it off, somebody. It makes me sick. Let's have some real music. Put on the ' Angelus.' " Two subalterns (in the Royal Welch a subaltern had to answer to the name of " wart ") sprang up, stopped the gramophone, and put on " When the Angelus is ringing." The young captain

[1] Published by Jonathan Cape, Ltd.

who had put on " We've been married " shrugged his shoulders and went on reading, the other faces in the room were blank.

" Who was that ? " I whispered to the Surrey-man.

He frowned. " That's Buzz Off," he said.

Before the record was finished the door opened and in came the colonel; Buzz Off reappeared with him. Everybody jumped up and said in unison: " Good morning, sir." It was his first appearance that day. Before giving the customary greeting and asking us to sit down, he turned spitefully to the gramophone: " Who on earth puts this wretched ' Angelus ' on every time I come into the mess ? For heaven's sake play something cheery for a change." And with his own hands he took off the " Angelus," wound up the gramophone and put on " We've been married just one year." At that moment a gong rang for lunch and he abandoned it. We filed into the next room, a ballroom with mirrors and a decorated ceiling. We sat down at a long, polished table. The seniors sat at the top, the juniors competed for seats as far away from them as possible. I was unlucky enough to get a seat at the foot of the table facing the commanding officer, the adjutant and Buzz Off. There was not a word spoken down that end except for an occasional whisper for the salt or for the beer—very thin French stuff. Robertson, who had not been warned, asked the mess waiter for whisky. " Sorry, sir," said the mess waiter, " it's against orders for the young officers." Robertson was a man of forty-two, a solicitor with a large practice, and had stood for Parliament in the Yarmouth division at the previous election.

I saw Buzz Off glaring at us and busied myself with my meat and potatoes.

He nudged the adjutant. " Who are those two funny ones down there, Charley ? " he asked.

" New this morning from the militia. Answer to the names of Robertson and Graves."

" Which is which ? " asked the colonel.

" I'm Robertson, sir."

" I wasn't asking you."

Robertson winced, but said nothing. Then Buzz Off noticed something.

"T'other wart's wearing a wind-up tunic." Then he bent forward and asked me loudly. "You there, wart. Why the hell are you wearing your stars on your shoulder instead of your sleeve?"

My mouth was full and I was embarrassed. Everybody was looking at me. I swallowed the lump of meat whole and said: "It was a regimental order in the Welch Regiment. I understood that it was the same everywhere in France."

The colonel turned puzzled to the adjutant: "What on earth's the man talking about the Welch Regiment for?" And then to me: "As soon as you have finished your lunch you will visit the master tailor. Report to the orderly room when you're properly dressed."

There was a severe struggle in me between resentment and regimental loyalty. Resentment for the moment had the better of it. I said under my breath: "You damned snobs. I'll survive you all. There'll come a time when there won't be one of you left serving in the battalion to remember battalion mess at Laventie." This time came, exactly a year later.

* * *

WITH the entry of Italy into the War in May, 1915, began one of the strangest campaigns in the history of modern warfare. The greater part of the battle-front lay along violently mountainous country, where the hostility of Nature was added to that of man.

ITALY COMES IN

From *At the War*.[1]

By LORD NORTHCLIFFE

As the sun rose the great peaks of the Dolomites stood out like pink pearls, set here and there in a soft white vapour. Coming through a Canadian-looking pine forest, with log-house barracks, kitchens, and canteens beneath one such peak, I was reminded of Dante's lines: "Gazing above, I saw her shoulders clothed already with the planet's rays." But

[1] Published by Hodder and Stoughton.

poetic memories soon faded before a sniper's bullet from a very near Austrian outlook.

At one spot the Austrian and Italian barbed-wire entanglements were clearly visible through glasses on a neighbouring summit at a height of over ten thousand feet. A few yards below in an open cavern, protected by an overhanging rock, the little grey tents of Italy's soldiers were plainly seen. It may be a consolation to our men on the Somme and in Flanders to know that the War is being waged here in conditions equally as dangerous as theirs.

The Italians have driven back the Austrians foot by foot up the almost vertical Dolomite rock with mountain, field and heavy guns, and especially in hand-to-hand and bomb fighting. Sniping never ceases by day, but the actual battles are almost invariably fought by night.

The only day fighting is when, as in the famous capture of Col di Lana and more recently at Castelletto, the whole or part of a mountain-top is to be blown off, because it is impossible to turn or carry it by direct assault. Tunnels, sometimes 800 yards long, are drilled by machinery through the solid rock beneath the Austrian strongholds, which presently disappear under the smashing influence of thirty or forty tons of dynamite. Then the Alpini swarm over the debris and capture or kill the enemy survivors and rejoice in a well-earned triumph.

One needs to have scaled a mountain side to an Italian gun emplacement or look-out post to gauge fully the nature of this warfare. Imagine a catacomb, hewn through the hard rock, with a central hall and galleries leading to a gun position 7000 feet up. Reckon that each gun emplacement represents three months' constant labour with drill, hammer and mine. Every requirement, as well as food and water, must be carried up by men at night or under fire by day. Every soldier employed at these heights needs another soldier to bring him food and drink, unless, as happens in some places, the devoted wives of the Alpini act nightly under organised rules as porters for their husbands.

The food supply is most efficiently organised. A young London Italian private, speaking English perfectly, whom I met by chance, told me, and I have since verified the information, that the men holding this long line of the Alps received special food, particularly during the seven months winter. Besides the excellent soup which forms the staple diet of the Italian as of the French soldiers, the men receive a daily ration of two pounds of bread, half a pound of meat, half a pint of red wine, macaroni of various kinds, rice, cheese, dried and fresh fruit, chocolate, and, thrice weekly, small quantities of Cognac and Marsala.

Members of the Alpine Club know that in the high Dolomites water is in summer often as precious as on the Carso. Snow serves this purpose in winter. Three months' reserve supplies of oil fuel, food, alcohol, and medicine must be stored in the catacomb mountain positions, lest, as happened to an officer whom I met, the garrisons should be cut off for weeks and months at a time. I have already pointed out that the Italians have driven the Austrians in most cases by sheer hard fighting to the very tops of the peaks. Unless the positions thus won were firmly held during the winter they might rapidly be lost at the melting of the snows. They form an essential portion of the great allied siege of Germany. Sir Douglas Haig has asserted that the war is a young man's game. Certainly, as far as concerns the fighting in the high Alps, men above thirty are of very little use.

* * *

AT the insistence of the French, the New Armies prepared for their first blood bath. On September 25th the battle of Loos opened with high hopes, which, unfortunately, could not be realised.

GUNS AT LOOS
From *Peter Jackson, Cigar Merchant*.[1]
By GILBERT FRANKAU

"*Three rounds battery-fire. One o seconds.*" "*Stop.*" "*Add twenty-five.*" "*Two rounds battery-fire. One o seconds.*" "*Go on.*" "*At battery-fire, sweep one five minutes.*"

[1] Published by Hutchinson & Co. (Publishers), Ltd.

Up and down the long line men stood shouting, men jerked triggers, muzzles roared and recoiled, shells leapt to open breech, breech-blocks twirled home, gunners—knees astride—clung to rocking seats. And round the rocking, roaring guns, deafened men still toiled with pick and shovel at the sandbag epaulments.

Batteries were firing independently: and Stark, mackintosh spread on the parados of a crumbling trench, watched them without a word. He felt a hand on his arm; saw two fingers and a cigar pointing over his shoulder, forward and upward through the gun-flashes. " See that sausage, sir? " shouted P. J. in his ear.

The Weasel looked round at his adjutant: the adjutant flicked an eye towards the crowded horse-lines.

" Behind those houses," rasped the Weasel. " Get 'em away quietly or they'll panic. And tell 'em to post a look-out man to watch for signals."

" Not bad for a civilian," thought the Weasel as he watched Peter stroll calmly to the haystack, tap Horrocks on the shoulder.

The balloon had gone down again; guns were still firing; and across the fields—veterinary officer's white breeches at their head—filed at a walk the horses of the headquarter staff. Now, in and out among the tethered teams at the battery horse-lines, strode a stocky figure, cigar in mouth, whispering, " Hook in and get away quietly. Behind those houses. At a walk, please, quartermaster-sergeant." Like figures in a quadrille the bays and browns and blacks of the teams, the dark green of the ammunition waggons curved to slow life, emerged into four long lines that unrolled steadily across the dun fields to safety. But as the lines drew clear they revealed, behind them, low dark bunches in the middle distance: other horses—hundreds and hundreds of horses. . . .

" *Ich kann nicht genau sehen*," mumbled a guttural voice three and a half miles away, " *aber am Dreiweg finden wir sircher etwas. Also, los damit, lieber Oberleutnant.* . . ."

Peter heard, above the roar of his own guns, a high shrill scream; saw a black fountain spurt from the ground 300 yards in front. Instantaneously the Weasel was on his feet, hands to mouth. "Take cover," roared the Weasel. "Take cover. All except gun-numbers into the trench." For the diggers had stopped work, stood staring at the dropping fountain.

Rose another scream up the sky. . . . "Get down, you bloody fools, get down." Now the Weasel was half-way along the flashing line. . . . The scream came shrieking to earth, stopped. A hundred yards in front, a few clods leapt from the ground. "Under cover. Under cover." Like rabbits to burrow men popped to earth. But still the guns went on.

Peter, kneeling behind quivering sandbags, was conscious of a mule-like bray high in air, of a second's deadly silence, of a thudding crash; felt a rush of air at his ears; saw something slice the sandbag at his side as knife slices cheese; plunge into the turf. . . . Then he heard fragments pattering on the hard earth behind him; looked up; and saw—a hundred yards away, standing upright, hands in his pockets, the Weasel: and the Weasel was still shouting: "Under cover, you bloody fools, get under cover." The gun behind which Peter knelt went off with a crash. . . .

"My aunt!" he thought.

Except for the colonel's figure nothing moved behind the guns. Purves and the doctor, noses to ground, were lying flat against the haystack. Very high in air, another shell went howling on its way. Peter, following the noise with his eyes, found dark clumps of horses; was conscious noise ceased; saw a great black earth-spout shoot up among the horses; heard the double crash of shell's alighting; saw terrified teams rear and plunge; saw little figures hurling themselves at bridles. . . .

Another shell swished over; and another; plunged to ground in rear of him. The whole middle distance seemed a mass of stampeding beasts that hurled themselves through black fountains across the plains.

"Didn't you hear me say get under cover, you sanguinary cigar merchant?" rasped a voice at his ear.

* * *

INFANTRY AT LOOS

From *A Generation Missing.*[1]

By Carroll Carstairs

The battery, which was in an enfilading position, had lost touch owing to a cut telephone wire. I was detailed to lay wire to a brigade headquarters. I began in the morning, but it was not until early the next morning that I had completed my task. We started along a communication trench down which the wounded Scottish soldiers of the 9th Division were coming—minute particles of the attacking waves drifting back with the ebb of the tide. They moved along the trench, weary and dazed, and suffering silently, the spent and broken remnants of those first fine Kitchener battalions. It was impossible to recognise in them the men who had swung so lustily along the roads behind the weird and plaintive, the almost prophetic wailing of their pipes. Some were being carried on stretchers, their ashen faces turned to the grey sky; others dragged along with gaping and bloody wounds, the lesser wounded helping the more helpless. Somehow I could hear again the low skirling of their pipes as, still under shell-fire, they crawled and shuffled away from their first murderous battlefield. . . . I gave one man a cigarette and he told me he had been in three bayonet charges the day before, and I thought the world should be draped in mourning for these mighty sufferers.

Soon it began to rain, a thin persistent rain. To make matters worse, the 7th Division, relieving the 9th, appeared, coming up the trench; meeting the wounded coming down, the congestion became terrible. There was no room for me, and I and my signallers continued laying the wire on top of the trench, although the chances of the wire getting cut or, incidentally, our getting hit was greater. Up the trench I kept pace with the 7th regular Division—jaunty, doughty Cockneys who scoffed with grim but good-humoured sarcasm at the failure of Kitchener's volunteers, and who felt a kind of pride that they, the regulars, should have been needed.

[1] Published by William Heinemann, Ltd.

"We 'ad to be called on to finish their job for 'em," I heard one say. Poor devils, little did they reckon on the morrow's massacre that awaited them. But I did not see them the following morning—I think of them still, cocky and sure, and ready to tackle what they considered was their own professional job.

Day changing into night found us still carrying our reel of wire, slipping along the ground that was rapidly becoming a morass. The rain, relentlessly continuing, blurred our vision so that we had to crawl along the very edge of the communication trench that we might not lose our way. Soaked to the skin (I had left my mackintosh behind), heavy with water and mud and weariness and lack of food (we had brought no rations), we moved along at a snail's pace. Our objective became an undreamed-of possibility. The men of the 7th, now silent or quietly cursing and dimly described in the night of rain, moved endlessly forward, choking the trench.

* * *

At the same time the French made fierce but abortive onslaughts at Champagne and Artois. Artillery duels paved the way for hand-to-hand fighting on a scale perhaps unknown before. Joffre described these attacks as "nibbles," but the dispassionate historian will see in their expensive failure a case of the biter bit.

BLOOD BATH IN CHAMPAGNE

From *Under Fire*.[1]

By Henri Barbusse

(Translated from the French by Fitzwater Wray.)

We are submerged in a mysterious smoke, and at first I can only see blue uniforms in the stifling gulf. We go one way and then another, driven by each other, snarling and searching. We turn about, and with our hands encumbered by knife, bombs and rifle, we do not know at first what to do.

"They're in their funk-holes, the swine!" is the cry. Heavy explosions are shaking the earth—underground, in

[1] Published by J. M. Dent & Sons, Ltd.

BLOOD BATH IN CHAMPAGNE

the dug-outs. We are all at once divided by huge clouds of smoke so thick that we are masked and can see nothing more. We struggle like drowning men through the acrid darkness of a fallen fragment of night. One stumbles against barriers of cowering clustered beings who bleed and howl in the bottom. Hardly can one make out the trench walls, straight up just here and made of white sandbags, which are everywhere torn like paper. At one time the heavy adhesive reek sways and lifts, and one sees again the swarming mob of the attackers. Torn out of the dusty picture, the silhouette of a hand-to-hand struggle is drawn in fog on the wall, it droops and sinks to the bottom. I hear several shrill cries of "Kamarad!" proceeding from a pale-faced and grey-clad group in the huge corner made by a rending shell. Under the inky cloud the tempest of men flows back, climbs towards the right, eddying, pitching and falling along the earthwork dark and ruined.

．　　．　　．　　．　　．　　．

And suddenly one feels that it is over. We see and hear and understand that our wave, rolling here through the barrage fire, has not encountered an equal breaker. They have fallen back on our approach. The battle has dissolved in front of us. The slender curtain of defenders has crumbled into the holes, where they are caught like rats or killed. There is no more resistance, but a void, a great void. We advance in crowds like a terrible array of spectators.

And here the trench seems all lightning-struck. With its tumbled white walls it might be just here the soft and slimy bed of a vanished river that has left stony bluffs, with here and there the flat, round hole of a pool, also dried up; and on the edges, on the sloping banks and in the bottom, there is a long, trailing glacier of corpses—a dead river that is filled again to overflowing by the new tide and the breaking wave of our company. In the smoke vomited by dug-outs and the shaking wind of subterranean explosions, I come upon a compact mass of men hooked on to each other who are describing a wide circle. Just as we reach them the entire mass breaks up to make a residue of furious battle. I see Blaire break away, his helmet hanging on his neck by the chin-strap and his face flayed, and uttering a savage yell. I stumble upon a man who is crouching at the entry to a dug-out. Drawing back from the black hatchway, yawning and treacherous, he steadies himself with his left hand on a beam. In his right hand, and for several seconds, he holds a bomb which s on the point of exploding. It disappears in the hole, bursts mmediately, and a horrible human echo answers him from the bowels of the earth. The man seizes another bomb.

Another man strikes and shatters the posts at the mouth of another dug-out with a pickaxe he has found there, causing a landslide, and the entry is blocked. I see several shadows trampling and gesticulating over the tomb.

Of the living rugged band that has got so far and has reached this long-sought trench after dashing against the storm of invincible shells and bullets launched to meet them, I can hardly recognise those whom I know, just as though all that had gone before of our lives had suddenly become very distant. There is some change working in them. A frenzied excitement is driving them all out of themselves.

"What are we stopping here for?" says one, grinding his teeth.

"Why don't we go on to the next?" a second asks me in fury. "Now we're here, we'd be there in a few jumps!"

"I, too, I want to go on."—"Me, too. Ah, the hogs!"

They shake themselves like banners. They carry the luck of their survival as it were glory; they are implacable, uncontrolled, intoxicated with themselves.

We wait and stamp about in the captured work, this strange demolished way that winds along the plain and goes from the unknown to the unknown.

Advance to the right!

We begin to flow again in one direction. No doubt it is a movement planned up there, back beyond, by the chiefs. We trample soft bodies underfoot, some of which are moving and slowly altering their position; rivulets and cries come from them. Like posts and heaps of rubbish, corpses are piled anyhow on the wounded, and press them down, suffocate them, strangle them. So that I can get by, I must push at a slaughtered trunk of which the neck is a spring of gurgling blood.

BLOOD BATH IN CHAMPAGNE

In the cataclysm of earth and of massive wreckage blown up and blown out, above the hordes of wounded and dead that stir together, athwart the moving forest of smoke implanted in the trench and in all its environs, one no longer sees any face but what is inflamed, blood-red with sweat, eyes flashing. Some groups seem to be dancing as they brandish their knives. They are elated, immensely confident, ferocious.

The battle dies down imperceptibly. A soldier says, "Well, what's to be done now?" It flares up again suddenly at one point. Twenty yards away in the plain, in the direction of a circle that the grey embankment makes, a cluster of rifle-shots crackles and hurls its scattered missiles around a hidden machine-gun, that spits intermittently and seems to be in difficulties.

Under the shadowy wing of a sort of yellow and bluish nimbus I see men encircling the flashing machine and closing in on it. Near to me I make out the silhouette of Mesnil Joseph, who is steering straight and with no effort of concealment for the spot whence the barking explosions come in jerky sequence.

A flash shoots out from a corner of the trench between us two. Joseph halts, sways, stoops and drops on one knee. I run to him and he watches me coming. "It's nothing—my thigh. I can crawl along by myself." He seems to have become quiet, childish, docile; and sways slowly towards the trench.

I have still in my eyes the exact spot whence rang the shot that hit him, and I slip round there by the left, making a detour. No one there. I only meet another of our squad on the same errand—Paradis.

We are bustled by men who are carrying on their shoulders pieces of iron of all shapes. They block up the trench and separate us. "The machine-gun's taken by the 7th," they shout. "It won't bark any more. It was a mad devil—filthy beast! Filthy beast!"

"What's there to do now?"—"Nothing."

We stay there, jumbled together, and sit down. The living have ceased to gasp for breath, the dying have rattled their last, surrounded by smoke and lights and the din of the guns that rolls to all the ends of the earth. We no longer know where we are. There is neither earth nor sky—nothing but a sort of cloud. The first period of inaction is forming in the chaotic drama, and there is a general slackening in the movement and the uproar. The cannonade grows less; it still shakes the sky as a cough shakes a man, but it is farther off now. Enthusiasm is allayed, and there remains only the infinite fatigue that rises and overwhelms us, and the infinite waiting that begins over again.

* * *

AFTER the failure of the Loos and Champagne attacks, the troops prepared for another weary winter in the trenches. Yet although all seemed " quiet on the Western Front," the trench lines were actually the scenes of incessant activity.

FRONT LINE SUPREMACY
From *Good-bye to All That*.[1]
By ROBERT GRAVES

The Second Royal Welch, unlike the Second Welsh, believed themselves better trench fighters than the Germans. With the Second Welsh it was not cowardice but modesty. With the Second Royal Welch it was not vainglory but courage : as soon as they arrived in a new sector they insisted on getting fire ascendancy. Having found out from the troops they relieved all possible information as to enemy snipers, machine-guns and patrols, they set themselves to deal with them one by one. They began with machine-guns firing at night. As soon as one started traversing down a trench the whole platoon farthest removed from its fire would open five rounds rapid at it. The machine-gun would usually stop suddenly, but start again after a minute or two. Again five rounds rapid. Then it usually gave up.

The Welsh seldom answered a machine-gun. If they did, it was not with local organised fire, beginning and ending in unison, but in ragged confused protest all along the line. There was almost no firing at night in the Royal Welch,

[1] Published by Jonathan Cape, Ltd.

except organised fire at a machine-gun or a persistent enemy sentry, or fire at a patrol close enough to be distinguished as a German one. With all other battalions I met in France there was random popping off all the time; the sentries wanted to show their spite against the War. Flares were rarely used in the Royal Welch; most often as signals to our patrols that it was time to come back.

As soon as enemy machine-guns had been discouraged, our patrols would go out with bombs to claim possession of No Man's Land. At dawn next morning came the struggle for sniping ascendancy. The Germans, we were told, had special regimental snipers, trained in camouflaging themselves. I saw one killed once at Cuinchy who had been firing all day from a shell-hole between the lines. He had a sort of cape over his shoulders of imitation grass, his face was painted green and brown, and his rifle was also green fringed. A number of empty cartridges were found by him, and his cap with the special oak-leaf badge. Few battalions attempted to get control of the sniping situation. The Germans had the advantage of having many times more telescopic sights than we did, and steel loopholes that our bullets could not pierce. Also a system by which the snipers were kept for months in the same sector until they knew all the loopholes and shallow places in our trenches, and the tracks that our ration-parties used above-ground by night, and where our traverses came in the trench, and so on, better than we did ourselves. British snipers changed their trenches, with their battalions, every week or two, and never had time to learn the German line thoroughly. But at least we counted on getting rid of the unprofessional German sniper. Later we had an elephant-gun in the battalion that would pierce the German loopholes, and if we could not locate the loophole of a persistent sniper we did what we could to dislodge him by a volley of rifle-grenades, or even by ringing up the artillery.

It puzzled us that if a sniper were spotted and killed, another sniper would begin again next day from the same position. The Germans probably underrated us and regarded it as an accident. The willingness of other battalions to let the Germans have sniping ascendancy helped us; enemy snipers often exposed themselves unnecessarily, even the professionals. There was, of course, one advantage of which no advance or retreat of the enemy could rob us, and that was that we were always facing more or less east; dawn broke behind the German lines, and they seldom realised that for several minutes every morning we could see them though still invisible ourselves. German night wiring-parties often stayed out too long, and we could get a man or two as they went back; sunsets were against us, but sunset was a less critical time. Sentries at night were made to stand with their head and shoulders above the trenches and their rifles in position on the parapet. This surprised me at first. But it meant greater vigilance and self-confidence in the sentry, and it put the top of his head above the level of the parapet. Enemy machine-guns were trained on this level, and it was safer to be hit in the chest or shoulders than in the top of the head. The risk of unaimed fire at night was negligible so this was really the safest plan. It often happened in battalions like the Second Welsh, where the head-and-shoulder rule was not in force and the sentry just took a peep now and then, that an enemy patrol would sneak up unseen to the British wire, throw a few bombs and get safely back. In the Royal Welch the barbed-wire entanglement was the responsibility of the company behind it. One of our first acts on taking over trenches was to inspect and repair it. We did a lot of work on the wire.

* * *

YPRES, 1915

From *Leaves from a Field Note-book*.[1]

By J. H. Morgan

Somewhere behind that ridge were the enemy's batteries and they were yet to find. But even as we searched the landscape with our field-glasses an aeroplane rose from behind our own position and made for the distant ridge, its diaphanous wings displaying red, white and blue concentric circles to our glasses like the scales of some huge magpie-

[1] Published by Macmillan & Co., Ltd.

moth, while a long streamer of petrol smoke made faint pencillings in the sky behind it. As it hovered above the ridge seven or eight little white clouds like balls of feathers suddenly appeared from nowhere just below it. They were German shrapnel. But the aeroplane passed imperturbably on, leaving the little feathers to float in the sky until in time they faded away and disappeared. In no long time the aeroplane was retracing its flight, and certain little coloured discs were speaking luminously to the battery, telling it of what the observer had seen beyond the ridge. Between the aeroplane, the observer, the telephone, and the guns, there seemed to be some mysterious freemasonry. And this impression of secret and collusive agencies was heightened by the vibration of the air above us, in which the shells from the batteries made furrows that were audible without being visible, as though the whole firmament were populated with disembodied spirits. The passivity of the toilers in the field below us, who, absorbed in their husbandry, regarded not the air above them, and the dreaming beauty of the distant city almost persuaded us that we were the victims of a gigantic illusion. But even as we gazed the city acquired a desperate and tragic reality. Voices of thunder awoke behind the ridge, the air was rent like a garment, and first one cloud and then another and another rose above the city of Ypres, till the white towers were blotted out of sight. A black pall floated over the doomed city, and from that moment the air was never still, as a rhythm of German shells rained upon it. The storm spread until other villages were involved, and a fierce red glow appeared above the roofs of Vlamertinge.

Yet the clouds and flame that rose above the white towers had at that distance a flagrant beauty of their own, and it was hard to believe that they stood for death, desolation, and the agony of men. Beyond the voluminous smoke and darting tongues of fire, our field-glasses could show us nothing. But we knew—for we had seen but yesterday—that behind that haze there was being perpetrated a destruction as mournful and capricious as that which in the vision upon the Mount of Olives overtook Jerusalem. Where two were in the street one was even now being taken and the other left; he who was upon the house-top would not come down to take anything out of his house, neither would he who was in the field return to take away his clothes. The great cathedral was crumbling to dust, and saints, apostles, prophets, martyrs were being hurled from their niches of stone, the Virgin alone standing unscathed upon her pedestal contemplating the ruin and tribulation around her. And we knew that while we gazed the roads from the doomed city to Locre and Poperinghe were choked with a terror-stricken stream of fugitives, ancient men hobbling upon sticks, aged women clutching copper pans, and stumbling under the weight of feather-beds, while whimpering children fumbled among their mothers' skirts. What convulsive eddies each of the shells, whose trajectory we heard ever and anon in the skies overhead, were making in that living stream were to us a subject of poignant speculation.

But as I looked immediately around me I found it ever more difficult to believe that such things were being done upon the earth. The carpenter went on hammering, stopping but for a moment to shade his eyes with his hand and gaze out over the plain, the peasants in the field continued to hoe, a woman came out of a cottage with a child clinging to her skirts, and said: " La guerre, quand finira-t-elle, M'sieu' ? " From far above us the song of the lark, now lost to sight in the aerial blue, floated down upon the drowsy air.

* * *

In flat country observation over enemy trenches was by means of captive " sausage " balloons. One of the objects of airplane attack was to bring these down in flames; in the early days inadequate equipment made this a matter of some difficulty.

AIR SKIRMISH

From *Peter Jackson, Cigar Merchant*.[1]

By Gilbert Frankau

Peter, sauntering back to Mess, heard the drone of engines far above, looked up, saw five biplanes winging towards him from the direction of Bailleul.

[1] Published by Hutchinson & Co. (Publishers), Ltd.

"Wonder what the deuce they're up to?" he thought; and ran upstairs for his glasses. . . .

By the time he came down, the five 'planes were over the Boche lines. Peter picked them up, hawk-like dots in a blue circle; saw the first shell burst between him and them. "Behind," thought Peter, "but why are they flying so low?" Now, the whole blue circle round the hawk-like dots grew hazy with the green flash and dark-grey puffs of anti-aircraft fire; the noise of the bursts resounded dull and hollow from the near distance. . . .

Suddenly, clean down the blue circle of his vision, dropped the black-winged shape of a sixth 'plane. Peter, whipping binoculars from his eyes, caught a glimpse of it diving behind tree line . . . saw a red hint as of flame . . . heard the intermittent thuds of the Archie shell rise to a crescendo of ineffectual clamour, heard the sudden rat-tat of machine-gun and rifle-fire burst out along the front . . . watched the five 'planes still wheeling among the smoke-puffs . . . was aware of another 'plane droning towards him from behind the trees.

"My aunt," thought P. J. "Never saw the Archies fire like that before. Wonder what it's all about?"

For how should groundsmen of those early days realise this latest marvel, or know that far dropping shape for his own brother: for Arthur—Arthur circling high above the five decoys, alone in the shriek and hum of the wind—Arthur peering overside, seeing neither hill nor valley, neither road nor trench-line, neither flash of gun nor puff of shell, but only his prey, only the blind and shapeless fish, tiny and dun against the flat ground 10,000 feet below—Arthur, watching his chance, taking his chance, setting her nose for earth, feeling her fuselage lift behind his shoulder-blades, seeing the blind fish and the flat ground leap at his face as he dived for them—Arthur, one with his wings, finger on the rocket-button. . . .

Downskies he came, a howling plummet; saw the dun shape below rush at him; touched button; felt the faint jar of rockets flashing from their struts; saw them, even as he wrenched at joystick, go crimson home; heard the wind howl through the banking wires above him, saw little figures tip-tilted against the blur below, felt the zip of bullets as he flattened her over the twirling trenches; saw the clouds drop down to him; knew his work accomplished. . . .

In after days, the R.F.C. did that work with Lewis gun and incendiary bullet; but Arthur Jackson had only rockets, rockets fastened to the struts between his roaring wings, rockets whose utmost range was the forty yards within which those roaring wings must bank, or perish with their flaming prey. Yet the work was accomplished!

* * *

An elaborate organisation for espionage was set up by each of the combatants. To cope with such activities, equally elaborate systems of counter-espionage were also operated.

ESPIONAGE

From *The German Secret Service*.[1]
By Colonel W. Nicolai

As the French Intelligence Service prepared for the theatre of war had collapsed, it was necessary to find ways and means to spread spies again in the French areas occupied by the Germans. It was natural that the enemy should try to get into touch by air with its own population. In May, 1915, it was discovered that spies, provided with carrier-pigeons, were being set down behind the German lines by French airmen. These spies were persons whose homes were in the occupied area, and they were landed in their native districts where they knew every highway and byway. Germans, too, were employed in this way. They were mostly Alsatians and Lorrainers, who had lived in France since before the War and had avoided military service in Germany, soldiers who had deserted, or prisoners of war. " Air-spies " of German nationality were more useful, because they were better acquainted with army conditions and could move with self-reliance among the German troops. Frenchmen, on the other hand, knew the population and could reckon on help from the people. All the

[1] Published by Stanley Paul & Co., Ltd.

"air-spies" were oldish men. Under their civilian clothes the French spies wore French uniforms and the Germans, German uniforms. The latter were instructed to take off their civilian clothes on landing and hide them, so as to appear in uniform among the German troops. The French spies kept their civilian clothes on in order to go about among the people; only when they were in serious danger were they to take off their civilian clothes so that, if arrested, they could be treated as prisoners of war and not as spies. The "air-spies" had very complete instructions and were well provided with French and German money. They were skilled in the handling of carrier-pigeons and generally brought six over with them for the purpose of sending back the information they gathered. The "air-spies" were landed at night, mostly near the lines of communication in quiet regions where there were few troops and, therefore, not a great deal of surveillance. From there they had to slip up to the fighting area. They were promised that, after a certain period, they would be picked up at the same spot by an aeroplane. Enterprises of this kind, it was noticed, greatly increased when big operations were about to take place, and so we could deduce where the enemy was going to undertake such moves or where they were expected from the German side. The statements of "air-spies" and the instructions found on them gave us information regarding the intentions and surmises of the enemy. In 1915 nine "air-spies," four of them in uniform, and five aeroplanes fell into our hands. Attempts to pick up the spies again were watched. The French aeroplanes would fly at the arranged time over the landing-place, kept under observation by German counter-espionage agents. But the airmen in such cases flew at a considerable height, because the sign agreed upon that the coast was clear was not given. It was often established, however, that the promised attempt to pick up the spy was not undertaken. In no case was it definitely ascertained that an "air-spy" was really taken off again. They were left to their fate, and either fell into the hands of the German authorities or reached Holland by a long and weary route.

· · · · · · ·

Even after they had been captured, the English retained their strict discipline. Up to the end of 1916 they were accustomed to be without shelter even at night. An iron discipline, maintained by a severe code of punishments, was in their very blood. We discovered in a captured army order that in one army alone, within a period of eleven months in 1917–18, several officers and sixty-five men had been shot, mostly for cowardice in face of the enemy, but also for lesser misdemeanours. All the English prisoners were convinced that their country would win the War as it had done all others. It was seldom that any of them showed any leaning towards the belief that England could come to an understanding with Germany. The idea of an arrangement between France and Germany found only odd supporters here and there among the French prisoners, and those few were chiefly from Southern France. It was remarkable that the Irish also sided with Great Britain in the War against Germany. The English battalions from South Africa were *élite* troops, and many pro-Germans were to be found among them. The English Colonial prisoners were annoyed that their valuable divisions should almost always be put into action where the fighting was hottest and used to the last man. The Australians wrathfully emphasised that they were dispatched presumably to Egypt, but were sent to the Front in France. All the Colonial troops were like the Irish, united in their feeling for Great Britain and in the view that England had never entered a war which she had not won.

* * *

COUNTER-ESPIONAGE

From *Queer People*.[1]

By Basil Thomson

During the first few days of the War I remember a staff officer remarking that we should repeat the experience of the Napoleonic Wars: we should begin the War with the worst Intelligence Service in Europe and end with the best. I was inclined to think that he was right about the first part of his

[1] Published by Hodder & Stoughton, Ltd.

prediction, and I now think that he was right about the second. But then, if he had gone on to say that the Germans started the War with the most elaborate Secret Service organisation in Europe and ended it with the worst, he would have been equally right. I have already related how at the vital moment of mobilisation the whole of the German organisation in the United Kingdom was broken up; how it was possible for us to dispatch our Expeditionary Force to France without the loss of a single man or a single horse, and without the knowledge of the Germans. It was, of course, not long before they attempted to make good. They had established espionage centres at Antwerp and Brussels, they had branch offices in connection with the German Consulate at Rotterdam. Unfortunately for them, there was great jealousy between the Navy and the Army, and each had been entrusted with a certain amount of Secret Service money, on which they entered into a sort of civil war of competition. Anything reported by a spy employed by the German naval authorities was at once ridiculed by the military Intelligence, and vice versa. This keen competition made them a very easy prey. On one occasion an adventurous Englishman actually passed into Belgium to take service in one of these Intelligence offices, and came back with useful information. They were prone also to engage quite unsuitable people—the sort of people who in war-time at once become what the French call *agents doubles*; that is to say, they attempt to serve both sides, either with the object of obtaining double pay or of making their lives safe in the event of detection. What these men do for a living in peace-time is hard to guess. I can imagine them running cheap gambling-hells, frequenting the docks to pick up some dishonest profit, resorting to a little blackmail, and performing the humbler offices for the White Slave trafficker. In war-time you will find them swarming in every capital, for war is their brief summer. The money they get by their complicated villainies is spent with both hands. They live like princes and dress like bookmakers' touts. The Germans were so easy to manipulate that quite early in the War some of these men came over and offered their services to us. They felt sure that any story, however improbable, would be swallowed.

Certainly the Germans got more interesting information from the *agents doubles* than they ever got from their own spies in England. Sometimes they acted upon it, and they paid quite liberally. When you come to think of it, not many private Englishmen were in a position to give naval or military information of importance, and still less a foreigner who dared not ask questions.

* * *

WHATEVER success the spies may have achieved, its effect was as nothing compared with the alarm and uneasiness they aroused. Anyone suspected of espionage, on the flimsiest pretext, was apt to receive a very short shrift. It was this nervousness which influenced the Germans in their decision to execute Edith Cavell—a Red Cross Nurse who was accused of using her privileged position to help in the escape of British soldiers.

NURSE CAVELL

From *Young Woman of* 1914.[1]

By ARNOLD ZWEIG

" Peace ? " he repeated. " I'm afraid, Herr Wahl, that we shall have to wait for that. The English don't want it, by all appearances, and England is not merely paying the cost of the War, as we are often told, they also provide a sort of moral backbone for the French."

Markus Wahl nodded : " Is that a bad thing ? England had more sense than the whole crowd of them. No other country has enough authority to open up negotiations. Haven't you seen how excited the *Norddeutsche Allgemeine Zeitung* became about peace rumours last October, and every six months since ? "

" This October, too ? Have you got a copy ? "

Markus Wahl pondered ; he could not remember that he had noticed it this month, but October was not yet over.

Sergeant Leo Brümmer shook his cropped head : " You

[1] Published by Martin Secker.

won't notice it this year, Herr Wahl, nor next April. We have made bitter enemies of the English at last."

"How is that?"

"Wasn't there anything in the German papers about Miss Cavell? Or in the *Züricher Zeitung?*"

Markus Wahl drew up his knees and clasped them with his arms, hunching himself into his chair with the air of an emaciated bird. In the last fortnight a few numbers of the Swiss paper had got lost in the post. What had happened?

"Wait a moment," said Lenore intently, "I remember reading something about it. Wasn't that the name of a female spy who was condemned to death in Brussels? Was she English?"

Sergeant Brümmer loosened his collar: "We shall have to pay for that girl's blood, and it will take a great many lives to avenge it. They tell me that the English newspapers are wild about it. Why were these people allowed to shoot a brave young woman because she helped prisoners to escape over the frontier? And after all, it didn't matter very much if they did join the French or Belgian Army. We shan't lose the War on that account."

"Was that why she was shot?" asked Lenore, and there was fear in her voice.

"She wasn't just an ordinary girl, she was a nurse, Fräulein Wahl. And she worked in a hospital where she had looked after a great many of our men, both officers and rank and file. I needn't tell you the story in detail, but it's the talk of all Belgium, and indeed the whole world just now. And I tell you it has raised a storm that will bring many hundreds of our Field Greys into their graves."

Lenore sat with wandering eyes, ready for flight. She remembered the Arch-Duchess, the first victim of this war. Shot in Sarajevo; and now another, and a woman, too—shot in Brussels. Had not all the thinkers in Germany, and indeed in all the world, conferred on women their charter of humanity? Couldn't she have been pardoned, or even imprisoned? This was too much....

Then Sergeant Brümmer told his tale. His source of information was unquestionable; orderlies, clerks, chauffeurs, telephonists, all the more passive agents of the military administration. Miss Cavell had taken the whole affair upon herself, admitted and confessed to every detail. She, and one or two other women had, in a certain sense, fought against Germany, and were guilty of treason; but no woman, no German woman, would have acted otherwise. The court-martial had an easy task; the sentence was, and had to be, death; though they recognised her high motives and her woman's feelings.

"You know," said Brümmer, standing up, and beginning to pace up and down the banker's narrow room, "we didn't believe that they would dare to do it; there were too many interests involved. For the execution of this woman, as we all understood, was worse than a crime, it was a folly of the very first order."

Markus Wahl banged his fist on the table: "Don't say what you can't answer for. A crime is a crime, and no folly can be worse than a crime."

"Oh, very well," said Brümmer uneasily, "but the world thinks otherwise. The world ignores crimes, but it avenges follies through their consequences."

The old man's face grew flushed and blotched like the face of a sick man. "Brümmer," he shouted, "I forbid you to talk such nonsense. Every crime, whatever else it is, is something that is beyond all sense and reason. You are a young man," he went on, calming down a little; "and you haven't seen much of the world yet. One day you will learn the truth of the words—He visits the sins of the fathers upon the children, unto the third and fourth generation, among those that hate me. We are all guilty; and we cannot expect to escape."

Lenore crushed her handkerchief in her right hand, which she held behind her back. She said nothing.

"The Governor-General was on leave, and that was the beginning of the trouble. The courts-martial for espionage are under the military authorities—which meant, for the time being, the Governor of Brussels, a General, who could act on his own responsibility. The German Government and the Foreign Ministry are represented in Brussels by the P.D.—

Political Department—just as in a branch of a business there is always a confidential man to look after the interests of the head office. This is in charge of a diplomat, a Baron, a man of sense and education, and he has a voice in everything that concerns policy. He knew exactly what was at stake in this matter; he realised that this would be a red rag to the English, and to the Americans, too. Nor did he have to fight alone— the neutral Ambassadors helped him. The American was in bed ill, but he sent his secretary; the Spaniard jumped up from a dinner-party when the news came, left his guests, and rushed off to the Baron. That very night they wrote out a petition for mercy—it's not yet a fortnight ago; they urged that the sentence should not be carried out until the real ruler of the land came back from leave. Then they drove in the Baron's car to the General's house, and the Spaniard waited outside for what he was sure would be a favourable answer. The Baron returned after a few minutes, looking pale and shaken. His car was a good one with a very silent engine, and the chauffeur, who told me the story, kept his ears open, and only his eyes on the slippery street. The General, you will understand, swept the petition off the table without so much as looking at it. The Baron was rather taken aback, but he controlled his feelings, bent down, picked up the paper, and laid it on the table again, keeping his hand on it this time. And now listen to this, Herr Wahl. It was nearly twelve o'clock, and the General wanted to go to bed, so he told the Baron pretty sharply that he did not receive communications from a Major. Do you understand? The representative of the Empire, of the Chancellor, and of all us tax-payers, was only a Major; and our employé, to whom we pay a couple of thousand marks a month to look after our affairs in Belgium, was a General, and could get his own back. Well, there was nothing more to be done. The Baron told him that the woman's blood would be upon his own and his children's heads. But the General was a man of iron: 'I was trained to take responsibility, Herr Major,' he said triumphantly, and went to bed. Well, if that's responsibility, I want to hear no more of it. Then came the dawn, the last walk to the execution yard, the rifle-shots and a grave. She did not complain, she did not cry, she knew how to face her end, and as none of us interfered, we shall all have to share the burden of what was done."

* * *

NURSE CAVELL was not, of course, the only victim of the anti-spy mania. The Germans occupying, as they did, a hostile territory were even subject to this mania to a greater degree than the other nations. The fate of the heroic nurse was undoubtedly shared by many another patriotic spirit.

CONDEMNED AS A SPY
From *Mrs. Warren's Daughter*.[1]

By SIR HARRY JOHNSTON

Moreover, the Red Placards of von Bissing were of increasing frequency. As a rule Vivie only heard what other people said of them, and that wasn't very much, for German spies were everywhere, inviting you to follow them to the dreaded Kommandantur in the Rue de la Loi—a scene of as much in the way of horror and mental anguish as the Conciergerie of Paris in the days of the Red Terror. But some cheek-blanching rumours she had heard on a certain Monday in October caused her to look next day on her way home at a fresh Red Placard which had been posted up in a public place. The daylight had almost faded, but there was a gas-lamp which made the notice legible. It ran:

CONDAMNATIONS

Par jugement du 9 Octobre, 1915, le tribunal de compagne a prononcé les condamnations suivantes pour trahison commise pendant l'état de guerre (pour avoir fait passer des recrues à l'ennemi):

1º Philippe BAUCQ, Architecte à Bruxelles;
2º Louise THULIEZ, professor à Lille;

[1] Published by Chatto & Windus.

3º Edith Cavell, directrice d'un institut médical à Bruxelles ;
4º Louis Severin, pharmacien à Bruxelles ;
5º Comtesse Jeanne de Belleville, à Montignies.
A la Peine de Mort.

Vivie then went on to read with eyes that could hardly take in the words a list of other names of men and women condemned to long terms of hard labour for the same offence—assisting young Belgians to leave the Belgium that was under German occupation. And further, the information that of the five condemned to death, *Philip Baucq* and *Edith Cavell* had already been executed.

The monsters! Oh, that von Bissing. How gladly she would die if she might first have the pleasure of killing him! That pompous old man of seventy-one with the blotched face, who had issued orders that wherever he passed in his magnificent motor he was to be saluted with Eastern servility, who boasted of his " tender heart," so that he issued placards about this time punishing severely all who split the tongues of finches to make them sing better. Edith Cavell—she did not pause to consider the fate of patriotic Belgian women—but Edith Cavell, directress of a nursing home in Brussels, known far and wide for her goodness of heart. She had held aloof from Vivie, but was that to be wondered at when there was so much to make her suspect—living, seemingly, under the protection of a German official. But the very German nurses and doctors at the Red Cross hospital had spoken of her having given free treatment in her Home to Germans who needed immediate operations, and for whom there was no room in the military hospitals.—And for such a trivial offence as *that*—and to kill her before there could be any appeal for reconsideration or clemency. Oh, *what* a nation! She would tend their sick and wounded no more.

· · · · · · ·

But for Vivie, that drive was an unforgettable agony. They went through suburbs where the roads had been unrepaired or torn up by shrapnel. The snow lay in places so thickly that it nearly stopped the motor. Still, it came to an end at last. The door on one side was wrenched open; she was pulled out rather unceremoniously; then, the pinioned Bertie, who was handed over to a guard; and the soldier escort after him, who took his place promptly by his side. Vivie had just time to note the ugly red-brick exterior of the main building of the Tir National. It reminded her vaguely of some hastily-constructed Exhibition at Earl's Court or Olympia. Then she was pushed inside a swinging door, into a freezing corridor; where the Prison Directeur and Monsieur Walcker were standing—irresolute, weeping. . . .

"Where is Bertie?" she asked.

"He is being prepared for the shooting-party," they answered. "It will soon be over . . . dear, dear lady . . . try to be calm——"

"I will be as calm as you like," she answered; "I will behave with the utmost correctitude or whatever you call it, if you—if they—the soldiers—the officer—will let me see him—as you promised—up to the last. But, by God—if there *is* a God—if you or they prevent me, I'll——"

Inexplicably, sheer mind-force prevailed, without the need for formulating the threat the poor grief-maddened woman might have uttered—she moved unresisted to a swing door which opened on to a kind of verandah. Here was drawn up the firing-party, and in front of them, fifteen feet away on snow-sodden, trampled grass stood Bertie. He caught sight of Vivie passing in, behind the firing-party, and standing beyond them at the verandah rail. He straightened himself; ducked his head aside from the handkerchief with which they were going to bandage his eyes, and shouted, "Take away your blasted handkerchief! *I* ain't afraid o' the guns. If you'll let me look at HER, I'll stand as quiet as a mouse."

The officer in command of the firing-party shrugged his shoulders. The soldier escort desisted from his attempts to blindfold the Englishman and stood aside, out of range. Bertie fixed his glowing eyes on the woman he had loved from his youth up, the rifles rang out with a reverberating bellow, and he fell out of her sight, screened by the soldiers, a crumpled body over which they threw a sheet.

What happened then to Vivie? I suppose you expect the time-worn trick of the weary novelist, anxious to put his pen down and go to his tea: " Then she seemed swallowed up in a cloud of blackness and knew no more "—till it was convenient to the narrator to begin a fresh chapter. But with me it must be the relentless truth and nothing but the truth, in all its aspects. Vivie was deafened, nearly stunned by the frightful noise of the volley in a confined space. Next, she was being unceremoniously pushed out of the verandah, into the corridor, and so out into the snow-covered space in front of the brick building; whilst the officer was examining the dead body of the fallen man, ready to give the *coup de grâce*, if he were not dead. But he was. Vivie was next conscious that she had the most dreadful, blinding headache she had ever known, and with it felt an irresistible nausea. The Prison Directeur was taking her hand and saying: " Mademoiselle: It is my duty to inform you that you are no longer under arrest."

* * *

GREAT as was the attention attracted by the romantic work of the spy—particularly of the Mata-Hari type of seductive female—it was of little significance compared with the solid " Intelligence " organisation functioning as a part of the army machine. This saw few dramatic moments, depending rather on a careful filtering of thousands of trickles of information, mostly of doubtful authenticity.

INTELLIGENCE

From *The Crater of Mars*.[1]

By FERDINAND TUOHY

An Intelligence Officer at Ypres at this stage had his hands fairly full. Popularly, our only job was supposed to be editing *Comic Cuts*, alias the daily summary of events in the Corps' sector; actually I often got this out in half an hour of an evening. Nor was *Comic Cuts*, despite its lapses and Olympian

[1] Published by William Heinemann, Ltd.

note, so exclusively humorous. As sole link between all branches—gunners, sappers, infantry, airmen—regarding the enemy and what he was up to, it could not have been dispensed with.

The senior I.O.'s job was exclusively the extremely important one of reading air photographs of the enemy's trench system, and mapping every alteration, even to a new mound of earth, my senior ultimately becoming so expert that he could follow with a magnifying-glass the tracks of buried cables. He also kept files, because I never could. Files of captured documents, of prisoners' statements, of agents' reports and of the expansion of the German Army. I, for my part, had to take on prisoners in examination; keep up the enemy's Order of Battle map; go out listening at night near the German wire; collect dud German shells for forwarding for laboratory research at St. Omer; tap the morale of our own men by opening green envelopes; liaison with our local Intelligence Police watching the civilian population; aid with *Comic Cuts* and in the general work of the office; and stand by for odd stunts.

Opening the green envelopes had its humours. Once I came across this (it had evidently been forwarded for information to someone in line who was now returning it to its authoress with scathing accompaniments):

Dear Sir respected Sir,

Though I take this liberty as it leaves me at present I beg to ask you if you will be kindly be kind enough to let me knew where is my husbin though he is not my legible husbin as has a wife though he says she is dead, but I do not think he knows for sure but we are not married though I am getting my alotment regular which is no fault of Mr. Lloy Georges who would stop it if he could or Mr. Makena but if you know where he is as he belongs to the Royal Fling Corps for since he joined in when he was sacked from his work for talking back to his Bos which was a woman at the laundry where he worked I have not had any money from him since he joined though he told Mrs. Harris which lives on the ground floor that he was a pretty ossifer for six shillings a week and lots of underclosse in for the bad weather and I have three children what he has been the father of. Hoping you will write to me soon and you are quite well as it leaves me at present I must close now hoping you are well.

(Signed) Mrs. JANE JENKINS.

With prisoners, I may have been among the first to dispose of armed guards and truculence, my system, such as it was, having been rather to seat the captive, offer him a cigarette, and chat, without dreaming of taking a note in his presence. A tone of good-natured raillery suited many captured Germans; moreover these could almost always be made to speak if you manœuvred them into boasting. Threats, or grilling, I found useless, in which connection I well recall an incident at Lôvie when a senior sahib of B Mess, whose unit had been gassed out of existence the previous April, insisted on making all preparations for the fake gassing of a German prisoner who refused to answer my questions. We were in a stable, and Major X had all present don gas-masks. He was about to bring in a hose and proceed with the mental torture, when I slipped out and rang the A.P.M., to whom all captives' bodies belonged, and so ended matters.

* * *

METAL SOLDIERS

From *Mr. Britling*.[1]

By H. G. WELLS

That diary-hunting strategy is just the sort of thing that makes this war intellectually fascinating. Everything is being thought out and then tried over that can possibly make victory. The Germans go in for psychology much more than we do, just as they go in for war more than we do, but they don't seem to be really clever about it. So they set out to make all their men understand the war, while our chaps are singing "Tipperary." But what the men put down aren't the beautiful things they ought to put down; most of them shove down lists

[1] Published by W. Collins, Sons & Co., Ltd.

of their meals, some of the diaries are all just lists of things eaten, and a lot of them have written the most damning stuff about outrages and looting. Which the French are translating and publishing. The Germans would give anything now to get back these silly diaries. And now they have made an order that no one shall go into battle with any written papers at all. . . . Our people got so keen on documenting and the value of chance writings, that one of the principal things to do after a German attack had failed had been to hook in the documentary dead, and find out what they had on them. . . . It's a curious sport, this body-fishing. You have a sort of triple hook on a rope, and you throw it and drag. They do the same. The other day one body near Hooghe was hooked by both sides, and they had a tug-of-war. With a sharpshooter or so cutting in whenever our men got too excited. Several men were hit. The Irish—it was an Irish regiment—got him—or at least they got the better part of him. . . .

Now that I am a sergeant, Parks talks to me again about all these things, and we have a first-lieutenant too keen to resist such technical details. They are purely technical details. You must take them as that. One does not think of the dead body as a man recently deceased, who had perhaps a wife and business connections and a weakness for oysters or pale brandy. Or as something that laughed and cried and didn't like getting hurt. That would spoil everything. One thinks of him merely as a uniform with marks upon it that will tell us what kind of stuff we have against us, and possibly with papers that will give us a hint of how far he and his lot are getting sick of the whole affair. . . .

There's a kind of hardening not only of the body but of the mind through all this life out here. One is living on a different level. You know just before I came away—you talked of Dower-House-land—and outside. This is outside. It's different. Our men here are kind enough still to little things —kittens or birds or flowers. Behind the front, for example, everywhere there are Tommy gardens. Some are quite bright little patches. But it's just nonsense to suppose we are tender to the wounded up here—and, putting it plainly, there isn't a scrap of pity left for the enemy. Not a scrap. Not a trace of such feeling. They were tender about the wounded in the early days—men tell me—and reverent about the dead. It's all gone now. There have been atrocities, gas, unforgettable things. Everything is harder. Our people are inclined now to laugh at a man who gets hit, and to be annoyed at a man with a troublesome wound. . . .

"You once wrote that all fighting ought to be done nowadays by metal soldiers. I perceive, my dear Daddy, that all real fighting is . . ."

* * *

THE BANGALORE TORPEDO

From *Old Soldiers Never Die*.[1]

By Private Frank Richards

We were in the Cambrin trenches and a Bangalore Torpedo was sent up to the Battalion, which had to be taken out and attached to the German barbed wire. This torpedo had been tried and proved a great success in some Back Area or other where there were no shells and bullets flying about and also no enemy waiting to ram a foot of steel through a man's chest. It was claimed that this torpedo would destroy more barbed wire than a battery of artillery would, firing for a week. Our comments were that if the inventor and the men who had tried it out in the Back Areas had the job of hitching it on the enemy's wire here at Cambrin they'd not reach half-way across no-man's-land before they'd be returning to change their under-pants.

Volunteers were called for from C Company; which met with no response. Everyone knew that the men who went out with the thing would be extraordinarily lucky to get back. There was every prospect of being spotted by a German patrol or listening-post, and even if they escaped these, there would probably be German working parties busy on the wire. There was also the danger of the torpedo being struck with a bullet as they were carrying it and blowing them to pieces. A second call came for volunteers, and three old soldiers,

[1] Published by Faber & Faber, Ltd.

as a matter of regimental *esprit de corps*, said that before anyone should be warned for the job as a duty they'd volunteer. One of the men was called " Freezer " : I knew him very well, having soldiered with him in India, and he was a hard case. He was continually being awarded Field Punishment Number One and getting the sentence washed out for some daring deed or other. What he didn't know about patrols and trench warfare in general was not worth knowing. The volunteers were shown how the torpedo was to be fixed and where to fix it, and before they left the trench it was set ready to explode at 1 a.m. that night. They went out at midnight with Freezer in charge, and perhaps forty minutes later we were glad to have the message passed along that they were safe back. A little group of officers was now in the front trench. They had their watches out and were anxiously studying the luminous hands. One of them commenced to reel the seconds off : five seconds to go, four, three, two—CRASH ! This was a German shell exploding five yards from them. But the Bangalore Torpedo failed to explode.

When day came and we stood-to, the torpedo could be distinctly seen where Freezer and his chums had put it on the enemy's wire. Some very beautiful remarks were made about it. One old soldier told a few young soldiers that the torpedo hadn't finished yet. It was liable to go off and when it did it would travel up and down the German Front, with a rage against barbed wire, blasting it all away without missing a single strand ; after which it would turn its attention to the barbed-wire dumps in Back Areas, and finally make for Germany where it would destroy the factories where the barbed wire came from until there wasn't a strand of barbed wire left in enemy territory large enough to stick a louse with.

It lay out on the wire all that day, but a message came through from Brigade Headquarters that it must be retrieved without delay. We all wanted to know what they wanted the thing back for, after calling for volunteers to get rid of it. I heard an officer remark that the reason was so as the enemy would not be able to get the Secret of it. So volunteers were again called for. The first journey had been dangerous enough, but this would be doubly so : the enemy would be on the watch, and have their machine-guns set. The same three men volunteered.

It was a quiet night. The Germans were not firing a shot in front of C Company, which made us think that they were waiting for whoever might come to fetch the thing back. But the men crept out, unhooked the torpedo and brought it back, much to everyone's surprise, without themselves or it being hit. Freezer, safe home in the trench, remarked that the torpedo seemed a damned sight lighter than when they took it out. He was right. Either that night or the night before, the Germans had got hold of it and brought it into their trench. They had taken it to pieces, removed the mechanism and hung the empty thing back on their wire for us to retrieve. That was why they had not fired—to invite us to come and fetch it. I expect they did a good grin over the Secret of that torpedo. It was the first and last Bangalore Torpedo that I ever saw come up the line.

* * *

ANOTHER mountain war, on a less homeric scale, was waged in the Balkan Peninsula. Although compared with the larger areas of battle, for which an hour's supply of ammunition would have sufficed the Serbian and Montenegrin Armies for the whole of their campaign, this minor zone gave an effect almost equivalent to that of *opera bouffe*, it none the less culminated in tragedy, with the crushing of these gallant States by a combined army of Germans, Austrians and Bulgars.

BALKAN FRONT

From *The Luck of Thirteen*.[1]

By JAN AND CORA GORDON

Here we left our horses and began to scramble through brambles along a narrow path, climbing up the back of a little hill on the crest of which were the machine guns. Just

[1] Published by John Murray.

before we got to the top we plunged into a tunnel which bored through the hill; at the end was the gun. The hero scrambled in, wriggled the gun about, and explained. He invited Jo to shoot. She squashed past him; there was a knob at the back of the gun on which she pressed her thumbs, and she immediately wanted another pair with which to stop her ears. The gun jammed suddenly. The hero pulled the belt about, and Jo set it going once more.

The Austrian machine-guns answered back and kept this up, so Jo pressed the knob again and yet again. Then we got into the trenches above. Whenever Jo popped her head over the trenches for a good look, there were faint reports from the mountain opposite. One or two bullets whizzed over our heads, and we realised that they were aiming at Jo's big white hat.

Jan climbed down the hill and took snapshots of Gorazhda; the enemy got a couple of pretty near shots at him.

When the Montenegrins thought this sport was becoming monotonous they remembered the business of the day. A big house in Gorazhda was said to be full of Hungarian officers, and they wanted to get the range of this with one of the big guns. This decision had been made a day or two before with much deliberation. This they thought the State could afford. The precious shell was brought out, and everyone fondled it.

Men were called out and huge preparations were made for sighting and taking aim. We scuttled round with field-glasses, and finally stood on tiptoe behind branches on a mound by the side of the gun. There were many soldiers fussing in the dug-out, and at last they pulled the string.

"Goodness! Now we've done it," Jo thought, as the mountains sent back the fearful report in decreasing echoes. We seemed to wait an eternity, and then "something white" happened far beyond the village.

The officers looked at each other with long faces. "A bad miss—the expense."

We felt the resources of the Montenegrin Empire were tottering. Awful! Could they afford another?

Finally, with great courage, they decided that it was better to spend two shells on getting a decent aim than to lose one for nothing. The terrific bang went off again, and this time the " something white " happened right on the roof of the house. The Hungarian officers all ran out, and the machine-guns below jabbered at them. Nobody was killed, as far as we know, but everyone was content and delighted.

* * *

THE AGONY OF SERBIA

From *With a Woman's Unit in Serbia, Salonica and Sebastopol*.[1]

By Dr. I. Emslie Hutton

Early next morning we knew the worst. All but the most seriously ill had been " evacuated," which really meant that they were put on their feet, sent out into the highroad, and staggered along, eating and sleeping where they could, until at length they arrived at their *selo* (village). An awful fate ! But terrible as it seemed to us then, we found that for many weeks we had to do likewise with men who were hardly fit even to leave their beds. There were four hundred and fifty cases left for us, each one severe and a problem in itself, and among them was a great number of pneumonias, for " Spanish influenza," a disease new to Serbia, was sweeping over the country.

It was bitterly cold and there was a good Scotch " on-ding " of snow, and those of the patients who were not in a raging fever shivered and tried vainly to adjust their tattered uniforms to gain a little warmth. They lay in blood-stained and torn uniforms, and had on their wounds a first dressing which had not been touched since its application in the field ; their clothing crawled with maggots and bugs and their bodies with lice. Dying men lay huddled so closely together on the floor that they touched each other. Others sat up gasping and blue in the throes of pneumonia. Blood and pus oozed from the wounds ; there was death already on many of the faces, and all showed the ravages of pain, cold and hunger. A few of the patients feebly extended their hands and a flicker of a

[1] Published by Williams and Norgate, Ltd.

smile lit their faces, but most of them were too ill to care what happened. None were more pleased to see us than the British Transport men, who were dotted here and there through the barrack-rooms, and I think our sympathy went out most of all to those of our race who were thus fighting for life against such odds.

I saw that when the building was cleaned up it would be capable of being transformed into a fine hospital; the spacious barrack-rooms would make excellent wards and the parade-ground would be ideal for the erection of tents when it was cleared of the litter of big guns and ammunition. There were great storehouses, stables, outhouses, and even a building suitable for an isolation ward. The kitchen and mess-rooms were conveniently separated from the main building by a grass square, and a great hall adjoined them; this had, no doubt, often been the scene of great military splendour, but now—seventy-odd Bulgars, in the last stages of dysentery, lay crouched along the walls, emaciated, dying, and some already dead. They bleated peevishly for *voda* (water), or just opened their eyes like starving dogs and glanced at us before their eyelids fell again. They crawled outside the hall from time to time, and the ground must have been alive with dysentery bacilli, for there were no sanitary arrangements, and the grass plot was foul.

In the barracks there was a drainage system of which Colonel Vladisavylevitch had spoken in terms of the highest praise, but all that happened was that the latrine material was collected in a cesspool, which was but imperfectly covered with a huge wooden lid. At once we proceeded to have all the inlets stopped up and to use the camp system and incinerators that we had employed with so much success at Ostrovo. These matters, no doubt, seem of little consequence, but in our campaign sanitation was all-important, and we always used to say that whenever British people got together in Serbia, every conversation began with lice and ended with latrines.

* * *

Throughout 1915, the Russians had sustained a series of colossal defeats, culminating in the loss of the greater part of Poland. Though they fought with the utmost gallantry, poor communications and woefully inadequate equipment led inevitably towards disaster.

THE RUSSIAN RETREAT
From *They Knew How to Die*.[1]
By Sophie Botcharsky and Florida Pier

Laughing, Schoura and I rose and said good night to our new friends. We had put our bed in the graveyard, as only there could we be sure of a little privacy, and it stood in an alley-way between the graves. We shared one sleeping-bag and slept deliciously. When we woke, Lala stood over us, saying we were to come at once, as wounded were already arriving at the hospital. We followed her and found the house in Bielsk empty of all equipment except the operating-tables. There were only a few beds belonging to the sisters, and, except for these, the wounded lay on piles of straw. We tried to make them comfortable, but as we worked we saw that the men changed. They were depressed and fretful. At night they were all taken away in the train, and again the hospital filled.

They did not stay long enough for us to learn what they needed, and they were dirtier than any of the men had been before. Insects covered them, and this distressed us. They still treated us with the same politeness and affection, but they were insistent in their demands, and they no longer seemed able or willing to endure. They had come from every direction, as small engagements were taking place on all sides. The Germans were sometimes ahead of us, sometimes level with us. They harried us as we moved, and now they began to press more sharply. There was no front line, but a confusion of weary, retreating men and those who followed them.

[1] Published by Peter Davies.

We fell back fighting, and then for days saw no sign of Germans. No one knew whether they could rest a moment, or when they must press on.

We worked on our knees, yet, kneeling beside the men, we could do little more than speak to them; they complained, but were otherwise silent. Wounded children were brought in to us, children of refugees who had been caught in the fighting, and this helped to unnerve us. The gloom of the hospital was made worse by our concern for Dolyn. His frail, delicate body was obviously tried beyond its capacity by the strain of the retreat. He was irritable, tortured by not knowing whether he dare operate or not, for any moment might come the word to move everyone, and he either risked lives by operating, or risked them equally by waiting to do so.

Lala and I sat in our tiny room by the light of a petrol lamp, and looking up, we saw a man standing staring in at us. He swayed from side to side, his coat was flung around his shoulders like a shawl, his eyes were blurred, and he muttered: "I am a deserter, I can't go on. Take my pulse, see if there's anything wrong. I'll go back if you tell me to."

I sprang up, recognising the engineer-officer who had snubbed Lala at Novo-Minsk. "It is all right, Lieutenant, it's all right. I am sure you are ill." I helped him to a chair, and taking his hand, found that it was burning. "You have typhus, I think."

・　　・　　・　　・　　・　　・

Lala had everything well arranged, and Dolyn was resetting a broken arm. I took charge of the next man to be done. When the bandage was off his fingers I saw that they were badly shattered, and one hung by a bit of muscle. I hid it from him with my shoulder, and he began to chatter. "I was wounded near Bielsk, Sister. The brothers were drunk, and the Germans almost surrounded us. As soon as I was hit, I got out of there. You have to look out for yourself. The station had been blown up, so I had to walk. But there's no harm for us in walking."

"Doctor, have a look here."

Dolyn nodded. "Cut it off; keep an eye on him."

THE RUSSIAN RETREAT

"How far did you walk?" I asked, as I cut the finger, letting it drop into a pail. "I'm afraid one of your fingers is gone, Brother!"

"Only one? That's not so bad." And he went on with his talk.

A bitter complaint came from a man who was sitting on a table while Dolyn cleaned a lot of small, but deep, wounds, in his chest. "What are they thinking about in the towns? How can we keep on without bread? We haven't been given bread for days. What do they think we live on? We've no boots, we're dirty and lousy, we're hungry——"

"We're retreating," said Dolyn. "You can't expect to have much during a retreat."

"Why should we retreat at all? Who's driving us back?" the man cried angrily. "We were a jolly good regiment before Warsaw, and we were ordered to retire. Why? We didn't see any Germans for days, and then, when the men grew tired, the Germans smelt it, and they began pushing us back." Dolyn said nothing, knowing the man needed to speak. "Who can fight, falling back? There's nothing to shelter us, and the people in the towns don't stand by us. They even leave us without ammunition, and the Germans have everything!" He turned passionately towards Dolyn. "Doctor, you can read. When will peace come?"

Dolyn's quiet voice grumbled as he worked. "I tell you, my boy, ammunition is almost ready; we shall soon be well equipped. We shall beat them. You will see!"

"They are too strong, Doctor, they are too strong."

"And we've Allies, they will help us!"

"They're far away. Who can tell if they're really fighting?"

"What is all this fighting for?" asked a soldier who sat waiting his turn to have his wound dressed. "What do we want from the Germans? We have everything in our villages. Our good, black earth gives us all we need."

Dolyn became irritated, and his voice rose shrilly: "Do you want the Germans to come and take your land and make you their serfs?"

A quiet, monotonous voice came from the corner. "Brother, it is all God's will."

Murmurs of assent came from all sides; the men were more reassured by these words than by what Dolyn had said.

• • • • • •

I was standing by a soldier in the half-dark, massaging his stiffened leg.

"Sister," he said, "what language were you and the other sister speaking between yourselves this morning? Was it French?" I nodded "Yes," and went on with the rubbing. "Did you understand all you said, Sister?" Again I nodded. "But tell me, Sister, why did they invent a French language?"

I laughed. "Oh, brother, they had to. There is a country called France, and they needed it there."

"You don't say so! Have they got towns? Have they got rivers? But they couldn't have got rivers, of course. Still, other countries are strange. The Japanese have a monkey instead of a Tzar!"

* * *

CANNON FODDER

From *The War in Eastern Europe*.[1]

By JOHN REED

Tarnopol Station was a place of vast confusion. From a long military train poured running soldiers, with tin teapots, to the *kipiatok*, hurtling a column of infantry that was marching across to another train. Officers shouted and cursed, beating with the flat of the swords. Engines whistled hysterically, bugles blared—calling the men back to their cars. Some hesitated and stopped, undecided whether to go forward or back; others ran faster. Around the hot-water tanks was a boiling, yelling mob. Clouds of steam rose from the pouring faucets.... Hundreds of peasant refugees—Poles, Moldavians, and Hungarians—squatted along the platform, waiting stolid and bewildered among their bundles and rolls of bedding; for as they retreated, the Russians were clearing the country of every living thing and destroying houses and crops. ... The stationmaster waved futile hands in the centre of a

[1] Published by Eveleigh Nash Company, Ltd.

bawling crowd of officers and civilians, all flourishing passes and demanding when their various trains departed. . . .

An armed sentry at the door tried to stop us, but we pushed by. He made a half-motion with his rifle, took a step and paused irresolutely, bellowing something about passes—and we went on. A hundred spies could have entered Tarnopol...

"*Na Stap!*" we cried to the cabby: "To the Staff!" Along the railroad yards on each side were mountains of sacks and boxes higher than the houses. Tarnopol was a city of solid Polish architecture, with occasional big, modern German buildings, and sudden vistas of narrow, busy streets lined with hundreds of shops, all painted with signs picturing the goods sold within; streets swarming with Jews in long, black coats and curly brimmed black hats. Here they looked better off and less servile than in Novo Sielitza. As everywhere in Galicia and Poland, there was a smell of combined *kosher*, boot-leather, and what we call *Polak*; it filled the air, tainted the food we ate and impregnated our very bedclothes.

Half-way down the street we met a column of soldiers marching four abreast toward the railway station, bound for the Front. Less than a third had rifles.

They came tramping along with the heavy, rolling pace of booted peasants, heads up, arms swinging—bearded giants of men with dull, brick-red hands and faces, dirty-brown belted blouses, blanket-rolls over their shoulders, intrenching-tools at their belts, and great wooden spoons stuck in their boot-tops. The earth shook under their tread. Row after row of strong, blank, incurious faces set westward toward unknown battles, for reasons incomprehensible to them. And as they marched, they sang—a plain chant as simple and tremendous as a Hebrew Psalm. A lieutenant at the head of the column sang one bar, the first sergeant took him up—and then, like a dammed-up river, burst the deep, easy voice of three thousand men, flung out from great chests in a rising, sudden swell of sound, like organs thundering:

"For the last time I walk with you, my friends—
For the last time!
And to-morrow, early in the morning,
Will weep my mother and my brethren,
For I am going away to the war!

And also will weep my sweetheart,
Whom I have loved for many, many years. . . .
She whom I hoped one day to go with to the church. . . .
I swear that I will love her until I die ! "

They passed, and the roaring slow chorus rose and fell crashing fainter and fainter. Now we rode between interminable hospitals, where haggard, white-draped figures leaned listlessly from the windows, bleached yellow from long confinement. Soldiers crowded the streets—wounded men on crutches, old Landwehr veterans, regulars, and boys who couldn't have been more than seventeen. There were three soldiers to every civilian ; though that may have been partly due to the fact that many Jews had been " expelled " when the Russians entered the town—a dark and bloody mystery that. On each corner stood an armed sentry, scrutinising the passers-by with the menacing look of a suspicious peasant.

* * *

As Cæsar would have said, the army in Gaul had now gone into winter quarters. The peasants in the war area were gradually learning the habits of their friendly invaders.

BILLETS

From *The Spanish Farm Triology*.[1]

By R. H. MOTTRAM

And now it was October, 1915 ; more troops than ever, especially infantry, were in the Commune, and an interpreter had warned Jerome Vanderlynden that he would have a whole battalion in the farm. He made no remark, but Madeleine had asked several questions. More awake mentally than her father, it had not escaped her close reading of the paper that a new sort of English troops were coming to France. They were described indifferently as " Territorials " and as " New Army " or " Kitchener's Army," and neither Madeleine nor, indeed, the newspapers of the Department du Nord knew of any difference between them and the Territoriaux of the

[1] Published by Chatto & Windus.

French system. Madeleine put them down as second-line troops and stored the fact in her vigilant mind.

She came and stood beside her father as the 10th Battalion Easthamptonshire Regiment broke up and moved off to its billets. Two of the sadly depleted companies went to adjacent farms, two remained on the premises. The officers—of whom only twelve had survived the Battle of Loos—were busy with non-coms., going through nominal rolls, lists of missing men or damaged equipment, trying to disentangle some sort of parade state and indent for replacements.

Madeleine did not bother about them. She said to her father: " I am going to find the *quarta-mastere* ! "

She found him, standing amid his stores in the hop-press, and knew him by his grey hair and white-red-white ribbon. She had long ago inquired and found out that this rank in the English Army were chosen from among the old soldiers, and were quickest at getting to business. It had been explained to her that the white-red-white ribbon was for length of good conduct, and secretly tolerant of men's foibles as of a child's, she stored this fact also, for identification purposes.

In this instance the Mess President having been killed, the old ranker, Lieutenant and Quartermaster John Adams, was acting Mess President, and doing nearly every other duty in the disorganisation and readjustment that followed the tragic bungle of the New Army's first offensive.

He greeted her with his professional aplomb: " Good day, Maddam, dinner for twelve officers ; *compris, douze* ! " He held up the fingers of both hands and then two fingers separately.

" All right ! " returned Madeleine in English. " Where are their rations ? "

He replied: " Ah, you're sharp ! " and called to his storekeeper : " Jermyn, officers' rations to Maddam, and tell the mess cook ! " He went on to bargain for other things—beds for the colonel, the adjutant and himself—and in the course of the argument, Madeleine informed him that, according to General Routine Orders, there was to be no smoking in the barns and no insanitary practices, that all gates must be kept closed, and no movables removed. Handing him her price list, she withdrew to her long, coffin-shaped stove in the brick-floored kitchen.

. . . .

Madeleine thought no more of the War, and the population it had brought to the Spanish Farm, until half-past seven, when the mess orderlies began to prepare breakfast. Obstinately refusing to allow anyone to touch her stove, she cooked that incomprehensible meal of oat-soup ("porridge" they called it!), and bacon and eggs, after which she knew, they ate orange confiture. She, her father and the farm hands, had long taken their lump of bread and bowl of coffee, standing. Her attention was divided between the hum of the separator in the dairy and her washing drying on the line, when she heard her father's voice calling: "Madeleine, *leinsche*!" ("Little Madeleine!"). She called out that she was in the kitchen.

The old man came, moving more quickly than usual, voluble in Flemish, excited. The soldiers had moved out all the flax-straw lying in the long wooden drying-shed behind the house, on the pasture, and all the machines, reapers and binders, drills and rakes. Moreover, they had taken for firewood hop-poles that had been expressly forbidden.

Madeleine washed her hands at the sink, saying she would see about it. But she was saved the trouble. Her father went out into the yard, unable to keep still in his impatience, and she heard him in altercation with old Adams. They drifted into the mess-room. As she was drying her hands, there was a knock on the kitchen door, and she saw her father ushering in the dark young officer of the evening before. Her brow cleared. She had not the least doubt she could "manage" the young man.

The young man surpassed expectations. Madeleine found it unnecessary to keep to her rather limited English. His French, while not correct, was expansive. He admitted her version of the farmer's rights under Billeting Law, but would not accept the sum, running into hundreds of francs, which Jerome Vanderlynden, typical peasant at a bargain, asked for compensation. It appeared that the quiet-looking young man knew something of flax culture and more of agricultural machinery. He quoted within a very little the cost of re-stacking the flax, oiling the machinery, with the price of two burnt hop-poles. He offered forty francs.

Old Vanderlynden made his usual counter: "What if I go to Brigade Headquarters about it!"

" Then you will get nothing at all. They are too busy, and we move on to-day ! "

The old man laughed and slapped his leg.

Madeleine, knowing by experience that the officer had been authorised to spend fifty francs (a sum which appealed to the English, being recognisable as a couple of sovereigns), began to respect him, took the money, and signed the receipt.

* * *

CRYING IN THE WILDERNESS
From *The Pope on Peace and War*.[1]
By HIS HOLINESS POPE BENEDICT XV.

APOSTOLIC EXHORTATION OF BENEDICT XV TO THE PEOPLES NOW AT WAR AND TO THEIR RULERS.

" When We, though all unworthy, were called to succeed on the Apostolic Throne the meek Pius X, whose life of holiness and well-doing was cut short by grief at the fratricidal struggle that had just burst forth in Europe, We, too, on turning a fearful glance on the blood-stained battle-fields, felt the anguish of a father, who sees his homestead devastated and in ruins before the fury of the hurricane. And thinking with unspeakable regret of our young sons, who were being mown down by death in thousands, We opened Our heart, enlarged by the charity of Christ, to all the crushing sorrow of the mothers, and of the wives made widows before their time, and to all the inconsolable laments of the little ones, too early bereft of a father's care. Sharing in the anxious fears of innumerable families, and fully conscious of the imperative duties imposed upon Us by the sublime mission of peace and of love, entrusted to Our care in days of so much sadness, We conceived at once the firm purpose of consecrating all Our energy and all Our power to the reconciling of the peoples at war : indeed, We made it a solemn promise to Our Divine Saviour, who willed to make all men brothers at the cost of His Blood.

. . . .

[1] Published by Catholic Truth Society.

" The abounding wealth, with which God the Creator has enriched the lands that are subject to You, allow You to go on with the struggle ; but at what cost ? Let the thousands of young lives quenched every day on the fields of battle make answer : answer, the ruins of so many towns and villages, of so many monuments raised by the piety and genius of your ancestors. And the bitter tears shed in the secrecy of home, or at the foot of altars where suppliants beseech,—do not these also repeat that the price of the long drawn-out struggle is great—too great ?

" Nor let it be said that the immense conflict cannot be settled without the violence of war. Lay aside your mutual purpose of destruction ; remember that Nations do not die ; humbled and oppressed, they chafe under the yoke imposed upon them, preparing a renewal of the combat, and passing down from generation to generation a mournful heritage of hatred and revenge.

" Why not from this moment weigh with serene mind the rights and lawful aspirations of the peoples ? Why not initiate with a good will an exchange of views, directly or indirectly, with the object of holding in due account, within the limits of possibility, those rights and aspirations, and thus succeed in putting an end to the monstrous struggle, as has been done under other similar circumstances ? Blessed be he who will first raise the olive-branch, and hold out his right hand to the enemy with an offer of reasonable terms of peace. The equilibrium of the world, and the prosperity and assured tranquillity of Nations rest upon mutual benevolence and respect for the rights and the dignity of others, much more than upon hosts of armed men and the ring of formidable fortresses.

" This is the cry of peace which breaks forth from Our heart with added vehemence on this mournful day ; and We invite all, whosoever are the friends of peace the world over, to give Us a helping hand in order to hasten the termination of the war, which for a long year has changed Europe into one vast battle-field. May the merciful Jesus, through the intercession of His Sorrowful Mother, grant that at last, after so horrible a storm, the dawn of peace may break, placid and radiant, an image of His own Divine Countenance. May hymns of thanksgiving soon rise to the Most High, the Giver of all good things, for the accomplished reconciliation of the States; may the peoples, bound in bonds of brotherly love, return to the peaceful rivalry of studies, of arts, of industries, and, with the empire of right re-established, may they resolve from now henceforth to entrust the settlement of their differences, not to the sword's edge, but to reasons of equity and justice, pondered with due calm and deliberation. This will be their most splendid and glorious conquest!"

* * *

THE Christmas truce of 1914 had naturally not been viewed with enthusiasm by the Higher Commands, who feared it might have led to a premature cessation of hostilities. Efficient steps were taken to ensure that there was no recurrence of this unmilitary celebration of the birth of the Prince of Peace.

CHRISTMAS, 1915

From *Up to Mametz*.[1]

By LL. WYN GRIFFITH

Another day of inactivity faded into a dull evening, and shortly after dusk we paraded on the road. We were to go to the front line, there to spend our Christmas. Last year there had been much fraternising with the enemy, but this year strict orders had been issued that we must confine our goodwill not only to our fellow-Christians, but to Christians of allied nationality. We were to remain throughout possessed by the spirit of hate, answering any advances with lead. This was the substance of the message read out to us on parade on Christmas Eve; it created no stir, nor did it seem in any way unreasonable at the time. Not one of us, standing on that road, had any desire to show cordiality to an enemy unseen and unknown, whose presence was manifested only in sudden moments of a great uprising of fear. Why should

[1] Published by Faber & Faber, Ltd.

we cherish any thought of sharing with this impersonal cause of our degradation even one arbitrary day of peace? I do not say that we marched up the rue Tilleloy inspired with a fresh determination to kill at every opportunity on Christmas Day, nor that we meditated a secret overthrowing of the orders that we had received. We reached the front line in a neutral mood, hoping rather for a quiet and uneventful spell of trench duty.

The night was fine and starry, with little wind. The front-line trench was wet and poor, flimsier even than Fort Erith—technically speaking it was a breastwork, not a trench. If Fort Erith seemed unfinished, this could not be rated higher than half-begun, with its evil-smelling wet walls, undrained sump-pits and ramshackle dug-outs. There were five officers to share the watch, and when the company commander allotted to me a two-hour period, from one in the morning till three, I felt proud to command a stretch of the front line on my first visit. At dinner that evening a bottle of champagne gave a spurious glow to an ordinary meal, if a first meal in the front line can ever be called ordinary. Towards midnight we heard voices from the German trenches and some snatches of song: they were making merry. The night was still, and its quiet was unbroken by rifle or machine-gun fire. The artillery on both sides sent over a few shells towards the rear of the lines. The firing could rightly be described as desultory, for there was little desire on either side to create trouble; some rounds must of course be fired, otherwise questions would follow.

The battalion on our right was shouting to the enemy, and he was responding. Gradually the shouts became more deliberate, and we could hear " Merry Christmas, Tommy " and " Merry Christmas, Fritz." As soon as it became light, we saw hands and bottles being waved at us, with encouraging shouts that we could neither understand nor misunderstand. A drunken German stumbled over his parapet and advanced through the barbed wire, followed by several others, and in a few moments there was a rush of men from both sides, carrying tins of meat, biscuits and other odd commodities for barter. This was the first time I had seen

No Man's Land, and now it was Every Man's Land, or nearly so. Some of our men would not go, and they gave terse and bitter reasons for their refusal. The officers called our men back to the line, and in a few minutes No Man's Land was once again empty and desolate. There had been a feverish exchange of " souvenirs," a suggestion for peace all day, and a football match in the afternoon, and a promise of no rifle-fire at night. All this came to naught. An irate Brigadier came spluttering up to the line, thundering hard, throwing a " court-martial " into every other sentence, ordering an extra dose of militant action that night, and breathing fury everywhere. We had evidently jeopardised the safety of the Allied cause. I suspect that across No Man's Land a similar scene was being played, for later in the day the guns became active. The artillery was stimulating the infantry to resume the War. Despite the fulminations of the Generals, the infantry was in no mood for offensive measures, and it was obvious that, on both sides, rifles and machine-guns were aimed high.

A few days later we read in the papers that on Christmas Day, 1915, there was no fraternising with the enemy—hate was too bitter to permit of such a yielding.

* * *

As the Army grew, the tangle of barbed wire before it was second in complexity only to the maze of the Red Tape in the back areas. Each grouping had its own " Headquarters," an office run chiefly by warriors more accustomed to the sword than to the pen.

THE WAR OF PAPER
From *The Gambardier*.[1]
By Mark Severn

He soon learnt how to play the Great Army Paper Game. It is called, " Passed to you, please," and consists in writing these magic words or alternatively, " For your Information and Necessary Action," on every memo or letter and sending

[1] Published by Ernest Benn, Ltd.

it on to somebody else. This military indoor game is of great antiquity, and is believed to have been initiated by Julius Cæsar during the second Gallic War as a means of keeping his staff employed, whilst he got on with the fighting. The advance of education has popularised the game, and it now forms an integral part of every properly organised military system.

The opening gambit usually starts from the very top or the very bottom. It is either up to Gunner Smith or the Quarter-Master-General to make the first move. Let us assume that Gunner Smith, in a moment of absent-mindedness, consumes his iron ration under the mistaken impression that by doing so he will stave off the pangs of hunger. The crime is duly discovered by the sergeant, or No. 1, of his section, who reports it to his section commander. The latter reports it to the B.C., who then writes to the Adjutant making a clean breast of the whole sordid story and asking for guidance as to how to obtain another iron ration. The Adjutant, an efficient young officer who knows his job, writes " Forwarded " on it and sends it to the Staff Captain! It is then purely a matter of volleying up and on through all the grades and formations until the correspondence finally reaches the august eye of the Q.M.G. Anyone who writes more than " Passed to you, please," or " Forwarded," automatically wastes time and loses the respect of the other players by branding himself a novice. The Q.M.G. delivers judgment, and issues a three-page memo of instructions as to the procedure to be adopted should such an unfortunate thing ever occur again. It is then passed back and the correct wording now is, " For your information and necessary action." Finally, the pile of papers returns to the battery commander and can go no further. Action has got to be taken. He sends for the quartermaster-sergeant and orders him to issue Gunner Smith with another iron ration out of store. The Q.M.S. then calls for his storeman and tells him to unpack that perishing case of tin rations and give one of them to that perishing perisher Gunner Smith. The net result is that, three months after the consumption of his original iron ration, Gunner Smith; should he still be alive, is provided with another, and everybody has enjoyed a very ably conducted rally of the Great Game in the interim.

At this period the Chief-of-Staff of the German Armies penned one of the most momentous documents of the War. In a masterly appreciation of the situation from the German point of view, he indicated the strategy of 1916. In his mind this was to be focussed on one word—VERDUN.

VERDUN: THE DECISION
From *General Headquarters, 1914-1916, and Its Critical Decisions*.[1]
By GENERAL ERICH VON FALKENHAYN

It is true that we have succeeded in shaking England severely—the best proof of that is her imminent adoption of universal military service. But that is also a proof of the sacrifices England is prepared to make to attain her end—the permanent elimination of what seems to her the most dangerous rival. The history of the English wars against the Netherlands, Spain, France and Napoleon is being repeated. Germany can expect no mercy from this enemy, so long as he still retains the slightest hope of achieving his object. Any attempt at an understanding which Germany might make would only strengthen England's will to war as, judging others by herself, she would take it as a sign that Germany's resolution was weakening.

England, a country in which men are accustomed to weigh up the chances dispassionately, can scarcely hope to overthrow us by purely military means. She is obviously staking everything on a war of exhaustion. We have not been able to shatter her belief that it will bring Germany to her knees, and that belief gives the enemy the strength to fight on and keep on whipping their team together.

What we have to do is to dispel that illusion.

With that end in view, it will not, in the long run, be enough for us merely to stand on the defensive, a course in itself quite worthy of consideration. Our enemies, thanks to their superiority in men and material, are increasing their resources much more than we are. If that process continues a

[1] Published by Hutchinson & Co.

moment must come when the balance of numbers itself will deprive Germany of all remaining hope. The power of our allies to hold out is restricted, while our own is not unlimited. It is possible that next winter, or—if the Rumanian deliveries continue—the winter after the next, will bring food crises, and the social and political crises that always follow them, among the members of our alliance, if there has been no decision by then. Those crises must and will be overcome. But there is no time to lose. We must show England patently that her venture has no prospects.

In this case, of course, as in most others involving higher strategic decisions, it is very much easier to say what has to be done than to find out how it can and must be done.

The next method would be an attempt to inflict a decisive defeat on England on land. By that I do not mean here the island itself, which cannot be reached by our troops. Of that the navy is profoundly convinced. Our efforts can therefore be directed only against one of the continental theatres where England is fighting.

. . . . . .

It is all the more necessary that we should ruthlessly employ every weapon that is suitable for striking at England on her own ground. Such weapons are the submarine war and the conclusion of a political and economic union between Germany and not her allies only, but all States which are not yet entirely under England's spell. The review is not concerned with the formation of such a union. The solution of that problem is the exclusive sphere of the political leaders.

The submarine war, on the other hand, is a weapon to itself. It is the duty of those who are conducting the war to explain their attitude on this question.

Submarine warfare strikes at the enemy's most sensitive spot, because it aims at severing his oversea communications. If the definite promises of the naval authorities, that the unrestricted submarine war must force England to yield in the course of the year 1916, are realised, we must face the fact that the United States may take up a hostile attitude. She cannot intervene decisively in the war in time to enable her to

VERDUN: THE DECISION

make England fight on when that country sees the spectre of hunger and many another famine rise up before her island. There is only one shadow on this encouraging picture of the future. We have to assume that the naval authorities are not making a mistake. We have no large store of experiences to draw on in this matter. Such as we have are not altogether reassuring. On the other hand, the basis of our calculations will be materially changed in our favour if we can increase the number of our submarines and make progress with the training of their crews. For all these reasons there can be no justification on military grounds for refusing any further to employ what promises to be our most effective weapon. Germany has every right to use it ruthlessly after England's unconscionable behaviour at sea. The Americans, England's secret allies, will not recognise that, but it is doubtful whether, in face of a determined diplomatic representation of Germany's standpoint, they will decide to intervene actively on the Continent of Europe. It is even more doubtful whether they could intervene in sufficient strength in time. If we refuse to adopt unrestricted submarine warfare, it means that we are abandoning what all competent experts assure us is a sure advantage of inestimable value for a draw-back which is serious but only problematical. In Germany's position that course is not permissible.

· · · · · ·

As I have already insisted, the strain on France has almost reached the breaking-point—though it is certainly borne with the most remarkable devotion. If we succeeded in opening the eyes of her people to the fact that in a military sense they have nothing more to hope for, that breaking-point would be reached and England's best sword knocked out of her hand. To achieve that object the uncertain method of a mass break-through, in any case beyond our means, is unnecessary. We can probably do enough for our purposes with limited resources. Within our reach behind the French sector of the Western Front there are objectives for the retention of which the French General Staff would be compelled to throw in every man they have. If they do so the forces of France will bleed to death—as there can be no question of a voluntary withdrawal—whether we reach our goal or not. If they do not do so, and we reach our objectives, the moral effect on France will be enormous. For an operation limited to a narrow front Germany will not be compelled to spend herself so completely that all other fronts are practically drained. She can face with confidence the relief attacks to be expected on those fronts, and indeed hope to have sufficient troops in hand to reply to them with counter-attacks. For she is perfectly free to accelerate or draw out her offensive, to intensify it or break it off from time to time, as suits her purpose.

The objectives of which I am speaking now are Belfort and Verdun.

The considerations urged above apply to both, yet the preference must be given to Verdun. The French lines at that point are barely twelve miles distant from the German railway communications. Verdun is therefore the most powerful *point d'appui* for an attempt, with a relatively small expenditure of effort, to make the whole German Front in France and Belgium untenable. The removal of the danger, as a secondary aim, would be so valuable on military grounds that, compared with it, the so to speak " incidental," political victory of the " purification " of Alsace by an attack on Belfont is a small matter.

* * *

VERDUN: THE ONSLAUGHT

From *Verdun*.[1]

By Marshal Pétain

On February 21st, 1916, a hurricane of iron and steel broke over the defences of Verdun. The Germans attacked with a force and violence never before equalled. The French accepted the challenge, for Verdun to them is even more than a great fortress, an outpost intended to bar the path of the invader on the east; it is the moral bulwark of France. The German onrush at first overwhelmed all our advanced positions, but

[1] Published by   Mathews & Marrot, Ltd.

VERDUN: THE ONSLAUGHT

we quickly found our feet, and from that time on we held in check by our unaided strength the formidable attacks that the Germans launched unremittingly for five months. Thus the Verdun region became the scene of a terrific duel between the two chief adversaries on the Western Front.

. . . . . .

The struggle was carried on with heroic courage, both by the troops and by their leaders. Bombardments by the German heavy artillery, during February 21st and the night of the 21st–22nd, preceded the charge of the shock divisions. Nowhere before, on any front, in any battle, had anything like it been seen. The Germans aimed to create a " zone of death," within which no troops could survive. An avalanche of steel and iron, of shrapnel and poisonous gas shells, fell on our woods, ravines, trenches and shelters, destroying everything, transforming the sector into a charnel field, defiling the air, spreading flames into the heart of the town, damaging even the bridges and Meuse villages as far as Genicourt and Troyon. Heavy explosions shook our forts and wreathed them in smoke. It would be impossible to describe an action of the kind. I believe that it has never been equalled in violence, and it concentrated the devastating fire of more than two million shells in the narrow triangle of land between Brabant-on-Meuse, Ornes and Verdun.

During the afternoon of the 21st and the morning of the 22nd, after a night in which the artillery had incessantly kept up its infernal pounding, the German troops advanced in small formations, the different waves pushing one another forward, hoping to progress without opposition. Imagine their amazement and their disappointment to see everywhere along their route the French rising from the wreck, exhausted and in tatters to be sure, but still formidable, defending the ruins from every possible point of vantage. . . .

The mass of combatants was composed of seasoned men, " grown old in experience of war," whose average age was from twenty-five to twenty-six years. Like the " grognards " of the First Empire, they constituted a generation of veterans whose physical vigour and moral strength were altogether extraordinary. They had made up their minds that they would save Verdun, and endured superhuman ordeals with stoicism, resigning themselves wholeheartedly, perhaps not without a touch of fatalism, to the strenuous tasks imposed upon them. Their spirit was not so much enthusiasm as virile determination, and their strength was founded principally on their inflexible purpose to defend their families and their homes from the invader. They were soldiers in the highest sense of the word, grim and resolute, accepting in their day's work both danger and suffering. When their time came to enter the line, they advanced with unfaltering steps to meet their fate, fully knowing what was in store for them. No one who saw these men at Verdun could ever forget them!

They had the implicit confidence of the French people, who thought of them as supermen, ready and able at any time to perform deeds of marvellous valour. There was something fantastic in the ideas of the general public, which, as it believed in the intervention of mysterious forces, was prone to underestimate the true wretchedness and suffering of our soldiers, and to over-estimate their powers. Hence came the feverish impatience with which a stroke of deliverance, for which the time was not yet ripe, was expected. Nevertheless we appreciated at its full value the high esteem in which we were held by our countrymen, and in order to be worthy of it we strove each day to do better than before.

Our superhuman resistance cast a beam of light beyond the bounds of our own land, and everywhere in the camps of the Allies new hope was born. Since France by herself was capable of accomplishing so much, it was felt that nothing was impossible to the united armies of the coalition. From the capital cities of the friendly nations and from the headquarters of their staffs, messages of congratulation poured in to Chantilly. The English were the first to join in our gratification and they attempted to hasten their entry into the lists at our side in the co-operative offensive that had been decided upon. General Cadorna visited the French front and spoke with admiration of the " calm tenacity " of our troops. The Italian Chamber of Deputies applauded the French Army and stated its conviction that we had saved Europe. Prince Alexander of Serbia, after having seen the battlefield of Verdun, expressed his enthusiasm to our Ministerial Council. Our ambassador at Petrograd received from our powerful eastern allies the most affecting expressions of admiration and the promise of prompt and vigorous collaboration.

To sum up, Verdun held.

* * *

VERDUN: THEY SHALL NOT PASS!
From *Verdun*.[1]
By Marshal Pétain

Three army corps were consequently hurled against our positions at Fort Vaux during the first part of June, the three being, in order from west to east, the First Bavarian Corps, the Tenth Reserve Corps and the Fifteenth Corps. All three had a thorough acquaintance with the terrain, where they had been fighting hard for weeks and months. They succeeded after a terrific bombardment in gaining a foothold for several groups of assault troops on the superstructure of the fort, and these men then attacked each of our isolated resistance centres in turn. Conditions were more favourable to them than they had been to us a few days earlier at Douaumont, and thanks to the fact that our position at that point formed a salient, they were able to surround the earthwork on three sides. Within a short time our communications with the rear were irremediably endangered. To attempt to hold their position under such circumstances was, on the part of our men, simply a matter of honour. Inspired by this noble ambition, Major Raynal and his heroic comrades in arms refused to yield the fort, and in recognition of their self-sacrifice, General Joffre sent them his congratulations and conferred upon their leader, as a reward, a high rank in the Legion of Honour. There can be no memory more affecting than that of their last stand, when, cut off from us with no hope of assistance, they sent us their final reports.

[1] Published by Elkin Mathews & Marrot, Ltd.

The following message came to us on the morning of June 4th by carrier-pigeon :

" We are still holding our position, but are being attacked by gases and smoke of very deadly character. We are in need of immediate relief. Put us into communication with Souville at once for visual signalling. We get no answer from there to our calls. This is our last pigeon ! "

Then during the morning of June 5th came this message, relayed by visual signal through Souville :

" The enemy is working on the west side of the fort to construct a mine in order to blow up the vaults. Direct your artillery fire there quickly."

At eight o'clock came another :

" We do not hear your artillery. We are being attacked with gas and liquid fire. We are in desperate straits."

Then this one, at nightfall on June 5th :

" I must be set free this evening, and must have supplies of water immediately. I am coming to the end of my strength. The troops, enlisted men and officers, have done their duty to the last, in every case."

On the 6th came only these few words :

" . . . you will intervene before we are completely exhausted. Vive la France ! "

And finally, on June 7th, at half-past three in the morning, these last words, whose meaning we could not make out :

" . . . must go on."

. . . .

ORDER OF THE DAY

" Every man of you should be mentioned by name, soldiers of Verdun, soldiers in the line and soldiers in the rear. For if I gave the place of honour, as is meet, to those who fell in the front of the battle, still I know that their courage would have availed nothing without the patient toil, continued day and night, to the last limit of their strength, on the part of the men to whose efforts were due the regular arrival of the reinforcements, of munitions, and of food, and the evacuation of the wounded : the truck-drivers along the Sacred Way, the railroad engineers, the ambulance force.

" Of what steel was forged the soldier of Verdun, the man whom France found ready in her need to meet the grave crisis that confronted her, the man who could calmly face the most severe of trials ? Had he received some special grace which raised him instinctively to the heights of heroism ?

" We who knew him can answer that he was but a man after all, with human virtues and human weaknesses. One of our own people, a man whose thoughts and affections still clung, after eighteen months of warfare, to his family, to his workshop, to his village, or to the farm on which he had been brought up.

" These same personal bonds, which, taken altogether, constituted his devotion to his country, laid him under obligation to protect those people and those things which in his eyes made life worth living. They inspired him to the complete sacrifice of himself. Other sentiments as well contributed to his state of mind—love of the soil, in the peasant who gave his life as a matter of course in defence of his ancestral field; devout submission to the decree of Providence in the heart of the true believer; the impulse to defend an ideal of civilisation in the intellectual.

" But the noblest feelings do not suffice to instil in men the ability to fight. This is something that comes only little by little, with a knowledge of what one goes through on a battle-field, and with experience in all the conditions of warfare. We must bear in mind that the War, already an old story, had in 1916 moulded our French everyday citizen and had made him a soldier in the fullest sense of the word.

" The suffering that he had already borne steeled him against emotion, and gave him extraordinary powers of endurance. The prospect of death, which he continually faced, filled him with a resignation that bordered on fatalism. Long practice in fighting had taught him that success is the most tenacious, and had developed in him qualities of patience and persistence. He had also learned that in a battle each man is one link in a chain that is forged of all, and he had sacrificed his individualistic ways and class prejudices, thus cementing the splendid spirit of comradeship that made our fighting men work as one.

" An experienced and tried soldier, believing in himself and in his comrades, proud of his renown, he went up into the line certainly without enthusiasm but also without hesitation. Feeling that he carried the burden of his country's need, more important than his own, he did his duty to the very limit of his powers.

"It is impossible to believe that the soldier could have risen to such heights of heroism if he had not felt behind him the inspiration of the whole nation. Our country as a whole took up the struggle and accepted all its consequences, material and moral. It was only because the soldier had the spirit of the nation behind him to drive him on that he won the battle. It was his country's will that he fulfilled."

* * *

ANOTHER subsidiary war was raged in Mesopotamia, the alleged garden of Eden, where Townshend's force, besieged in Kut, was compelled to surrender. The march of British and Indian prisoners across the desert is one of the most heart-rending stories of the campaign.

GUESTS OF THE UNSPEAKABLE

From *Golden Horn*.[1]

By FRANCIS YEATS-BROWN

Our destination was Afionkarahissar, a town in the centre of Anatolia.[2]

I remember little of the journey thither. When vitality goes, memory follows it. I was worn out, more dead than alive. Vaguely I recollect a crowded train, a stage by carriages, carrying my quilt—which seemed to weigh a ton—up a mountain-path, and fainting on the way, a dead Indian whom we

[1] Published by Victor Gollancz, Ltd.
[2] Afionkarahissar (Black Opium Rock) is reached by the Aleppo–Constantinople railway, but in 1916 there were two breaks in the ine, at Islahie and Bozanti, where the sections across the Taurus Mountains had not been completed.

GUESTS OF THE UNSPEAKABLE 155

thought the guards had killed, and a doctor whom we questioned as to whether lice would give us typhus; he had opened the collar of his tunic and said, " Don't worry: I'm swarming with them myself and haven't got it yet." At Bozanti I implored the Turks to leave me and let me die. I lay on some sacks in the railway-station, a bundle of skin and bone that might not have been human at all. Porters threw more sacks on the pile and I was soon almost covered. I lay still: as my bodily weakness increased, so did my mind range out beyond normal consciousness, deep into myself and wide into the world. I thrilled to this strange strength, which seemed to mount to the throne of Time, surveying life from a great height. I saw then something which happened three months later, at this station.

I saw some hundred men, prisoners from Kut and mostly Indians, gathered on the platform: one of them was sitting on this heap of sacks: he was sitting here rocking himself to and fro in great pain and sorrow, for a guard had struck him with a rifle butt and broken his arm. Not only his bone but the spirit within him was shattered: no hope remained: he had done that which is most terrible to a Hindu, for he had eaten the flesh of cows and broken the ordinances of his caste. His companions had died in the desert without the lustral rites prescribed by the Vedas, and he would soon die also, a body defiled, to be cast into outer darkness. For a time the terror of that alien brain was mine: I shared its doom and knew its death.

· · · · · ·

All of us were the survivors of some strange experience and had lived through bad moments. Out of four hundred officers reported missing on Gallipoli, only seventeen had survived, and among the men the proportion was about the same: small wonder that we were restless.

One of the Dardanelles prisoners had been dragged as a supposed corpse to the Turkish trenches and there built into the parapet. He was not dead, but stunned; when he came to life the Turks began to bayonet him to avoid disturbing the earthwork, but orders had been issued by Liman von Sanders that a few prisoners were required for Intelligence purposes, and he was spared. He was none the worse now for his experience except that he suffered slightly from deafness, as his ear had formed the base of a loophole.

Then there was a boy of nineteen, who had been left as dead after an attack; he also had recovered consciousness, but not the use of his limbs until some time afterwards: for an hour he had lain helpless, in the path of the Turkish retreat. Passers-by prodded him with bayonets, so that he now had twenty-seven wounds, and a gap in his bottom where there should have been solid flesh. From the brink of the valley of the shadow he had returned to life: he told one of us that in his experience the most unpleasant place to be stabbed was the stomach. No doubt he knew.

Again, there was a young Frenchman, who had remained four days and nights between the lines, disembowelled and tortured by thirst; by a miracle he had survived, and now at night, sometimes, when will lost its grip on consciousness, he would live those ninety-six hours again. . . .

. . . .

We had heard and seen something of the Kut prisoners. Thirteen thousand had been captured: scarce five thousand survived their marches and prisons: they had been clubbed, stripped, mutilated: their bones were strewn in the deserts between Baghdad and Aleppo.

Some of the survivors had arrived so dazed that they could not speak, so enfeebled by hunger that they could not carry their tiny bundles. Sometimes a group of four or five emaciated men had passed underneath our windows bearing a coffinless corpse on a stretcher: skeletons alive, carrying a skeleton to the end of its long journey.

* * *

The Irish Revolution, which ended in the establishment of the Irish Free State as a Dominion of the British Commonwealth of Nations in 1921, began with a rebellion by about one thousand men in Dublin at Easter, 1916, and a few minor affrays in the provinces. The rebellion was suppressed after a week's fighting.

THE BATTLE OF DUBLIN
From *The Wasted Island*.[1]
By Eimar O'Duffy

Dublin has reason to be proud of Easter Week, for the gay, shabby, majestic old city bore herself bravely during her six days' agony. While her young volunteers, sleepless, hungry, and bewildered, fought heroically against overwhelming odds, her citizens faced the horrors which had so suddenly and unexpectedly fallen upon them with calmness and fortitude. Indeed, their principal feeling throughout was one of curiosity, and they were foolhardy in the extreme in their desire to satisfy it. Tradesmen went about their humdrum and necessary business with matter-of-fact courage in face of every danger. So long as there was milk to deliver the milkmen delivered it; so long as there was bread it did not remain undistributed; and it was the same with all the providers of necessities. When the fires began to add a new horror to the situation, the fire brigade crossed bullet-swept zones to fulfil their duty and so saved the city from certain destruction. Of panic there was no sign anywhere.

On Wednesday the bombardment began. In the morning the gunboat *Helga* steamed up the Liffey, pounded Liberty Hall into ruins, and proceeded to drop shells into Sackville Street. Rifle-fire at the same time began afresh, and the machine-guns recommenced their infernal racket. To those who listened it seemed that the whole city must inevitably be destroyed, for what buildings could possibly survive the fearful tornado that smote upon their ears? As soon as the din

[1] Published by MacMillan & Company.

slackened in one quarter it burst forth even more vigorously in another. Thus, when the dwellers on the south side noticed a slight diminution in the distant roar from Sackville Street, with shattering suddenness crashed forth a violent fusilade close at hand: where troops newly arrived from England, and on the march from Kingstown, had fallen upon the Volunteer outposts in the Pembroke area and been repulsed with heavy loss. And even as the sounds of this conflict died away, from the south-east, with redoubled intensity, burst out the cannonade which the *Helga* was directing against the stronghold of Boland's Mill. Then it too gave place to the sounds of a fresh attack from the north. So all day long the thunder of battle rolled unceasingly; it went on muttering even after dark; and there were vicious bursts at intervals during the night.

Thursday brought hunger and the fires. There was no milk that day, and no bread: people counted themselves lucky to scrape together a meal of black tea, stale crusts, and scraps of meat. The sun shone brilliantly as it did all through the week. The battle roar boomed forth again, more heavily than ever, but it had ceased to terrify. It had become monotonous. All count of time had been lost; people felt almost as if the rebellion had always been, and came to accept it as a thing of custom and part of the natural order of the day. On Monday, Tuesday and Wednesday people had asked each other incessantly: "How long is it going to last?" On Thursday they asked it no more.

About midday came the first of the fires. Following the fall of a succession of shells a thin wisp of smoke rose up from a shattered house in Abbey Street. Almost simultaneously a second appeared farther on. There was no pause in the shooting. Flames began to leap out of the windows of some of the houses, and still shell after shell dropped in the area. A dense column of flame-reddened smoke came billowing up out of the wrecked buildings, and with a crackle and roar and the thunderous fall of beams and masonry, the fire began to spread in every direction. Soon the whole block of buildings bounded by Abbey Street, Sackville Street and Eden Quay was ablaze. Great black-and-ruddy pillars of smoke rose up into the sultry air, eddying and bulging and spreading themselves into a vast canopy aloft. As night fell the terrified inhabitants saw the sky lit by a lurid glare, and so immense was the conflagration that even in the outlying districts the spectators received the impression that it was close at hand. It was generally believed that the whole city was doomed, and that night nobody slept.

. . . .

"Things are quieter this morning," observed Hugo McGurk on Friday.

He and his section held a house commanding one of the canal bridges. Every window-pane in the building had been smashed and the embrasures were fortified with sand-bags, mattresses, and articles of furniture. These ramparts had been riddled and splintered by bullets, and the front of the house was chipped and spotted and scarred all over, for the position had been under fire most of the previous day. The garrison had originally numbered eight, but two had been slain, and three of the survivors wore bandages. Smoke-grimed, hungry, and exhausted, they had scarcely left their posts at the windows for close on eighteen hours, but their spirits were still undaunted. No heart could fail under McGurk's cheery command.

Grimmest and most fearless of all the garrison was the grizzled recruit John Malone. Firing with deadly speed and accuracy, he had done more to repel yesterday's assaults than all the rest of his companions put together. Towards the end of the day a bullet had pierced his right forearm, but he had barely given time to allow it to be bandaged before he was back at his post dealing out death once more. It was to him that McGurk's remark had been addressed.

"I guess things will be all the hotter when they come," he replied. "I tell you, sergeant, this has been some fight. Well worth living for, my son."

The sentry from the roof entered the room just then and saluted McGurk.

"Troops massing at the end of the road," he reported.

McGurk made the round of his defences.

"Hold your fire till you're sure to hit, boys," he said. "Mulligan, keep your head down. We can't afford any more casualties.... Kelly, don't waste your ammunition.... Now, boys, they're coming...."

A tornado of firing burst forth as he spoke. Bullets came through the windows and pattered on the opposite walls. The rooms were filled with smoke and dust. A motor lorry came down the street and on to the bridge. Then there was an explosion and it came to a standstill. Malone had emptied his magazine into the bonnet. Soldiers poured out from it and made a rush for the house. Down went three of them: a few ran back: half a dozen came storming at the garden gate. The man at the window over the hall door dropped his empty rifle and fired both barrels of a shot-gun loaded with buck-shot into the midst of them. Four fell, and the remainder ran away screaming with pain. More soldiers came pouring over the bridge. Malone, hurrying not at all, but still firing with the same monotonous regularity, picked off man after man and drove the survivors behind the waggon for shelter. Some of them began shooting from this piece of cover, and Mulligan fell dead with a bullet in his brain.

"Steady, boys!" cried McGurk. "Heads down! Shoot slow."

There was a lull in the combat. A bandaged warrior stepped up to McGurk.

"Ammunition nearly gone," he said.

"Well, well," said McGurk. "We'll have to retreat, I suppose." He thought a moment. "Have you any ammunition left, Malone?" he shouted.

"Plenty," called back Malone.

"Well, the rest of you fall back over the roofs," said McGurk. "You take command of them, Mick. Me and Malone will hold the rear for a bit. Carry on now."

The man saluted and marched off with his three comrades.

"Here they are again," cried Malone, and reopened fire. McGurk dropped behind a sand-bag and did the same. His shooting was wilder than Malone's and not so effective, but he did some damage all the same. It was, however, hopeless for these two to stop the enemy's rush. Over the bridge it came

THE BATTLE OF DUBLIN

and into the garden. A terrible explosion told of bombs flung at the door, and at that moment Malone gave a cry of pain and rolled over. McGurk rushed to his side.

"I'm done," said Malone. "You'd better git." And he died.

It was too late to retreat. Down went the door with a crash and the enemy surged into the hall and up the stairs. McGurk rushed out on to the landing. Bang! went his last cartridge and the foremost soldier dropped. On came the others, a tall man and a little man at their head. McGurk, at the stair-head, crossed bayonets with the tall man, and the little man tried to run in under his guard. McGurk knocked up the tall man's rifle and dealt the little man a kick in the stomach that sent him reeling. Back and forward went McGurk's bayonet like the tongue of a snake, jabbing the tall man in the chest. Before he could withdraw it another man leapt over the body of the little man and stabbed McGurk in the side. McGurk uttered a curse and went back a step. Another man thrust at him, wounding his thigh. With a roar of anger, McGurk clubbed his rifle and smashed in his assailant's head, but at the same moment he was wounded again by another foe. Then at last he fell, and the whole band swarmed up and over him, trampling the life out of him. . . .

Once more the tumult of war crashed over the city. With redoubled intensity the big guns boomed and the machine-guns rattled, and gallantly the diminishing rifles of the Volunteers answered back. The Post Office, heart and brain of the insurrection, was being shelled. After twenty minutes of intense bombardment those who watched saw the Republican Flag become obscured by a cloud of smoke. Up from the roof rushed a swirling black column, and soon afterwards a long flame curled up out of one of the windows and licked at the foot of the flagstaff. Little figures could be discerned running about on the roof desperately fighting the flames amid a hail of bullets. Their efforts were useless. Out of the windows and through the roof leaped the red blaze. Soon the whole interior was irretrievably involved, and the building had become a vast raging furnace. With a crash the whole internal structure fell in and a gigantic pillar of smoke and flame and sparks and incandescent fragments shot up into the sky. Down came the sparks again in a glittering cascade; up rushed another fury of flames; down rolled the smoke in coiling, fuming billows, spreading themselves abroad or dissipating themselves in filmy clouds. Soon nothing was left of the building but the four bare walls, from one corner of which the flag still flew. It was still flying over the red glowing embers when night fell. For an hour after dark it still fluttered feebly in the breeze. Then suddenly the staff lurched forward and went down.

· · · · · ·

All hell seemed loose in Dublin on Saturday. One after another the Volunteer outposts had been swamped or driven in, and now the main positions were isolated one from another, while the cordon was closing tighter and tighter on the centre of the city, where, somewhere in the mean streets behind the Post Office, the chief command had sought fresh quarters. On this position the enemy's artillery was now concentrated. From ten o'clock in the morning till four in the afternoon the bombardment went on relentlessly, still answered feebly by the rifles of the defenders, until the west side of Sackville Street, Henry Street, and part of Moore Street was made fuel for a conflagration which rivalled that of Thursday. Once more the unfortunate people of Dublin saw imminent destruction lowering over their city. Despair at last took possession of them.

"Is this going on for *ever*?" they asked each other, and even as they waited for an answer, the boom of the big guns ceased and the rifle-fire diminished in volume and was no longer continuous. The rebel commanders had surrendered.

Then those who watched from a distance saw a strange sight. A little band of men, not quite a hundred in number, weary, tattered, and grimy, came marching down Sackville Street under a fluttering white flag. They were met at the bridge-head by a party of military, and there at the foot of O'Connell's statue, with the flaming buildings forming a lurid background to the scene, they laid down their arms. The insurrection was over.

THE BATTLE OF DUBLIN

Amongst those who surrendered was Fergus Moore. Throughout the fighting this man had performed deeds which would have been heroic had they not been inspired by suicidal determination. When the flag was shot away it was he who had fixed it up again amid a hail of bullets; when the Post Office was in flames it was he who was foremost in the futile attempts to extinguish them; when volunteers had been called for to storm a British barricade he had been the first to offer himself and the only one to return unscathed. He had sought for death and it had been denied him, and now he handed in his arms and equipment with the same bitter smile still hovering on his war-stained countenance.

· · · · · ·

In his refuge in Glencoole, Stephen read of the collapse of the rebellion; of the minor skirmishes in Galway, Wexford and Fingall, where evidently the countermanding orders had gone astray or been disobeyed; and of the quiescence of the rest of the country. It was quite clear that Ireland was both puzzled and annoyed by the whole affair; she repudiated the insurrection and its authors with anger and disdain; and contemplated their possible punishment with indifference. It seemed for a time as if militant nationalism had slain and discredited itself.

Then came the executions. The insurrectionary leaders undid by their death much of the harm which the insurrection had done to their cause, for Ireland roused herself in rage when her sons were slain by the foreigner.

News came in slowly to Stephen, for his father dared not visit him too often. First the lists of the executed trickled in; then he heard of the death in action of The O'Rahilly, McGurk, Malone and others; then of the arrest of Casement; and finally, of the rounding up of the Volunteers all over the country. Crowley and Umpleby and Moore were amongst those deported and interned at Frongoch; Brian Mallow and Hector O'Flaherty received sentences of twenty and ten years penal servitude. Saddest fate of all was that of Bernard Lascelles.

"What a catalogue of wasted material!" he muttered.

There was no news of O'Dwyer. Presumably he had escaped arrest. One vaguely familiar name hovered hither and thither through the newspapers. Mr. Molloy, the rising young solicitor, rose higher and higher on the wreckage. . . .

"And now," said Michael Ward to his son, "now that everything has turned out as I told you it would, what do you mean to do?"

"I suppose," replied Stephen, "we must begin all over again."

* * *

THE Russians, planning a great offensive in Poland, directed General Brussilov and his Southern Army to stage a preliminary diversion in order to draw off the enemy reserves. With no obvious preparations, and therefore with the incalculable advantage of surprise, Brussilov fell upon the heterogeneous Austro-Hungarian Army and swept it like chaff before him. In a few days over three hundred thousand prisoners were taken.

THE LAST GRIP OF THE BEAR
From *Siberian Garrison*.[1]
By RODION MARKOVITS

When the Russian colonel told him that he might sleep in the house, all the excitement and all the fatigue of two days and a night descended upon him at once. Infinite weariness closed his eyelids, and by the time he had stretched himself out on the floor, he was already fast asleep. He awoke with a start; someone was mercilessly shaking him. He thought he had been lying thus collapsed for a few minutes only, but he must have been sleeping a long time, for it was morning now and the sun shone brightly.

He was ordered to leave the room.

The open field swarmed with prisoners. With an immense number of prisoners. There were officers among them now, and yesterday's lethargy was supplanted by a strange liveliness. Russian N.C.O.'s were searching the prisoners. They took the

[1] Published by Peter Davies.

THE LAST GRIP OF THE BEAR 165

cameras away from the officers, tore up their papers and the pink field post-cards they found in the pockets of the ranks. But the Russians could not search all of them; there were too many. It was a haphazard examination.

They then had to take off their boots and the Russians felt inside them, they had to unbutton their tunics and the Russians searched under their shirts. A Russian soldier ordered him to open his mouth. Meekly he obeyed and the Russian thrust his filthy fist into his mouth and he felt the touch of the cold and dirty fingers on his tongue. The Russian tried to break the gold crown of one of his teeth off, but then he began to yell at the top of his voice. The Russian soldier ran away, and officers arrived who put an end to the looting and searching. But by that time, something had been taken away from practically every one of them.

Food, blankets, safety-razors and the little bags which hung round their necks and in which they kept their money under their shirts.

The Russian officers ordered mounted Cossacks to mount guard over them, and the Cossacks surrounded them with their seven-foot lances and herded them together. He lost the three men with whom he had been captured; he was now in the midst of strangers. They set off, in huge masses, intimidated and stumbling at every step, driven on by the yells, the lances and the knouts of the Cossacks.

He had only one wish: he would have liked to get to the outer edge of the marching masses. There he would not tread on anyone's heel, there no one would tread on his heels, there he would not be suffocated with the foul stench of the mob. But those at the edge held on to their positions and those inside would not let him go. A second lieutenant was somehow swept next to him; one of his eyes was bandaged, the other one half closed. He tried hard to keep it open, but could not. "My name is Lányi, let me lean on you, I am half blinded," said the second lieutenant, and took him by the arm and leaned on him. The masses just marched on, no one knew where; no one knew either the country, or the road, or their destination. Painfully he staggered along with the second lieutenant on his arm; he could hardly drag himself, and now there was this second lieutenant too. He remembered he had been taught at school about Samaritans, but when one read of them sitting on a school-bench, or at home in bed, one merely smiled, deprecatingly. What of it, to help a wounded comrade? It's a duty, and something of an effort, one said, and waved it aside.

That was just what he was doing now, and how insufferable it was, what an incredible effort. It was maddening, the fatigue was driving him insane, he could hardly drag his blind comrade any longer, he thought that they would both collapse in a second, and then they would be trampled to death by those who came behind them.

The colossal weight of the second lieutenant hung on his arm and on his chest and on his shoulders, the silent second lieutenant pulled him down. He tried to get to the side, at least, to get air, to have just a little more elbow-room to drag him along: but they roughly pushed him back and cursed him; don't shove, don't kick, stay where you are.

Sweat and stench of perspiration and suffocating stink whirled about them. There spread the infinite Samaritan steppes. Yet all the choking, foul odour settled on this narrow strip of a road where the prisoners marched.

They marched, and their throats became dry: they marched and they put their feet mechanically one before the other: they marched, and the road had nowhere an end. They marched, and little pools of water glistened in the sun, and thirst tormented them. He had never known this, either: what it meant to be thirsty, as it was described in novels and in the Bible; to be thirsty, he had never known that sensation. All feeling of nausea, all feeling of fastidiousness disappeared, the men looked longingly and covetously at the pools covered with weed; they imagined that they would be instantaneously transported to Heaven if only they could drink of them.

It was noon. The Cossacks stopped the column.

An interpreter announced that those who drank out of the ruts or puddles would be immediately shot to death. This water spread typhus.

They squatted and knelt and sat in the dust, and stared longingly and covetously at the water in the ruts and the mossy pools.

THE LAST GRIP OF THE BEAR

He told Lanyi that he had chocolate in his bag, and suggested to him that they should eat some.

Lanyi covered his mouth with his palm, and whispered back to him to keep silent.

" There are others who also have food. There are even some who have water in their flasks. Can't you see that no one touches his bag; they are all afraid of the others——"

There he sat, on the road to Kiev, and there was chocolate in his bag, but he dared not take it out because of the other starving men. The Samaritan dared not take the chocolate out of his bag because there were other hungry men around him. And there were some who had water in their flasks, and they dared not drink it, either.

There they sat, quivering and shivering with hunger, and looking squarely in each other's eyes, and watching jealously and anxiously each other's every gesture, and no one dared touch his food, his drink; they dared not drink nor eat for fear of each other. The man who showed that he had a bite of bread would have been torn to pieces on the spot. There they sat, and not even the sick men, the men suffering from fever, could have a gulp of water. Those who still had something sat indifferently, they would not betray even with their eyes that they had something. There they sat and hated each other with deadly hatred. They would have liked to run off to distant forests, to hide there in order to gobble up their chocolate undisturbed, greedily, with saliva oozing out of their mouths. They stared at each other with protruding eyes, and the hidden food and the hidden flask of water burned them like lit fuses.

When they rose, they were more tired than they had been before the rest. But they marched on mechanically and shattered. The colossal weight of Second Lieutenant Lanyi pulled him down with incredible force. He felt as if his right side where Lanyi hung on to him had been torn out of his body.

" Please, comrade, come round to my left side, let's change places."

After many efforts and experiments Lanyi managed to come to his left, but after a few minutes of relief, he felt the weight even more than before. Now he would have liked to have

Lanyi back in the original position, for there his side was already wholly numb, but this would have been a very daring and very dangerous experiment.

He had to go on, because those behind him trod on his heels and his ankles with their spiked boots, whenever he fell out of step, whenever he slowed down even for a second.

When they saw a village from afar, their hopes rose, they thought it was their goal. They dragged themselves on and they reached the village, and then they left the village again, the few miserable houses and the small church with its garlic-shaped roof. And they marched on with burnt-out hopes. In every tree, in every hovel they saw the castle of their hopes, they approached deserted barns as if they had been sacred walls.

The silent, wordless march went on for ever, with the mercilessness and certainty of the grave.

Late in the afternoon, in the desperate struggle of the march, he turned to Lanyi : " What happened to your eyes ? "

" They beat me."

" Who did ? When ? "

" When they got my machine-gun. They are infuriated with machine-gunners."

" They've got machine-guns themselves. Why should they complain of ours ? "

" Makes no difference. They are furious with them."

* * *

RUSSIAN PRISONERS

From *All Quiet on the Western Front*.[1]

By Erich Maria Remarque

(Translated from the German by A. W. Wheen.)

This thin, miserable, dirty garbage is the objective of the prisoners. They pick it out of the stinking tins greedily and go off with it under their blouses.

It is strange to see these enemies of ours so close up. They have faces that make one think—honest peasant faces, broad foreheads, broad noses, broad mouths, broad hands and thick hair.

[1] Published by G. P. Putnam's Sons.

They ought to be put to threshing, reaping, and apple picking. They look just as kindly as our own peasants in Friesland.

It is distressing to watch their movements, to see them begging for something to eat. They are all rather feeble, for they only get enough nourishment to keep them from starving. Ourselves we have not had sufficient to eat for long enough. They have dysentery: furtively many of them display the blood-stained tails of their shirts. Their backs, their necks are bent, their knees sag, their heads droop as they stretch out their hands and beg in the few words of German that they know—beg with those soft, deep, musical voices, that are like warm stoves and cosy rooms at home.

Some men there are who give them a kick, so that they fall over;—but those are not many. The majority do nothing to them, just ignore them. Occasionally, when they are too grovelling, it makes a man mad and then he kicks them. If only they would not look at one so—— What great misery can be in two such small spots, no bigger than a man's thumb—in their eyes!

They come over to the camp in the evenings and trade. They exchange whatever they possess for bread. Often they have fair success, because they have very good boots and ours are bad. The leather of their knee boots is wonderfully soft, like suede. The peasants among us who get tit-bits sent from home can afford to trade. The price of a pair of boots is about two or three loaves of army bread, or a loaf of bread and a small, tough ham sausage.

But most of the Russians have long since parted with whatever things they had. Now they wear only the most pitiful clothing, and try to exchange little carvings and objects that they have made out of shell fragments and copper driving bands. Of course, they don't get much for such things, though they may have taken immense pains with them—they go for a slice or two of bread. Our peasants are hard and cunning when they bargain. They hold the piece of bread or sausage right under the nose of the Russian till he grows pale with greed and his eyes bulge and then he will give anything for it. The peasants wrap up their booty with the utmost solemnity, and then get out their big pocket-knives, and slowly and deliberately cut off a slice of bread for themselves from their supply and with every mouthful take a piece of the good, tough sausage and so reward themselves with a good feed. It is distressing to watch them take their afternoon meal thus; one would like to crack them over their thick pates. They rarely give anything away. How little we understand one another!

* * *

CONFORMING to Joffre's idea of a simultaneous offensive on all fronts, the Italians also made gallant, but ineffectual, attempts to advance on the Carso and Isonzo fronts. Difficulty of terrain reduced the battle to an inconclusive struggle which dragged on for many months.

MOUNTAIN WARFARE!
From *A Farewell to Arms*.[1]
By ERNEST HEMINGWAY

I ate the end of my piece of cheese and took a swallow of wine. Through the other noise I heard a cough, then came the chuh-chuh-chuh-chuh—then there was a flash, as a blast-furnace door is swung open, and a roar that started white and went red and on and on in a rushing wind. I tried to breathe but my breath would not come and I felt myself rush bodily out of myself and out and out and out and all the time bodily in the wind. I went out swiftly, all of myself and I knew I was dead and that it had all been a mistake to think you just died. Then I floated, and instead of going on I felt myself slide back. I breathed and I was back. The ground was torn up and in front of my head there was a splintered beam of wood. In the jolt of my head I heard somebody crying. I thought somebody was screaming. I tried to move but I could not move. I heard the machine-guns and rifles firing across the river and all along the river. There was a great splashing and I saw the star-shells go up and burst and float whitely, and rockets going up and I heard the bombs, all this in a moment, and then I heard close to me someone saying:

[1] Published by Jonathan Cape.

"Mama mia! Oh, mama mia!" I pulled and twisted and got my legs loose finally and turned around and touched him. It was Passini and when I touched him he screamed. His legs were toward me and I saw in the dark and the light that they were both smashed above the knee. One leg was gone and the other was held by tendons and part of the trouser and the stump twitched and jerked as though it were not connected. He bit his arm and moaned: "Oh, mama mia, mama mia," then: "Dio te salvi, Maria. Dio te salvi, Maria. Oh, Jesus shoot me. Christ shoot me, Mama mia, mama mia, oh, purest lovely Mary, shoot me. Stop it. Stop it. Stop it. Oh, Jesus lovely Mary, stop it. Oh, oh, oh, oh," then choking: "Mama, mama mia." Then he was quiet, biting his arm, the stump of his leg twitching.

"Porta feriti!" I shouted, holding my hands cupped. "Porta feriti!" I tried to get closer to Passini to try to put a tourniquet on the legs, but I could not move. I tried again and my legs moved a little. I could pull backward along with my arms and elbows. Passini was quiet now. I sat beside him, undid my tunic and tried to rip the tail of my shirt. It would not rip and I bit the edge of the cloth to start it. Then I thought of his puttees. I had on wool stockings, but Passini wore puttees. All the drivers wore puttees. But Passini had only one leg. I unwound the puttee and while I was doing it I saw there was no need to try and make a tourniquet because he was dead already. I made sure he was dead. There were three others to locate. I sat up straight and as I did so something inside my head moved like the weights on a doll's eyes and it hit me inside behind my eyeballs. My legs felt warm and wet and my shoes were wet and warm inside. I knew that I was hit and leaned over and put my hand on my knee. My knee wasn't there. My hand went in and my knee was down on my shin. I wiped my hand on my shirt and another floating light came very slowly down and I looked at my leg and was very afraid. "Oh, God," I said, "get me out of here."

· · · · · ·

Outside the post a great many of us lay on the ground in the dark. They carried wounded in and brought them out.

I could see the light come out from the dressing-station when the curtain opened and they brought someone in or out. The dead were off to one side. The doctors were working with their sleeves up to their shoulders and were red as butchers. There were not enough stretchers. Some of the wounded were noisy, but most were quiet. The wind blew the leaves in the bower over the door of the dressing-station, and the night was getting cold. Stretcher-bearers came in all the time, put their stretchers down, unloaded them and went away. As soon as I got to the dressing-station Mahera brought a medical sergeant out and he put bandages on both my legs. He said there was so much dirt blown into the wound that there had not been much hæmorrhage. They would take me as soon as possible. He went back inside. Gordini could not drive, Manera said. His shoulder was smashed and his head was hurt. He had not felt bad, but now the shoulder had stiffened. He was sitting up beside one of the brick walls. Manera and Gavuzzi each went off with a load of wounded. They could drive all right. The British had come with three ambulances and they had two men on each ambulance. One of their drivers came over to me, brought by Gordini who looked very white and sick. The Britisher leaned over.

"Are you hit badly?" he asked. He was a tall man and wore steel-rimmed spectacles.

"In the legs."

. . . . . .

Captain doctor (interested in something he was finding): "Fragments of enemy trench-mortar shell. Now I'll probe for some of this if you like, but it's not necessary. I'll paint all this and—does that sting? Good, that's nothing to how it will feel later. The pain hasn't started yet. Bring him a glass of brandy. The shock dulls the pain; but this is all right, you have nothing to worry about if it doesn't infect and it rarely does now. How is your head?"

"It's very bad," I said.

"Better not drink too much brandy then. If you've got a fracture you don't want inflammation. How does that feel?"

Sweat ran all over me.

"Good Christ!" I said.

JUTLAND—NIGHT ONSLAUGHT

" I guess you've got a fracture all right. I'll wrap you up and don't bounce your head around." He bandaged, his hands moving very fast and the bandage coming taut and sure. " All right, good luck and Vive la France."

* * *

ONLY once during the four years of the War did the Grand Fleet of Britain and the High Seas Fleet of Germany meet in conflict. Each made periodic " sweeps " in the North Sea, and on May 31st, 1916, their scouting ships chanced to meet. Battle was immediately joined : at first the brunt was borne by Beatty's battle cruisers, which had the worst of the opening rounds. Jellicoe and his mighty fleet of battleships were racing to the scene, but mist and failing light ended the main action almost as soon as it was begun. At the end of the day, the British Fleet lay between Scheer and his bases, and there were high hopes of a Trafalgar on the morrow. During the night, however, the German Fleet slipped through the cordon, and regained its harbours.

Because the losses of the combatants were approximately equally shared—the British actually somewhat heavier than the German—the battle of Jutland has frequently been described as " indecisive." The real results of the battle, however, were that the British blockade continued unrelaxed, and that the next time the German Fleet crossed the North Sea was in November, 1918, when it was on its way to an ignominious surrender.

JUTLAND—NIGHT ONSLAUGHT

From *The Fighting at Jutland*.[1]

The Personal Experiences of Sixty Officers and Men of the British Fleet—edited by H. W. Fawcett, R.N., and G. W. W. Hooper, R.N.

By the NAVIGATING OFFICER OF H.M.S. " BROKE "

We now found ourselves steaming full-speed into the darkness, with nothing in sight except a burning mass on the

[1] Published by Hutchinson & Co. (Publishers), Ltd.

starboard quarter, which must have been the remains of the unfortunate *Tipperary*. The captain accordingly ordered me to bring the ship back to the original course south and to reduce to 17 knots, the speed of the fleet, in order to have a look round and see if we could collect our destroyers together again. His intention was to attempt another attack on the three enemy ships before they had time to get too far away, and we hoped that the rest of our destroyers had fired torpedoes when we did, and would, therefore, not be far off. As we turned *Sparrowhawk* was sighted, and took station astern of us.

Almost as soon as the ship was steadied on her course south, the hull of a large ship was sighted on the starboard bow on a more or less parallel course, but this time well before the beam and not more than half a mile away. The captain immediately gave the order to challenge, but almost as he spoke the stranger switched on a vertical string of coloured lights, some green and some red, an unknown signal in our service.

" Starboard 20 ; full-speed ahead both ; starboard foremost tube fire when your sights come on ; all guns—Green 40—a battleship," and various other orders were simultaneously shouted down the various voice pipes on the bridge, but the German had evidently been watching our movements and we were too late.

Within a few seconds of our seeing his recognition signal, he switched on a blaze of searchlights straight into our eyes, and so great was the dazzling effect that it made us feel quite helpless. Then after another interval of about a second, shells could be heard screaming over our heads, and I vaguely remember seeing spashes in the water short of us and also hearing the sound of our 4-inch guns returning the fire of this German battleship, which we afterwards had strong reason to believe was *Westfalen*. I then remember feeling the ship give a lurch to one side as a salvo hit us, and hearing the sound of broken glass and débris flying around, after which the searchlights went out, and we were once more in the darkness.

At this moment I became conscious of the fact that I could get no answer from the quartermaster at the wheel, so shouting to the captain that I was going below, I jumped down on to the lower bridge. There, in the darkness, I found complete chaos. The quartermaster and telegraph-man were both killed, and the wheel and telegraphs were shattered and apparently useless. I found our midshipman had followed me down to assist, and we were both just starting to strike matches to make certain that communication with the engine-room was gone, when I heard the captain's voice down the pipe shouting: "Full-speed astern both."

I looked up for an instant and saw a green bow light of some other ship just ahead of us, and then with a terrific crash the ship brought up all standing, and we were hurled against the bridge screens by the force of the collision.

On picking myself up I at once saw that we had one of our own destroyers bumping alongside, and an ugly-looking rent in her side abreast of the bridge showed where we had hit her. Steam was roaring out of our foremost boiler-rooms, and it was extremely difficult to see or hear anything. Our ship appeared to be settling by the bow, and at intervals gave unpleasant lurches from side to side, which for the moment made me feel that she might be sinking.

* * *

JUTLAND—HUMAN FLOTSAM
From *The Fighting at Jutland.*[1]

The Personal Experiences of Sixty Officers and Men of the British Fleet—edited by H. W. Fawcett, R.N., and G. W. W. Hooper, R.N.

By the COMMANDING OFFICER OF H.M.S. "ARDENT"

A terrible scene of destruction and desolation was revealed to me as I walked aft (with some difficulty). All boats were in pieces. The funnels looked more like nutmeg graters. The rafts were blown to bits, and in the ship's side and deck were holes innumerable. In the very still atmosphere, the smoke and steam poured out from the holes in the deck perfectly straight up into the air. Several of my best men came up and tried to console me, and all were delighted that we had

[1] Published by Hutchinson & Co. (Publishers), Ltd.

at length been in action and done our share. But many were already killed and lay around their guns and places of duty. Most of the engine-room and stokehold brigade must have been killed outright.

I walked right aft and sat down on the wardroom hatch. I could do no more as my leg was very stiff and bleeding a lot. My servant and another seaman, both of whom had been with me over two years, came aft to look for me and to help me. I sent them forward and told them to pass the word for each man to look out for himself. For a moment or two I was quite alone; the smoke cut me off from those farther forward, and there was absolute quiet and stillness. Then all of a sudden we were again lit up by searchlights, and the enemy poured in four or five more salvoes at point-blank range, and then switched off her lights once more. This would be about ten minutes from the time we were first hit.

The *Ardent* gave a big lurch, and I bethought myself of my "Gieve" waistcoat. I blew and blew without any result whatever, and found that it had been shot through. Another lurch, and the ship heeled right over and threw me to the ship's side. I could feel she was going, so I flopped over into the sea, grabbing a lifebuoy that was providentially at hand. The *Ardent's* stern kept up a few moments, then she slowly sank from view. As the smoke and steam cleared off I could see many heads in the water—about forty or fifty I should think. There was no support beyond lifebelts, lifebuoys and floating waistcoats, so I was afraid that few of us could possibly survive, especially as I realised that all the destroyers had gone on, and that no big ship would dare to stop, even if they saw us in the water.

I spoke to many men, and saw most of them die one by one. Not a man of them showed any fear of death, and there was not a murmur, complaint or cry for help from a single soul. Their joy was, and they talked about it to the end, that they and the *Ardent* had "done their bit," as they put it. While there were still many alive, a German came close and fired a star-shell over us. I could see her distinctly and was all for giving her a hail, but the men all said "No"; they would sooner take the remote chance of being saved by an English ship than be

JUTLAND—RETROSPECT

a prisoner in Germany. I was nearly done in once or twice in the first hour by men hanging on to me in the last stages of exhaustion, and I was separated from my lifebuoy and was pulled right over in the water, but managed to recover myself and the buoy. None of the men appeared to suffer at all; they just seemed to lie back and go to sleep.

After a long, weary while the sun came up, and then I was feeling much more comfortable than two hours previously. I found a skiff's oar floating past, and put it under my arms. I began to feel very drowsy, and dropped off into a sort of sleep several times, only to be awakened again by waves slapping into my face. There was quite a swell, but the surface of the water was smooth, owing to the masses of oil floating about from sunken ships. I woke again, after what I felt to be a long time, to hear a shout, and could see ships a long way off. I took a sort of detached interest in them, heard and gave an answering shout to " Stick it, *Ardent's!* " to someone in the water nearby, but whom I could not see, and watched the ships disappear again without much interest and dozed off again.

Once more I woke to find a flotilla leader—the *Marksman* close alongside me. I sang out for help, and in reply got a welcome and reassuring shout: " You're all right, sir; we're coming," and once again relapsed into unconsciousness, and have no recollection at all of being actually got on board.

* * *

JUTLAND—RETROSPECT

From *The World Crisis*, 1916–1918. Part I.[1]

By The Rt. Hon. WINSTON S. CHURCHILL, C.H., M.P.

So ended the Battle of Jutland. The Germans loudly proclaimed a victory. There was no victory for anyone; but they had good reason to be content with their young Navy. It had fought skilfully and well. It had made its escape from the grip of overwhelming forces, and in so doing had inflicted heavier loss in ships and men than it had itself received. The British Battle Fleet was never seriously in action. Only one ship,

[1] Published by Thornton Butterworth, Ltd.

the *Colossus*, was struck by an enemy shell, and out of more than 20,000 men in the battleships only two were killed and five wounded. To this supreme instrument had been devoted the best of all that Britain could give for many years. It was vastly superior to its opponent in numbers, tonnage, speed and, above all, gun-power, and was at least its equal in discipline, individual skill and courage. The disappointment of all ranks was deep; and immediately there arose reproaches and recriminations, continued to this day, through which this account has sought to steer a faithful and impartial passage. All hoped that another opportunity would be granted them, and eagerly sought to profit by the lessons of the battle. The chance of an annihilating victory had been perhaps offered at the moment of deployment, had been offered again an hour later when Scheer made his great miscalculation, and for the third time when a little before midnight the Commander-in-Chief decided to reject the evidence of the Admiralty message. Three times is a lot.

* * *

ONLY a few days before his " New Armies " were to advance on the Somme to the greatest battle in the history of British arms to that date, Lord Kitchener was drowned in the *Hampshire*, which struck a mine off the Orkneys.

KITCHENER

From *Politicians and the War*, 1914–1916.[1]

By The Rt. Hon. LORD BEAVERBROOK

What were the reasons for the appointment of the first great general since the Duke of Wellington to hold high civil office, and what was the nature of the man in whose favour this breach with ordinary tradition was made? The two questions are really indisseverable, for it was the personality of Lord Kitchener which gave him the immense prestige which compelled the Government to employ him at any cost. All this immense reputation was partly substance and partly that

[1] Published by Thornton Butterworth, Ltd.

KITCHENER

longer shadow which concrete objects cast in the rays of a setting sun. Lord Kitchener was a great and obscure figure. He had always been successful in everything which he had undertaken in distant lands.

The overthrow of the Khalifa, the final pacification of South Africa, the reorganisation of the Indian Army, the kindly and successful despotism he practised in Egypt, stood as bright and solid milestones marking the progress of his career. Other men have perhaps achieved as much without achieving adoration. But Lord Kitchener was the best-advertised man in the Empire, because he refused to advertise; he had found a royal road by which the Press was compelled to talk about him, if only in sheer annoyance at his silence. And something of the mystery and fatalism of the East was added to the hard practicality of his mind.

He was a stranger in England, and had the power and attraction of strangeness. On the Christmas Day of 1914 a visitor found him as usual during the War in his own large room at the War Office. Two huge fires blazed at either end, and the room was hot and sluggish. The new-comer commented on the appalling state of the atmosphere. "Very likely," said Kitchener, with a shiver. "I have not spent a Christmas in England for forty years." This touch of loneliness always struck the mind of the people, and also explains much in his Whitehall career. The low haze of the desert mist concealed his feet, and threw the rest of the figure up in huge proportions till it loomed gigantic above the mirage like a fabled and superhuman being in some Arabian tale.

The people did not reason about Kitchener, they just trusted, and that mere trust was a priceless asset in days when life was being torn up by the roots and the firmest mind might well fall into doubt or fear. Men simply said: "Kitchener is there; it is all right." The final proof of this contention is to be found in the myths which surrounded his death. In all the black ages of time men have looked for a deliverer, and when the deliverer has died with his work only half accomplished, his real death has always been denied, and his return confidently predicted. The belief comes to us from behind the earliest dawn of history, and education has fortunately tried to kill these credulous hopes in vain. It is the last crown of popular worship, and when people said that Lord Kitchener was really a prisoner in Germany they ranked him with King Arthur and all the other heroes who come no more.

All this was the source of his strength, and of his appointment to office. He added to his prestige immensely by his prophecy of the scope and duration of the War. No other Secretary of State would have imagined it, and so no other would have prepared for it; certainly no other man could have induced his colleagues to act on his conclusions or the public to accept them. A short war was in everyone's mouth. But as events worked out at the outset along the lines he predicted—as the Germans failed to reach Paris, while the Russian steam-roller, instead of rushing upon Berlin at the speed of a motor-car, reeled back in confusion from Tannenberg, and the lines settled down in the west from the Alps to the sea, his outside reputation for prophecy rose to a towering height.

A subtle touch of the dramatic in the way in which he did business added to this impression, even in the inner circle of Government. In the first days of August the Government proposed to ask the House of Commons for power to increase the Army by 50,000 men. When the requisition came to the War Office Kitchener simply struck out the figure 50,000 and wrote in 300,000! And if prestige in England was great, so was his position in Europe. The French and Russian Ambassadors, M. Cambon and Count Benckendorf, gave him their complete confidence and received his in return.

But when one has said this one has drawn the picture at its brightest; henceforward the lights begin to fade, and the rest is a melancholy story of the gradual whittling away of an immense reputation. From the very start the presence of Lord Kitchener produced a curious atmosphere in the Government. The wit who invented the tale that after a long exposition of the military position Kitchener leant back, lit a cigar, and remarked to the assembled Cabinet: " And now let's talk about the Welsh Church," did not get altogether away from the truth. Kitchener was frightened of the politicians, and ill at ease with nearly all of them. He had the soldier's professional and professed distrust of the class—and only Grey and Asquith surmounted the prejudice. Consider his career, his military upbringing, his prolonged absences from English life, the Oriental reticence in which he had dipped his mind. To him the men of law, of persuasion, of the energy of speech, were like some strange animals out of another world. Mr. Asquith seemed to understand him.[1]

Kitchener was a shy man, and though on some unbidden occasion sentences of great power and simplicity would rise suddenly to his lips in the intimacy of a private conversation, he added to the soldier's inability to explain that curse of nervousness which prevents a man speaking at the moment when he should and must speak if he is to prevail in council. This failing produced by degrees a dismal impression. Lloyd George once said to me that Kitchener talked twaddle, and then, as though striving to be just added: "No! He was like a great revolving lighthouse. Sometimes the beam of his mind used to shoot out, showing one Europe and the assembled armies in a vast and illimitable perspective, till one felt that one was looking along it into the heart of reality—and then the shutter would turn and for weeks there would be nothing but a blank darkness."

. . . . . .

I have said that this is a story of diminishing lights, and now nearly all the candles but one—that of life itself—are out. Even Kitchener's great popularity had not survived altogether intact the hard and disastrous year of 1915. Neuve Chapelle, Loos, the Dardanelles were not names of good omen; and the strain of war was beginning to tell. In the early days the crowds had come down in the morning to see him enter the War Office: they came no longer. Partly, no doubt, his manner discouraged these demonstrations; he did not seem to care whether people gazed at him or not—hardly indeed to be aware of their presence; unlike Lloyd George, who borrowed an open car to drive from Downing Street to the Mansion House because he could not be seen in a closed one! So the crowds, too, fell away as the Cabinet Ministers had done.

[1] "Asquith had the confidence, even the attachment, of Kitchener in a way that no one else in the Cabinet had then." Cf. *Twenty-five Years*, by Viscount Grey of Fallodon, Vol. II, p. 241.

To him the Russian Mission was a disguised banishment—for he knew that from it he would never return to Whitehall. He did not conceal from himself that the sun of his military activities was setting, although he could not foresee with what suddenness it would be plunged into darkness.

So, on a day in June, unnoticed, uncheered, almost unattended, the greatest living soldier of the Empire, a man who had become even in his lifetime a legend both to East and West, drove down to King's Cross. He arrived a minute and a half before the train was due to depart, and on the platform Kitchener had one of his curious and sudden gusts of impatient irritation over the delay. Then the engine pulled out, and the train, with its load of human greatness, vanished into the night.

* * *

AFTER a week's artillery preparation, British and French attacked astride the Somme on July 1st, 1916. In the southern sector the attack was moderately successful, but on the left the grim German defence held out against every onslaught On this one day the British casualties alone were more than 60,000 men. The battle continued with varying intensity until November, when the advance—achieved at enormous cost in men and material—was something less than the objectives of the first day. Almost the entire weight of the battle had been carried by Britain's new levies, fighting under conditions of which no old soldier ever dreamed. Added to the menace of the rifle, the domination of the machine-gun and the ever-growing weight of artillery was the emergence of a new fighting arm—the air force.

THE SOMME–MAMETZ WOOD
From *Up to Mametz*.[1]
By LL. WYN GRIFFITH

Before the Division had attempted to capture Mametz Wood, it was known that the undergrowth in it was so dense

[1] Published by Faber & Faber, Ltd.

that it was all but impossible to move through it. Through the middle of the wood a narrow ride ran to a communication trench leading to the German main second line of defence in front of Bazentin, a strong trench system permitting of a quick reinforcement of the garrison of the wood. With equal facility, the wood could be evacuated by the enemy and shelled, as it was not part of the trench system.

My first acquaintance with the stubborn nature of the undergrowth came when I attempted to leave the main ride to escape a heavy shelling. I could not push a way through it, and I had to return to the ride. Years of neglect had turned the wood into a formidable barrier, a mile deep. Heavy shelling of the southern end had beaten down some of the young growth, but it had also thrown trees and large branches into a barricade. Equipment, ammunition, rolls of barbed wire, tins of food, gas-helmets and rifles were lying about everywhere. There were more corpses than men, but there were worse sights than corpses. Limbs and mutilated trunks, here and there a detached head, forming splashes of red against the green leaves, and, as in advertisement of the horror of our way of life and death, and of our crucifixion of youth, one tree held in its branches a leg, with its torn flesh hanging down over a spray of leaf.

Each bursting shell reverberated in a roll of thunder echoing through the wood, and the acid fumes lingered between the trees. The sun was shining strongly overhead, unseen by us, but felt in its effort to pierce through the curtain of leaves. After passing through that charnal house at the southern end, with its sickly air of corruption, the smell of fresh earth and of crushed bark grew into complete domination, as clean to the senses as the other was foul. So tenacious in these matters is memory that I can never encounter the smell of cut green timber without resurrecting the vision of the tree that flaunted a human limb. A message was now on its way to some quiet village in Wales, to a grey farm-house on the slope of a hill running down to Cardigan Bay, or to a miner's cottage in a South Wales valley, a word of death, incapable, in this late century of the Christian era, of association with this manner of killing. That the sun could shine on this mad cruelty and on the quiet peace of an upland tarn near Snowdon, at what we call the same instant of Time, threw a doubt upon all meaning in words. Death was warped from a thing of sadness into a screaming horror, not content with stealing life from its shell, but trampling in lunatic fury upon the rifled cabinet we call a corpse.

.   .   .   .   .   .

" How did you come to find that telephone ? " asked the general.

" I happened to notice that artillery officer on my way down, and I went to ask him if his line back was working. Don't you remember my leaving you ? "

" No, I don't remember. . . . Well, it saved the lives of some hundreds of men, but it has put an end to me."

" Why do you say that ? "

" I spoke my mind about the whole business . . . you heard me. They wanted us to press on at all costs, talked about determination, and suggested that I didn't realise the importance of the operation. As good as told me that I was tired and didn't want to tackle the job. Difficult to judge on the spot they said! As if the whole trouble hadn't arisen because someone found it so easy to judge when he was six miles away and had never seen the country, and couldn't read a map. You mark my words, they'll send me home for this : they want butchers, not brigadiers. They'll remember now that I told them before we began that the attack could not succeed unless the machine-guns were masked. I shall be in England in a month."

He had saved the brigade from annihilation. That the rescue, in terms of men, was no more than a respite of days was no fault of his, for there is no saving of life in war until the eleventh hour of the last day is drawing to an end. It was nearly midnight when we heard that the last of our men had withdrawn from that ridge and valley, leaving the ground empty, save for the bodies of those who had to fall to prove to our command that machine-guns can defend a bare slope. Six weeks later the general went home.

* * *

THE SOMME—RED BATTLE
From *Her Privates We*.[1]
By Private 19022 (Frederick Manning)

They were singularly brave men, these Prussian machine-gunners, but the extreme of heroism, alike in foe or friend, is indistinguishable from despair. Bourne found himself playing again a game of his childhood, though not now among rocks from which reverberated heat quivered in wavy films, but in made fissures too chalky and unweathered for adequate concealment. One has not, perhaps, at thirty years the same zest in the game as one had at thirteen, but the sense of danger brought into play a latent experience which had become a kind of instinct with him, and he moved in those tortuous ways with the furtive cunning of a stoat or weasel. Stooping low at an angle in the trench, he saw the next comparatively straight length empty, and when the man behind was close to him, ran forward, still stooping. The advancing line, hung up at one point, inevitably tended to surround it, and it was suddenly abandoned by the few men holding it. Bourne, running, checked as a running Hun rounded the further angle precipitately, saw him prop, shrink back into a defensive posture, and fired without lifting the butt of his rifle quite level with his right breast. The man fell, shot in the face, and someone screamed at Bourne to go on; the body choked the narrow angle, and, when he put his foot on it, squirmed or moved, making him check again, fortunately, as a bomb exploded a couple of yards round the corner. He turned, dismayed, on the man behind him, but behind the bomber he saw the grim bulk of Captain Malet and his strangely exultant face; and Bourne, incapable of articulate speech, could only wave a hand to indicate the way he divined the Huns to have gone.

Captain Malet swung himself above ground, and the men, following, overflowed the narrow channel of the trench; but the two waves, which had swept round the machine-gun

[1] Published by Peter Davies.

post, were now on the point of meeting; men bunched together, and there were some casualties among them before they went to ground again. Captain Malet gave him a word in passing, and Bourne, looking at him with dull, uncomprehending eyes, lagged a little to let others intervene between them. He had found himself immediately afterwards next to Company-Sergeant-Major Glasspool, who nodded to him swiftly and appreciatively; and then Bourne understood. He was doing the right thing. In that last rush he had gone on and got into the lead, somehow, for a brief moment; but he realised himself that he had only gone on because he had been unable to stand still. The sense of being one in a crowd did not give him the same confidence as at the start, the present stage seemed to call for a little more personal freedom. Presently, just because they were together, they would rush something in a hurry instead of stalking it. Two men of another regiment, who had presumably got lost, broke back momentarily demoralised, and Sergeant-Major Glasspool confronted them.

"Where the bloody hell do you reckon you're going?"

He rapped out the question with the staccato of a machine-gun; facing their hysterical disorder, he was the living embodiment of a threat.

"We were ordered back," one said, shamefaced and fearful.

"Yes. You take your bloody orders from Fritz," Glasspool, white-lipped and with heaving chest, shot sneeringly at them. They came to heel quietly enough, but all the rage and hatred in their hearts found an object in him now. He forgot them as soon as he found them in hand.

"You're all right, chum," whispered Bourne to the one who had spoken. "Get among your own mob again as soon as there's a chance."

The man only looked at him stonily. In the next rush forward something struck Bourne's helmet, knocking it back over the nape of his neck so that the chin-strap tore his ears. For the moment he thought he had been knocked out, he had bitten his tongue, too, and his mouth was salt with blood. The blow had left a deep dent in the helmet, just fracturing the steel. He was still dazed and shaken when they reached some building ruins, which he seemed to remember. They were near the railway station. . . .

He wished he could sleep, he was heavy with it; but his restless memory made sleep something to be resisted as too like death. He closed his eyes and had a vision of men advancing under a rain of shells. They had seemed so toy-like, so trivial and ineffective when opposed to that overwhelming wrath, and yet they had moved forward mechanically as though they were hypnotised or fascinated by some superior will. That had been one of Bourne's most vivid impressions in action, a man close to him moving forward with the jerky motion a clockwork toy has when it is running down; and it had been vivid to him because of the relief with which he had turned to it and away from the confusion and tumult of his own mind. It had seemed impossible to relate that petty, commonplace, unheroic figure, in ill-fitting khaki and a helmet like the barber's basin with which Don Quixote made shift on his adventures, to the moral and spiritual conflict, almost superhuman in its agony, within him. Power is measured by the amount of resistance which it overcomes, and, in the last resort, the moral power of men was greater than any purely material force which could be brought to bear on it. It took the chance of death, as one of the chances it was bound to take; though, paradoxically enough, the function of our moral nature consists solely in the assertion of one's own individual will against anything which may be opposed to it, and death, therefore, would imply its extinction in the particular and individual case. The true inwardness of tragedy lies in the fact that its failure is only apparent, and as in the case of the martyr also, the moral conscience of man has made its own deliberate choice, and asserted the freedom of its being. The sense of wasted effort is only true for meaner and more material natures. It took the horrible chance of mutilation. But as far as Bourne himself, and probably also, since the moral impulse is not necessarily an intellectual act, as far as the majority of his comrades were concerned, its strength and its weakness were inseparably entangled in each other. Whether a man be killed by a rifle bullet through the brain or blown into fragments by a high-explosive shell may seem a matter of indifference to the conscientious objector, or to any other equally well-placed observer, who in point of fact is probably right; but to the poor fool who is candidate for posthumous honours, and necessarily takes a more directly interested view, it is a question of importance. He is, perhaps, the victim of an illusion, like all who, in the words of Paul, are fools for Christ's sake; but he has seen one man shot cleanly in his tracks and left face downwards, dead, and he has seen another torn into bloody tatters as by some invisible beast, and these experiences had nothing illusory about them: they were actual facts. Death, of course, like chastity, admits of no degree; a man is dead or not dead, and a man is just as dead by one means as by another; but it is infinitely more horrible and revolting to see a man shattered and eviscerated than to see him shot. And one sees such things; and one suffers vicariously, with the inalienable sympathy of man for man. One forgets quickly. The mind is averted as well as the eyes. It reassures itself after that first despairing cry: "It is I!"

"No, it is not I. I shall not be like that."

And one moves on, leaving the mauled and bloody thing behind: gambling, in fact, on that implicit assurance each one of us has of his own immortality. One forgets, but he will remember again later, if only in his sleep.

After all, the dead are quiet. Nothing in the world is more still than a dead man. One sees men living, as it were, desperately, and then suddenly emptied of life. A man dies and stiffens into something like a wooden dummy, at which one glances for a second with a furtive curiosity. Suddenly he remembered the dead in Trones Wood, the unburied dead with whom one lived, he might say, cheek by jowl, Briton and Hun impartially confounded, festering, fly-blown corruption, the pasture of rats, blackening in the heat, swollen with distended bellies, or shrivelling away within their mouldering rags; and even when night covered them one vented in the wind the stench of death. Out of one bloody misery into another, until we break. One must not break. He took in his breath suddenly in a shaken sob and the mind relinquished its hopeless business. The warm smelly darkness of the tent seemed almost luxurious ease. He drowsed heavily, dreaming of womanly softness, sweetness; but their faces slipped away from him like the reflections in water when the wind shakes it, and his soul sank deeply and more deeply into the healing of oblivion.

* * *

THE SOMME—A "PREMATURE"

From *Medal Without Bar*.[1]

By RICHARD BLAKER

Suddenly, in a single gesture, they ducked and were crouched on their knees and elbows.

" God Almighty ! " exclaimed Reynolds. And Cartwright, slowly and very thoughtfully, said, " Christ ! "

He knew that sound now, that had followed the sergeant's peaceable, " Number three, fire."

In it the report of the gun, expected by a slight tightening of muscles that raised and held the shoulders a little towards the ears, by the suspension—for an instant—of breathing and the postponement of the answer to the remark of Reynolds—the report of the gun never came.

It was swallowed and annihilated in the stark burst of the shell itself.

A premature.

Reynolds said so, raising his face slowly to look in Cartwright's, and then aside from it and beyond to the gun-pits at Cartwright's back. . . . " Premature."

Cartwright was in no great hurry to turn and follow the gaze of Reynolds upon the foul black cloud uncoiling over the stricken gun-pit and the quiet crew. . . .

" Uncle. . . . Come on . . . it's got some one . . ." he heard Reynolds entreating through the fumes of shattering noise that lingered still somewhere inside his head. ". . . Uncle. . . ."

" All right, Rennie." And they lurched across the fifty yards

[1] Published by Hodder and Stoughton, Ltd.

to number three pit, pushing aside from its entrance the sergeant and a corporal and a man or two who had scrambled across from the other guns.

Browne was sitting under the dial sight, facing them, his right shoulder humped up and tightly propped against the wheel. His legs stretched out under the trail. His hands, palms upward and neither clenched nor open, but slack in complete repose, lay on his thighs.

Simpson, from his position on the right of the breech, was flung over it, anyhow. His arms hung limply down—like the arms of a shirt tossed over a clothes-line except for the wrists and hands sticking out of them—and from the broken crown of his head there dripped to Browne's knees a froth of brains and blood and God knew what.

Sergeant McCorkindale, engine-driver from Saskatchewan, sat huddled against the back of the pit with his hands tightly clasped upon his stomach; half his face, gone to the colour of drying mud from the colour of good bright leather, was fringed in a dark moving whisker from a gash under his ear. He, from whom the faintest smile had been occasion for comment and report, was smiling now—grinning with the grin of a goblin—as he stopped his breath into a ripple that was neither moan nor croon nor chuckle.

Reynolds turned upon Upton who had been loading at the gun. "Shut up, you fool!" he snapped. "We can *see* that for ourselves. Clear out!"

Upton shut up and cleared out. He had been standing and looking at nothing in particular, mumbling, ". . . never touched me . . . never touched me. . . ."

Browne's eyelids never flickered to lift from their drooping over his eyes. The pull was gone that had stretched the two straps of muscle from beside his nostrils to the boundaries of his meticulously shaven chin. Gone was the little downward twist of the lips that had framed for every triviality and every monstrosity a comment. The sardonic mask was melted and reset. The eyes behind drooping lids were resting upon an open skull that dripped into his lap; and Browne was silent.

Smiling a smile of utter, gentle innocence, he was silent.

No more was there a man to shun the commonplace, the

cliché of " Fritz " for Germans in the mass and to claim the aloofness of his own individuality by referring to them, unsmiling, as " old Lud-wigg." No more would lice, with their hundred common nicknames, be distinguished with the same individualistic touch by the gentle names of " twilight toddlers " or " prahling Percy."

They patched up McCorkindale, painting and stanching the hole in his neck, padding and loosely binding the rent in his stomach. Cartwright gave him a tablet and they hurried him away on the stretcher, while the other three guns finished the series.

They carried out Simpson and Browne, emptying out their pockets, wiping the contents of Browne's; and they took the appropriate disk from the breast of each. The splinter that had stabbed Browne's heart in two was one of half a dozen that could equally have killed him; Simpson, too, was half a dozen times destroyed and a thigh was broken.

They washed in Richards's bucket and had a drink.

" I wish to God," said Reynolds, " that Dad would hurry up, so that we can get out before Dicky comes back. . . ."

" It never seemed to strike one," he said later, when Cartwright had been filling his silence for some time with gratitude that there was a letter in his pocket to Dorothy, already written that morning; " it never seemed to strike one that *Browne* might get done in. . . . Somehow . . ."

Jackman, from his vigil, came down to tell them that Mr. Whitelaw was just coming across from the road. They went up, and at the top Reynolds said, " Half a tick," and went over to the guns to say something to Upton.

Then they went across to meet Whitelaw and to take their road. Stopping for a moment, they glanced back at the two blanketed and neatly tied shapes behind number three pit. Then they moved on, silent till Reynolds said, " Uncle . . . we shall not look upon his like again. . . . Dicky will give the job to old Riding, I expect, and we'll have to find someone else to help the quarter-bloke. . . ."

* * *

THE SOMME—ENEMY PRISONERS
From *Twelve Days*.[1]
By Sidney Rogerson

We had now more energy to look about us and to note details of the vast concentration of men, beasts and machines which spread as far as the eye could see across the countryside. We saw strange-looking guns, great hump-backed howitzers being drawn along by tractors. We looked out eagerly but without success for those new monsters, the "tanks," which had burst so dramatically upon friend and enemy alike at Flers some six weeks before. So far we had not seen one, and our only idea of what they looked like had been gleaned from very foggy newspaper illustrations. We passed through lines of Australians, seeing them at close quarters for the first time, and marvelled at the difference in their physiognomy, their stature and their equipment. The slouch-hats we knew already, but how odd their shirt-like jackets looked! We commented on their dirty, slipshod appearance, which we did not then realise masked a deadly efficiency as fighting men, and on the curious lope of their long-maned horses. German prisoners were working on the roads under lanky Anzac guards. Few of them were our idea of "Square-heads." Some were mere boys, others myopic be-spectacled scarecrows. Many were bearded, some having fringes of whiskers framing their faces after the manner of the great-crested grebe. All wore the long-skirted field-grey coats, the trousers stuffed into clumsy boots. It gave us a strange feeling to see our enemies at such close range. Except for dead ones, for an occasional miserable prisoner dragged back half-dead with fright from some raid, or for groups seen through field-glasses far behind their lines, many of us had never seen any Germans. That was one of the oddest aspects of the War. There must have been hundreds of men who were in France and in the trenches for months, even years, who never set eyes on the men they were fighting. The

[1] Published by Arthur Barker, Ltd.

enemy early became a legend. The well-wired trenches that faced ours, frequently at a distance of only a few yards, gave shelter, we understood, to a race of savages, Huns, blond beasts who gave no quarter, who crucified Canadians and bayoneted babies, raped Belgian women, and had actually built kadaver works where they rendered down the bodies of their dead into fats! It was perhaps as well that we should believe such tales. But were these pallid, serious youths really capable of such enormities?

* * *

THE SOMME—THE O.P.
From *Medal Without Bar*.[1]
By Richard Blaker

That day saw the end of those lusty and prodigious assaults that wrung the so-called "heights" from an enemy that pressure could bend but no pressure seemed able to break.

And the "heights" were found, as yet, to be illusion. A man standing erect on a parapet of Stuff Redoubt could, perhaps, have seen over the dun wreckage and tumble of the immediate foreground; but a man projected cautiously upwards to the extent only of his cheekbones above the dank bags—or even adding, precariously and inch by inch, the dozen or eighteen inches of the length of his cloaked and muffled periscope—was face to face with the foreground only. A corpse and a battered water-bottle; a helmet and a bent rifle; crags sculptured in miniature, knolls and hummocks and cañons, flat deserts and ranges of tiny mountains fashioned from the churning and ceaseless tossing of the drab, yielding mud; shards of metal and jags of fractured timber.

"Can you see Grandcourt?" Richards had asked when croakings and squeaks had at last died away from the three frail miles of wire that connected the wheezing instruments.

"Grandcourt?" said Cartwright, shocked by the sudden eagerness of such expectancy. "No, Dicky. Not yet."

For the frontier of the minutely limned foreground in his

[1] Published by Hodder and Stoughton, Ltd.

periscope was the rust and dustbin-coloured smear and tangle of enemy wire.

Conquest, as yet, had brought no breadth of vision; and—around a twist of trench where men moved warily with lips sedately pursed and fingers alert near the safety-ring of a grenade—conquest abruptly ended. It ended in a sniper's shield built across the trench in a frame of sandbags. A man leaned alone against the shield in the manner of a theatrical eavesdropper in some corridor scene. The men nearest to him, at the traverse, had bayonets fixed, and two grenades apiece on the parapet beside their rifles—as it were on the mantel-piece. The eavesdropper had a bomb-proof canopy above his head—timbers and boxes, expanded metal and hump of bags.

The validity of its right to this title of "bomb-proof" Cartwright did not himself see tested.

He slunk forward to the plate and glanced, for some moments, through its eye. It looked into the similar eye of another plate—a dozen, or twenty, or eighty feet away. The space between was a distorted drainful of entanglements. The bodies therein were flung in the expansive postures of death from shell-fire or bombs; and huddled—"collected," as one would say of a horse's pose—where a bayonet thrust had left them. Between them and about them were the bric-à-brac of stakes and tumbled knife-rests; beds hacked out of the nearest dug-out; a twist that might equally have been the relic of some ancient plough as the carriage of a flame-thrower; and tangles of wire.

Carnage would have been inconspicuous in the mean squalor, the menace and wreckage that submerged that day into the gloom of evening. The cautious traversing of Cartwright's periscope was suddenly arrested once and struck still by the pale impassive jowls of a German in the shadow of his low helmet. It was some seconds before Cartwright realised that his instrument was a magnificent telescope, that the face could not be five but must be a hundred or two hundred yards away. Still, he wondered that no one saw that reckless, prying head, to drive it down to cover. He brought an infantry subaltern to the eyepiece of the periscope; and someone thereafter did drive it down. The someone (a bony corporal) in due course slithered to the fire-step again with a neat hole in his throat and a frayed tear at the back of his neck; and Cartwright interfered no more in matters strictly concerning the infantry.

The touchy atmosphere of the afternoon found him slipping a carefully examined grenade into the pocket of his tunic and explaining (with academic exactness) the mechanism of grenades to Whittle.

The double telephone line to Zollern made only this difference to the patrolling—there were two wires to be repaired from time to time instead of one. One signaller or the other was always gone upon this errand—to Zollern Redoubt, and beyond it to the Wonder-Work. (Beyond the Wonder-Work the line was being maintained by the battery.) The recurrence of this duty signified little, however, to the linesmen; Stuff Redoubt, even in a dug-out, was no more kindly a spot than Sammy's much-hated trench or the clinging puddle of Zollern and the Wonder-Work.

Everywhere the air was rain and metal and haggard expectancy. Information was scarce, save that which was arrived at by inference. From this it was clear, with persistent lucidity, that whatever else might have happened in quarters more distant, the situation at Regina Trench was still unchanged. Sammy prowled about with Black and without him, placing his guns, fidgeting and worrying. The battalion commander went round, scrubby-faced and dirty; assuring himself in passing that Cartwright's line to the battery was kept in order and repair. Alarms were given; black din hurtled up from behind upon Stuff Trench and Regina. Sammy's guns loosed off upon their appointed lines (and saw fit, immediately thereafter, to change their places). Fresh, answering din was added to the wretchedness of the garrison of Stuff; and—nothing happened.

Each time, whether the formation of the counter-attack was broken by the barrage, or whether, as some august and sardonic portent-readers had it, " he " could not be made to come over; whether, again as Sammy's stalwarts had it, " he " did indeed begin to come until caught by Sammy's guns—the incredible fact remains that nothing happened.

The unobtrusively killed and wounded went their unobtrusive ways. Every man was damp where he was not wet; and dug-outs inhabited with such men sleeping were uninhabitable for dainty-stomached men awake.

* * *

THE SOMME—KNIGHTS OF THE AIR
From *The Seventh Vial*.[1]
By Frederick Sleath

" Jove ! I knew the fellow was a sport," he exclaimed suddenly.

Far ahead of him a black speck showed against the sky, circling round and round as though waiting for someone. He knew that it was the blue-striped aeroplane. The message which he had dropped yesterday had contained a challenge for the German to meet him in single combat; and there his antagonist was, ready to accept the challenge.

Joyously Tiny throttled full out, driving his machine to the utmost in his anxiety to engage the German before any intruders might appear. But he was no hare-brained schoolboy rushing heedlessly into a playing-field scrum. He had accurately estimated the calibre of his opponent. Even as the distance between him and his adversary rapidly closed he carefully tested every part of the machine within reach to see that nothing was wanting or defective.

He felt the flexibility of his controls, earnestly listened to the rhythmic hum of his engine, and watched the revolution pointer to note if it moved an undue hair-breadth. Then he examined his guns, and fired a round or two from each to make sure that they were in working order. Everything was perfect. Never before had his gallant little scout appeared such a splendid fighting machine. He leaned back contentedly behind his windscreen, and gave all his attention to the waiting Hun.

The German had started to climb as soon as he saw his enemy approaching. He was now fully a thousand feet above the British scout, in splendid position for the first attack.

[1] Published by Herbert Jenkins, Ltd.

KNIGHTS OF THE AIR

But Tiny did not worry. He had fought and drowned a score of Huns who had come at him from every point in space; and he had a counter ready for whichever way the German liked to attack him. None knew better than he how best to turn a defensive into an offensive position. He flew steadily onward and waited for his opponent to make the first move.

The German did not leave him long in doubt as to his intention. Down came the bulbous blue nose of the Albatross, its fin and rudder rose to view above the upper plane. Swift as a swallow, it swooped to the attack.

Tiny pushed forward his joystick and went down also, but only for a few hundred feet. Then deftly pulling back the control, he flattened out and swept upward on the ower curve of the loop.

It had been his intention to loop right over and rake the Hun with his upper Lewis gun as his aeroplane sped upside down round the zenith. But the German was too wily for him. He swerved away in his dive out of the line of fire, and Tiny's heart thrilled at the cleverness of the man in so quickly divining his intention.

But he had the German beneath him now, and instantly he pressed the advantage home. Down he went after him, opening fire at a long range, seeing his bullets go tearing through his enemy's tail plane. The German twitched round and rolled into safety. Tiny went swooping past a wing's breadth away.

He flattened out madly and looped, for the Hun was after him. But when he again flattened out his enemy was coming straight for him on his own level. The fellow was a master airman. Tiny even began to have some inward trepidation as to the result of the fight. He banked away only just in time from the path of the German's rush, and throttled full out in an attempt to shake off his relentless pursuer.

The German performed a manœuvre which Tiny would never have believed possible if he had not actually witnessed it. Instead of overshooting the mark as Tiny turned away, the Hun somehow managed to swing his aeroplane round like a weight on the end of a string attached to his opponent's machine, and all the time his two forward guns poured in their concentrated fire on the British scout. By a miracle Tiny himself was not struck. Pushing his joystick forward, he dropped like a stone to a safer distance.

The manœuvre had evidently been the German's master stroke, and he circled round above Tiny, seemingly quite disconcerted at its failure. Tiny let him circle. He, too, had a master stroke in reserve, if only the Hun would give him the opportunity to use it. He wanted the German to dive on him; and the German soon gratified his wish.

As the tail of the Albatross lifted into the air, he drew back his joystick and started to climb. The Hun flattened out a little to suit his aim to his opponent's altering position. But just as he got to shooting distance, Tiny stalled and slipped back into a tail dive.

The German lunged wildly sideways. But no human skill could save him. Tiny gently slewed his rudder-bar round, his aeroplane languidly tilted over on its wing tip, its nose still pointing in the air, until above him, straight over his gunsights, sailed the Hun machine.

He saw the bullet spray from all three guns slash up through the undercarriage and into the heart of the enemy plane, slicing off great splinters from the V-shaped struts, and smoking into the fuselage from engine bearings to tail skid as the Hun glided forward through the heart of the zone of fire. The Albatross quivered slightly, like a pigeon shot in full flight. A moment later it was flashing past him in an almost perpendicular dive.

Instantly Tiny dived in pursuit. Like two giant hawks joined together by an invisible leash, swooping down on the same quarry, the two planes dashed earthward together, barely thirty yards apart. Had Tiny wished to make absolutely certain he could have raked the German again and again. But no such thought entered his mind. Instead, he was fervently hoping that his gallant adversary would regain sufficient control to be able to come to earth safely.

Just as it looked as though he were going to crash, the German flattened out and landed on a stretch of level meadow land. He clambered out of the cockpit and began to crawl painfully away from the machine. Tiny waited till the German had reached a safe distance, then he opened fire on the derelict plane, and poured in burst after burst until the spurts of flame and the curling blue smoke showed that it was well alight.

All the while the enemy pilot sat at the end of the field, coolly dressing his wounds. Tiny was glad to note that he did not seem badly injured. He flew towards him, and waved a friendly greeting as he sped past. " Jove ! He is a sport," he murmured, as the German stopped his dressing to return the salutation.

How great a sport the German was Tiny did not realise until some time afterwards, for the next few minutes were the most thrilling of his crowded career. He was full a field away when it suddenly occurred to him that the German had stopped his wave abruptly to point up into the sky, the while gesticulating wildly with the other arm. Tiny looked hurriedly up into the heavens. There, behind him, diving down full tilt on his tail, were four enemy aeroplanes. They had been attracted by the sound of his shooting while destroying the blue-striped machine, and but for the German's friendly warning, they would have sent him crashing before he was aware of their presence.

* * *

THE SOMME—THE BLOOD BATH OF THE NEW ARMIES

From *The World Crisis*, 1916–1918.[1]

By THE RT. HON. WINSTON S. CHURCHILL, C.H., M.P.

A young army, but the finest we have ever marshalled; improvised at the sound of the cannonade, every man a volunteer, inspired not only by love of country but by a widespread conviction that human freedom was challenged by military and Imperial tyranny, they grudged no sacrifice, however unfruitful, and shrank from no ordeal however destructive. Struggling forward through the mire and filth of the trenches, across the corpse-strewn crater fields, amid the flaring, crashing, blasting barrages and murderous machine-gun fire, conscious of their race, proud of their cause, they seized the most

[1] Published by Thornton Butterworth, Ltd.

formidable soldiery in Europe by the throat, slew them and hurled them unceasingly backward. If two lives or ten lives were required by their commanders to kill one German, no word of complaint ever rose from the fighting troops. No attack, however forlorn, however fatal, found them without ardour. No slaughter, however desolating, prevented them from returning to the charge. No physical conditions, however severe, deprived their commanders of their obedience and loyalty. Martyrs not less than soldiers, they fulfilled the high purpose of duty with which they were imbued. The battle-fields of the Somme were the graveyards of Kitchener's Army. The flower of that generous manhood, which quitted peaceful civilian life in every kind of workaday occupation, which came at the call of Britain, and, as we may still hope, at the call of humanity, and came from the most remote parts of her Empire, was shorn away for ever in 1916. Unconquerable except by death, which they had conquered, they have set up a monument of native virtue which will command the wonder, the reverence and the gratitude of our island people as long as we endure as a nation among men.

* * *

THE most significant feature of the Somme fighting was not the slow gain of ground or the enormous casualties, but the introduction of a new weapon designed to break through the trench lines. Prematurely introduced, the tank immediately justified its existence and gained the confidence of the troops—though not of the higher command.

THE NEW WARFARE
From *A Saga of the Sword*.[1]
By F. BRITTEN AUSTIN

That emplacement was still firing—other now suddenly revealed emplacements were also firing in a furious unusually prolonged hammering—but the bullets no longer came in his direction. He delayed for a glance at their target. Was

[1] Published by Arrowsmith, Ltd.

another attack following? He saw no rush of men who stumbled and fell. The desolation was empty of human beings. What was it? Fritz was shelling too—shelling his own trenches. From a smoke-smother of shell-bursts, he saw something emerge—a weirdly monstrous shape that crawled snoutingly onwards, lurching into shell-holes and trenches, climbing out of them, wallowing over the soft ground. One of the machines he had seen last night! More than ever it was like some prehistoric pachyderm, blind-eyed, sniffing its way, ponderously dragging itself over every obstacle. He could hear the clatter of its steel tracks as they passed down on either side of its uplifted nose, could see the bullets of those frenziedly firing machine-guns splashing bright on its fantastically painted sides. A gun protruded from each flank, and every now and then they spurted in a whiff of smoke and a loud report. It came on like a sentient thing—now as it were hesitating—now resuming a slow but relentless progress, uncannily suggestive of some small-brained primeval monster awakened to a dull vindictiveness against a puny humanity that had usurped the earth.

It became at last aware of those furiously raging machine-guns. It stopped, and then with a mighty roar—one track not moving—it turned, began to crawl towards them. The adjutant watched breathlessly, fascinated. Its camouflage-mottling was streaked and scored, splashed all over, by that hail of bullets. It ignored them in a contemptuous invulnerability, disdained to reply with its similar weapons. Ominously purposeful, exhaling, as it were, angry puffs of vapour from behind its head, roaring and clattering, it lurched and wallowed straight towards the nearest emplacement. The machine-gun within it continued to hammer desperately. The monster approached, was only a yard or two away. It reared a little to climb the mound—very little—rolled over it. Behind it the machine-gun was silent. Roaring and clattering it swung towards the next. That also continued to fire. It fired until the monster heaved and lurched and left it flattened. The adjutant sprang recklessly to his feet, waved and pointed to that murderous machine-gun nest he had failed to silence. It also was still firing. A brain within the monster perceived and understood. Again the great bulk swung ponderously, commenced to crawl deliberately upon its prey. The adjutant called up some riflemen from the trench, ready in case that doomed machine-gun crew should attempt to bolt. They did not. Their weapon continued to hammer until the great snout lifted above the little mound, until the noisily-running steel tracks came down upon it and the huge squat body slithered and lurched. The adjutant waved and cheered as never before in his life he had waved and cheered. By his side his men cheered and waved also, as though demented with delight.

The monster turned again, moved along the edge of the trench towards the enemy position. The adjutant yelled and gesticulated. "Follow on, men! Follow on behind!" Cheering, shouting and laughing like a crowd of excited schoolboys, they followed this roaring, clattering, grotesquely formidable marvel along the trench—not only the original few men with the adjutant, but a constantly increasing throng. It was extraordinary how many isolated individuals, how many little groups, had been hiding themselves in the shell-holes, waiting until night or another attack should deliver them from those deadly machine-guns, vigilant to hammer out annihilation at the first sign of life upon that corpse-strewn crater field. Now, assured of a local security, they streamed across in a wild enthusiasm, eager for close proximity with this weirdly-novel machine which rolled over machine-gun nests as though they were ant-heaps. The adjutant led them, in a soldierly impulse, to gain and consolidate as much ground as possible. They ran suddenly into men in deep-fitting helmets and grey uniforms.

The enemy was massing for a counter-attack. There was a recoil, a moment of confusion among the khaki-clad enthusiasts. It was a moment only. Instantly, the monster opened a devastating fire with her machine-guns, with her quick-firing six-pounders, came slithering heavily down into the trench. There was a wild shriek of horror and astonishment. Some few brave men rushed close in under her weapons, hurled bombs that exploded pettily, harmlessly. There were those who tripped and fell, failed to get from under as she clambered in deafening noise up to the farther and firmer bank. The most turned to rush away, crowding and jamming around the traverses of this trench comparatively untouched by the bombardment. The machine-gun bullets, the six-pounder shells, overtook them. The survivors put up their hands. The adjutant hurriedly detailed escorts for squads of prisoners, rushed on again. All the way up the trench the enemy was surrendering in batches. It was a triumphal progress.

The trench was empty of any enemy. The monster stopped. A steel door opened and an officer, his clothes soaked in oil, his face black, crawled out. The adjutant ran up to him. It was the officer of last night. Now, sweating and blowing, he mopped his face with a dirty rag. He grinned, white-teethed, at the adjutant.

" I think that'll do for the present," he said. " We're pretty far forward and we haven't got much in the way of supports. Also, we haven't too much petrol. I should hang on and consolidate if I were you."

The adjutant congratulated him, reminded him of their talk the previous night.

" You were quite right ! " he exclaimed excitedly. " This thing alters everything. Epoch-making isn't the word for it ! There's nothing to prevent us going on and on ! "

The officer grinned again.

" Except that we haven't enough machines. But that'll come. This is only the beginning."

. . . . . .

That morning of September 15th, 1916, when, for the first time, the Tank appeared upon the battle-field, indeed signalised the end of one epoch and the beginning of another.

* * *

BREAKING THE NEWS
From *All Our Yesterdays*.[1]

By H. M. TOMLINSON

" His father was so proud of that boy."

Proud of him ! My eyes roved to the china dogs on the

[1] Published by William Heinemann, Ltd.

mantelpiece. The portrait of Lord Beaconsfield stared down at us from over the mantelpiece. I wanted to be active, to blaspheme aloud; to cry out something. But kept still.

"What shall we do now?" his mother asked.

Yes, what should we do! She sat down again, and pulled a handkerchief about quickly. She stopped, and touched the head of the cat with one finger. After a spell of silence she got up again.

"Mr. Bolt will be wondering who is here. Come you up to him. But he mustn't know. He might die if he knew, the state he's in."

"Hullo, mother," called the deep voice of the old shipwright, as we entered his room. "What's been keeping you?"

He was up on his elbow, to see who was with her.

"What, you? Where have you been all this time? What have you been talking about? Here, come and sit here." He touched, with a brown hand, that had lost some of its substance, the edge of his bed. He lay back.

"Well, what's the best news?" He kept a hold on me.

We gossiped of this and that, lightly. He made a show of his old vivacity, rebuking mother for her food, starving him at his age, and me for the time I had been away. His eye was arrested by a needle of light, as the shaft of a searchlight went by the parting of his heavy window curtains.

"That girl in yet?" he asked sharply.

"Not yet, Tom, it is hardly her time."

"What's this night like?" He turned to me.

"Oh, quiet now. No wind. But the glass has dropped. It looks as if we might get a south-westerly blow."

"Huh! Is that so? I hope we do. We could do with it. But what are those searchlights up for?"

"Practising, I should say. I know of no warning."

"Well, then, that's all right," commented Mrs. Bolt cheerfully. "I'll see if Annie is coming along." She went out of the room.

Old Tom Bolt plainly was glad I was there. His big body had collapsed, his eyes were hollow, but something of his old fire was burning. It could flash up, with sardonic humour. He touched on the great affair, yet casually, as though he were wearied by it, yet still must consider it, for there it still was. What did I think of it?

The time came when I guessed that I had better be off. This energetic talking might do him no good.

"Going? Not you, you've only just come. Sit down. You will wait till Annie comes in. Sit down."

He was quiet for a time, watching the passing and re-passing of the splinter of light. The night without was soundless. Then he got up on his elbow, and looked at the door.

"That door shut?"

The door was all right.

"Now I'll show you what puts me here. Over there!" He pointed peremptorily to a coat behind the door. "Go and feel in the pocket."

I could find nothing, except his tobacco pouch.

"No, no, not that one." He was testy. "Inside, inside!"

I drew out some papers, and letters. "Show me," ordered Mr. Bolt. "That one," he said. "Read it." He thrust it at me, and sank back.

It was from France. It said how sorry . . . Jack was a gallant fellow . . . wounded and missing . . . all were sorry. It was signed: F. Gillow, Captain.

"Put it where it was, right to the bottom. Put that coat straight. As it was."

The minutes were interminable. I sat by him again, and waited, trying to form an answer. Then Mr. Bolt spoke.

"Now you know," he rumbled. "But his mother doesn't. She's not to know. Can't tell her about her baby. Luckily I took it in when she was out."

"She will have to know, though," he added. "Something will have to be done. What is it? But it will kill the old girl. It will kill her. I know she couldn't stand it."

We both watched the flickering of the searchlights where the curtains barely met. If there was anything to be said it was unknown to me.

"That's the door key," he muttered in relief. "There's Annie. That child is home."

Then he turned to me, as if with the sudden thought of important news. "I don't know what we should do without that girl."

She came up at once with her mother, and some light nonsense passed between her and her father. It was not long before I felt the discomfort of an intruder, and took my leave.

From the outer gate, when I left the house, Annie walked with me a little down the street. She paused under one of the blobs of purple.

" Did either of them tell you anything ? "

" Both told me."

She gazed into the night with that expression I saw last in a trench somewhere near Ypres.

" What am I to do ? " she pleaded. " Each has told me and I'm to keep it secret from the other. How long ? "

* * *

HIGH COMMAND—THE IDEAL

From *Foch Talks*.[1]

By COMMANDANT BUGNET

" You must have knowledge ; it is the foundation with which you cannot dispense. You must have the power of accomplishment, and to that end you must develop your faculties of thought, of judgment, of analysis, and of synthesis. But what is the use of all these things, if they function in a vacuum ? You must make up your mind with determination, and work towards your object, without swerving. Most important of all is action, if you are to bring your theories to fruition, to produce results. Work ; set stone upon stone ; keep on building. You must do something, you must act, you must obtain results. Results !—that is all I consider."

* * *

HIGH COMMAND—THE REAL

From *Realities of War*.[2]

By SIR PHILIP GIBBS

I came to know G.H.Q. more closely when it removed for fresher air to Montreuil, a fine old walled town, once within

[1] Published by Victor Gollancz, Ltd.
[2] Published by Hutchinson & Co. (Publishers), Ltd.

sight of the sea, which ebbed over the low-lying ground below its hill, but now looking across a wide vista of richly cultivated fields where many hamlets are scattered among clumps of trees. One came to G.H.Q. from journeys over the wild desert of the battle-fields, where men lived in ditches and "pill-boxes," muddy, miserable in all things but spirit, as to a place where the pageantry of war still maintained its old and dead tradition. It was like one of those pageants which used to be played in England before the War, picturesque, romantic, utterly unreal. It was as though men were playing at war here, while others, sixty miles away, were fighting and dying, in mud and gas-waves and explosive barrages.

An "Open Sesame," by means of a special pass, was needed to enter this City of Beautiful Nonsense. Below the gateway, up the steep hillside, sentries stood at white posts across the road, which lifted up on pulleys when the pass had been examined by a military policeman in a red cap. Then the sentries slapped their hands to their rifles to the occupants of any motor car, sure that more staff-officers were going in to perform those duties which no private soldier could attempt to understand, believing they belonged to such mysteries as those of God. Through the narrow streets walked elderly generals, middle-aged colonels and majors, youthful subalterns all wearing red hatbands, red tabs, and the blue-and-red armlet of G.H.Q., so that colour went with them on their way.

Often one saw the Commander-in-Chief starting for an afternoon ride, a fine figure, nobly mounted, with two A.D.C.'s and an escort of Lancers. A pretty sight, with fluttering pennons and all their lances, and horses groomed to the last hair. It was prettier than the real thing up in the Salient or beyond the Somme, where dead bodies lay in upheaved earth among ruins and slaughtered trees. War at Montreuil was quite a pleasant occupation for elderly generals who liked their little stroll after lunch, and for young Regular officers, released from the painful necessity of dying for their country, who were glad to get a game of tennis down below the walls there, after strenuous office work in which they had written "Passed to you" on many "minutes," or had drawn the most comical caricatures of their immediate chief, and of his immediate chief, on blotting pads or writing-blocks.

It seemed at a mere glance, that all these military inhabitants of G.H.Q. were great and glorious soldiers. Some of the youngest of them had a row of decorations, from Montenegro, Serbia, Italy, Roumania, and other States, as recognition of gallant service in translating German letters (found in dug-outs by the fighting men), or arranging for visits of political personages to the back areas of war, or initialling requisitions for pink, blue, green, and yellow forms which in due course would find their way to battalion adjutants for immediate filling-up in the middle of an action. The oldest of them, those white-haired, bronze-faced, grey-eyed generals in the administrative side of war, had started their third row of ribbons well before the end of the Somme battles, and had flower borders on their breasts by the time the massacres had been accomplished in the fields of Flanders. I know an officer who was awarded the D.S.O. because he hindered the work of industrious men with the zeal of a hedge-sparrow in search of worms, and another who was the best decorated man in the army because he had presided over a visitors' château and entertained royalties, Members of Parliament, Mrs. Humphry Ward, miners, Japanese, Russian revolutionaries, Portuguese ministers, Harry Lauder, Swedes, Danes, Norwegians, clergymen, Montenegrins, and the Editor of *John Bull*, at the Government's expense—and I am bound to say he deserved them all, being a man of infinite tact, many languages and a devastating sense of humour. There was always a Charlie Chaplin film between moving pictures of the Battles of the Somme. He brought the actualities of war to the vistiors' château, by sentry boxes outside the door, a toy tank in the front garden, and a collection of war trophies in the hall. He spoke to high personages with less deference than he showed to miners from Durham and Wales, and was master of them always, ordering them sternly to bed at ten o'clock (when he sat down to bridge with his junior officers), and with strict military discipline insisting upon their inspection of the bakeries at Boulogne, and boot-mending factories at Calais, as part of the glory of war which they had come out for to see.

So it was that there were brilliant colours in the streets of Montreuil and at every doorway a sentry slapped his hand to his rifle, with smart and untiring iteration, as the Brains of the Army, under brass hats and red bands, went hither and thither in the town, looking stern, as soldiers of grave responsibility, answering salutes absent-mindedly, staring haughtily at young battalion officers who passed through Montreuil and looked meekly for a chance of a lorry-ride at Boulogne, on seven days' leave from the lines.

The smart society of G.H.Q. was best seen at the Officers' Club in Montreuil, at dinner-time. It was as much like musical comedy as any stage setting of war at the Gaiety. A band played ragtime and light music while the warriors fed, and all these generals and staff officers, with their decorations and arm-bands and polished buttons, and crossed swords, were waited upon by little W.A.A.C.'s with the G.H.Q. colours tied up in bows on their hair. Such a chatter! such bursts of light-hearted laughter! such whisperings of secrets and intrigues and scandals in high places! such careless-hearted courage when British soldiers were being blown to bits, gassed, blinded, maimed and shell-shocked in places that were far—so very far—from G.H.Q.!

* * *

THE death of the aged Emperor of Austria-Hungary, on November 21st, 1916, was far more significant than is commonly realised. Loyalty to his person and fear of his power had held together a ramshackle Empire for sixty-six years. No sooner had he passed from the scene than the forces of disintegration gained ever-increasing momentum.

END OF AN EPOCH
From *The World Crisis, The Eastern Front*.[1]
By THE RT. HON. WINSTON S. CHURCHILL, C.H., M.P.

The time was now come for the Emperor Francis Joseph to die. He had witnessed with frigid satisfaction the vast recoil

[1] Published by Thornton Butterworth, Ltd.

of Russia in 1915. The dismissal of the Grand Duke Nicholas from the command of the Russian armies had seemed to him a signal of Teutonic victory more indubitable even than the fall of Warsaw. He had followed with measured approval the over-ripe, but at last condign chastisement of Serbia. He had welcomed the Kaiser on his way to the celebrations of that joyous event. All was then a feast of mutual congratulation. Yet intimate observers had noticed that the high spirits of both potentates had seemed rather forced, and Baron Margutti, to whose records we are indebted, felt at the time that both really wanted peace. They looked upon victory as the means of gaining peace, not, like their generals, as the means of further victories. They had preoccupations not shared by their servants. Nations may fall and rise again; but dynasties in modern times can only stand or fall. Still at the beginning of 1916 the sun shone so brightly on the bristling bayonets of the Central Empires that the general staffs were everywhere in the ascendant. Falkenhayn, it was said, had new wonders to produce, and Conrad, too, as we have seen, had his plans.

The Emperor lived long enough to endure the news of Brusilov's offensive, to receive the Roumanian declaration of War which he had so long dreaded, to see Falkenhayn, the glittering deliverer of the spring, dismissed by the Kaiser in the autumn. The old man's inveterate pessimism and deeply ingrained expectation of misfortune returned with doubled force. How often had he not seen these false dawns before? True, the Prussian military flame seemed unquenchable, and Roumania was already suffering the penalty of her faithlessness. But the clouds had gathered again. The summer of success had been bright, but also brief. Evidently, as he had always been convinced, and so often declared, the road was to be uphill to the very end. The end had now come for him.

Since the War began, he had scarcely been seen in public. He refused all holidays and ploughed methodically through his daily routine at Schönbrunn. The care of the Court Chamberlain had forbidden the Park before the Imperial windows to the public. It was widely rumoured that the Emperor was already dead, and was being preserved as a fetish and a symbol. Unpleasant details about the social and economic life of his Peoples were sedulously kept from him; but his immense experience enabled him to understand better than his courtiers or his generals how grave the food-shortage and popular discontents had become; and when his Prime Minister, Count Stürgkh, was pistolled to death by the son of the leader of the Democratic Party, Francis Joseph formed a perfectly clear resolve to make peace as soon as possible. He determined to make peace by any means at latest in the spring of 1917. As a first step he replaced his murdered minister by a politician of the Left, Koerber, a man who was honoured by the hungry millions, and distrusted by the well-fed tens of thousands. This was his last contribution to the affairs of the Austro-Hungarian Monarchy.

Bronchitis at eighty-five is always serious. The Emperor coughed much and passed bad nights. Nevertheless, the dawn of November 20th saw him already seated in his old blue uniform at his writing-desk. It was the practice to send him three portfolios a day. The first was punctually discharged. Before the second was completed his condition of weakness and fever was such that his granddaughter brought him a special blessing from the Pope and persuaded him to receive the sacraments. Four chickens were made into a broth for him at noon. He could not eat it. But the midday files were duly dispatched to the departments. In the afternoon the doctors succeeded in inducing him to go to bed. He rose from his table, but had to be supported to the neighbouring room. The immense fatigue of years of care overwhelmed him. Sleep and death drew quickly near. With an effort he said to his valet, " Call me at seven. I am behindhand with my work," and sank almost immediately into coma. The Departments inquired about the evening portfolio. The aide-de-camp on duty replied that it would not be delivered that night. A few hours later the sixty-six years' reign of Francis Joseph was completed. He died in harness.

Although the War weighed oppressively upon Vienna the funeral of the departed ruler was magnificent. The populace, sorely tried, silent, helpless, hungry, understood that a long chapter in the history of Central Europe had closed.

New pages must be turned; nay, a new volume must open. The aged Count Paar would not see this volume. " I died yesterday," he said to Margutti on the morrow of his master's death. In fact he expired during the memorial service two days later. The ties of a lifetime which had been snapped were also the heartstrings of this faithful servitor.

But the war rolled on.

* * *

IN THE TRENCHES
From *A Soldier's Diary of the Great War*.[1]
By Henry Williamson

The trench-mortar is a horrible engine; the concussion of the shell is terrific; it blows your heavy muddy kilt about your thighs even when bursting a long distance out of harm's way, and whole stretches of trench may be blown in by it. One thing, you hear the faint thud of the discharge, look up, see it coming, whirling and twisting in the air, and scuttle along the trench away from it. But this gets on your nerves after a while; it is so tiring dodging up and down the trench like that.

Many good officers, N.C.O.'s and men have gone west.

Etched in my brain is the picture of one of our officers lying dead, sprawling on his back, head down, mouth open, eyes staring in the middle of what was once a section of trench, now a jumble of upturned earth and ruptured sandbags; a pitiful sight.

One morning I had a mug of tea and a biscuit and jam, and was just going to begin breakfast when I was seized with a momentary nausea, followed by a fit of coughing. My eyes began to smart and run. I walked along and found my men coughing and crying too. " Whatever is the matter with us all ? " said I. " It's the gahss, sir-r ! " replied a corporal. Gas ! Something new in war.

. . . . .

Wiring is a rotten job, and everyone is glad to come in when it is over. You get out of the trench, preferably on a

[1] Published by Faber & Faber.

dark night, and wander off some yards in front with a party loaded up with stakes and coils of barbed wire. The stakes have to be driven in as noiselessly as possible; sometimes we have a sort of trestle shaped like a knife-rest, and wire is festooned and tangled up on the wood. In the early days one fancied that when the Verey lights went up one *must* be seen, but in fact the bright light has a very restricted area of illumination, and if you stay still you will most likely be unobserved.

Talking of Verey lights, to-night I went by myself to a deserted trench which ran out towards the enemy, just to reconnoitre and see whether it need be manned. One of these rockets suddenly landed almost at my feet, fizzled flaring on the ground, and leapt at me. I turned and fled down the sap with this thing fizzing and bouncing at my heels till it at length expired, and I stopped in utter darkness, cursing myself for getting windy at nothing.

A typical day in these trenches begins at dawn with " Stand to." The N.C.O.'s jerk the men out of their heavy sleep—the private soldier seems to have the power of dropping off into deep slumber in the most uncomfortable positions—and plant them on the fire-step, where they yawn and rub their eyes and begin to clean their rifles before the inspecting officer comes round. One or two men in every fire-bay has been by turns on sentry duty all night. I make the round of my platoon accompanied by my platoon sergeant, inspecting rifles, bombs and gas-masks.

This duty over, " Stand down " is given, day sentries are posted, and I go off to my dug-out for a shave, provided things are quiet. The men prepare their breakfast, and we officers have ours and settle down for the day's routine. This may be quite peaceful, or we may be harassed by trench-mortars or some five-nines.

If so annoyed, there is no rest for anyone, and it is no use ringing up the artillery for retaliation, for we seem to have nothing heavier behind us than divisional four-fives, which seem unable to knock out the trench-mortar emplacement. I have spotted exactly where it is and have tried the divisional artillery on it, but their ammunition seems rationed, and nothing they can do seems any good. It is said that the heavy stuff has left us for an "unknown" destination. Everywhere are rumours of the Big Push. To-day I was on company duty till two o'clock, snatching a bite of lunch nevertheless. Then a blessed rest tea at five, though personally I can seldom sleep in the front line.

At dusk we all "stood to" again, and got ready for the night's work. One of us is in charge of a wiring party, another of a trench-repairing gang, while a third—my turn to-night—will go round the company front, inspect all posts and sentries, and be generally responsible. And it is going to rain!

So it goes on, day after day and night after night, when we get our rations and evacuate our casualties, if any.

* * *

The last rumbles of the Somme offensive having subsided, the British Army prepared for its third winter. By this time trench warfare had become a matter of routine, with multifarious specialists in all departments. Bombs thrown by hand were supplemented by several varieties of trench-mortar, of which the "minenwerfer" was perhaps the most hated.

MINNIES

From *Grey Dawn—Red Night*.[1]

By James Lansdale Hodson

That part of the Cambrin Front known as the Brickfields introduced them to "minenwerfers": they called them "minnies." Hardcastle learnt that noise may have a more devastating effect on your morale than an accurate estimation of dangers. The tearing, crashing roar of a minnie was horrible in the extreme. They made a crater five to ten yards across; if they hit a trench they demolished it—and all in it or about it. It was a pleasant German custom to toss them over after breakfast. You could imagine the German minenwerfer experts yawning and saying, "Dear me! A trifle liverish this morning. Must have some exercise. Let's set off a few squibs." And shortly afterwards a succession of

[1] Published by Victor Gollancz, Ltd.

whistle blasts in Hardcastle's neighbourhood would spread the news that the ugly canister-shaped engines were being tossed into the air and were wobbling over in a devilish, drunken lurch towards the British lines. So far as Hardcastle could see we were thoroughly nonplussed by them. We had nothing to hurl back in return—and we dodged them as best we could. The plan devised was to post sentries who blew whistles. Two blasts for a bomb to the right, one blast for a bomb to the left. But, as Thorndike was at pains to point out, one sentry's right was another's left, so that you got the same bomb heralded by two whistles and by one whistle, and in consequence men running in all directions, colliding and falling over one another; and if you happened to be up on a working party carrying planks and wearing a long waterproof cape, the spectacle of men treading, as they ran, on their capes and falling in the mud with planks atop of them was most diverting—to the gods above. But Hardcastle and company ran and tripped and . . . yes, they laughed. The bubble or whatever it may be that, when broken, spurts laughter into your eyes and your bowels so that you are convulsed functioned a yard from death quite readily. Nevertheless, Hardcastle was alarmed: he had, as they had begun to phrase it, "the wind up." Men said to one another, "I can stand anything but minnies." But Hardcastle didn't find them so totally awful at night, perhaps because watching their fiery tails arcing through the night commanded your interest —they followed one another in " column of route " as the description had it—or perhaps because by night you had grown more accustomed, were less on edge. It was astonishing how many might drop in your vicinity without any serious damage: but the law of averages worked at last—a sergeant killed; one or two wounded. Word came round: men spoke of it in subdued tones. Hardcastle never saw the dead; he walked past the crater; it reminded him somehow of a slag-heap . . . one of those curious tricks of the mind; it was an eyesore, an offence against Nature, disembowelling the earth . . . and disembowelling men. He had seen two men dead the previous day. They had been up on a working party doing gentle fatigue—carrying gas cylinders that weighed one and a half hundredweights and, standing in the support lines, had seen a mine go up. It was as though you saw an eruption on the films—a quivering of the earth that shook beneath their feet and beneath the hands that rested on the trench-sides, a rending of the ground, a column of steam and smoke a hundred feet high, and then, as if answering a signal, a crackle of rifle-fire, vicious, viperous, and the rattle of machine-guns, the incredulous whistle and crash of shells, the boom of bombs, the hurtle of death at man in jagged shape and frightening sound, and now the hiss and fall of bits of metal all about you. Hardcastle and his companions were " out of it," and they were glad of it : at least, *he* was. He had no urge to dash to the mine crater a quarter of a mile away. Not their job. Maybe theirs would come to-morrow. So, the gas cylinders deposited in proper place, they trudged stolidly back, silent, occupied with watching the feet of the man in front that you might avoid the pitfalls he avoided—or didn't avoid. And then as they emerged from the trench they saw it—the shattered house, window-frames still burning, woodwork scorched black, immense holes rent in walls ; the roadway with three large holes, a motor-car, its screen broken, bonnet bent ; a grocer's cart toppling on to the horse that, foul and bloody, was collapsed dead in the shafts. And on the pavement two huddled nameless things, wearing equipment, rent in pieces . . . foul, unspeakably foul. The sight was an offence. Why weren't they buried, at once, at once, made decent, the place cleansed ? This was what was happening, then, when you heard the guns booming, saw the horizon flickering with dancing flashes, looked on it and thought it had beauty. Beauty ! At the other end . . . where the shells fell . . . what was there ?

* * *

SNIPERS
From *The Red Horizon*.[1]
By Patrick MacGill

Little mercy is shown to a captured sniper ; a short shrift and swift shot is considered meet penalty for the man who

[1] Published by Herbert Jenkins, Ltd.

coolly and coldly singles out men for destruction day by day. There was one, however, who was saved by Irish hospitality. An Irish Guardsman, cleaning his telescopic rifle as he sat on the trench banquette and smoking one of my cigarettes, told me the story.

" The coal slack is festooned with devils of snipers, smart fellows that can shoot round a corner and blast your eye-tooth out at five hundred yards," he said. " They're not all their ones neither, there's a good sprinkling of our own boys as well. I was doing a wee bit of pot-shot-and-be-damned-to-you work in the other side of the slack, and my eyes open all the time for an enemy's back. There was one near me, but I'm beggared if I could find him. ' I'll not lave this place till I do.' I says to meself, and spent half the nights I was there prowlin' round like a dog at a fair with my eyes open for the sniper. I came on his post wan night. I smelt him out because he didn't bury his sausage skins as we do, and they stunk like the hole of hell when an ould greasy sinner is a-fryin'. In I went to his sandbagged castle with me gun on the cock and me finger on the trigger, but he wasn't there; there was nothin' in the place but a few rounds of ball an' a half-empty bottle. I was dhry as a bone, and I had a sup without winkin'. ' Mother of Heaven,' I says, when I put down the bottle, ' it's little ye know of hospitality, stranger, leaving a bottle with nothin' in it but water. I'll wait for ye, me bucko,' and I lay down in the corner and waited for him to come in.

" But sorrow the fut of him came, and me waiting there till the colour of day was in the sky. Then I goes back to me own place, and there was he waiting for me. He only made one mistake, he had fallen to sleep, and he just sprung up as I came in be the door.

" Immediately I had him by the big toe. ' Hands up, Hans ! ' I said, and he didn't argue, all that he did was to swear like one of ourselves and flop down. ' Why don't ye bury yer sausages, Hans ? ' I asked him. ' I smelt yer, me bucko, by what ye couldn't eat. Why didn't ye have something better than water in yer bottle ? ' I says to him. Dang a Christian word would he answer, only swear, and swear with nothin' bar the pull of me finger betwixt him and his Maker. But, ye know, I had a kind of likin' for him when I thought of him comin' into my house without as much as yer leave, and going to sleep just as if he was in his own home. I didn't swear back at him, but just said : ' This is only a house for wan, but our King has a big residence for ye, so come along before it gets any clearer,' and I took him over to our trenches as stand-to was coming to an end."

* * *

As a trench pest, both mortar and sniper faded into insignificance before the common or garden louse. In all theatres of war an unsuccessful campaign was raged against it. This paragraph is chosen as being, so far as is known, the one case of effective de-lousing.

LICE

From *A Roumanian Diary*.[1]

By Hans Carossa

At seven o'clock we went on again in rain and mist. Three men, suspected of typhus, had to be left behind in Oitóz. The louse, that disseminator of pestilence, till lately only ludicrous and disgusting, manifests itself gradually as a diabolical, unconquerable foe. For months it has tormented our bodies, so that often our skins seem to be inflamed at a thousand separate points ; it scatters our thoughts and dreams ; now it is trying to kill. On Kishavas I was struck by the fact that the patch on my shirt, over which were pinned the sprays given me by the woman of Szentlelek, remained almost free from lice. I concluded from this that the natural oils of certain plants must be still more inimical to the vermin than naphthaline, the supply of which, in any case, is becoming scarcer and scarcer ; and I plucked some wild mints which were growing there in abundant, thick bluish-green clumps. Twice a day I rubbed my skin with the leaves and stalks, and I have taken a good supply with me as well. At first the itching and burning increased ; but the final effect has, so far, been beneficial.

[1] Published by Martin Secker.

* * *

In spite of all hardships, the spirit of the troops was high.

P.B.I.

From *War Letters to a Wife*.[1]

By ROWLAND FEILDING.

December 14th, 1916.

I have for many weeks past been working to get some good company sergeant-majors out from home. One in particular, I have been trying for—a Sergeant-major McGrath, reputed to have been the best at Kinsale. His commanding officer very kindly agreed to send him to me, although he wrote that he regretted parting with him. McGrath arrived the day after I returned from leave, and within half an hour of his reaching the fire-trench was lying dead, a heavy trench-mortar bomb having fallen upon him, killing him and two others, and wounding two more. Now, is not that a case of hard luck " chasing " a man, when you consider how long others of us last? I never even saw him alive.

I visited the fire-trench just after the bomb had fallen. It had dropped into the trench, and the sight was not a pleasant one. It was, moreover, aggravated by the figure of one of the dead, who had been blown out of the trench on to the parapet, and was silhouetted grotesquely against the then darkening sky.

But what I saw was inspiring, nevertheless. The sentries stood like statues. At the spot where the bomb had burst—within forty yards of the Germans—officers and men were already hard at work in the rain, quietly repairing the damage done to our trench, and clearing away the remains of the dead; all—to outward appearance—oblivious to the possibility—indeed the probability—of further trouble from the trench-mortar, trained upon this special bit of trench, that had fired the fatal round.

What wonderful people are our infantry! And what a joy it is to be with them! When I am here I feel—well, I can hardly describe it. I feel, if it were possible, that one should

[1] Published by The Medici Society, Ltd.

never go away from them: and I contrast that scene which I have described (at 1s. 1d. a day) with what I see and hear in England when I go on leave. My God! I can only say: "May the others be forgiven!" How it can be possible that these magnificent fellows, going home for a few days after ten months of this (and practically none get home in less), should be waylaid at Victoria Station, as they are, and exploited, and done out of the hard-earned money they have saved through being in the trenches, and with which they are so lavish, baffles my comprehension. It is unthinkable: and that, I think, is the opinion of most officers who go on leave.

I can never express in writing what I feel about the men in the trenches; and nobody who has not seen them can ever understand. According to the present routine, we stay in the front line eight days and nights; then go out for the same period. Each company spends four days and four nights in the fire-trench before being relieved. The men are practically without rest. They are wet through much of the time. They are shelled and trench-mortared. They may not be hit, but they are kept in a perpetual state of unrest and strain. They work all night and every night, and a good part of each day, digging and filling sandbags, and repairing the breeches in the breastworks; that is when they are not on sentry. The temperature is icy. They have not even a blanket. The last two days it has been snowing. They cannot move more than a few feet from their posts: therefore, except when they are actually digging, they cannot keep themselves warm by exercise; and when they try to sleep, they freeze. At present, they are getting a tablespoon of rum to console them, once in three days.

Think of these things, and compare them with what are considered serious hardships in normal life! Yet these men play their part uncomplainingly. That is to say, they never complain seriously. Freezing, or snowing, or drenching rain; always smothered with mud; you may ask any one of them, any moment of the day or night: "Are you cold?" or "Are you wet?"—and you will get but one answer. The Irishman will reply—always with a smile—"Not too cold, sir," or "Not too wet, sir." It makes me feel sick. It makes me think

I never want to see the British Isles again so long as the War lasts. It makes one feel ashamed for these Irishmen, and also of those fellow-countrymen of our own, earning huge wages, yet for ever clamouring for more; striking, or threatening to strike; while the country is engaged upon this murderous struggle. Why, we ask here, has not the whole nation, civil as well as military, been conscripted?

The curious thing is that all seem so much more contented here than the people at home. The poor Tommy, shivering in the trenches, is happier than the beast who makes capital out of the War. Everybody laughs at everything here. It is the only way.

* * *

A "BLIGHTY"

From *Other Ranks*.[1]
By W. V. TILSLEY.

For hours, it seemed, a procession of stumbling figures passed Bradshaw unheedingly as he gazed into the sky. The ground revolved round him. Everything seemed detached; distant. The company had left him lying there! The back of his head felt blown away, aching dully. He knew he wasn't dying, because there were no half-measures about head wounds. He'd his leave to go on, too.

He'd been wounded! He remembered now. Something had hit him on the head, yet lifted him off his feet into the air and laid him, jarringly, on his back—a flattened bundle. He remembered Mr. Hautz and Cavalry Joe looking round as he fell, but carrying on. Then it felt as if his head were being rolled about the battle-field, and he went to sleep. . . .

He cautiously touched the back of his head. His hair was matted, fingers came away sticky. He raised himself; a trickle of blood changed its course down his neck. Why, the guns were still at it! He stood up gingerly, then fell again, wondering. His tin hat jerked forward and rolled off, revealing an ugly gash about three inches wide. The broken edges, jagged and uneven, showed the thickness of the metal.

[1] Published by R. Cobden-Sanderson, Ltd.

Field dressing, of course! Then leave. . . .

He crawled to the nearest hole, clutching the tin hat by its chin-strap, and rolled in almost on top of Whelan, with his Lewis gun.

"Have you stopped one, too?" asked Bradshaw.

Whelan felt round his hip, said he thought so. Bradshaw pulled out his field dressing and broke the iodine phial. Amateurishly he coiled a bandage round his head and adjusted the gashed helmet, now a few sizes too small. It had saved his life. That, and his shortness. If he'd been three inches taller the shell-piece would have passed below his steel helmet's rim into an unprotected neck.

For months he had hoped to be wounded; not too badly. Primarily to gain the respite, however brief, of civilised living; and secondly because there was something tangible about a scar gained in battle. A branding of the skin is much easier to bear than scarless mental branding. But now his wound would rob him of leave! And he'd been so looking forward to being at home to-morrow.

Bradshaw left Whelan to his own devices. The Lewis gunner wasn't the only man that morning, hit by a clod of earth, who dropped out to investigate. There seemed little to choose between volunteers and Derby men. Each, after doing his painful bit to the last gasp, was off like a shot the moment he was hit. The days had gone when men disregarded their wounds and carried on.

He felt steadier. The wounded lay in shell-holes held up by Jerry's box barrage, fearful lest, after all, they wouldn't get back to the safety now within reach. For Jerry plastered the old lines and supports with an appalling shower of missiles: a belt of liveliness too dangerous to cross. Bradshaw had one interest only: to get to the nearest aid post. Dozens like him cowered at the fringe of the hostile barrage, Blighty passports on the hands and feet, legs, arms, and bodies; awaiting the slightest cessation to scurry through. Some of them had been hit several times whilst waiting there; several killed. Must he, sheep-like, join them or make an effort to get through? Stay here, and risk being hit, or make a bold dash for absolute safety?

A "BLIGHTY"

Another Fritz came through, arms fixed upwards, mechanical, dead-eyed. A man cried "Bastard," and levelled his rifle at the Jerry. Bradshaw snatched the barrel aside and rose to his feet.

He set off towards the splashing earth, heart in mouth, gasping and choking, making a drunken bee-line for a disabled tank. Another lad followed, hanging on Bradshaw's heels, but soon the corporal was compelled to drop back and assist him. Crocked in the left leg, another piece of shell had entered his forearm whilst waiting for the firing to lift. They carried on more slowly, arms around each other's shoulders . . . entered the barrage, heads down to ward off showers of damp earth.

CRRRUMP! CRRRUMP!

Elliott, Bradshaw's companion, cried "Oh!" as a third splinter hit his hand, then they carried on luckily between the shell-bursts. A fourth wound came, on the shoulder, and simultaneously Bradshaw felt a tug at his water-bottle. The bottom half hung limp, cut away as if guillotined. Elliott gasped, trembling and frightened, complaining in a plaintive, childish voice that two were enough. He licked away the blood from his hand. They reached the tank, breathless and choking; sheltered a moment under one of its huge, tilted diamond sides. The worst was over; shells dropped behind. A far-pitched one burst on the other side; the tank heaved over them, and settled. They pushed on, reaching the muddy road. Through!

The hubbub before and behind went on unabated. Bradshaw took one look back at the misty rise and bursting smoke-clouds, then set his face steadfastly towards Ypres. The ground was unrecognisable; filthily churned. A few dead men lay around, pale but not inhuman; a horse here; a splintered limber there. One man, half buried in the road-banking, looked so natural that both moved forward instinctively to help him. The part they thought buried was blown away. An officer came up the road—the first human being they had seen on the safe side of the barrage, and the only one in sight: an artillery officer who might have been greeting friends at home on a Sunday morning stroll.

"Hello, boys! How have they gone on at the Schuler galleries?"

Neither of them knew. Both were tempted to say: "The lads are going on fine, sir!" Bradshaw looked apologetic, and said he was afraid he didn't know. Some strong point, it appeared.

The officer passed on.

Bradshaw vaguely imagined that behind the attackers would be a force actively backing them up. Not only guns, but parties of men feverishly energetic. There wasn't a sign of anybody. The guns were nearer, and not so angry now, but before them only a stretch of unoccupied, uninviting land; a gap that got Bradshaw in the stomach. It appeared as if every effort to back up the attackers was not being made. By then the different waves were lapping each other, perhaps over-lapping, on the beach of pill-boxes. How were they going on? Everything about was unbelievably clayed up and dirty, as if spurned; left dead. A closer examination revealed that an army had recently passed that way. Several times Bradshaw's helmet fell off its swollen perch, disturbing the unworkman-like bandage. His colleague rearranged it, and during one stoppage spotted in the mud a neat silver wristlet watch. A peculiar yet perhaps natural place to find such a souvenir. "I was slow then," thought Bradshaw.

The guns still hammered away as the wounded pair reached the first aid post, though less fantastically than that uproarious, spectacular outburst at zero. Thousands of shells were falling expensively, extravagantly, and uselessly on the unoccupied ground between the pill-boxes. Down a few steps to be greeted by a kindly-faced *padre*, who, smiling, said: "Well done, boys! Why, doc, this one's a corporal!"

"Yes," thought Bradshaw; "a sergeant, really." Very few wounded had arrived; others, apparently, had been more decorous in leaving the attack. Looking round the dim dug-out, he saw two Germans, one particularly ill looking. The pulverising barrage had missed them.

Innoculation. Dressings. The *padre* again. A bespectacled, quiet-voiced orderly directed them to a grey marquee. Delighted amazement! A trestle counter of several tables groaned, and certainly wilted, under a most appetising array of sweets and other eatables. Chocolate bars and sandwiches were piled in perilously high erections. There were mounds of cakes and buns; a profusion of square, round, and oblong packets of biscuits; and, most acceptable of all at first, big urns of steaming hot tea.

Bradshaw and his companion started an offensive immediately, hastily wolfing. It must have appeared a greedy orgy to the Salvation Army attendants. They paused for breath, then noticed the two Jerries sitting aside on a form. They lolled dejectedly with the demeanour of criminals brought to justice, dreading a sudden revenge; expecting to be bullied and kicked about. Bradshaw got tea for them; and, after an enquiring look at the S.A. helpers, invited them to tuck in at the sandwiches. A whole bulwark of hatred fell from their already opening eyes. Tears trickled down the cheeks of the younger, more badly wounded one, yet he showed exceptional control in mastering his emotion before drinking the much-desired tea.

They returned to where a South African worked trucks on a single uncamouflaged rail track, having gained a better appreciation of these voluntary Salvation Army workers—obviously not A1, yet working within shell range. They clambered inside a good, low-sided roofless truck, followed by a fair, upstanding German boy wearing an Iron Cross. Other men came in ones and twos, one a lance-corporal from " A " Company, loud-voiced and aggressive. He climbed up, noticing immediately the Iron Cross, and peremptorily demanded it. The German clicked his heels to attention, but looked defiant. To Bradshaw's disgust, the lance-corporal quickly proved himself a blustering bully threatening to throw the Jerry out of the truck if he didn't part with the decoration. But Fritz stood up to Tommy. For a few apprehensive moments Bradshaw feared trouble, then a private said contemptuously:

" Leave him be, fathead. Happen that'll find thi'sen like him afore this lots o'er wi' ! "

And Bradshaw wondered why he hadn't said it. How had the German won his medal? Up with the rations? Probably by killing one, or more, of our chaps. Or, better thought, perhaps by saving one of his own companions. A man, anyway!

* * *

TRENCH BREAKFAST
From *Twelve Days*.[1]

By SIDNEY ROGERSON

There are those who deny that breakfast is, as its name implies, the most important meal of the day, but in the trenches no one could question it for a moment. No matter how violent, sulphurous, or bloody the night, no matter how tense the grim ceremonial of " stand-to " which ushered in the day, the command " stand-down " was almost invariably followed by a lull along the whole front. Hostilities were temporarily suspended by mutual, if mute, consent, and for what reason except that after the strained hours of darkness English and German alike turned with relaxation to break their fast? For anything from an hour to two hours the most vicious noise to be heard in the trench was the sizzling of frying bacon. Then some machine-gunner, cheerful from his meal, would break the spell with the " Pop-pop-op-pop-pop ! " call on his Vickers, which never failed to evoke the slower " pop-pop " from some heavy machine-gun within the German lines.

There was something very refreshing about this breakfast truce. Above all, is it associated in my mind with a brief triumph of the kindly smells of Nature over those more sinister ones of man's making. For a few minutes the sun and dew distilled a faint fragrance even from the freshly turned earth or the coarse weeds bruised by the night's shelling, before the moisture evaporated and allowed the normal odours of trench life to assert themselves. Even then the all-pervading reek of chlorate of lime would be overcome for a while by the homely acrid smell of the cook's wood fire, and —oh, most welcome !—of bacon.

But as I reached my headquarters my nose registered none

[1] Published by Arthur Barker, Ltd.

of these things. No. 7 platoon were starting the day as each man, except the sentry on the high fire-step, thought best. Some were asleep, others busy with their breakfast. What miserable breakfasts we were compelled to during those four days! Bread, whiskery with strands of sand-bag, butter, and a dollop of cold " Maconochie " or bully beef, washed down, if we were lucky, with a half-cupful of neat rum. Tea was even harder to go without than bacon, but it was impossible to light a fire during daylight without giving the enemy gunners a fresh target. Lunch, tea, and dinner were repetitions of breakfast, except that at nightfall the old-soldier's ingenuity triumphed over circumstances. " Buggy " Robinson contrived a kind of oven in the side of the trench, covering the hole with a ground-sheet pegged into the earth with rifle cartridges. Inside he put his stove, made of a tin of whale-oil—" trench feet, for the prevention of," to use the language of the period—soaked in which was a piece of " four-by-two " rifle rag. The heat given out was not very intense, but was enough to warm up one tin mug of liquid at a time, without any light showing in the trench. During the day Robinson improved his patent, and dug into the trench one of the salved German machine-gun belt boxes, which, with a lid that could be propped open, was most effective.

* * *

WINTER QUARTERS
From *Undertones of War*.[1]
By Edmund Blunden

And now, as I lie in bed in my billet, after a conversation on infant schools with the lady teacher whose house it is, with trees softly swaying almost to the window, and only the odd night voices of an ancient town about me, I conjecture briefly, yet with a heaving breast, of that march southward which begins to-morrow morning. It will be a new world again. The past few months have been a new world, of which the succession of sensations erratically occupies my

[1] Published by Messrs. Cobden-Sanderson.

mind; the bowed heads of working parties and reliefs moving up by " trenches " framed of sacking and brushwood; the bullets leaping angrily from charred rafters shining in greenish flarelight; an old pump and a tiled floor in the moon; bedsteads and broken mattresses hanging over cracked and scarred walls; Germans seen as momentary shadows among wire hedges; tallowy, blood-dashed, bewildered faces— but put back the blanket; a garden gate, opening into a battle-field; boys, treating the terror and torment with the philosophy of men; cheeky newspaper-sellers passing the gunpits; stretcher-bearers on the same road an hour after; the old labourer at his cottage door, pointing out with awe and circumstance (the guns meanwhile thundering away on the next parish) his eaves chipped by anti-aircraft shrapnel; the cook's mate digging for nose-caps where a dozen shells have just exploded; the " Mad Major " flying low over the Germans' parapet and scattering out his bombs, leaving us to settle the bill; our own parapet seen in the magnesium's glare as the Germans were seeing it; stretchers or sooty dixies being dumped round trench corners; the post cards stuck on the corner of Coldstream Lane; the diction of the incoming and outgoing soldiers squeezing past one another in the pitch-black communication-trench; the age that has gone by since I read Young's *Night Thoughts* in the dug-out at Cuinchy. And, now I think of it, I forgot to rescue that edition (1815) when it slipped down behind the bunks ! We may go back again, of course, but—

> Time glides away, Lorenzo, like a brook,
> In the same brook none ever bathed him twice.

．　　　．　　　．　　　．　　　．

Then we went into the trenches round about Thiepval Wood, which not long before had been so horrible and mad; but now they had assumed a tenderer aspect, were voted " a rest-cure sector," and we were envied for them. The land in front was full of the dead of July 1st and other days of destruction, but our own casualties were happily few, and there was cover for all. Occasionally heavy shells blocked

WINTER QUARTERS

up parts of Inniskilling Avenue, or the waterside path to Mill Post (opposite our old mill at Hamel) which Lapworth, the mild-looking boy who had so stalwartly endured the pandemonium of Stuff Trench, now commanded. At battalion headquarters it was like old times, everyone having time and means to appear with shining face and even shining buttons, and arguments about ghosts, Lloyd George's ammunition, the German Emperor and the French artillery rising into sonorous eloquence until some near explosion put out the acetylene lamp, or "paper warfare" warmed up with the receipt of large envelopes from Brigade. Those not in the front trench were sheltered in medieval-looking archways hewn through the chalk and the roots of trees; the forward posts were chiefly manned from tunnels called Koyli West and East; and in truth everyone seemed disposed to be satisfied. In Paisley Valley, alongside the wood, some tanks were lying veiled with brown nets, and one might have translated the fact; but a week or so passed, and nothing had happened except rain and fog. Had it not? With the aid of the sergeant cook I had built four ovens in the wood, which Wren himself would have eaten his dinner out of—or gone without.

In spite of the sylvan intricacies (a trifle damaged) of Thiepval Wood, and a bedroom in the corridored chalk bank, and the tunes of the "Bing Boys" endlessly revolved, one was not yet quite clear of Stuff Trench; my own unwelcome but persistent retrospect was the shell-hole there used by us as a latrine, with those two flattened German bodies in it, tallow-faced and dirty-stubbled, one spectacled, with fingers hooking the handle of a bomb; and others had much worse to remember. We were merry when at length the relief was sent in and we emerged from the Ancre mists to form up and march in pale daylight to Senlis, a village six or seven miles behind the line. The road wound and twisted, but we liked it well, and as at one point the still lofty stump of Mesnil Church tower showed above the dingy trampled fields it was hard not to shout aloud. "Not gone yet," signalled the tower. We heard the church bell ring in Senlis, we bought beer and chocolate, and we admired with determination the girls who sold them; so vital was the hour of relaxation, so kindly was the stone of the road and the straw of the barn. We envied the troops employed as road-sweepers and ditchers in their drains and puddles. Fatuous groups of dug-outs, tin and matchboard, seemed unfair luxury. We heard the high-velocity gun shooting at the Bouzincourt Road with no anxiety. But, prime gift of eccentric heaven, there was the evening when Harrison took all the old originals and some others to the divisional concert-party performing in the town. The barn roof ought indeed to have floated away in the pæans and warblings that rose from us, as the pierrots chirruped and gambolled there. In sweet music is such art—and never was music sweeter than the ragtime then obtaining, if appreciation indexes merit. " Take me back to dear old Blighty " was too much for us—we roared inanely, and when a creditable cardboard train was jerked across the stage and the performers looking out of the windows sang their chorus, " Birmingham, Leeds or Manchester," the force of illusion could no further go. " Mr. Bottomley—Good old Horatio " was a song scarcely less successful, though Mr. Bottomley was blamed for several things scarcely under his control—as,

" When you're deep in a decline,
Who provides the Number Nine?
Mr. Bottomley—John Bull."

" On the day on which Peace is declared," a neat little skit, and " When you're a long, long way from home " will never cease to ring pathetically through the years between. All the performers had been over the top. Glum and droll clown, where can I now find your equal? Will time yield you such a " house " again? and you, graceful tenor, with what glorious air can you now awaken such a sigh as when in that farmstead you sang the " cheap sentiment " of those newly from the outer darkness? " When you're a long, long way from home "—we seemed to be so.

* * *

After taking two years in persuading Roumanians to come in, the Allies allowed them to be knocked out within a few weeks. Here, in the defiles of the Carpathians, was fought a war vastly different from that of France and Flanders—a war of movement, of tactical advance and grand strategy.

BATTLE IN ROUMANIA
From *A Roumanian Diary*.[1]
By Hans Carossa

Our road was now continuously uphill. The adjutant said it was only about ten miles to the trenches, but we heard no firing. The pine trees became sparser, and juniper, rich with violet-green berries, grew luxuriantly among the crags. We came on rows of graves which from the inscriptions could only have been five days old. Carp, a Roumanian lieutenant, was the name on one of the wooden crosses. Towards two o'clock we traversed a bare hollow streaked with mist, and saw a terrible and bewildering spectacle. Where a solitary house in the middle had been burned down, the embers were still smoking. The blackened walls were still standing, and one could see that they had been of the usual blue; but nothing was left of the roof save its charred ribs. Behind a wooden shed untouched by the fire lay two graves without crosses but decked with juniper; and a tall, very old woman, naked to the waist, with Magyar features, her grey hair wild and filthy, glided round and round the two hummocks talking confidentially to an invisible something. As we came nearer she drew herself up and made a forbidding gesture with her hand as if to warn us from the place; then she suddenly turned away and wrung her hands towards the east with a piercing wail. Trusting to his smattering of Hungarian, Lieutenant F. tried to speak to her, but she bent down, gathered a handful of earth from the nearest grave and flung it at him, more as an exorcism and a warning than as a hostile act. Half in vexation, half in horror, Lieutenant F. started back and returned

[1] Published by Martin Secker.

to the column. None of the other officers or men halted. They did, indeed, wonder aloud what could have happened to the old woman; but most of them felt that here a tragedy had taken place which no facile sympathy could alleviate, and went on marching silently into the mists which soon blotted out the terrible grandeur of the scene.

. . . . . .

The mountain we climbed was a mountain of blindness and death. From the eastern slope, where the battle was not yet decided, wild cries rang through the rattle of the musketry; and up here, in the position we had captured, the enemy were wreaking their vengeance on the conquerors. Like a swarm of hornets the shells dashed against the rocks, tearing the flesh from the limbs of the living and the dead. Sometimes German wounded called to us, sometimes Roumanian, who were now being mutilated for a second time by the fire of their comrades. Some of them suffered in silence; others twisted like wounded snakes. Through the zone of death we saw Germans lightly wounded descending the mountain, a few white and shaken, but others walking jauntily, dressed up as if for a fancy-dress ball in the gay-coloured belts, jackets and military decorations of their dead enemies. One had brought back a gramophone with him from the Roumanian lines; now an idea suddenly struck him, he placed it on a stone and set it going, the page in *Figaro* began to sing, and like the voice of a mad soul Mozart's music rose in a world of ruin. The despatch orderly Glavina was leaning against a granite block near the commander's dug-out; he was still breathing, but on his face was already the prescient look of the dead. We could see no trace of blood. Fighting down our sorrow and apprehension, we searched for the wound and found at last a tiny splinter driven into the nape of the neck. Soon his breathing ceased. A few closely written sheets of paper, which must have fallen out of his pocket, I took with me to hand over to the adjutant; but I noticed on the way back that they did not contain anything official, so I kept them beside me for the time being. We told the major that the Bosnian stretcher-bearers who had been arranged for had not yet come; he promised to communicate with the Division and sent us back to Hallesul.

Meanwhile the sky had darkened; snow began to fall. A flowing white veil shut off the guns from the targets they were firing at; one after another they fell silent, and we descended almost in safety. A Roumanian stretched between two birch trunks lay across my path; I thought he was dead and was stepping over him, when I heard a groan and felt a feeble but perceptible tug at my cloak. Turning round, I looked down on the dying face of a man of about thirty; his eyes were closed, his mouth terribly twisted with pain. His fingers still clutched the fast hem of my cloak. Through a grey cape which covered his breast a slight vapour was rising. R. threw it back; under his torn ribs his lungs and heart lay exposed, the heart beating sluggishly. A number of silver and copper medals of saints, which he had been wearing on a black ribbon round his neck, were driven deep into his flesh, some of them much bent. We covered him up again. The man half-opened his eyes, his lips moved. Simply for the sake of doing something I filled my morphia syringe, and then I saw that this was what he seemed to want: he pushed the cloak aside and tried to stretch out his arm to me in readiness—behaviour hard to account for in a man already almost dead! But perhaps there is an infinitely keen, infinitely poignant anguish which a man conscious of approaching death desires to be rid of at any price, because it holds him fast to life in burning pain and hinders a free and clean parting: who knows? After the injection he laid his head back against the birch almost in comfort and closed his eyes, in whose deep sockets large snowflakes were already beginning to fall.

. . . . .

At daybreak rifle-firing, which soon fell silent. After sunrise the overcast sky cleared; one could see behind a transparent veil of cloud the waning moon like an embryonic golden shape. The stretcher-bearers have come, and in relays all the wounded are being carried away. Pirkl must remain here; his pulse is almost imperceptible and he would most probably reach Oitóz as a corpse. His brother had obtained an hour's leave to visit him. As Pirkl cannot speak any longer his brother is employing his time in digging a grave for the still living man, and carving a cross, on which he is very carefully printing in blue pencil the name of the fallen.

* * *

ENGLAND's traditional system of voluntary recruitment having proved inadequate, conscription was introduced in January, 1916. Within a few months its victims were fighting on many fronts side by side with men of the New Armies, the Territorials and the scanty survivors of the peace-time regular army.

CONSCRIPTS
From *Disenchantment*.[1]
By C. E. MONTAGUE

Even in trenches and near them, where most of the health was, time had begun to embrown the verdant soul of the army. "Kitchener's Army" was changing. Like every volunteer army, his had sifted itself, at its birth, with the only sieve that will riddle out, even roughly, the best men to be near in a fight. Till the first of the pressed men arrived at our front, a sergeant there, when he posted a sentry and left him alone in the dark, could feel about as complete a moral certitude as there is on the earth that the post would not be let down. For, whatever might happen, nothing inside the man could start whispering to him, "You never asked to be here; if you do fail it isn't your doing."

Nine out of the ten conscripts were equally sound. For they would have been volunteers if they could. The tenth was the problem, the more so because there was nothing to tell you which was the tenth and which were the nine. For all that you knew any man who came out on a draft, from then on, might be the exception, the literal-minded Christian who thought it wicked to kill in a war; or an anti-nationalist zealot who thought us all equally fools, the Germans and us, to be out there pasturing lice instead of busy at home taking the

[1] Published by Messrs. Chatto & Windus.

hide off the *bourgeois*; or one of those drift wisps of loveless critical mind, attached to no one place or people more than another, and just as likely as not to think that the war was our fault and that we ought to be beaten. *Riant avenir*! as a French sergeant said when, in an hour of ease, we were talking over the nature of man, and he told me, in illustration of its diversity, how a section of his had just been enriched with a draft of neurasthenic burglars.

These vulgar considerations of military expediency never seemed to cross the outer rim of the consciousness of many worthies who were engaged at home in shooting the reluctant into the army. If a recalcitrant seemed to be lazy, spiritless, nerveless, if there was every sign of his making a specially worthless and troublesome consumer of rations in a trench, then a burning zeal to inflict this nuisance and danger on some unoffending platoon in France seemed to invade the ordinary military tribunal. Report said that the satisfaction of this impulse was called, by the possessed persons, " giving Haig the men," and sometimes, with a more pungent irony, " supporting our fellows in the trenches." *Non tali auxilio nec defensoribus istis*. Australia's fellows in the trenches were suffered to vote themselves out of the risk of getting any support of the kind. Australia is a democracy. Ours were not asked whether they wanted to see their trenches employed as a penal settlement to which middle-aged moralists in England might deport, among other persons, those whom they felt to be morally the least beautiful of their juniors. So nothing impeded the pious practice of " larning toads to be toads." For the shirker, the " kicker," the " lawyer," for all the types of undesirables that contribute most liberally to the wrinkled appearance of sergeants, those pious men had the nose of collectors. Wherever there was a spare fifty yards of British front to be held, they, if anyone, could find a man likely to go to sleep there on guard, or, in some cyclonic disturbance of spirit, to throw down his rifle and light out for the coast across country.

Such episodes were reasonably few. The inveterate mercy that guards drunken sailors preserved from the worst disaster the cranks who had made a virtue of giving their country every bad sailor they could. And the abounding mercy of most courts-martial rendered few of the episodes fatal to individual conscripts. Nor, indeed, was the growth in their frequency after conscription wholly due to the more fantastic tricks played before high Heaven by some of the Falstaffs who dealt with the Mouldies, Shadows and Bull-calves. Conscription, in any case, must be dilution. You may get your water more quickly by throwing the filter away, but don't hope to keep the quality what it was. And the finer a New Army unit had been, to begin with, the swifter the autumnal change. Every first-rate battalion fighting in France or Belgium lost its whole original numbers over and over again. First, because in action it spared itself less than the poor ones; secondly, because the best divisions rightly got the hard jobs. Going out in the late autumn of 1915, a good battalion with normal luck might have nearly half its original volunteer strength left after the Battle of the Somme. Drafts of conscripts would fill up the gap, each draft with a listless or enigmatic one-tenth that volunteering had formerly kept at a distance. The Battle of Arras next spring might leave only 20 per cent of the first volunteers, and the autumn battles in Flanders would pretty well finish their business. Seasons returned but not to that battalion returned the spirit of delight in which it had first learnt to soldier together and set foot together in France and first marched through darkness and ruined villages towards the flaring fair-ground of the front. While a New Army battalion was still very young, and fully convinced that no crowd of men so good to be with had ever been brought together before, it used to be always saying how it would keep things up after the War. No such genial reunions had ever been held as these were to be. But now the few odd men that are left only write to each other at long intervals, feeling almost as if they were raising their voices in an empty church. One of them asks another has he any idea what the battalion was like after Oppy, or Bourlon Wood, or wherever their own knock-out came. Like any other battalion, no doubt—a mere G.C.M. of all conscript battalions; conscription filed down all special features and characters.

* * *

The task of converting civilians, willing or unwilling, into soldiers was not an easy one, particularly when entrusted to a certain type of N.C.O.

DISCIPLINE

From *A Private in the Guards*.[1]

By STEPHEN GRAHAM

The officers had very little to do with us in the initial stages of training. A very great personage to us was the brigade sergeant-major, with the Royal Arms embroidered on his sleeve. He was kind to the recruits, but a terror to the non-commissioned officers. His sharp eye often detected a corporal or sergeant in the act of striking the men. He seemed to regard it as one of the worst offences possible, and he never failed to administer a sharp reprimand to an offender. The men had no greater grievance than that of being struck whilst on parade, and it made the blood boil to be struck oneself, or to see men near forty years of age struck by corporals or sergeants of twenty-three or twenty-four without the possibility of striking back. The sergeant-major also tried to stop the more exuberantly filthy language that was used, but in that he was much less feared by the instructors. Even when he was near them, the latter had a way of standing quite close to you and delivering a whispered imprecatory address on adultery, the birth of Jesus, the sins of Sodom, and what not. The instructors, who had a very free hand whilst " knocking civvies into shape," said the sort of things which every man instinctively feels can only be answered by blows. Descriptive justice can never be done to this theme, so important in itself, this particular aspect of the training. For although there is a French book in which such obscenity as is used has been set down as heard, it is not really possible in English. It is not even desirable, except for one reason—that reason being the assumption that bad language, the " hard swearing," is only a trait of which we may be indulgently proud, a few bloodies and damns, and that's all. It is much more than that, and it is

[1] Published by William Heinemann, Ltd.

frantically disgusting and terrible. It could not be helped in the middle of a great war, and no one naturally would find fault with the old peace-time professional army, whatever language it found most convenient, but it is different when the whole nation is brought under the military yoke. If conscription is going to survive, let us remind all private soldiers who have come through the obscenity and detested it all the while, lest as fathers of the rising generation they should regard it in a more lenient spirit, and think it harmless for their sons when, at eighteen or nineteen, they leave the purer atmosphere of home or school or factory or office for the training ground. Army life has many compensations, but there are thousands of quiet youths in every generation who would be corrupted and spoiled by the sort of treatment received during the Great War. And among these quiet youths would be found most of the really gifted and promising. The Army is an institution somewhat like a public school, in that each fresh generation going into it inherits the undying part of the language and manners of those who have gone before. The old controls the new, and it is impossible to escape traditions which, besides being manifest and glorious, are often secret and evil as well. It is impossible to make a fresh start and train the young nation in a completely wholesome positive, and ideal atmosphere. It seems strange, however, that " the red little, dead little army " should now set the way of life and expression for the whole nation in arms, and that we should all have gone through such a miserable eye of a needle. But at the moment, when practically all have been brought in, it is possible to look around and see that the whole system is staffed by the survivors of the pre-1914 army. They have made the tone. The hope is that if military service comes in as a national feature of our life after the War, we shall purify the system and make the Army a decent continuation school, where a young man can grow nobly to manhood among his fellows.

.   .   .   .   .

Another great pain which is suffered is in learning to be impure. It is only a strong character that can resist the infection of impurity. Inevitably you say or think things which are obscene and brutal, and many go and do the sort of things they say and think. With what a pang do you relinquish the sacredness of your manhood. You often hear it said in a jocular way : " What would the missus think if she could hear me now ! " But oh ! the grief in the secret places of the heart when you first begin to swear, when you first say indecent things, when, perchance, in a moment of confraternity a man says an indecent thing about his own wife !

. . . .

The defects in the Little Sparta system are the humiliation of recruits by words or blows, the use of glaringly indecent language, the possibility 'of squaring punishment, the use by N.C.O.s, even by lance-corporals, of recruits as batmen. I believe these were recognised as defects in peace time, and some of them had been eradicated, others endured in secret. But in war time the problem of breaking in those who were never intended by Nature to be soldiers was so difficult that some of these ugly things become useful. Constant humiliation and the use of indecent phrases took down the recruit's pride, and reduced him to a condition when he was amenable to any command. It is impossible not to think less of yourself when a sergeant has bawled before a whole squad : " Well, I think you're about the ugliest thing ever dropped from a woman," or, " Are you married ? Fancy a decent woman having children by a man like you."

To be struck, to be threatened, to be called indecent names, to be drilled by yourself in front of a squad in order to make a fool of you, to be commanded to do a tiring exercise and continue doing it whilst the rest of the squad does something else ; to have your ear spat into, to be marched across parade ground under escort, to be falsely accused before an officer and silenced when you try to speak in defence—all these things take down your pride, make you feel small, and in some ways fit you to accept the role of cannon-fodder on the battleground. A good deal of it could be defended on grounds of usefulness. But, of course, it doesn't make a Christian army, and it's hell for the poor British soldier.

* * *

STILL harder was the lot of those who refused military service on conscientious grounds. Unable to convince the Military Tribunals of the honesty of their objections to bloodshed, they proved their courage by their steadfastness in the face of imprisonment and even of torture.

"CONCHIES"
From *Conscription and Conscience—a History*, 1916-1919.[1]
By JOHN W. GRAHAM, M.A.

Alec Baxter, William Little and Garth Ballantyne received a sentence of five years' hard labour for disobeying an order. These long sentences, however, were given to terrify the others; and were all changed to two years on arrival at the prison; for it was not legal to keep a man abroad with longer sentence than that. These men went to a military prison camp, on the exposed low-lying swampy shore near Dunkirk. It was Prison No. 10, and though the smallest, held about four hundred men. The inmates were not criminals, but had broken discipline in some form. It seems worth while to describe a military prison, not because its hardships specially fell upon conscientious objectors, but because they were, on the contrary, the doom of ordinary soldiers. No doubt the reply of the army would be that discipline is essential to success in war, and must be maintained, if necessary, by terror. If this be so—and probably the military know their own business —so much the worse for military discipline, and therefore so much the worse for war.

The prisoners in this camp occupied bell tents, about sixteen men to each. Two long, low, corrugated iron sheds, with small windows high up in the wall, were the punishment cells. The whole was surrounded by two high barbed-wire fences, with sentries walking between them. The prisoners received a bullying reception in order to cow them down, and thirty of them had to have a bath in two small tubs of lukewarm water. It was December, but all their woollen underclothing was taken away from them. The three then refused to obey an order, and were put into solitary confinement, with bread and

[1] Published by George Allen & Unwin, Ltd.

water, wearing figure of eight handcuffs for about twelve hours a day. Their food was eight ounces of dry bread at seven in the morning, with water, and the same at five in the evening. The cells were seven feet square, and the iron walls were dripping with frost. Ballantyne writes (quoted from *Armageddon or Calvary*) :

" During the first morning I sat down on the floor to rest my legs, but I rapidly became so cold and stiff that without the help of my hands I had the greatest difficulty in getting on my feet again. This was a lesson to me, and during the remainder of my punishment I walked from corner to corner of my cell, three short strides each way, for the full twelve hours each day. My arms and shoulders ached almost intolerably, and became so numbed with cold that when the handcuffs were removed they hung powerless at my sides. For weeks and weeks afterwards I felt the effect of this punishment in my arms.

" This much was the authorised punishment, but during the time that a prisoner was in the cells he was in the hands of the warder in charge, who administered by kicks and blows such punishments as he deemed necessary for the ' maintenance of good order and discipline in the cells.' Generally, when a prisoner was sent to the cells for punishment he was first taken into a cell, stripped naked, sometimes handcuffed ; then the warder would proceed to administer a sound thrashing, using both his hands and feet, one warder, during his turn in charge of the cells, going so far as to use a heavy leather belt. Then, when the prisoner was beginning to get groggy, buckets of freezing cold water would be thrown over him to revive him, and finally he would be given a bucket and cloth and be told to dry up his cell before he would be given back his clothes. Often the bumps and thuds of the poor prisoner against the iron walls and his yells and cries for mercy could be heard all over the compound.

" The next form of punishment we experienced was shot drill. This is an old form of punishment, abolished years ago in the Navy as being inhuman. It is still good enough, however, for our up-to-date military prisons. The shot in this case consisted of a round bag of about nine inches in diameter, filled with sand, and supposed to weigh twenty-eight pounds;

although when the sand became wet it was usually heavier. To do the drill the prisoner stands with the shot between his feet. The warder stands with a whistle, and in time to his blasts the prisoner first bends down, picks up the shot, and balances it on the palms of his hands in front of himself; then, on the next whistle, he takes three quick steps forward, on the following whistle placing it down between his feet again and standing up, straight; then down, up, three paces forward, down; and so on for perhaps an hour, with only one or two short rests of a few minutes. Each movement has to be made distinctly and sharply, and the warder's whistle is generally a bit ahead each time, so that the prisoner has to go his hardest in order to keep up. It is, in fact, just an ingenious device to tax absolutely the man's strength to the utmost. The effect, I found, was to make me horribly giddy and to produce terrible pains in my back and forearms. This punishment was often given in conjunction with No. 1 Field Punishment.

"The prisoner sentenced to No. 1 Field Punishment was put with his back to a post and his hands handcuffed behind the post, and he was held practically immovable by three straps, one around his chest, another around his knees, and the other around his ankles. I have seen men kept thus in driving snow and sleet for two hours, and when released they could scarcely stand. They would then almost immediately be put on to shot drill 'to loosen their joints.'"

* * *

At the end of 1916, the question of man-power having become acute, a Labour Corps was created. It consisted of men unfit for actual duty in the line, who could carry out what were vaguely described as "garrison duties" in the back areas, thus releasing fighting troops.

THE LABOUR CORPS

From Chorus to Adventurers.[1]

By Roger Pocock

It was just after Christmas, 1916, that I was ordered to report at Taunton, where I found myself to be one of four

[1] Published by John Lane, the Bodley Head, Ltd.

platoon commanders, mobilising a Labour Company. When we had worked our heads off for three days, the Officer Commanding turned up and was turned down. So I was given the command, my Captaincy, and France.

For young and able-bodied men it was their right to serve in the fighting line, but for us of the Labour Corps, the aged, the disabled, the wreckage of the army and of the nation, it was a privilege to be allowed within the danger areas. The coloured men of the Labour Corps were young, with thrice our strength, but they were not permitted as we were within the range of shells. Almost every man in my five hundred had been disabled, or claimed some mortal disease and gloried in it. We were an amazing mixture of volunteers up to seventy years of age, of conscripts drawn from sedentary life, of Jews from the slums, and gipsies from the highways, roughs, tramps, company directors, public entertainers, pavement artists, navvies, rich, poor, destitute, but all of us alike, rated unfit. Nobody as yet seems to have thought it worth while to tell the story of the dregs of England put to the test of war.

The parade was not so bad, the marching fairly good, the entraining free from muddle, there were no absentees. Crossing from Southampton to Boulogne, the weather being rather rough, men were perhaps too sea-sick to care about mines or torpedoes. We did not like the Base Wallahs at Boulogne, with plenty of decorations and no manners, but all went well in the night-train to Hazebrouck, and in the morning we marched about three miles to a couple of farms assigned to us as a billet. I think it would have been still nicer if the decorated Base Wallahs had mentioned to the Second Army that we might need food, fuel, blankets, while the snow drove through our barns before a yelling gale. In the morning we found two men dead.

On each highway I posted an officer, with orders to stop all army vehicles, plunder them, and turn them loose to report the robbery with the utmost possible speed. Meanwhile, I tramped through the drifts to Hazebrouck, found a telephone, and made its ears burn with the whole vocabulary of the Wild West. Would the Authorities send rations, or should I slaughter cows to feed my men? What with my perfect frankness and one or two highway robberies, we got fuel that morning, rations in the afternoon, indignant Staff Officers in the evening, and the next day a medical inspection which invalided a score of men to Blighty. Then transport arrived in force, and we were carried to the finest camp in Flanders. It was a prisoner-of-war camp evacuated in haste, because the German Government objected to its nationals being under shell-fire, and threatened reprisals upon British captives. We did not mind the shells which screamed overhead, addressed to Poperinghe, but we did like the hot baths, the comfortable stoves, the luxurious rations, and most of all the kindness of Captain Wallace, the Staff Officer in charge of our affairs. We had left behind us the areas of harsh discourtesy.

Our work was unloading trains, building light railways, or mending roads which shells had made untidy; and steadily our invalids gained in strength from outdoor living, good food, and moderate labour. I am told that under gusts of shell-fire the Chinese and Negro Companies had panicked so badly that they had to be withdrawn; but our men would walk to the nearest cover, smoke cigarettes, and watch the shelling with interest while they rested. The spell improved their work; but of much greater value was their interest in the drum-fire, in the movements of troops, in the aerial dog-fights overhead, in the burning of kite balloons and parachute descents, but most especially in the processions of German prisoners, to whom they would give the whole of their cigarettes. Interest in the army led to pride in the Service, eagerness to help, a sporting rivalry between platoons, and the discovery that the 178th Labour Company was not to be beaten by any sort of unit in the field.

When a strange Staff Officer came to inspect our camp with a view to taking it over for a General, I had grave misgivings, realised when I received a Movement Order. "At noon, your unit will move to M36b48, where a Guide will meet you at 2 p.m., conducting you to your destination. Acknowledge." The point of the joke was that the number of the map sheet was not mentioned, nor had I any maps, nor had the order arrived until three hours after my time of departure. I took that as a test, and sent off my three officers at the double to beg, to borrow, or if possible to steal maps while the men had their dinner. So that is how we found M36b48, and were conducted to Toronto Camp. The place was famous for rats. They went catting, and got my cat. They bit the sergeant-major's ear, an act of unheard-of insolence. The men tried poison gas, and smoked out the officers' mess while we sat at dinner. I used to ask all adjacent Staff Officers and even mere unit commanders, to my ratting parties. But that reminds me of the mess at dinner on an evening of steady downpour, when I heard a nightingale singing in the rain. That was unusual, but when a skylark followed I sent an officer to make inquiries about an event not foreshadowed in King's Regulations. In due course it was reported that Private So-and-so, who was So-and-so the eminent Bird Impersonator, was perched on a waggon, giving his entertainment.

* * *

Partly as a result of the Battle of the Somme, the Germans retired during the winter to the skilfully prepared " Hindenburg " line. The retirement was carried out with great skill, and the Allied Command—possibly unable to understand the mentality of a general who was willing to sacrifice a few miles of worthless ground—showed needless and unnecessary caution in following up the retreating enemy.

ACCORDING TO PLAN
From *A Fatalist at War*.[1]
By Rudolf Binding
(Translated from the German by Ian F. D. Morrow.)

The withdrawal of the line from the hopeless positions on the Somme has been effected without loss. A fearful zone of deliberately devastated territory has been left as a barrier between us and the enemy. The expulsion of the inhabitants from their little towns and villages was a heart-rending business, more ghastly than murder. The thought that their houses and homes, with all that they had tended through a

[1] Published by George Allen & Unwin, Ltd.

lifetime, were to be destroyed drove many of them out of their wits. The priest of the little place where I was billeted had a stroke at the news. Women hurled themselves out of the windows, and among the disorderly processions of refugees streaming to the rear one could see cases for whom this fate was as good as death.

It is an eternal shame for England that this operation cost us no losses. It was a safe calculation to assume that the immensity of the facts would leave Sir Douglas Haig entirely without inspiration. For four days and four nights the troops were passing through our village. For hours the overloaded motor-lorries thundered through in a cloud of fumes, until the cobble stones were reduced to a sort of moraine of irregular rubble. A retreat is a fearfully costly business; that no lives were lost this time is really great.

What does this Russian revolution mean? I take it that the Tsar has driven so deep into the mud that even a new driver will take some time to get out again. It is extraordinary how long a nation will allow itself to be misgoverned.

. . . . . .

I have already written about the result of the withdrawal of the Somme Army to the Siegfried Line (sounds uncommonly like the theatre!). Although we can flatter ourselves on the helplessness of the English, our own becomes now unpleasantly apparent. Our troops have had no successes; everybody wanted to get away as quick as possible; they were not going to risk fighting. In St.-Pierre-Vaast Wood, according to the latest reports, there seems to have been a sort of tacit understanding between our people and the Scottish: " Set no traps for us and we'll let you out." Although our troops knew the ground, no prisoners were taken (with a few exceptions). It was thought that there would be plenty. Once again, as formerly in Flanders, we should have had a cavalry brigade on our flank. When it arrived it was much too late (not from any fault of its commanders). The English had cavalry on the spot at once, and the day before yesterday our G.O.C. and one of the A.D.C.'s nearly rode into them and got captured. Unfortunately I was not there.

The English speak of an enthusiastic reception by the inhabitants, but that only means about twenty thousand old women and cripples who had been left concentrated at one or two points. All the rest of the inhabitants, who were transportable and whose services might have been useful to the enemy on the spot, were evacuated. So the shouts of joy must have been on rather a cracked note, and there cannot have been many fair maidens to welcome the victors.

In the meantime there is no sign of the end.

* * *

THE Allies were massing troops for a great offensive in 1917, and reinforcements were being hurried overseas in everincreasing numbers.

THE BASE CAMP

From *War is War*.[1]

By Ex-Private X

The base camp was close to Harfleur, and we started on the march through the rain, not quite in the footsteps of Henry the Fifth, for, of course, Captain Jinks got himself lost. " Follow the tram-lines and they'll lead you home " is not true of the environments of Le Havre, for the tram-lines lead everywhere. For some reason we were not expected to sing —perhaps because Captain Jinks realised that we were now in France and had a theory that the Germans might hear us. It was as well, because nobody wanted to. Wet through, tired, hungry and utterly fed up we reached the camp at about half-past three in the morning.

Anybody knowing the army will guess at once what happened there. We were not expected. There was no accommodation for us. My suggestion that we should return home was coldly received by the magnificent base-wallah sergeant who had been dug out of his bunk to come and look at us. We were herded into a Black Hole of Calcutta, which they had the nerve to call a " reception hut," and remained there until half-past five, when we were harried into some wet bell tents on a greasy slope—sixteen or so to each tent.

[1] Published by Victor Gollancz, Ltd.

It's funny how experience changes one's point of view. Cold, sodden, hungry, sleepless and already home-sick, we thought we could never be more miserable. Yet this was heaven to what most of us went through later. It was no use trying to go to sleep, for réveillé was at six, and although nobody took the least notice of us for the next three hours we had to stand by our tents until somebody did.

At about nine o'clock we were called on parade for breakfast and conducted to a so-called mess hut. We had cheered up a little, but as soon as we were inside our faces fell. I forget what was offered us to eat, but I know it was quite uneatable. The tea was cold and about as foul as the cooks could brew it. And our bread ration—our half a loaf of white bread a day, ha ! ha !—consisted of a small handful of crumbs, bread and biscuit, tossed into the top parts of our mess-tins by a filthy little swine of an orderly with dirty fingers.

Looking back across the years, and a great deal mellowed by time, I still say that those who were responsible for the administration of the base camps in France should be hanged as high as Haman. Rations were always shortest where there was no excuse for a shortage, and cooking was always at its worst where there was every appliance to hand. Moreover, the " permanent base " people of all ranks were indeed permanently base. The unofficial motto of the Army, " — you, Jack, I'm all right ! " was screamed at one on every hand.

I gave up trying to count the decayed dug-out old colonels who ought to have died in their beds years since. There they were, purple, alcoholic, pompous, over-fed, strutting and preening, getting in everybody's way and doing nothing except eat a good man's food and draw a good man's money. The N.C.O.'s were futile, brazen-voiced asses, clinging to their jobs as drowning men are supposed to cling to straws. An N.C.O. of that particular type could often get a job at the base and bully the poor fools of better men who were going up the line to die for him. The rank and file consisted largely of professional footballers, pugilists and other athletes who were naturally too delicate to endure life in the trenches. But I will say as little as possible about the base because the memory of it still makes me angry.

HORSES

From *All Quiet on the Western Front*.[1]
By Erich Maria Remarque
(Translated from the German by A. W. Wheen.)

Things become quieter, but the cries do not cease. "What's up, Albert?" I ask.

"A couple of columns over there have got it in the neck."

The cries continue. It is not men, they could not cry so terribly.

"Wounded horses," says Kat.

It's unendurable. It is the moaning of the world, it is the martyred creation, wild with anguish, filled with terror, and groaning.

We are pale. Detering stands up. "God! For God's sake! Shoot them!"

He is a farmer and very fond of horses. It gets under his skin. Then as if deliberately the fire dies down again. The screaming of the beasts becomes louder. One can no longer distinguish whence in this now quiet, silvery landscape it comes; ghostly, invisible, it is everywhere, between heaven and earth it rolls on immeasurably. Detering raves and yells out: "Shoot them! Shoot them, can't you? Damn you again!"

"They must look after the men first," says Kat quietly.

We stand up and try to see where it is. If we could only see the animals we should be able to endure it better. Müller has a pair of glasses. We see a dark group, bearers with stretchers, and larger black clumps moving about. Those are the wounded horses. But not all of them. Some gallop away in the distance, fall down, and then run on farther. The belly of one is ripped open, the guts trail out. He becomes tangled in them and falls, then he stands up again.

Detering raises his gun and aims. Kat hits it up in the air. "Are you mad——?"

Detering trembles and throws his rifle on the ground.

We sit down and hold our ears. But this appalling noise, these groans and screams penetrate, they penetrate everywhere.

[1] Published by G. P. Putnam's Sons.

We can bear almost anything. But now the sweat breaks out on us. We must get up and run, no matter where, but where these cries can no longer be heard. And it is not men, only horses.

From the dark group stretchers move off again. Then single shots crack out. The black heap is convulsed and becomes thinner. At last! But still it is not the end. The men cannot overtake the wounded beasts which fly in their pain, their wide-open mouths full of anguish. One of the men goes down on his knee, a shot—one horse drops—another. The last one props himself on his forelegs and drags himself round in a circle like a merry-go-round; squatting, it drags round in circles on its stiffened forelegs, apparently its back is broken. The soldier runs up and shoots it. Slowly, humbly, it sinks to the ground.

We take our hands from our ears. The cries are silenced. Only a long-drawn dying sigh still hangs on the air.

Then again only the rockets, the singing of the shells, and the stars—and they shine out wonderfully.

Detering walks up and down cursing. " Like to know what harm they've done." He returns to it once again. His voice is agitated, it sounds almost dignified as he says : " I tell you it is the vilest baseness to use horses in the war."

* * *

THE spring operations, which, like all their predecessors, were designed to break through the German front, were under the control of the new French commander, Nivelle. Preceding a French attack on a tremendous scale in Champagne, the British launched a subsidiary assault in front of that quaint old city of Spanish Flanders, Arras.

ARRAS

From Unhappy Far-off Things.[1]
BY LORD DUNSANY

On the great steps of Arras Cathedral I saw a procession, in silence, standing still.

[1] Published by Elkin Mathews.

ARRAS

They were in orderly and perfect lines, stirring or swaying slightly. Sometimes they bent their heads, sometimes two leaned together, but for the most part they were motionless. It was the time when the fashion is just changing, and some were newly all in shining yellow, while others still wore green.

I went up the steps amongst them, the only human thing, for men and women worship no more in Arras Cathedral, and the trees have come instead; little humble things, all less than four years old, in great numbers thronging the steps processionally, and growing in perfect rows just where step meets step. They have come to Arras with the wind and the rain; which enter the aisles together whenever they will, and go wherever man went; they have such a reverent air, the young limes on the three flights of steps, that you would say they did not know that Arras Cathedral was fallen on evil days, that they did not know they looked on ruin and vast disaster, but thought that these great walls open to stars and sun were the natural and fitting place for the worship of little weeds.

Behind them the shattered houses of Arras seemed to cluster about the cathedral as, one might fancy easily, hurt and frightened children, so wistful are their gaping windows and old grey empty gables, so melancholy and puzzled. They are more like a little old people come upon trouble, gazing at their great elder companion and not knowing what to do.

But the facts of Arras are sadder than a poet's most tragic fancies. In the western front of Arras Cathedral stand eight pillars rising from the ground; above them stood four more. Of the four upper pillars the two on the left are gone, swept away by shells from the north: and a shell has passed through the neck of one of the two that is left, just as a bullet might go through a daffodil's stem.

The left-hand corner of that western wall has been caught from the north by some tremendous shell which has torn the whole corner down in a mound of stone: and still the walls have stood.

I went in through the western doorway. All along the nave lay a long heap of white stones, with grass and weeds on the top, and a little trodden path over the grass and weeds. This is all that remained of the roof of Arras Cathedral and of any chairs or pews there may have been in the nave, or anything that may have hung above them. It was all down but one slender arch that crossed the nave just at the transept; it stood out against the sky, and all who saw it wondered how it stood.

In the southern aisle panes of green glass, in twisted frame of lead, here and there lingered, like lonely leaves on an apple tree after a hailstorm in spring. The aisles still had their roofs over them which those stout old walls held up in spite of all.

Where the nave joins the transept the ruin is most enormous. Perhaps there was more to bring down there, so the Germans brought it down: there may have been a tower there for all I know, or a spire.

I stood on the heap and looked towards the altar. To my left all was ruin. To my right two old saints in stone stood by the southern door. The door had been forced open long ago and stood as it was opened, partly broken. A great round hole gaped in the ground outside, it was this that had opened the door.

Just beyond the big heap, on the left of the chancel, stood something made of wood, which almost certainly had been the organ.

As I looked at these things there passed through the desolate sanctuaries, and down an aisle past pillars pitted with shrapnel, a sad old woman, sad even for a woman of Northeast France. She seemed to be looking after the moulds and stones that had once been the cathedral: perhaps she had once been the bishop's servant, or the wife of one of the vergers; she only remained of all who had been there in other days, she and the pigeons and jackdaws. I spoke to her. All Arras, she said, was ruined. The great cathedral was ruined, her own family were ruined utterly, and she pointed to where the sad houses gazed from forlorn dead windows.

* * *

AFTER initial successes the British Army, in order to relieve pressure on the French, continued a series of bitter and costly attacks.

ATTRITION

From *Death of a Hero*.[1]

By Richard Aldington

The inner gas-curtain was lifted, and Evans' servant stumbled in, taking off his mask.

"Report at once, fighting order, Winterbourne!"

Winterbourne hurriedly put on his boots and puttees, struggled into his equipment, snapped on his mask and jog-trotted over to the officers' cellar, through the now familiar hail of gas shells. He was amazed and distressed, and ashamed to find how much his flesh instinctively shrank when a shell dropped close at hand, how great an effort he now needed to refrain from ducking or cowering. He raged at himself, called himself coward, poltroon, sissy, anything abusive he could think of. But still his body instinctively shrank. He had passed into the final period of war strain, when even an air-raid became a terror.

Evans was laboriously writing. The large cellar looked very cellar-like and empty, with one man in place of the six who had lived there less than a fortnight before.

"You know Mr. Thompson's killed?"

"Yes, sir. Henderson told me."

"I can't carry on as a company by myself with less than forty available men." Evans spoke bitterly. "There's a chit from Division complaining that we are doing far less work than a month ago. They don't seem to know there's been a battle and that we're worn out and reduced to a third our strength!"

He was silent, re-read his despatch, folded it, and handed it to Winterbourne.

"Take this down to Battalion Headquarters. I've marked it Special Urgency. Make them get the colonel up if he's

[1] Published by Chatto & Windus.

asleep. If he questions you, tell him our position. I haven't seen him for three weeks. And refuse to leave without an answer."

"Very good, sir."

"And, Winterbourne."

"Sir?"

"There's another chit here somewhere urging us to get two volunteers for infantry commissions in each company. Henderson's going—he's a stout little tyke. The other volunteers are that filthy cook's mate and the sanitary man. Idiotic. I won't recommend them. But I want you to volunteer. Will you?"

Winterbourne hesitated. He didn't want the responsibility; it was contrary to his notion that he ought to stay in the ranks and in the line, take the worst and humblest jobs, share the common fate of common men. But then, he had consented to be a runner. And then, he was sorely tempted. It meant several months in England; it meant seeing Fanny and Elizabeth again; it meant a respite. He was amazed to find that he didn't want to leave Evans, and suddenly saw that what he had done in the past months had been chiefly done from personal attachment to a rather common and ignorant man of the kind he most despised, the grown-up public school boy.

"What are you hesitating about?"

"Well, sir," said Winterbourne whimsically, "I was wondering how you'd get on without me."

"xxxxxxxxxx!" said Evans. "Besides, at this rate I shan't last much longer. Now, shall I put your name down?"

"Yes, sir."

He afterwards regretted that "Yes."

Evans's sharp note brought an abrupt change in their lives. They exchanged places with one of the other Pioneer companies in a quieter section of the line. Evans marched his forty men down as one platoon, and they passed successively the four platoons of the relieving company. The men exchanged ironical jibes as they passed.

Their new quarters were a great improvement. They were joined by a captain, who took nominal command, and two subalterns. But no men. There appeared to be no men available. They lived in shelters and dug-outs in the reserve line. Winterbourne, Henderson, and two other runners lived in a two-foot shelter just outside the officers' dug-out. Winterbourne was now officially company runner. He lived one fortnight in the line, and one at battalion H.Q. The sacking bed at H.Q., the comparative absence of shelling, the better food, the rest, made it seem like paradise. He did not know that his application for a commission had been passed at once, and that he was being looked after.

Two days after they got to their new quarters, in the line, Evans's servant poked his head excitedly into the runners' shelter.

"Winterbourne!"

"Yes."

"You're to come at once. Mr. Evans is sick."

"Sick!"

Winterbourne found Evans leaning against the side of the trench, a ghastly green pallor on his face.

"Whatever's the matter, sir?"

"Gas. I've swallowed too much of the beastly stuff. I can't stand it any longer. I'm going to the dressing station."

"Shall I get a stretcher, sir?"

"No, damn it, I'll walk down. I can still stand. Take my pack and come along."

Every few yards Evans had to stop and lean against the trench wall. He heaved, but did not vomit. Winterbourne offered his arm, but he wouldn't take it. They passed two corpses, rather horribly mutilated, lying on stretchers at the end of the communication trench. Neither said anything, but Evans was thinking: "Well, gas is better than that," and Winterbourne thought: "How long will it be before someone puts me there?"

He finally got Evans to the dressing station, supporting him with his right arm. They shook hands outside.

"You'll get your commission, Winterbourne."

"Thanks. Are you all right, sir? Shall I come down with you further?"

"No; go back, and report that you left me here."

"Very good, sir."
They shook hands again.
"Well, good-bye, old man ; best of luck to you."
"Good-bye, sir, good-bye."
He never saw Evans again.

* * *

The first structure to collapse under the colossal strain of the War was the jerry-built Russian Tsardom. The first Republic under Kerensky attempted to continue the War against Germany, but on the advent of Lenin Russia, for all practical purposes, dropped out of the conflict. The Russian troops mutinied *en masse* and returned to their homes.

RUSSIA IN REVOLUTION—THE GERMAN REASONING

From *The German Secret Service*.[1]

By Colonel W. Nicolai

It was, therefore, under the Kerenski Government that an anti-German propaganda first began among the Russian troops. For this service such old and well-known revolutionaries as Plechanow, Amphitheatrow, and the notorious Breschko-Breschkowskaja offered themselves. In speech and in writings they worked among the troops in favour of the continuation of the War. Everyone who took the word "Peace" on his lips was at once stamped as a German agent. Nothing was said, of course, about the shedding of more Russian blood for foreign aims. For six weeks after the revolution the army was formally in the hands of the new Government, and the prisoners we took showed a strong anti-German bias. Their belief in victory was roused afresh. While these developments were taking place we entered into negotiations with numerous Russian commanders, including the calvary general, Dragomirow, commander-in-chief on the North Front. Our aim was to stop the progress of these

[1] Published by Stanley Paul & Co., Ltd.

developments, but our efforts led to no result. French propaganda had triumphed.

The prospects of a military victory, however, had not improved. The Kerenski Government had reached power by means and with aims which, from the Russian national standpoint, could only be regarded as reprehensible, and its fall was to be foreseen. As successors, the Bolshevists were lying in wait. Their leader, Lenin, was in Switzerland. After the fall of the Tsar's Government, which had exiled him, he was free to return to Russia. He had the choice of two ways. One, through Entente countries, was, however, barred. He turned to the Germans. The German Foreign Office favoured his travelling through Germany and Russia because it hoped to create difficulties for the anti-German Kerenski Government. At first, however, the German High Command was against the idea, but later agreed, on the condition that Lenin and his companions should not be given an opportunity for propaganda on their way through Germany. Its co-operation in the matter was limited, therefore, to providing anti espionage agents to see that Lenin was kept isolated while in Germany, and to accompany him on his journey through the country.

* * *

RUSSIA IN REVOLUTION—THE JOURNEY OF LENIN

From *Memories of Lenin*.[1]

By NADEZHDA K. KRUPSKAYA

The defensists raised a hullabaloo about the Bolsheviks travelling through Germany. Of course, in giving us permission to travel, the German Government was under the impression that revolution was a terrible disaster for a country and thought that by allowing *émigré* internationalists to pass through to their native country they would help to spread this "disaster" in Russia. The Bolsheviks were very little concerned with what the *bourgeois* German Government thought. They considered it their duty to spread revolutionary propaganda

[1] Published by Martin Lawrence.

in Russia and set as the aim of their activities the achievement of the victorious proletarian revolution. They knew that the defensists would throw mud at them, but they knew also that the masses would finally follow their lead. On March 27th the Bolsheviks alone risked the route through Germany, but a month later, more than two hundred emigrants, including Martov and other Mensheviks, followed the same route.

In boarding the train, no questions were asked about the baggage and passports. Ilyich kept entirely to himself, his thoughts were in Russia. *En route*, the conversation was mainly trivial, Robert's cheerful voice could be heard through the whole car. He particularly liked Sokolnikov and did not want to talk to the women. The Germans tried to show us that they had plenty of everything, the cook prepared exceptionally big meals, to which our emigrant fraternity were not greatly accustomed. Through the car window we noticed a surprising absence of adult men; some women, boys and girls in their teens and children could be seen at the stations, on the fields and city streets. I was often reminded of this picture during the first days in Petrograd, where I was surprised that the street cars were so crowded with soldiers.

On arrival in Berlin our train was shunted on to a siding. Near Berlin several German Social-Democrats entered a special compartment. No one of our people spoke to them, except Robert, who looked into their compartment and asked in French: " What does the conductor do ? " I do not know whether the Germans answered Robert, but I do know that they were not able to put the questions they wanted to go to the Bolsheviks. On March 31st we arrived in Sweden. At Stockholm we were met by the Swedish Social-Democratic deputies, Lindhagen, Carlson, Ström, Ture Nerman and others. A red flag was hung up in the waiting-room and a meeting was held. I remember little of Stockholm; all thoughts were in Russia. The Russian Provisional Government did not permit Fritz Platten and Radek to enter Russia, but did not dare to stop the Bolsheviks. From Sweden we crossed to Finland in small Finnish sledges. Everything was already familiar and dear to us—the wretched third-class cars, the Russian soldiers. It was terribly good. It was not long before Robert was in the arms of an elderly soldier, clasping his neck with his small arms, chattering to him in French and eating Easter cheese with which the soldier fed him. Our people were huddled against the windows. The station platforms we passed were crowded with soldiers. Usyevich leaned out of the window and shouted: " Long live the world revolution! " The soldiers looked at him puzzled. A pale-faced lieutenant passed us a few times, and when Ilyich and I went into a nearby empty car, he sat down beside Ilyich and spoke to him. The lieutenant was a defensist, and they started an argument. Ilyich put his point of view—he, too, was dreadfully pale. Soldiers began squeezing into the car until there was no room to move. The soldiers stood on the benches so as the better to see and hear the one who was speaking so convincingly against the predatory war. And as the minutes passed they became more attentive and their faces became more tense.

Maria Ilyinishna, Shlyapnikov, Stahl and other comrades and women workers met us at Beloostrov. Stahl urged me to say a few words of greeting to the women workers, but all words had left me, I could say nothing. Ilyich asked the comrades who sat with us if we would be arrested on our arrival; they smiled. Soon we arrived in Petrograd.

The Petrograd masses, workers, soldiers and sailors came to meet their leader. Among the many close comrades there, was Chugurin—a student at the Longjumeau school, his face wet with tears, wearing a wide red sash across his shoulder. There was a sea of people all around.

Those who have not lived through the revolution cannot imagine its grand, solemn beauty. Red banners, a guard of honour of Kronstadt sailors, searchlights from the Fortress of Peter and Paul illuminating the road from the Finland station to the Kshesinsky Mansion,[1] armoured cars, a chain of working men and women guarding the road.

Chkheidze and Skobelev met us at the Finland station as the official representatives of the Petrograd Soviet of Workers' and Soldiers' Deputies. The comrades led Ilyich to the Tsar's

[1] The former residence of the Tsar's mistress, the ballet dancer Kshesinskaya. The mansion became the headquarters of the Bolshevik Party.—Ed.

rest-room where Chkheidze and Skobelev were. When Ilyich came out on the platform a captain came to him and, standing at attention, reported something. Ilyich, a little taken aback with surprise, saluted. Ilyich and all our emigrant fraternity were led past a guard of honour which was on the platform. Ilyich stood on an armoured car, the rest were seated in automobiles and thus we drove to Kshesinsky Mansion. " Long live the Socialist world revolution ! " Ilyich called out to the huge crowd of many thousands surrounding us.

Ilyich sensed the beginning of this revolution in every fibre of his body.

* * *

RUSSIA IN REVOLUTION—MUTINY
From *A Soldier's Note-Book*, 1914–1918.[1]
By General A. A. Brussilov

In any case my front remained staunch until my departure for Mogilev, and there was not a single case of murder of officers, which is more than other fronts could say. Further, I can say that the men trusted me and believed that I was the soldiers' friend and would not betray them. Accordingly, when, as occasionally happened, some division or other, or some army corps, declared that they would not remain any longer at the front but were going home, drove out their officers, and threatened to kill any general who dared to show himself among them, I went straight off to these disaffected troops, and they greeted me enthusiastically, listened to my reproaches, and promised to take back the officers they had turned out and obey them, and not to leave their posts, but to defend them if the enemy attacked. But I never succeeded in getting them to promise to advance or to attack the enemy positions. I was always met by the words " No annexations and no reparations," and one could get no further, for this was only an excuse for avoiding a question they did not wish to discuss. I could understand the attitude of the Bolsheviks when they preached " Down with the War ! Peace at once

[1] Published by MacMillan & Co., Ltd.

and at any price!"; but I could not comprehend the tactics of the Social Revolutionaries and the Mensheviks, who on the one hand wished to destroy the army for fear of a counter-revolution—which does not say very much for their understanding of the mentality of the troops and of the masses—and on the other wished to carry the War to a successful conclusion. It was for this reason that in the spring of 1917 I invited Kerenski, then Minister of War, to visit the South-West front and support at meetings, in the name of the Petrograd Soviet of Workers' and Soldiers' Deputies, the movement in favour of an offensive. The fact is that at this period the bulk of the troops refused to recognise the Imperial Duma, considering it opposed to their interests, whereas they would still, more or less, listen to the Workers' and Soldiers' Soviet. Sokolov, the author of the accursed *Prikaz No. 1*, accompanied him.

In May the troops on all the fronts began definitely to refuse to obey orders, and no steps could be taken to stop them. Even the Commissars they themselves had appointed were only given a hearing when they were in agreement with the men; if they took any other line, the men refused to listen to them. For example, the VII Siberian Corps, which had been taken out of the line for a rest in the rear, flatly refused to return to the front when their time was up. They told Boris Savinkov, the Commissar of this Army Corps, that they wanted to go and rest further back at Kiev, and all his harangues and threats could not dissuade them, for this was only an excuse based on reluctance to continue fighting. There were numbers of similar cases on all the fronts. At the time when Kerenski went over the front, he was warmly welcomed almost everywhere, and various promises were given him; but when it came to carrying them out, the men, after capturing the enemy trenches, came back the next day of their own accord, saying that since they wished for neither annexations nor reparations, it was no use bothering about a victorious finish to the War, and that consequently they were returning to their old positions. Then when the enemy attacked our troops they left their lines without resisting and retreated. It is obvious that both Kerenski and the Soviet of Workers' and Soldiers' Deputies had also for the moment lost all control over the mass of the troops, and that we were hastening towards anarchy, in spite of the feeble efforts of the powerless Provisional Government; to tell the truth, the Government did not really know itself what it wanted.

* * *

As a preliminary to the main assault planned by the British for the autumn of 1917, an ingenious siege operation was executed at the Messines Ridge, captured at small cost following the explosion of nineteen great mines!

THE CRATER
From *The Brown Brethren*.[1]
By Patrick MacGill

At that moment the earth trembled like a wind-shaken leaf. The men rushed to the parapet and looked over. Out in front a great lump rose on the level like a whale breaking up from the sea, and a livid flash lit the world. The soldiers sank into cover, mute, pale, hesitating. The roar of an earthquake filled their ears, and a million flying fragments filled the sky. . . . An almost incoherent order passed along the trench, and on the right men clambered over the sandbags into the open field. . . . They had to take possession of the mine crater. Snogger, Bowdy Benners and Bubb were across and in the next minute they were conscious of many things. Bubb slipped twice in getting over the top, and panted wearily as he rushed towards the spot where the earth was lumped up black and raw. Other men rushed along at his side, shouting and yelling. Rifles were discharged wildly at no particular objective, and a group of voluble guns chorused in dizzy harmony.

The men clambered down the steep sides of the newly-formed valley, a hundred feet deep or more, and up the crest again, where it looked over the enemy's trenches. The

[1] Published by Herbert Jenkins, Ltd.

Germans were already advancing in extended order several hundred strong. The advance was done at the double through the lurid flashes of curtain fire which the English guns had opened. The Germans were falling, and the sight steadied the men somewhat, and they trained their rifles with precision and a certain amount of calmness on the oncomers.

The English guns were now speaking with furious vehemence and the shrapnel hissed at the grey forms which were still rising over the rim of the trench in front. Bubb and Benners lay down with their mates on the slope of the parapet and fired, a bit wildly perhaps, but it was impossible to miss. A machine-gun, already in position, swayed its snout from side to side, snapped viciously, and extracted its toll from the attackers.

They came forward, rushing wildly, their bayonets in air, their legs clumsily cutting off the distance between their trench and the crater. Many in the first line of attackers were falling and several were crawling back to their own lines on their bellies. Our bombers stood waiting, fingering their bombs nervously. The stench of explosives was suffocating. Several who were overcome with the gases dropped to the ground and rolled down the slope into the bottom of the pit. Bill Hurd stood up on the verge of the crater, where the wet, glistening machine-gun peeped forth.

"Steady, boys, steady!" he cried. "Take careful aim! Don't waste a round! Make every bullet tell! We'll beat them off! We'll beat them back, back, well back! Begorrah, we'll show them."

He looked enormous, standing there, shouting vehemently and waving his arms.

"Beat them back!" he yelled, repeating the same remark over and over again. His rifle lay against the rim of the crater; the bayonet, rusty and grim, peered over the top as if in waiting.

"Take good aim," he shouted, running along the rim of the crater. "Be sure of your min. . . . Don't get flurried. . . We'll bate thim back easily! . . . Keep cool and don't get flurried. If ye do you'll be damned unlucky. Don't get excited," he shouted. "If you do it won't be no good."

He held his peace then and Bubb looked round to see where he had sought cover. He was lying on his face and a very tiny red scar showed on his forehead.

Although the enemy advanced at the double, the time dragged slowly for the men on the parapet. They waited in agonised suspense for closer combat; somehow the firing seemed to have very little effect on the attackers. Hundreds fell and hundreds took the place of the fallen. The rim of the foemen's parapet was like the lip of a waterfall; the men came across in waves, got dashed to pieces, and waves followed only to meet with a similar fate. The successive lines of men were endless, eternal as a running brook.

The German first line drew nearer; the English could almost see the expressions of the men's faces; felt that the soul of the attackers was not in their work. It was impossible to miss them now. The attacking lines withered like waves on a beach. One man who came in front flung down his rifle, raced towards the crater with his hands in air and jumped on top of Bill Hurd's bayonet, a ludicrous fixture.

"Pull it out!" he yelled in agony, speaking in good English. "Pull it out, for Gott's sake!"

But there was not time to spare at that moment; the English were fighting to save their own skins. The German rolled down to the bottom of the crater with the bayonet on which he had sat still stuck in his body.

A second and a third wave of attack followed; but the concentrated fire of the defenders cut great gaps in the attackers' lines, which became merged one with the other, when half-way across. The men had no heart for further movement; they drew themselves to earth, and dug holes in the ground for safety. The English artillery fire prevented them from going back, the rifles would not allow them to come forward; they were caught between two fires.

Now and again an entrenching tool could be seen rising in air, and it was fired at. When a figure in grey moved, a questing bullet reminded it forcibly of the indiscretion. At times one would rise and walk round in an unconcerned and indifferent manner; probably he had gone insane, or perhaps the pain of a wound put death out of reckoning. The end was in all cases the same, the bullet found the man, and the ghastly fury of destruction held its sway.

On the right they reached the wires and the boys went out and met them; there the bayonet was at work.

They came up in big droves and some fumbled through. The defenders rushed out and gave fight. . . . An excited machine-gunner played for a minute on the crush of friend and foe. . . .

The Germans lost heart, retreated and were followed with bayonet, bludgeon and bomb. Tripping on the wires and stepping in flesh and blood, they went back, tramping on dead and wounded. The latter groaned piteously and shrieked for mercy.

The retreat became general, the front wave of attackers receded, those which followed stood still undecided. Here and there isolated parties made great fight, holding out until the last men fell. . . .

* * *

OCCUPIED FLANDERS
From *A Fatalist at War*.[1]

By RUDOLF BINDING

(Translated from the German by IAN F. D. MORROW.)

There exists somewhere a Food Supplies Board, but its ways are dark. We both of us seem to have been taking private lessons from it, for does it not look as if we were following one of its rules when you send me chocolates to the Front and I simultaneously send you chocolate from the Front? I thought I should be supplying a want; you thought the same; in the same way all over Germany potatoes are journeying for mysterious reasons from Hamburg to Breslau, while at the same time, for equally mysterious reasons, other potatoes are journeying from Breslau to Hamburg. This sort of thing is not a laughing matter. If they tried their very hardest human beings could not do more to obstruct.

Reason is everywhere being turned to folly. The Supreme

[1] Published by George Allen & Unwin, Ltd.

Army command is bound to economise. For this reason it offers prize money for valuable war material which is found and salvaged—particularly for gun ammunition, such as, for instance, gets left behind when a battery changes position in a hurry, or falls out of an overturned or wrecked limber at night, or gets lost on the way by transport going up to the front. This has resulted in the troops organising salvage parties. And now this is what happens. The salvage parties steal the gun ammunition from the forward positions for the sake of the prize money. Suppose that an ammunition column has hauled its shells painfully and laboriously through mud and slime under fire from the enemy to somewhere in the neighbourhood of a battery, and deposited them there as best it may; the next night the salvage parties haul them back again to the dumps at the peril of their lives, through the same mud and slime, and again under the enemy's fire, and so earn their prize money.

FLANDERS,
June 10th, 1917.

Once again I am quartered in the same dead-alive town, strangely and unnaturally waked to life by the War, in which I got my first impression of this country. Perhaps I shall end the War here, where I began it. The town has become poorer, the old curiosity shops have been bought out, and are now filled again with things that are old indeed but bad, for at all times people made both good stuff and bad stuff. The food supplies are scarce and dear, but, even so, much more plentiful than at home.

The English are supposed to be going to make some sort of an attack from the sea, either against Holland or Ostend. Our divisions were originally intended for an attack on the ill-fated Wytschaete salient, now only a vain dream. There, once again, we made the terrible mistake of collecting too many troops in a space which was threatened from both sides, without letting them attack at the right time. The English launched their offensive at the two extremes of the salient, leaving the point untouched. They were successful on both sides, and cut off everything which was gripped between the two claws of the great pincers. Fortunately as this was anticipated, it only amounted to a few hundreds, certainly not more than five thousand men.

In Flanders the country is now in the plenitude of its fertility. The wheat stands higher than a man, the pasture is fat, and the cattle are fat; in the meadows, which are cut up by narrow dykes, graze mares with foals of colossal proportions; everywhere the soil of the fields and gardens is carefully weeded and kept free from stones. How often have I described it all! It almost makes me melancholy to see it all; all this blue and silver, these people, these beasts. We have as our provisional headquarters a great baroque hall, with one hall after another, and room upon room. For years it has been sound asleep. Now it is being stirred out of its repose and is perhaps waking up; but its new tenants don't understand it; it would be better if it went to sleep again.

* * *

The battles classed by the British soldier under the general term of Passchendaele were fought under incredible conditions. Weeks of rain saturated the already water-logged ground, so that ordinary movement was impossible. The terrible conditions went further to breaking the spirit of the British Army than anything the Germans ever did, and never was British morale so low as after these battles in mud.

The abnormal conditions were not appreciated at G.H.Q. *After* the battles were over, the highly placed General Staff Officer responsible for their initiation and continuance visited the battle-front for the first time. When he saw the appalling state of the ground he exclaimed: " What! Do you mean to say that we sent men to fight in this ? " And when the junior officer who was showing him around assured him that he had, he sat down by the side of the track and burst into tears!

The sufferings of the German troops were almost as terrible as those of the British. Their defence was greatly aided, however, by belts of pill-boxes—concrete shelters of great strength, manned by machine-gunners—which replaced the normal trench system.

PASSCHENDAELE—THE MUD BATH

From *The Fifth Army*.[1]

By GENERAL SIR HUBERT GOUGH, G.C.M.G., K.C.B., K.C.V.O., Etc.

The Battles of Ypres, 1917, are, at first sight, the most unsatisfactory of the British major operations in France. It is true that they were not popular among the troops which took part in them. This feeling was not due to the casualties—which, though high, were by no means so grossly excessive as has sometimes been represented—but to the terrible conditions under which the battles were fought. Many pens have tried to describe the ghastly expanse of mud which covered this water-logged country, but few have been able to paint a picture sufficiently intense. Imagine a fertile countryside, dotted every few hundred yards with peasant farms and an occasional hamlet; water everywhere, for only an intricate system of small drainage canals relieved the land from the ever-present danger of flooding; a clay soil which the slightest dampness turned into clinging mud, and which, after rain, resembled a huge bog. Then imagine this same countryside battered, beaten, and torn by a torrent of shell and explosive—a torrent which had lasted without intermission for nearly three years. And then, following this merciless scourging, this same earth was blasted by a storm of steel such as no land in the world had yet witnessed—the soil shaken and reshaken, fields tossed into new and fantastic shapes, roads blotted out from the landscape, houses and hamlets pounded into dust so thoroughly that no man could point to where they had stood, and the intensive and essential drainage system utterly and irretrievably destroyed. This alone presents a battle-ground of tremendous difficulty. But then came the incessant rain. The broken earth became a fluid clay; the little brooks and tiny canals became formidable obstacles, and every shell-hole a dismal pond; hills and valleys alike were but waves and troughs of a gigantic sea of mud. Still the guns churned this

[1] Published by Hodder and Stoughton.

PASSCHENDAELE—MUD BATH

treacherous slime. Every day conditions grew worse. What had once been difficult now became impossible. The surplus water poured into the trenches as its natural outlet, and they became impassable for troops: nor was it possible to walk over the open field—men staggered warily over duckboard tracks. Wounded men falling headlong into the shell-holes were in danger of drowning. Mules slipped from the tracks and were often drowned in the giant shell-holes alongside. Guns sank till they became useless; rifles caked and would not fire: even food was tainted with the inevitable mud. No battle in history was ever fought under such conditions as that of Passchendaele.

Was it worth it? It is still too early to say. We, as contemporaries, can only pass opinions. It must be left to posterity to pronounce judgment. It was a temptation for the unfortunate actors to take a superficial view in those days, and even now critics can still follow that easy path. Three months' bitter fighting resulted in the capture of a few square miles of mud and some trifling ridges of no great tactical value, and these at the cost of over 200,000 casualties. Was Haig right, therefore, in fighting this battle?

It is of the greatest importance that the British people should cast aside this purely superficial outlook when viewing such important events as these. Haig's strategy in this attack was sound. The disadvantage of the lateness of the season could not have been avoided, but nevertheless he was entitled to expect normal weather for the rest of the " summer." Had he got it, both conditions and results would have been vastly different. Weather is becoming increasingly important in warfare. With the continuous development of scientific devices for use in war, with the complexity and delicacy of the mechanisms which are essential to a battle, good weather becomes the best friend a general can have. This tendency will probably become even more pronounced, and the meteorological expert may soon rank as a Senior Staff Officer of the highest importance.

* * *

PASSCHENDAELE—THE PILL-BOX

From *A Generation Missing*.[1]

By Carroll Carstairs

Our new company headquarters was an exceptionally large and powerfully built pill-box. A hole in its side made by a direct hit from a British heavy enabled one to measure the thickness of its walls—three to four feet in depth. The floor was uneven with fallen debris and masonry and the air was foul. Eaton was writing a requisition of some sort in his notebook. The pay sergeant had arrived about rations. The room was crowded with runners, orderlies, servants, stretcher-bearers and the sergeant-major. I observed them with a kind of expectancy as the first British shell, like tearing silk, came whizzing overhead. In a breathless second every gun in the crowded British area had opened fire. It was a signal for which the Boche was waiting, as shell after shell came crashing around us. Our pill-box, solid though it was, trembled like a frightened man when a shell landed with more than ordinary proximity. On and on it went, this demoniac uproar that sundered air particles and spun them into everlasting reverberations. The earth was splitting up—splitting its sides—what a joke! Blinding flash after flash lighted up the faces of the men, too appalled to be scared. The angry clang of metal struck against the exterior of the pill-box or whined through the air in an agony of search, while we waited for the shell that would send us to eternity. But hell itself can get out of breath, and there came a gradual let up.

Dawn showed no paler than the faces of officers and men.

With the morning light we found a German corpse in our pill-box half-buried in clay and mortar. Hence the terrible stench. With great difficulty he was dug up, and given as decent a burial outside as haste permitted.

Eaton and I went along slits that had now a welter of fresh shell-holes around them, while the company itself had miraculously escaped. The men gazed at us with white

[1] Published by William Heinemann, Ltd.

expressionless faces and I thought how like death a face became when utterly wearied out.

About four in the afternoon our artillery was hard at it again. Guns—guns—guns—the whole world was made up of them. Thunder cut up for cannon mouths, thunder at last free of the heavens and running wild over the earth—lightning, sneaking under the earth and kicking it full of holes. All night the earth shook and the air vibrated with the noise of guns and shells—English guns and German shells in an endless terrifying din of reiteration.

A direct hit on our pill-box rocked the place like a boat caught in the trough of the sea.

There was no sleep for anyone. Through the long hours the nightmare persisted until at 5.40 a.m. the division on our right went over the top to the tune of the most mighty cannonade conceivable, and my life reached a peak of auricular experience. It was at last the whole world crashing about our ears. Gun-fire had, at a moment, leaped into an intensity no human being could have realised without hearing. A veritable crescendo of sounds, so continuous as to merge and blend into a single annihilating roar, the roar of a train in a tunnel magnified a million-fold; only the rattle of the machine-gun barrage, like clocks gone mad, ticking out the end of time in a final breathless reckoning, rose above it, while the accelerating blasts of enemy shells added weight to the crowning catastrophe. One imagined the very air ripped and torn by the flight of numberless shells, the very sky to have become a tattered blue garment.

I went to the entrance of our pill-box to see what I could of the battle and never was spectator so thrilled, so awed. Beyond the enemy lines, behind the high dust of battle, colour stole shamefacedly into the sky; the rising sun appeared, a blurred and murky mass. The light of another day crept chill and faint over a scene too desolate for further destruction. Great clouds of smoke and dirt spouted into the air and drifted like a dirty morning mist along the horizon line. Showers of sparks, made by incendiary shells, burst like monster fire crackers, while enemy rockets, signalling that the attack had begun, shot into the sky, breaking from red into green lights, like dragon's eyes changing colour. Of troops I could see little. Specks too much the tone of the earth over which they were moving. For me the battle continued, a hurling and crashing of huge projectiles. . . .

After a little, orderlies appeared coming back at the double, while soon after zero the sky was dotted with our contact aeroplanes. One came down in our lines.

The very day, made restless by its predecessors, gave us no peace, and shelling kept up, heavy as ever, while a tour of the company's front revealed the fact that it had escaped the terrible bombardment of the night with one man killed and a man " buried."

All day the firing went on, until 6 p.m., when it turned again from scattered knocks into the prolonged, concerted bang of gun-fire—attack or counter-attack? But one heard nothing and knew nothing except what was happening to one's own company—and not always much of that.

* * *

PASSCHENDAELE—GAS
From *The Land-locked Lake*.[1]
By Lt.-Col. A. A. Hanbury-Sparrow

Scream—over—phut! Scream—over—phut! We know the sound well of those gas shells. They're pouring them by the hundred into the valley just behind, building up a concentration in the still night air. Suddenly Wheewh! Wheewh! Wheewh! Wheewh! A salvo of heavies straight into the middle of the concentration, breaking it up, blowing its deadly poisons over the acres, like a stroke of Death's scythe.

Creeping Death climbs the bank; its antennæ coil round the pill-box groping for the entrances. Sniff! Look out! Gas!

Masks on in the instant. We gaze at one another like goggle-eyed, imbecile frogs. Presently you look at your wrist-watch. It's barely half-past eight. What a night we're in for!

The gas-mask makes you feel only half a man. You can't think; the air you breathe has been filtered of all save a few

[1] Published by Arthur Barker, Ltd.

chemical substances. A man doesn't live on what passes through the filter, he merely exists. He gets the mentality of a wide-awake vegetable if one can conceive such an impossibility. Whatever be in the air that really gives vitality—cosmic rays and forces perhaps—all that is cut off in this purified atmosphere. Anyhow, you yourself were always miserable when you couldn't breathe through your nose, and the clip on the gas-mask prevents that. Better far one mouthful of the melinite-tainted corpse-stenched air outside than half a dozen of this filtered stuff.

You always felt this poison-gas was so mean and treacherous. It wasn't so much the harm it did to the body, which was always much over-estimated in the popular imagination, as the harm it did to the mind. A shell might make terrible wounds, but its burst was all over in an instant. It was a case of hit or miss which left no ill-will behind. But this harmless-looking, almost invisible, stuff would lie for days on end lurking in low places waiting for the unwary. It was the Devil's breath. It was Ahrimanic from the first velvety phut of the shell-burst to those corpse-like breaths that a man inhaled almost unawares. It lingered about out of control. When he fired it, man released an evil force that became free to bite friend or foe till such time as it died into the earth. Above all, it went against God-inspired conscience. In using it the user degraded himself, for war even more than peace should be inspired by moral law. The greater the power of the user the greater the need of restraint. Restraint is essentially something that must be perceived by the moral senses, for by the time the necessity of it is grasped by the intelligence the power to be controlled has gained a quasi-independent life of its own. Whether one takes sex, drink, machinery, or war, all need a restraint that must first be suggested by the conscience, for the intellect cannot at first perceive the necessity. War pushed to its logical conclusions—to gas and air bombing—means either race suicide or the tyranny of the dead hand of a hide-bound treaty. All things need restraint—even logic—even gas.

Slowly the gas clears. We remove our masks. Then it starts again in the valley. Scream—phut, scream—phut. " Is dinner ready ? " you shout. " Yes, sir," calls the mess corporal. "Then bring it in." We'd better eat it quickly before the gas comes again. So in it came, those fids of fried meat on the enamel plates, those boiled potatoes, the dish of tinned fruit, and the can of Ideal milk masquerading as cream. As a rule we fed like decent Christians, the comic batman and messman beloved of the stage hadn't got to the point of their joke before they were buzzed off back to duty. You wouldn't stand that kind of insubordinate impertinence. But to-night the meal is below standard. Conditions are absolutely impossible. Twice have we put on our gas-masks before the meat course is finished—the pill-box sustains another direct hit which jars over the fruit juice and puts out the candle—and within you and without you is the almost unbearable tension of tight suppressed fear that meets the food and curdles it before ever it reaches the end of the gullet.

Two signallers go out to repair the telephone line to brigade. Hardly are they back before it's cut in half in a dozen more places, and out they have to go again.

It's obvious the Boche are making a dead set at this pill-box. It was theirs once, it's ours now. They know its position to an inch, know its entrances are facing towards them, and—as they built it—presumably know how much of this treatment it will stand. Oh, but he's made it strong, as he has made them all strong. The ground is too wet to dig dug-outs as he did on the Somme. So he has taken a tip from Verdun and built these things of ferro-concrete. In a way he made them too good. His idea was to use them simply as dug-outs above ground. The moment the barrage lifted the troops were to rush out and man the trenches. That was his theory, and therefore he provided them with no loop-holes. The wall facing the English was solid blank. But because these dug-outs were so safe and our fire so terrifying his men wouldn't run out when the moment came and, unable to resist within the eyeless shelter, got captured. He had realised his mistake, and his latest orders had directed that all the new structures were to be loopholed for machine-guns. Of course, once they were loopholed his men would never have faced the music outside, and had it gone on the fight would have been an attack against mutually supporting machine-gun emplacements. How blockaded Germany found the concrete was a marvel. We never could.

Because their location was known and their entrances faced the wrong way, these pill-boxes were not as safe for us as for the Boche. But how we welcomed them! Despite all their disadvantages they were as oases in a desert, solid tussocks in a quagmire, termite heaps in a world of decaying slime. But how much hammering would they stand? Nobody knew. What were the chances of a shell finding the entrance? Too good to bear thinking about.

* * *

PASSCHENDAELE—SHELL-FIRE

From *A Subaltern's War*.[1]

By Charles Edmonds

Though the day had started well, it was to turn out the most wretched of my life. The three of us crouched happily enough in our circular pit, 5 feet in diameter, and dug it down till it was 5 feet deep. We talked of what people do talk of in such situations, " shop," the chance of relief, yesterday's adventures, to-day's expectations, details of food supply, and sometimes reminiscences. We knew there would be heavy shelling sooner or later, but felt disinclined to discuss that. One had a curious undefined superstition that to mention it might attract it.

As we were in full view of the enemy on the right front, along the valley of the Stroombeek, the movement of men in and near our position drew its reward. When the German gunners really settled down to their day's shooting they gave us their fullest attention. There was no drumfire, no hurricane barrage, but a steady, slow bombardment of the whole valley with heavies; all day the fire grew in intensity and accuracy; and occasionally the area was raked over with a finer shower of field-gun shells. We had nothing to do but to sit and listen for the roar of the 5·9's, lasting for five seconds each, perhaps twice a minute. One would be talking aimlessly of some unimportant thing when the warning would begin. The speaker's

[1] Published by Peter Davies, Ltd.

voice would check for an infinitesimal fraction of a second; then he would finish his sentence with a studied normality marvellously true to life. Everyone listened hard to the conversation, but with more than half an ear cocked in the direction of the enemy. If the shell were coming close, one would crouch down against the side of the pit, apparently as a mere perfunctory precaution, actually with delight that one could take cover unashamed. When the shell had burst in a smother of black smoke, and the clods and whining splinters had ceased to fall pattering around, one went on with the conversation.

It was a kind of round game, in which a man felt he had lost a point every time a grunt or a remark about the danger was fetched out of him.

Thorburn won easily; of course, he had been through nothing yet but a night in a safe, dry trench. Yet this trial might well have finished off a fresh man. The shells fell consistently among our men (who, however, were well scattered and in the deepest shell-holes); every other one would fling a shower of mud on to our helmets. About one in five or six would fall near enough to shake the parapet, blast its pungent fumes in our faces, and set every nerve in our bodies jangling. Wolfe came out in an unexpected light; he was a tall, pale, flabby medical student in spectacles, and until that day I had had but a poor opinion of him. Every time a shell fell near he proceeded to tell us that he had a very strong presentiment: nothing was going to hit him that day. He said it so often, with such conviction, and so ingenuously, that it cheered me wonderfully, even at the worst moments. He did nothing and seemed to care little, but was quite contented about himself.

I needed some cheering up. I had had very much worse times than either of the others, but cannot deceive myself, all the same; I never could stand shell-fire. I got into a thoroughly neurotic state during the day. Enduring a bombardment is the opportunity for that kind of nervous disease which made Dr. Johnson touch every post as he walked along Fleet Street. You think of absurd omens and fetishes to ward off the shell you hear coming. A strong inward feeling compels

PASSCHENDAELE—SHELL-FIRE

you to sit in a certain position, to touch a particular object, to whistle so many bars of a tune silently between your teeth. If you complete the charm in time you are safe—until the next one. This absurdity becomes a dark, overpowering fatalism. You contemplate with horror that you have made a slip in the self-imposed ritual, or that the augury sign of your own invention shows against you. You imagine that the shells are more deliberate and accurate than could be possible. They seem to have a volition of their own, and to wander malevolently until they see a target on which to pounce; they seem to hurl themselves with intention sounding in the fierce roar of their near approach; they defy your mute relief when they fall far away, by sending slivers of jagged steel sighing and murmuring hundreds of yards towards you, long after the shock of the explosion is spent and gone.

Every gun and every kind of projectile had its own personality. Old soldiers always claimed that they knew the calibre of a shell by its sound, and could always foretell which shells were going to fall dangerously close. Yet far more than they calculated depended on the range and the nature of the intervening ground. Sometimes a field-gun shell would leap jubilantly with the pop of a champagne cork from its muzzle, fly over with a steady buzzing crescendo, and burst with a fully expected bang; sometimes a shell would be released from a distant battery of heavies to roll across a huge arc of sky, gathering speed and noise like an approaching express train, ponderous and certain. Shells flying over valleys and woods echoed strangely and defied anticipation; shells falling in enclosed spaces simply arrived with a double bang and no warning at all. Some shells whistled, others shrieked, others wobbled through space, gurgling like water poured from a decanter.

So all the day you listened, calculated, hoped or despaired, making imaginary bargains with fate, laying odds with yourself on the chances of these various horrors. One particular gun would seem to be firing more directly on you than the others. You would wait for its turn so intently as to forget other perhaps more real dangers. At last it comes. You hold frenziedly on to the conversation; you talk a little too fast; your nerves grow tense, and while you continue to look and talk like a man, your involuntary muscles get a little out of hand. Are your knees quivering a little? Are you blinking? Is your face contorted with fear? You wonder and cannot know. Force yourself to do something, say something, think something, or you will lose control. Get yourself in hand with some voluntary action. Drum out a tune with your finger-tips upon your knee. Don't hurry—keep time—get it finished, and you will be safe this once. Here superstition and neurasthenia step in. Like the child who will not walk on the lines in the pavement and finds real safety in putting each foot on a square stone, you feel that your ritual protects you. As the roar of an approaching shell rises nearer and louder you listen in inward frenzy to the shell, in outward calm to the conversation. Steady with those nervous drum-taps on your knee; don't break time or the charm is broken and the augury vain. The shell roars nearer. What is Thorburn saying?

"Oh, yes! The rations came up at nine o'clock, enough for twice our numbers." (Explosion!)

Thank God, the tune was finished soon enough. But then comes an overwhelming rush of panic. The next shell will be the nearest, the climax of the day. What is the next shell when the air is never free from their sound? The next that is at all near. But how near? Which is near enough to break the tension? Thorburn is saying: "We haven't issued the rum to-day. Best do it at dusk, don't you think?" (Terrific explosion!) "God," you say with a gasp, dropping for an instant the mask of indifference. You eye the others guiltily and wonder if they are going through the same performance.

At least, are you keeping up appearances as well as they do? What a comfort that Wolfe's augury is so optimistic.

Once in the afternoon I was on the point of breaking down. My luck turned; the self-deluding charm failed; omens were bad and a shell roared into the mud, throwing clods and whining splinters on our heads. I swore and moved nervously and lost control of my features.

"Steady," said Thorburn, putting a hand on my arm.

That was my nadir. The shelling slackened and stopped, until between Wolfe's optimism and Thorburn's unconcern, I revived my good spirits.

* * *

PASSCHENDAELE—WAR FROM THE AIR

From *Into the Blue*.[1]

By Captain Norman Macmillan, M.C., A.F.C.

The day of attack dawned.

But, long before the dawn, the hum of aero-engines being run on test vibrated upward to the stars.

It was the day for the single-seater fighters—they were detailed for " low strafing." They were to become the fighting advance guard for the infantry upon the ground. And they were to work, not in big formations, but singly or in pairs. Ever individualists, they were not absolutely so.

With the first grey streaks flittering through the starlight, two scouts left the aerodrome. They could just be discerned as they rushed away into the windless dawn. Little flashing accolades of fire accompanied the powerful roar of their engines—the fiery spumes from the exhaust. Overhead, they became grey blurs droning across the starscape.

They swung round east; the sound of their engines was lost in a swelling murmur as of distant thunder that rolled down the dawn wind stealing westward at the first flush upon the eastern sky. The four mechanics attached to the machines stood silently watching and listening until the distant thrum of the engines died away. They loved these two machines and the pilots who flew with them.

Away ahead, through the half-grey twilight of the early dawn, the pilot saw the carpet pattern of fire which overlaid the field of battle. It was a wonderful sight. Little spumes of vivid flame danced and hovered over all the earth. Overhead, the dawn mist hazed the stars. In the air, long spurts of fire threw streams of light that flamed and died. The pattern was ever changing, never alike, with shell and mortar drawing the threads for weft and warp. It was the most wonderful picture of war. Its ugliness, its horror, was camouflaged in beauty. It was as a river of fire, foaming and spraying over hidden rocks and snags. It was the masterpiece of the devil

[1] Published by Gerald Duckworth & Co.

artist of war. And the background of hanging haze and smoke threw it into weird relief.

Low down, the two tiny fighting aeroplanes flew straight into the fury of the inferno. The noise of the drum-fire penetrated even the roaring of their engines. They swung to the right. The barrage was too heavy to fly straight through. They turned southward, above the angry mouths of the flaming guns, their frail machines rocking and pitching in the air-swirls from the concussions of discharge. They rounded the extreme southern end of the barrage, then turned east and north. They surged through the invisible air-storm on the enemy side of the barrage. The pilots' eyes, strained to the uttermost, searched the shell-torn earth below. They were human hawks winging to swoop upon the humbler fowl. The light grew in the sky.

Suddenly one of the machines turned over in the air and dived. The crackle of his guns sounded in the pilots' ears above the other noises of the battle. Down in the earth, where the double stream of bullets struck, a tumbled, shell-cratered line of trenches was filled with grey-clad men. They huddled in their holes, trying to grub themselves deeper with their finger-nails. They gazed upwards over their shoulders in fascinated fright. The bullets crackled round them in hissing menace. Some of them wriggled and twisted where they crouched, then lay still. On their faces was the imprint of fear. The rushing, roaring scout-fighter passed over their heads, the bullets enfilading the shell-holes beyond. As the living rose the second machine came down. They flung themselves into the mud of their funk-holes again.

The two aeroplanes screamed at full speed along the line of battered trenches. They zoomed upwards, at intervals, only to descend in fiercer swoops. The two pilots, crouching forward in their tiny scouts, followed their tracer bullets downwards to the very earth. They sat tense in their seats, concentrated in the every movement of their controls, conscious of the danger of their job, but risking everything.

From the redoubts and pill-boxes on the nearer ground machine-guns rattled out against them. They heard the duller sound as some found their billet in the plane. The crackle dimmed as they swerved away, then sharpened as they straightened out. Again they dived. The British barrage had crept forward on to the ground below. Shells burst out all round them. Clods of earth and fragments of shell pierced their wings and fuselage. They hurtled downwards for the final burst.

As they zoomed, a shell struck one machine and sent it tumbling earthward. The pilot pulled wildly at his joystick. The bus struck one wing first, whirled on to its nose, and crumpled up.

The other machine was entombed in the creeping barrage. The invisible shells moaned all around the plane, and burst below it on the right. The craft rocked amid the whirling currents of the air. Above, the sky was shut out by a roof of smoke. It was like a living tomb of torment.

The pilot did the only thing he could. He dived for the ground, westward for the ground. He prayed that the shells might pass overhead, not short. But, as he flattened out above the ground, the enemy machine-gun barrage caught him. The bullets pierced the petrol tanks, the engine. One tore through his arm. He had not time to land. In the front of him was a shell-hole. The bus plunged into the soft mud.

The pilot loosened his belt, jumped out, and ran onward. Shells whistled and crashed around him, but still he ran, pulling one foot after another from the clinging mud. And as he ran, the blood reddened on his sleeve. He stumbled. A spume of shrapnel burst above him. He lay where he fell.

* * *

Not until November, 1917, did the tanks get a real chance to exploit their possibilities. Then, without warning, a swarm of armoured monsters burst through the German lines.

TANKS AT CAMBRAI
From *A Company of Tanks*.[1]
By Major W. H. L. Watson, D.S.O., D.C.M.

Until the 17th, the enemy apparently suspected nothing at all; but on the night of the 17th–18th he raided and captured

[1] Published by William Blackwood and Sons.

some prisoners, who fortunately knew little. He gathered from them that we were ourselves preparing a substantial raid, and he brought into the line additional companies of machine-gunners and a few extra field-guns.

The 19th came with its almost unbearable suspense. We did not know what the Germans had discovered from their prisoners. We could not believe that the attack could be really a surprise. Perhaps the enemy, unknown to us, had concentrated sufficient guns to blow us to pieces. We looked up for the German aeroplanes, which surely would fly low over the wood and discover its contents. Incredibly, nothing happened. The morning passed and the afternoon—a day was never so long—and at last it was dusk.

At 8.45 p.m. my tanks began to move cautiously out of the wood and formed into column. At 9.30 p.m., with engines barely turning over, they glided imperceptibly and almost without noise towards the trenches. Standing in front of my own tanks, I could not hear them at two hundred yards.

By midnight we had reached our rendezvous behind the reserve trenches and below the crest of the slope. There we waited for an hour. The Colonel arrived, and took me with him to pay a final visit to the headquarters of the battalions with which we were operating. The trenches were packed with Highlanders, and it was with difficulty that we made our way through them.

Cooper led the tanks for the last half of the journey. They stopped at the support trenches, for they were early, and the men were given hot breakfast. The enemy began some shelling on the left, but no damage was done.

At 6.10 a.m. the tanks were in their allotted positions, clearly marked out by tapes which Jumbo had laid earlier in the night....

I was standing on the parados of a trench. The movement at my feet had ceased. The Highlanders were ready with fixed bayonets. Not a gun was firing, but there was a curious murmur in the air. To right of me and to left of me in the dim light were tanks—tanks lined up in front of the wire, tanks swinging into position, and one or two belated tanks climbing over the trenches.

TANKS AT CAMBRAI

I hurried back to the Colonel of the 6th Black Watch, and I was with him in his dug-out at 6.20 a.m. when the guns began. I climbed on to the parapet and looked.

In front of the wire, tanks in a ragged line were surging forward inexorably over the short down grass. Above and around them hung the blue-grey smoke of their exhausts. Each tank was followed by a bunch of Highlanders, some running forward from cover to cover, but most of them tramping steadily behind their tanks. They disappeared into the valley. To the right the tanks were moving over the crest of the shoulder of the hill. To the left there were no tanks in sight. They were already in among the enemy.

Beyond the enemy trenches the slopes, from which the German gunners might have observed the advancing tanks, were already enveloped in thick, white smoke. The smoke shells burst with a sheet of vivid red flame, pouring out blinding, suffocating clouds. It was as if flaring bonfires were burning behind a bank of white fog. Over all, innumerable aeroplanes were flying steadily to and fro.

The enemy made little reply. A solitary field-gun was endeavouring pathetically to put down a barrage. A shell would burst every few minutes on the same bay of the same trench. There were no other enemy shells that we could see. A machine-gun or two were still trained on our trenches, and an occasional vicious burst would bring the venturesome spectator scrambling down into the trench.

Odd bunches of men were making their way across what had been No-Man's Land. A few, ridiculously few, wounded were coming back. Germans, in twos and threes, elderly men for the most part, were wandering confusedly towards us without escort, putting up their hands in tragic and amazed resignation, whenever they saw a Highlander.

The news was magnificent. Our confidence had been justified. Everywhere we had overrun the first system and were pressing on.

A column of tanks, equipped with a strange apparatus, passed across our front to clear a lane through the wire for the cavalry.

On our left another column of tanks had already disappeared

into the valley on their way to Flesquieres. It was Ward's company, but Ward was not with them. A chance bullet had killed him instantly at the head of his tanks. When we heard of his death later, the joy of victory died away....

* * *

THE failures of the year were relieved by one success—the considerable advance in Palestine. Following the second battle of Gaza, the Turks retreated hastily before the victorious British and Indian Troops, and on December 11th, 1917, General Allenby entered Jerusalem.

THE FALL OF JERUSALEM
From *How Jerusalem Was Won*.[1]
By W. T. MASSEY

I have asked many men who were engaged in the fight for Jerusalem what their feelings were on getting their first glimpse of the central spot of Christendom. Some people imagine that the hard brutalities of war erase softer elements of men's natures; that killing and the rough life of campaigning, where one is familiarised with the tragedies of life every hour of every day, where ease and comfort are forgotten things, remove from the mind those earlier lessons of peace on earth and goodwill toward men. That is a fallacy. Every man or officer I spoke to declared that he was seized with emotion when, looking from the shell-torn summit of Nebi Samwil, he saw the spires on the Mount of Olives; or when reconnoitring from Kustul he got a peep of the red roofs of the newer houses which surround the old City. Possibly only a small percentage of the Army believed they were taking part in a great mission, not a great proportion would claim to be really devout men, but they all behaved liked Christian gentlemen. One Londoner told me he had thought the scenes of war had made him callous, and that the ruthless destruction of those things fashioned by men's hands in prosecuting the arts of peace had prompted the feeling that

[1] Published by Constable & Co., Ltd.

THE FALL OF JERUSALEM

there was little in civilisation after all, if civilisation could result in so bitter a thing as this awful fighting. Man seemed as barbaric as in the days before the Saviour came to redeem the world, and whether we won or lost the War, all hopes of a happier state of things were futile. So this Cockney imagined that his condition showed no improvement on that of the savage warrior of two thousand years ago, except in that civilisation had developed finer weapons to kill with and be killed by. The finer instincts had been blunted by the naked and unashamed horrors of war. But the lessons taught him before war scourged the world came back to him on getting his first view of the Holy City. He felt that sense of emotion which makes one wish to be alone and think alone. He was on the ground where Sacred History was made, perhaps stood on the rock the Saviour's foot had trod. In the deep stirring of his emotions the rougher edges of his nature became rounded by feelings of sympathy and a belief that good would come out of the evil of this strife. That view of Jerusalem, and the knowledge of what the Holy Sites stand for, made him a better man and a better fighting man, and he had no doubt the first distant glimpse of the Holy City had similarly affected the bulk of the Army. That bad language is used by almost all troops in the field is notorious, but in Jerusalem one seldom heard an oath or an indecent word.

. . . .

For succinctness it would be difficult to improve upon the Commander-in-Chief's own description of his Official Entry into Jerusalem. Cabling to London within two hours of that event, General Allenby thus narrated the events of the day:

(1) At noon to-day I officially entered this City with a few of my staff, the commanders of the French and Italian detachments, the heads of the Picot Mission, and the Military Attachés of France, Italy, and the United States of America.

The procession was all on foot.

I was received by Guards representing England, Scotland, Ireland, Wales, Australia, India, New Zealand, France, and Italy at the Jaffa Gate.

(2) I was well received by the population.

(3) The Holy Places have had Guards placed over them.

(4) My Military Governor is in touch with the Acting Custos of Latins and the Greek representative has been detailed to supervise Christian Holy Places.

(5) The Mosque of Omar and the area round it has been placed under Moslem control and a military cordon composed of Indian Mahomedan officers and soldiers has been established round the Mosque. Orders have been issued that without permission of the Military Governor and the Moslem in charge of the Mosque no non-Moslem is to pass this cordon.

(6) The proclamation has been posted on the walls, and from the steps of the Citadel was read in my presence to the population in Arabic, Hebrew, English, French, Italian, Greek and Russian.

(7) Guardians have been established at Bethlehem and on Rachel's Tomb. The Tomb of Hebron has been placed under exclusive Moslem control.

(8) The hereditary custodians of the Wakfs at the Gates of the Holy Sepulchre have been requested to take up their accustomed duties in remembrance of the magnanimous act of the Caliph Omar who protected that Church.

.   .   .   .   .   .

The Proclamation read from the steps of David's Tower on the occasion of the Commander-in-Chief's Official Entry into Jerusalem was in these terms :

To the inhabitants of Jerusalem the Blessed and the people dwelling in its vicinity :

The defeat inflicted upon the Turks by the troops under my command has resulted in the occupation of your City by my forces. I therefore here and now proclaim it to be under martial law, under which form of administration it will remain as long as military considerations make it necessary.

However, lest any of you should be alarmed by reason of your experiences at the hands of the enemy who has retired, I hereby inform you that it is my desire that every person should pursue his lawful business without fear of interruption. Furthermore, since your City is regarded with affection by the adherents of three of the great religions of mankind, and its soil has become consecrated by the prayers and pilgrimages of multitudes of devout people of those three religions for many centuries, therefore do I make it known to you that every sacred building, monument, holy spot, shrine, traditional site, endowment, pious bequest, or customary place of prayer, of whatsoever form of the three religions, will be maintained and protected according to the existing customs and beliefs of those to whose faiths they are sacred.

* * *

THE fall of Jerusalem did not end the Palestine operations, for the British continued to advance, occupying many ancient cities of Biblical renown. The conditions of the campaign were severe, yet a complete contrast to those prevailing at Passchendaele, since lack of water was the greatest hardship.

CAMPAIGNING IN PALESTINE
From *Red Dust*.[1]
By DONALD BLACK

Gun-shot wounds take their toll, but mostly it is the malaria; many would willingly have wounds in exchange for this cursed fever. It brings about a see-sawing temperature. One minute its victims are sweating with heat, the next rolled shivering in blankets, shivering when the shade temperature is one hundred and twenty or more. Often the blood turns jet black, they cannot eat, just lie in the shade doing nothing but drink huge quantities of water. It is not possible for everyone developing fever to be removed, as this would mean the line becoming deserted; only the very bad cases go out. The others hang on, some get worse and go away, others recover and take their accustomed place in the line again. Occasionally variation is provided by someone going off his head, to be carried away raving. Usually they recover, but a few probably never will, the canker of the valley biting too deeply into their brains.

[1] Published by Jonathan Cape

Is it any wonder that men go this way? Mentally we are all dulled, the heat clouds our faculties so that they function spasmodically. The food, too, is insufficient and bad; we are only half nourished. It is not the Powers' fault this; they do what they can for us; it is our location right up here which makes transport so difficult.

Our diet has little variation, mostly bully beef and mildewed bread with onions, sometimes a tin of jam as a luxury. The heat turns the beef-fat into oil. We place the tins in wadi beds to cool, but the water is half-tepid, so it is not much use. Usually when we prod a tin with the bayonet preparatory to opening, the liquid fat squirts out.

The bread is made a long way off, and comes to us in sacks as large as chaff bags, always broken, seldom more than a few whole loaves in each sack, dried and hard with mould penetrating right through. We have long been used to this mould and scarcely notice it; hunger has overcome any squeamishness we may have once had; the bread is too precious to waste by scraping the green away. Day in day out, diet is the same, and our stomachs revolt against so much repetition, but there is nothing else unless it be an occasional tin of mixed vegetable and meat. This makes us rejoice, and we treat it with well-merited honour. We have ways of disguising the inevitable bully. Mixing it with bread or, when we have it, flour, frying the lot and calling the result rissoles. The flour is never enough to make a damper, but enough to provide a cloak for the constant bully so that we may think it something else and hope to deceive our stomachs thereby.

The great consolation is that tea, our mainstay, is regular. Without this we would indeed be lost; it helps keep our thirst down and is very comforting in many ways. When we have jam we only get what it suits the flies to leave for us. When a tin is opened they swarm over the surface and though we beat the air about the opening tin, they nevertheless get in, swarming over the surface and completely coating it. As quickly as we remove them others take their place. As we spread the jam on bread, they swarm around so that it is impossible to avoid eating them too or else lose the food. What does it matter anyway, we are not epicures that we should grumble; some say that our meat supply is thereby increased; at least it's the only fresh meat we get.

At a small canteen at Jericho various tinned foods are obtainable. Whenever anyone goes there they always bring back what they can carry. Without this service we would not exist at all, the army ration would surely finish us.

Smith was removed this morning; he went off his head during the night. He put up a good struggle, too good—he must pay for his courage. How thin he has grown, his ribs sticking out like xylophone keys, one could almost strike matches on them! I will miss his cheery face, his ever-ready wit, but above all his wonderful comradeship. I shall never forget his worn and emaciated appearance, tribute to the greathearted soldier he always was. His indomitable courage and determination to stick it through have claimed payment for his fortitude. Never virtuous or troubled about his morals, sincere in what he did for others, a hard liver, but, above all, a man. His loss to me is the greatest personal calamity of the campaign. I loved him.

* * *

By this time the Allied propaganda machine was working at full strength. Generally it was very effective, not only in its subversive effect in enemy countries but in the maintenance of the proper righteous indignation at home.

THE CORPSE FACTORY

From *Falsehood in War-time*.[1]

By Arthur Ponsonby, M.P.

A series of extracts will give the record of one of the most revolting lies invented during the War, the dissemination of which throughout not only this country but the world was encouraged and connived at by both the Government and the Press. It started in 1917, and was not finally disposed of until 1925.

(Most of the quotations given are from *The Times*. The

[1] Published by George Allen & Unwin, Ltd.

references in the lower strata of the Press, it will be remembered, were far more lurid.)

"One of the United States consuls, on leaving Germany in February, 1917, stated in Switzerland that the Germans were distilling glycerine from the bodies of their dead."

The Times, April 16th, 1917.

"Herr Karl Rosner, the Correspondent of the Berlin *Lokalanzeiger*, on the Western Front . . . published last Tuesday the first definite admission concerning the way in which the Germans use dead bodies.

"We pass through Everingcourt. There is a dull smell in the air as if lime were being burnt. We are passing the great Corpse Exploitation Establishment (Kadaververwertungsanstalt) of this Army Group. The fat that is won here is turned into lubricating oils, and everything else is ground down in the bone-mill into a powder which is used for mixing with pig's food and as manure—nothing can be permitted to go to waste."

The Times, April 16th, 1917.

There was a report in *The Times* of April 17th, 1917, from *La Belgique* (Leyden), via *l'Independance Belge*, for April 10th, giving a long and detailed account of a Deutsche Abfallverwertungsgesellschaft factory near Coblenz where train-loads of the stripped bodies of German soldiers, wired into bundles, arrive, and are simmered down in cauldrons, the products being stearine and refined oil.

In *The Times* of April 18th, 1917, there was a letter from C. E. Bunbury commenting and suggesting the use of the story for propaganda purposes, in neutral countries and the East, where it would be especially calculated to horrify Buddhists Hindus, and Mohammedans. He suggested broadcasting by the Foreign Office, India Office, and Colonial Office; there were other letters to the same effect on April 19th.

In *The Times* of April 20th, 1917, there was a story told of Sergeant B——, of the Kents, that a prisoner had told him that the Germans boil down their dead for munitions and pig and poultry food. "This fellow told me that Fritz calls his

THE CORPSE FACTORY

margarine 'corpse fat' because they suspect that's what it comes from."

 . . . . . .

In reply to a question in the House of Commons on May 23rd, Mr. A. Chamberlain stated that the report would be "available to the public in India through the usual channels."

A corpse factory cartoon appeared in *Punch*.

Kaiser (to 1917 recruit): And don't forget that your Kaiser will find a use for you alive or dead. (At the enemy's establishment for the utilisation of corpses the dead bodies of German soldiers are treated chemically, the chief commercial products being lubricant oils and pig food.)

The story had world-wide circulation and had considerable propaganda value in the East. Not until 1925 did the truth emerge.

"A painful impression had been produced here by an unfortunate speech of Brigadier-General —— at the dinner of the National Arts Club, in which he professed to tell the true story of the war-time report that Germany was boiling down the bodies of her dead soldiers in order to get fats for munitions and fertilizers.

"According to General ——, the story began as propaganda for China. By transposing the caption from one of two photographs found on German prisoners to the other, he gave the impression that the Germans were making a dreadful use of their own dead soldiers. This photograph he sent to a Chinese newspaper in Shanghai. He told the familiar story of its later republication in England and of the discussion it created there. He told, too, how, when a question put in the House was referred to him, he answered it by saying that from what he knew of German mentality, he was prepared for anything.

"Later, said General ——, in order to support the story, what purported to be the diary of a German soldier was forged in his office. It was planned to have this discovered on a dead German by a war correspondent with a passion for German diaries, but the plan was never carried out. The diary was now in the War Museum in London."

 The Times, October 22nd, 1925. From *New York Correspondent*.

   * * *

The idea that troops marched into battle exclusively to the strains of " Tipperary " was probably due to the imagination of a journalist. Tommy's songs were of great variety, but the most popular type was the parody—most frequently, let it be said regretfully, set to hymn tunes. Probably the most popular of all was sung to an adaptation of the air of the old revivalist hymn, " Whiter than the snow." It ran :

" Whiter than the whitewash on the wall,
Whiter than the whitewash on the wall,
Wash me in the water where you wash your dirty daughter,
And I shall be whiter than the whitewash on the wall."

It would be impossible to calculate how many hundreds of thousands of miles were marched by weary troops to this inspiring ditty !

TOMMY'S SONGS

From *War is War*.[1]

By Ex-Private X

It seems a pity that many of the soldier's songs, probably because of their obscenity, will in time be lost as irretrievably as those that were sung in the Napoleonic wars. Some were merely foul, but others were quite funny, and one or two showed signs of genuine literary craftsmanship.

" The lady she was dressing, Dressing for the ball——"— what Tommy took this straight from the Decameron and put it into verse in the true ballad form ? It was very amusing, admirably executed and, to me, not offensively dirty ; but no modest pen could quote one single stanza.

" I Love my Girl " was simply filthy. A bawdy song ought to be at least partly redeemed by humour.

One of the division's favourites, set to a good marching tune, consisted only of one verse. I give a Bowdlerised version of it.

[1] Published by Victor Gollancz, Ltd.

> I 'aven't seen the Kayser for a 'ell of a time,
> I 'aven't seen the Kayser for a 'ell of a time.
> I bin on the Somme to see what 'e's bin doin',
> The — —rd Division will be the bastard's ruin.
>
> I' aven't seen the Kayser for a 'ell of a time,
> 'E's the leader of 'is Army—Army,
> 'E's the leader of the whizz-bang band,
> So damn 'im, 'e's no cousin of mine!

I did not hear " Mademoiselle from Armentières " until I got back to England, and I think it must have derived from another song we used to sing which had the same tune and burden. Having politely altered a few of the words—which ones the initiated will easily guess—I can jot down a few of the verses from memory.

> A German officer crossed the Rhine, parly-voo!
> A German officer crossed the Rhine, parly-voo!
>   A German officer crossed the Rhine
>   To know the women and drink the wine—
> Inkey-pinkey-parly-voo.
>
> Oh, landlord, have you a daughter fine? Parly-voo!
> Oh, landlord, have you a daughter fine? Parly-voo!
>   Oh, landlord, have you a daughter fine
>   Fit for an officer from the Rhine?
> Inkey-pinkey-parly-voo!
>
> My daughter, sir, she's much too young, parly-voo!
> My daughter, sir, she's much too young, parly-voo!
>   My daughter, sir, she's much too young
>   To be messed about by a son of a gun—
> Inkey-pinkey-parly-voo!
>
> Oh, father dear, I'm not too young—parly-voo!
> Oh, father dear, I'm not too young—parly-voo!
>   Oh, father dear, I'm not too young,
>   You can go and ask the gardener's son!—
> Inkey-pinkey-parly-voo.

Tommy's songs varied extraordinarily. There was the frankly obscene, the mawkishly sentimental, the utterly ridiculous and inconsequent, the humorously funky, and occasionally the good stuff. I am no musical critic, except that I know that anything that appeals to me is pretty sure to be extremely bad. I like Molloy's "Boys of the Old Brigade," and I don't care who knows I like it. I heard it sung once in an *estaminet*, and after the usual songs, sung in self-mockery, such as "I want to go Home" and "Take me Back to Blighty," this old song swept over us like summer fire over a parched common. We felt like men while we were singing it.

Nobody ever invented more boring and idiotic songs than those about the man and his dog who went to mow a meadow, the grasshopper that jumped over another grasshopper's back, and John Brown's Baby who was afflicted with a pimple on an un-named part of his anatomy. We are wedded by sentiment to "Tipperary," but was there ever a lousier or more whining tune?—and the words speak for themselves. I recollect the song before it was famous, when it used to be sung on the music-halls by a lady in tights with the largest pair of thighs I have ever yet seen exposed to the simple inhabitants of these islands.

Tommy loves singing songs about how he hated the War, and didn't want to die, and wanted to go home. The psychology of this is simple. We were all more or less "windy," and though we tried to hide it from each other with varying degrees of success, most of such secrets were open secrets. Since we knew each other so well it was better to own to fear and make fun of ourselves than try to run a bluff which wouldn't have deceived a blind infant.

One song was always sung with real feeling. It properly belonged to the Scotch, that hardy race of savages who continued to hate the Boche and lust for battle long after we soft Southerners would willingly have laid down our arms and accepted a *status quo*. Most of us had wives or sweethearts waiting for us at home, and it was very moving to hear a crowd of men whose lives were worth about ninepence in the pound, singing "Loch Lomond."

> For I and my true love will never meet again
> On the bonny, bonny banks of Loch Lomond.

I was with some hundreds of men who will never again meet their true loves, unless the all-loving God has provided in the after-world a trysting-place for soldiers and soldiers' lasses.

* * *

On a somewhat higher intellectual plane, ingenious spirits produced real newspapers under conditions that would make any ordinary editor throw a fit. The circulation of these newspapers was small, and their very existence precarious, since Editorial office and printing-room were liable at any moment to be wrecked by a shell.

TRENCH NEWSPAPERS
From *The Crater of Mars*.[1]
By Ferdinand Tuohy

As winter set in I was lucky to have, among battalion intelligence officers to instruct, two former colleagues. Both were in the alleged trenches before Ypres, and we evolved the notion of getting out a Christmas number of some kind. This later emerged, with a Roneo-d circulation of a couple of hundred or so, as *The Salient*, from which I take these haphazard contributions as being perhaps of interest for their resuscitation of the humour and outlook of that distant day:

AN A.B.C. TO THE ARMY

No. 1. Regular.
A totally extinct force which flourished before the War. It consisted of pipe-clay and metal polish with a man inside to give it more effect. Strange as it may seem, after the War broke out the man was discovered to be of more importance than the pipe-clay.

No. 1 (a). Yeomanry.
These are horse-soldiers, and can only be differentiated from fraudulent wearers of riding-breeches by spurs.

No. 2. Territorial Force.
An apparatus whereby an undeserving War Office may be able to summon a complete army in division at twenty-four hours' notice. By the terms of its formation, it is forbidden that it should ever receive any credit for its work. Its official designation is " Saturday night soldiers."

[1] Published by William Heinemann, Ltd.

No. 3. Kitchener's Army.

This is a large departmental internment camp for young men between the ages of 19 and 38. Monotony of existence is relieved by movement to different places in England. Isolated units have been found in France.

No. 4. City Battalion.
(*See* England's Last Hope.)

No. 5. R.A.M.C.

A party of men lured into Belgium under false pretences. Ostensibly for the purpose of practising the healing art, they lead a precarious existence with a spade. For further particulars see " Navvies' Battalion " (except pay).

No. 6. A.S.C.

(Technically known as the " Strawberry Jam Pinchers.") Predatory pirates who lead a life of filibustering. They have a habit of becoming "attached" to regiments, which may account for their habit of attaching themselves to rations. Act as " clearing station " for all rations.

No. 7. M.T.

A collection of eccentrics from Scotland, Ireland, Wales, Wiltshire, Lancashire and London. Very little is known of these, as an interpreter is needed to speak to any of them.

No. 8. A.O.C.

Ordnance is ancient English for cannon. In consequence, this unit is rarely found within sound of the guns. Though frequently found " in the dumps," they are, on the whole, a cheerful crew. They affect bright buttons and are the arbiter of fashion in the Army.

No. 9. Engineers.

Otherwise known as the " Press-gang." Isolated members of this Corps have been known to imprison large numbers of other regiments and act as task-masters to them in making dug-outs and roads. Troops get into the habit of instinctively taking cover from all Engineers.

TRENCH NEWSPAPERS

RECENT DISCOVERIES IN THE RHINE VALLEY. FROM THE "LEADSWINGER," OCTOBER 20TH, 3915

As most of our readers are aware Prof. Dug-out has been busy for some time past on the work of excavation in the basin of this ancient river, and we have just received from the publishers a small brochure on the results of the work up to the present, from which we are privileged to make a few extracts.

Many interesting finds have been made, some of which throw grave doubts on the theories hitherto held regarding the habits of the early inhabitants of this part of the Continent of Urop. The vast army of workers, under the personal supervision of a trained staff of scientific experts, have unearthed ruins of what at one time must have been a village or town of some size, but the evidence is curiously conflicting, and will require much careful sifting before any definite conclusion can be drawn. A few hypotheses, however, have been suggested by Prof. Dug-out, one of which is based on the finding of certain inscriptions. Several broken fragments of metal, it appears, have been discovered bearing letters which may well be assumed to indicate the name of the town. Prof. Dug-out thinks that possibly the letters represent a word Yppts or Ypres, the latter being the more likely reading. Large fragments of timber have also been found bearing other characters and letters, apparently burned into the wood. Most of these are quite unintelligible, such combinations of letters appearing as R.A.M.C., R.G.A., D.A.D.M.S. One fragment bears two inscriptions, and its appearance suggests that its use may have been to direct traffic to the town. We reproduce a facsimile of this fragment. The upper part of the two words is very similar to the one appearing on the metal fragment, and is almost certainly the name of the town in an alternative spelling, and it is not improbable that the word Wipers refers to the same place, and may be a dialectic variation of the name. This evidence points to the fact that the town was inhabited by a mixed people speaking different languages, or, at any rate, variant dialects of a possibly common stock.

There are very few suggestions of the presence of those conical structures built of hardened clay blocks, which we are wont to associate with the domiciliary habits of our ancestors, instead there have been found long rows of cave-like dwellings situated along the banks of a depression which may have been at one time the bed of a river, and assuming such to have been the case, it might be supposed that the inhabitants of these cave-dwellings were a race of fishermen, naturally living close to the water.

Both lines of dwellings face the setting sun, and as Prof. Dug-out acutely remarks, the reason for this is probably to be sought for in some ancient religious rite. Besides these cave-dwellings, other strange objects have been discovered apparently buried in square pits usually about four metres, cubic capacity. It is difficult to describe the heterogeneous contents of these pits, but the commonest are small cubical or truncated blocks of some thin metallic substance surrounding a softish material, which, when examined, appears to be of animal origin. The outer covering or carapace is occasionally suggestive of colour, and in some cases is ribbed at one end. Various suggestions have been made as to the origin of these collections, but the most likely is that put forward by Mons Bulibeef, who thinks that these cube-like masses of soft matter with a thin hard outer covering, may be the remains of some early crustacean creature.

A regrettable incident occurred during the excavation of a patch of ground a little to the east of the main works, involving the death of six men, who, whilst digging, were suddenly hurled into space by a violent explosion, the nature of which is at present quite inexplicable. In an article in this Journal last year we drew attention to the frequency of explosions which occurred two thousand years ago, when records show that it was not uncommon for agricultural labourers in Urop to be killed whilst ploughing or digging and the cause was supposed to be due to the sudden impact of the plough or spade with a peculiar form of stone or shale (occasionally spelled "shell"), which was found in great profusion at this time in this locality. From their appearance and situation, "shales" or "shells" were supposed to be of meteoric origin, and it is not improbable that the explosion at Ypres, or Wipers, may have been of this nature.

* * *

LEAVE

From *Grey Dawn—Red Night*.[1]
By JAMES LANSDALE HODSON

He sat on the edge of the taxi-cab seat all the way from London Road Station to Miss French's house that stood near St. Peter's Church, its bow window (the only one in the row) protruding over the flagged pavement. His heart was pounding and the cab seemed unconscionably slow. It bumped over the setts of Chapel Street and caused his tin hat and metal drinking-cup to clank. The first milk-carts were galloping about. Up very early. So they thought. How funny it was. The same old life going on. The cab swung across the street, lurching him on one side, and then, as it swung round to the left, tossing him back again. It pulled up, squeaked, and stopped with a jerk that flung him on to the glass partition. He began to mutter: " Of all the blo——" and stopped. This wouldn't do. He had wanted to step out calmly, as if coming home on leave were an everyday affair, and here he was, all over the place, rifle on floor, cap on one side. . . . He crawled out as if from a dug-out. Before he could reach the door Miss French had flung it open, trotted down the steps, said: " How are you, dear? " waited for no reply, taken his rifle from him, told him: " Go on, dear, she's waiting," and taken charge of the driver. Hardcastle was conscious of a trace of moisture in his eyes. He took the steps in a flying leap and saw Stella. She was leaning against the lintel of the drawing-room door, her left hand holding her heart, her eyes luminous and large and blue, her face pale, her lips parted, and, he thought, a-quiver. And then she was in his arms, his arms tenderly encompassing her, his lips pressed firmly, almost fiercely, to hers, which were trembling and soft, and which not for a long time took shape and returned his pressure. That kiss told him everything, how she had suffered and sorrowed and longed and almost been overborne by waiting. He was murmuring: " My sweet, my beautiful, my very dear one." Her eyes were closed and the

Published by Victor Gollancz, Ltd.

lids were veined with a dim azure tint. When he removed his lips from hers she lay spent in his arms, her head supported by his arms behind her neck, her mouth slightly open and sighs breaking from it. He kissed her again, more softly and gently now, kissed her tired eyes, smoothed her eyebrows with his lips, buried his face in her bosom. After a while her lips took shape and returned his kisses, as if life were being poured back into her veins. She opened her eyes, and when he saw the love shining there, and the pride and faith in him, he had to fight to keep his tears from falling. "My dearest love, my beautiful," he was saying, and she was murmuring: "Darling, darling sweetheart, my beloved."

They sat there a long time in the large chair, her arms about his neck, their cheeks pressed close, no words being spoken. His mind was empty of everything save Stella's presence: no thoughts of the morrow, of their future, of the War, of the child. Presently Stella spoke, but he could barely catch the words. She said: "Dearest, it has seemed so long," and as she spoke a stifled sob shook her form. He brought her lips to his again, and as they kissed her eyes became suffused with tears. They streamed down her cheeks and lodged where their cheeks met, and ran in a tiny rivulet to the right and past his ear. He soothed her and stroked her hair, and she wept unrestrainedly for a while, till, as a child might quieten, she became quiet, the sobs ceased, and she lay still and tired and sleepy.

* * *

A COMMON penalty for military "crimes" was Field Punishment No. 1. For more serious offences there were the tortures of the military prison and death by shooting.

FIELD PUNISHMENT

From *Red Dust*.[1]

By DONALD BLACK

"Why? Don't you remember the Tommy we found spreadeagled when out here in a patrol?" the first queries.

[1] Published by Jonathan Cape.

"Oh, yes, I remember that, and when we rode up and began to cut him down, he asked to be left, saying his punishment would only be increased if we interfered!"

"We cut him down though," the first speaker interrupted, "and a Tommy officer came up and threatened to report us, and we told him that we had a good mind to put him up as a substitute for the Tommy. I wonder what happened to the poor devil, we never came back that way again."

"Whoever introduced that bloody torture should be crucified himself, but with real nails," broke in a burly artilleryman of the H.A.C.

It is a fact, and an abhorrent one too, but none the less true for that, that this barbarous practice should survive as a means to inflict inhuman torture on undefensive soldiery. Invented two thousand years ago, used for the crucifixion of Christ, condemned through history's pages as an everlasting blot on Jewry, yet perpetrated now in a modified form by those who condemn.

Often the crime was not of great proportions. The guilty man would be tied to a limber wheel so as to form the letter "X" with his limbs and left to the mercy of the broiling sun. A little while and the strength is sapped; the prisoner droops, then hangs by his hands, his feet no longer able to support him. What pain it inflicts only those who have seen it practised know.

* * *

CONDEMNED TO DEATH

From *The Secret Battle*.[1]

By A. P. Herbert

But he got no mercy. The sentence was confirmed by the higher authorities. I heard afterwards that the officers of the court-martial were amazed and horrified to hear it.

I cannot pretend to *know* what happened, but from some experience of the military hierarchy I can imagine. I can see those papers, wrapped up in the blue form, with all the right

[1] Published by Methuen & Co., Ltd.

information beautifully inscribed in the right spaces, very neat and precise, carefully sealed in the long envelopes, and sent wandering up through the rarefied atmosphere of the Higher Formations. Very early they halt, at the Brigadier, or perhaps the Divisional General, someone who thinks of himself as a man of " blood and iron." He looks upon the papers. He reads the evidence—very carefully. At the end he sees " Recommended to Mercy."—" All very well, but we must make an example sometimes. Where's that confidential memo we had the other day? That's it, yes. ' Officer who fails in his duty must be treated with the same severity as would be awarded the private in the same circumstances.' Quite right, too. Shan't approve recommendation to mercy. Just write on it, ' See no reason why sentence should not be carried out,' and I'll sign it." Or, more simply perhaps : " Mercy! mercy be damned ! Must make an example. I won't have any cold feet in my Command." And so the blue form goes climbing on, burdened now with that fatal endorsement, labouring over ridge after ridge, and on each successive height the atmosphere becomes more rarefied (though the population is more numerous). And at long last it comes to some Olympian peak—I know not where—beyond which it may not go, where the air is so chill and the population so dense, that it is almost impossible to breathe. Yet here, I make no doubt, they look at the blue form very carefully and gravely, as becomes the High Gods. But in the end they shake their heads, a little sadly, maybe, and say, " Ah, General B—— does not approve recommendation to mercy. He's the man on the spot, he ought to know. *Must* support *him*. Sentence confirmed."

Then the blue form climbs sadly down to the depths again, to the low regions where men feel fear.

· · · · · ·

The thing was done seven mornings later, in a little orchard behind the Casquettes' farm.

The Padre told me he stood up to them very bravely and quietly. Only he whispered to him, " For God's sake make them be quick." That is the worst torment of the soldier from beginning to end—the waiting.

He was shot down by his own men, by men of D Company.

* * * * * *

This book is not an attack on any person, on the death penalty, or on anything else, though if it makes people think about these things, so much the better. I think I believe in the death penalty—I do not know. But I did not believe in Harry being shot.

That is the gist of it; that my friend Harry was shot for cowardice—and he was one of the bravest men I ever knew.

* * *

SHOT AT DAWN
From *A Brass Hat in No Man's Land*.[1]

By Brig.-Gen. F. P. Crozier, C.B., C.M.G., D.S.O.

Now, in peace-time, I and the rest of us would have been very upset indeed at having to shoot a colleague, comrade, call him what you will, at dawn on the morrow. We would not, in ordinary circumstances, have slept. Now the men don't like it, but they have to put up with it. They face their ordeal magnificently. I supervise the preliminary arrangements myself. We put the prisoner in a comfortable warm place. A few yards away we drive in a post, in a back garden, such as exists with any villa residence. I send for a certain junior officer and show him all. "You will be in charge of the firing-party," I say; "the men will be cold, nervous and excited, they may miss their mark. You are to have your revolver ready loaded and cocked; if the medical officer tells you life is not extinct you are to walk up to the victim, place the muzzle of the revolver to his heart and press the trigger. Do you understand?" "Yes, sir," comes the quick reply. "Right," I add, "dine with me at my mess to-night." I want to keep this young fellow engaged under my own supervision until late at night, so as to minimise the chance of his flying to the bottle for support. As for Crocker, he leaves this earth, in so far as knowing anything of his surroundings is concerned, by midnight, for I arrange that enough spirituous

[1] Published by Jonathan Cape.

liquor is left beside him to sink a ship. In the morning, at dawn, the snow being on the ground, the battalion forms up on the public road. Inside the little garden on the other side of the wall, not ten yards from the centre of the line, the victim is carried to the stake. He is far too drunk to walk. He is out of view save from myself, as I stand on a mound near the wall. As he is produced I see he is practically lifeless and quite unconscious. He has already been bound with ropes. There are hooks on the post; we always do things thoroughly in the Rifles. He is hooked on like dead meat in a butcher's shop. His eyes are bandaged—not that it really matters, for he is already blind. The men of the firing-party pick up their rifles, one of which is unloaded, on a given sign. On another sign they come to the "Present" and, on the lowering of a handkerchief by the officer, they fire—a volley rings out—a nervous ragged volley it is true, yet a volley. Before the fatal shots are fired I had called the battalion to attention. There is a pause, I wait. I see the medical officer examining the victim. He makes a sign, the subaltern strides forward, a single shot rings out. Life is now extinct. We march back to breakfast while the men of a certain company pay the last tribute at the graveside of an unfortunate comrade. This is war.

* * *

BENEATH the frightful strains of modern warfare there was always danger of the nerves' collapsing. If the victim of this malady were fortunate he might be classed as shell-shock and sent home to England; if unfortunate he might find himself facing a court-martial and a firing-party.

SHELL-SHOCK

From *Unwilling Passenger*.[1]

By ARTHUR OSBURN

It was a depressing experience. The shelter we were in had only been a temporary one, constructed for the crews of the German artillery before they had been driven back. So the

[1] Published by Faber and Faber.

side facing their line was naturally quite unprotected from their fire. Long abandoned and out of repair, a single hit would have undoubtedly brought the half-rotten "roof" and tons of bricks and rubble down on top of us. We literally cowered in the mud, feeling quite helpless. Suddenly three men of the Brigade Signals appeared in the entrance carrying or rather dragging a Staff Officer. Breathlessly they flung him inside and, shouting something about "the General's orders," bolted out again. There was no chance of getting further explanations, for the piece of ground that lay between our shelter and the ladder leading underground to the good German dug-out which Brigade Headquarters had annexed was being well plastered with shell.

The Staff Officer, a biggish man, somewhere between twenty-five and thirty, lay moaning on the ground. We could find no wound. In the din I tried to question him, thinking he had been seized with a fit or with acute internal pain. But he only moaned and jibbered and shook his head, grovelling on the ground at my feet with his face pressed to the muddy floor. While I questioned him we were suddenly assailed by a more then usually heavy burst of shelling. A perfect hurricane of whizz-bangs, skimming just over the roof and bursting on a bank only about ten yards away, the splinters rattling on the roof or flying back through the entrance.

The grovelling object appeared now to be suddenly seized with a fresh access of terror. Wildly and incoherently he made efforts to conceal himself between the remains of a broken chair and the mud wall of the shelter. Then suddenly, spasmodically, he began to dig furiously with his fingers. The huddled men, mostly stretcher-bearers of the R.A.M.C., stared at him in amazement, the pink tabs on his collar, and a decoration on his smart uniform, seemed strangely inconsistent with this extraordinary behaviour. It was a case of complete loss of nerve and self-control. Driven mad with terror, slobbering and moaning, he clawed and scrabbled violently in the mud, his head under the chair. It was like a terrified and overrun fox going to ground, trying to dig his way back to safety through the very bowels of the earth. His behaviour was simply less than human. Extreme terror had driven him back through a thousand generations to some pre-human form of life. I suppose some cringing prehistoric half-human thing, making futile efforts to escape from rending beak and steely claw of hovering pterodactyl, may once have burrowed and behaved thus. Not wishing to have my men, who were in any case not enjoying the shelling, demoralised by this exhibition of terror from an officer, who had himself passed orders on to me, I made renewed attempts to quiet him. Above the roar of shelling I shouted in his ear:

"You're all right—safe here! Keep still—be quiet! In a moment, as soon as this shelling stops we'll carry you to an ambulance! Quite close! You'll go back—straight to the Base—Home—and have a long rest! Try and sit up and swallow some brandy."

But one might as well have spoken to a mad dog. At last, the shelling abating a little, I got three of the biggest men I had with me to lay hold of this pathetic, scrabbling incoherent animal that had once been a British Staff Officer, and we tried to drag him, or carry him out. He resisted violently.

At last after several efforts we got rid of him. Half-way to the ambulance that would carry him to safety he tried to bolt back to us! The three men had to risk their lives to get him across the hundred and fifty yards of comparatively open ground and across a road into an old gun-pit where I had had a Ford motor-ambulance concealed. I do not know what became of him; possibly he never reached home alive, or perhaps he is in an asylum. Perhaps, recovered, he shoots partridges now in Norfolk, dines at Claridges, hunts with the North Cotswold, or keeps a chicken farm in Surrey. But when one thinks of how we treated this Staff Officer, and how, on the other hand, some poor, half-educated, blubbering ploughboy, whose nerves had likewise given way, and who was not much more than half this Staff Officer's age, was sent back to face the enemy or be shot for cowardice . . . But that is war. It must often be luck; it can never mean justice.

* * *

Not merely soldiers taken in battle were prisoners of war, but thousands of interned civilians. In every country helpless and unoffending men were penned behind iron bars like wild beasts.

BARBED-WIRE SICKNESS
From *Time Stood Still*.[1]
By Paul Cohen-Portheim

Soldiers led a dangerous and terrible life, prisoners led a helpless and senseless one. Soldiers fought, they were active, they had an aim. They were protecting their country, they were trying to achieve an object, they felt (the great majority felt this, I think) that they were doing something indispensable and very praiseworthy, and all was done to strengthen that conviction in them. The interned civilians were doing nothing, were completely useless. They were quite passive, they suffered in their way, but their suffering was of no use to anybody, nor were they glorified for it. They were quite helpless and quite superfluous, their existence was utterly aimless, their lives perfectly futile. That sense of *complete futility* is the second great horror of internment life. One day these men had been torn from their homes, from their occupations and interests and put in a cage for no purpose but to wait months, a year, many years, till the end of their lives—who knew—until war should be over. There to do what they pleased, provided it was of no earthly use to anybody. The British, of course, could not allow anything that might help the Germans, the Germans interdicted all work of any kind as it might be helpful to the British. They were there with no object whatsoever in view, they just had to wait and wait and wait.

And, strange as it may appear, impossible as it appeared in the first few months, one gets used even to that. One gets used to it because time is a mirage. Time passes slowly when days are full of activities, that is to say after a few very varied days a long time seems to have passed. If you are travelling

[1] Published by Gerald Duckworth, & Co., Ltd.

about, seeing many cities, sights, people, in a few weeks it will seem to you as if you had travelled for months; if, on the other hand, you spend the same number of days in great monotony, let us say lying on the sands and gazing at the sea, time will seem to have passed very quickly. And if you get the incredible sameness and monotony of a prisoner's life, what happens is not so much that time seems short (a day may seem endless) but that you lose all count, all sensation of time. *Time stands still.* Days, weeks, months, years, all these artificial divisions follow each other in endless monotony, time has ceased to have any signification; where there is no aim, no object, no sense, there *is* no time. One gives in, one surrenders, one's will is broken. All is prescribed, regulated, inevitable. All is senseless and hopeless, but one no longer realises it. Only contrast and change create sensation, monotony kills it. Such monotony is a state very near death and very near that of Nirvana; it is the most unnatural state one can be in while still alive—but it is, to some natures at least, paradoxical as it may sound, a state as near complete happiness as one can obtain. But such happiness is for monks and nuns, and if you have ever been near it you will distinguish its reflection in their calm faces.

For that happiness is not for you in a prisoners' camp. You recognise its possibility, but you cannot approach it— for you are not alone. And that is the horror of horrors of that life, the one which not only does not lessen with time, but goes on increasing, and the one no one can imagine who has not been through it: *you are never alone.* Not by day, not by night, not for an hour, not for a second, day after day, year after year. During the War the term *maladie du fil de fer barbelé*, barbed-wire sickness, became a recognised medical designation under which were grouped all sorts of mental symptoms observed in prisoners of war; but it is not the barbed wire which is their cause, it is the monstrous, enforced incessant community which inevitably breeds the malady. There is nothing like it to be found anywhere else. Monks retire to their cells, soldiers have their days or weeks off; here it continues for ever, and the longer it continues the more you suffer from it. No privacy, no possibility of being alone,

BARBED-WIRE SICKNESS

no possibility of finding *quietude*. It is inhuman, cruel and dreadful to force people to live in closest community for years; it becomes almost unbearable when that community is abnormally composed like that of a prisoners' camp. There are no women, no children, there is no old age and next to no youth there, there is just a casual rabble of men forced to be inseparable. Try to imagine—though it is impossible really to understand without having experienced it—what it means, *never* to be *alone* and *never* to know *quiet*, not for a minute, and to continue this for years, and you will begin to wonder that there was no general outbreak of insanity, that there yet remained a difference between lunacy and barbed-wire nerves. The space allotted to a prisoner in a hut was exactly six feet by four (a coffin is six feet by two); besides that there was a space set aside for meals, etc., at the end of the hut, which just held the tables and necessary number of chairs. In your own " space " you were as far removed from the next man as you can be in the hut, and that is a few feet. Nearly all people enclosed their space as time went on, converting it into a cubicle for one or possibly for more, but even then you naturally heard every sound through the thin matchboards which formed the partitions. You heard, in fact, every single noise in the hut, heard people talking, laughing, quarrelling, reading the paper aloud, practising the violin or some other instrument (often several at it at the same time), and they in their turn heard every word you spoke, every movement you made. And if you could have got used to the noise there was the vibration, which I found quite impossible ever to get accustomed to, for the floor consisted of thin, badly joined boards laid on rafters, and whenever anyone walked in the hut or moved a chair it set up vibration right through the hut. At night you heard the breathing, snoring or whispering of thirty men (there is an incredible variety of such noises); some talked in their sleep, and every half (or was it quarter?) hour you heard the guards cry out to each other and your ears followed the sound right round the camp.

No one could stand staying in the hut for long; one soon developed a habit of rushing out every ten minutes or so. That habit became so much of a second nature that I found it very difficult to get rid of again in later years. One rushed round, one walked round, one walked or ran round the camp a hundred times a day, one walked across it or between the huts by way of change, and wherever you went there were people just in front of you, just behind you, just beside you or just coming towards you, and they were always the same people. You could not talk to a friend without being overheard, you could not make a movement that was not watched. The control exercised by the prisoners over each other was infinitely more irritating and galling than the superficial outside control.

No one escaped the effects of such an existence. Its most inevitable results were of two kinds. There were the men who sank into an unlimited mutual intimacy based on mutual contempt. They lost all reserve, all sense of decency, they let themselves go altogether and gave up all that makes life in common tolerable to civilised men. They became what one calls beastly, though I don't know what beasts really behave in such a manner.

* * *

SOME of the liveliest literature of the War is provided by the story of escapes. The best stories—of which the following are typical—are those of young British officers captured by the Germans. The light-hearted way in which these ingenious and courageous men defied every prison device makes ordinary fiction appear tame.

TUNNELLING TO FREEDOM

From *Escapers All*.[1]

By HUGH DURNFORD

Now let us follow one of the shifts behind the trap-door and see them actually at work. The tunnel is progressing steadily if slowly. A stratum of very hard, large stones has been encountered, much worse than that earlier stratum of yellow clay. The man on the job at the tunnel face lies on his

[1] Published by John Lane, The Bodley Head, Ltd.

stomach in a strained and cramped position. The tunnel is only eighteen inches in diameter. He has two tools—a trowel and a cold chisel—within reach of his hand and a candle in the wall beside him. He prods, levers and finally wrenches out the big stones till they lie in a heap up to his chin, large enough to be removed. He pulls in a rope which is attached to him. At the other end of the rope is a basin which he gets past and in front of him and fills up with the stones. Then with incredible difficulty he gets the full basin somehow behind his body again. Now one of his mates who is working the pump at the tunnel mouth does his share. He also has hold of another length of rope attached to the basin and at the signalling jerk from the excavator he pulls the basin towards him. And so, backwards and forwards, while the third man packs away the stones in the rapidly filling chamber.

The pump consists of bellows home-made from wood and the leather of a flying-officer's coat. It has to keep the air tolerably clean at the tunnel face so that the tunnellers can breathe and the candle can stay alight. It is fixed on wooden uprights and discharges its blast into a pipe of tin tubes made out of biscuit boxes which have come in parcels from home. The pipe is sunk in the tunnel floor and grows, of course, with the tunnel. Later on—as the twists and irregularities of the tunnel increased—the rope and basin method gave place to merely filling sacks with the earth and stones and pulling them out from the face. It isn't a popular pastime to wriggle fifty yards back, fifty yards forward, on elbows and toes in clean air in the open. In foul air, in a tortuous and uneven hole, pulling a heavy sack out behind you, it is still less so.

* * *

EXPLOITS OF THE ESCAPING CLUB
From *Escapers All*.[1]
By A. J. Evans

The carriage was crowded, and both racks were full of small luggage, and, noticing this, I had an idea. I arranged with the

[1] Published by John Lane, The Bodley Head, Ltd.

others to act in a certain way when the train next went slowly, and I gave the word by saying to the sentry, in German: " Will you have some food ? We are going to eat." Five or ten minutes of tense excitement followed. Suddenly the train began to slow up. I leant across and said to the sentry, " Will you have some food ? We are going to eat." Immediately everyone in the carriage stood up with one accord and pulled their stuff off the racks. The sentry also stood up, but was almost completely hidden from the window by a confused mass of men and bags. Under cover of this confusion, Buckley and I stood up on our seats. I slipped the strap of my haversack over my shoulder, pushed down the window, put my leg over, and jumped into the night, I fell—not very heavily— on the wires at the side of the track, and lay still in the dark shadow. Three seconds later Buckley came flying out after me, and seemed to take rather a heavy toss. The end of the train wasn't yet past me, and we knew there was a man with a rifle in the last carriage ; so when Buckley came running along the track calling out to me, I caught him and pulled him into the ditch at the side. The train went by, and its tail lights vanished round a corner and apparently no one saw or heard us.

I have not space to say much about our walk to the German-Swiss frontier, about 200 miles away. We only walked by night, and lay up in hiding all through the hours of daylight— which was, I think, the worst part of the business and wore out our nerves and physical strength far more than the six or seven hours' marching at night, for the day seemed intolerably long from 4.30 a.m. to 9.30 p.m.—seventeen hours—the sun was very hot, and there was little shade, and we were consumed with impatience to get on. Moreover, we could never be free from anxiety at any moment of those seventeen hours. The strain at night of passing through a village when a few lights still burnt and dogs seemed to wake and bark at us in every house, or of crossing a bridge when one expected to be challenged at any moment never worried me so much as a cart passing or men talking near our daytime hiding-places.

We went into hiding at dawn or soon after, and when we'd taken off our boots and put on clean socks we would both drop asleep at once. It was a bit of a risk—perhaps one of us ought to have stayed awake, but we took it deliberately since we got great benefit from a sound sleep while we were still warm from walking. And it was only for about an hour, before we woke again shivering, for the mornings were very cold and we were usually soaked with dew up to our waists. Then we had breakfast—the great moment of the day—and rations were pretty good at first, as we underestimated the time we would take by about four days. But later on we had to help things out with raw potatoes from the fields, which eventually became our mainstay. All day long we were pestered with stinging insects. Our hands and faces became swollen all over, and the bites on my feet came up in blisters which broke and left raw places when I put on my boots again.

On the fifteenth day our impatience got the better of us, and we started out before it was properly dark, and suddenly came upon a man in soldier's uniform scything grass on the side of the road. We were filthily dirty and unshaven and must have looked the most villainous tramps; it was stupid of us to have risked being seen; but it would have aroused his suspicion if we'd turned back, so we walked on past him. He looked up and said something we didn't catch. We answered " Good evening " as usual. But he called after us, and then when we took no notice, shouted " Halt! Halt! " and ran after us with his scythe.

We were both too weak to run fast or far, and moreover we saw at that moment a man with a gun about fifty yards to our right. There was only one thing to be done, and we did it.

We turned haughtily and waited for our pursuer, and when he was a few yards away Buckley demanded in a voice quivering with indignant German what the devil he meant by shouting at us. He almost dropped his scythe with astonishment, then turned round and went slowly back to his work. Buckley had saved the day.

The end of our march on the following night brought us within fifteen kilometres of the Swiss frontier, and we decided to eat the rest of our food and cross the next night. However, I kept back a few small meat lozenges. We learnt the map by heart so as to avoid having to strike matches later on, and left all our spare kit behind us in order to travel light for this last lap. But it wasn't to be our last lap.

We were awfully weak by now and made slow progress through the heavy going, and about two hours after we'd started a full, bright moon rose which made us feel frightfully conspicuous. Moreover, we began to doubt our actual position, for a road we'd expected to find wasn't there. However, we tramped on by compass and reached a village which we hoped was a place named Riedheim, within half a mile of the frontier. But here we suddenly came on a single-line railway which wasn't on our map. We were aghast—we were lost—and, moreover, Buckley was fearfully exhausted for want of food, so we decided to lie up for another night in a thick wood on a hill. The meat lozenges I'd saved now came in very handy and we also managed to find water and some more raw potatoes. Then we slept, and when daylight came studied our small-scale map and tried to make head or tail of our situation.

We had a good view of the countryside from our position, but could make nothing of it. Perhaps we were already in Switzerland? It was essential to know and it was no good looking for signposts since they'd all been removed within a radius of ten miles of the frontier. I think we were both slightly insane by now from hunger and fatigue; anyhow I decided to take a great risk. I took off my tunic and walking down into the fields asked a girl who was making hay what the name of the village was. It was Riedheim—as I'd originally thought. The railway, of course, had been made after the map was printed. I don't know what the girl thought of my question and appearance; she gave me a sly look, but went on with her work. I returned to Buckley, and when it was quite dark we left our hiding-place. We had three-quarters of an hour to cross the frontier before the moon rose—and we had to go with the greatest care. For a time we walked bent double, and then we went down on our hands and knees, pushing our way through the thick, long grass of water meadows. The night was so still—surely the swishing of the grass as we moved through it must be audible for hundreds of yards. On and on we went—endlessly it seemed—making for a stream which we had seen from our hill and now knew must be the boundary-line. Then the edge of the moon peered at us over the hills. We crawled at top speed now, until Buckley's hand on my heel suddenly brought me to a halt. About fifteen yards ahead was a sentry. He was walking along a foot-path on the bank of a stream. *The* stream. He had no rifle, and had probably just been relieved. He passed without seeing us. One last spurt and we were in the stream and up the other bank. " Crawl," said Buckley. " Run," said I, and we ran. It was just after midnight when we crossed into Switzerland and freedom on our eighteenth night out.

* * *

INVETERATE ESCAPERS
From *Escapers All*.[1]
By Duncan Grinnell-Milne

There were two rows of wire at Ströhen: one row, tall, close-meshed, surmounted by barbed wire; the other, the inner row, a fence some three or four feet high, designed to keep us away from the outer row. The space between was called the " Neutral Zone "—anyone found itside it got shot! Wherever there was a gate in the outer wire fence, there was naturally a smaller gate in the inner one; and it was my job to open this small gate, at the crucial moment, so as to let the " battering-ram " party go through at speed. I also had to watch the sentries, lest they should smell a rat—meaning me !

On the evening of the appointed day, the gallant party assembled behind a nearby hut—iron bar, rucksacks, escaping kit and all, in readiness. As it grew dark I commenced pacing up and down near the wire, trying to look happy, with an eye on the sentry. Presently, when no Germans were looking, I gave the signal to " stand by." Then I strolled up to the small gate, unlatched it and pulled it open. It squeaked horribly, but I couldn't let go or it would have swung to—and I had already waved and whistled for the charging-party to start. I couldn't see much in the dark, but I heard a

[1] Published by John Lane, The Bodley Head, Ltd.

scuffling sound as they got under way; and a second later they came thundering past. I have a recollection of feeling at that moment exactly like an old man at a level-crossing holding open the gates for an express to go by; and the next moment the express was derailed and I was left looking stupidly at the accident.

There was a tremendous crash as the front man of the party hit the gate. In the darkness he had missed the lock with the end of the ram and it was his face that charged the framework. But in spite of the five strong men behind him, his face wasn't hard enough to push down the obstruction, and he let forth a yell that must have curdled the blood of all the sentries round the camp. The iron bar was immediately dropped with a loud clang, and the party having picked itself up made off at top speed in the direction of the huts. I fancy I was rather dazed at the rapidity of these happenings, for I stood for a moment, still holding the little gate open, gaping at the "battering-ram" on the ground, until a loud report close behind brought me suddenly to my senses and I just managed to dodge into a hut before the infuriated guards came streaming into the camp, ready to start the inevitable search.

And not long afterwards, when numerous attempts had driven the commandant to the verge of insanity, a properly organised search for escaping kit was made with the help of detectives from Berlin. We all felt very sorry for those poor detectives! From the time they entered the camp to the time they left, the unfortunate men were given no peace. Impeded at every turn, they were harried from one room to another; contraband captured in one hut was recaptured by the prisoners in the next. On leaving, surrounded by a band of cheering British officers, several of them complained that their pockets had been picked; their identity cards and police papers stolen. And one wretched man walked out with a notice pinned to his coat-tail: "You know my methods, Watson!"

Next day more prisoners escaped.

* * *

Many men faced death more easily than the loss of limbs, for there is no sight more poignant than a strong man who has lost his strength. Affecting as is this to the onlooker, still more insistent is the self-consciousness to a sensitive man.

LIMBLESS

From *The Whistlers' Room*.[1]

By Paul Alverdes

It was not, however, for their cracked notes that the whistlers blushed, but for this to-do with lifting their bibs and feeling with their fingers for their secret mouthpiece; and this predicament they tried every means to disguise. Were a stranger to address them on the roads through the park, or in the wide passages and halls of the great building where in bad weather they sometimes took their walks, they usually forbore returning an immediate answer. They looked in meditation down at their toes, or with head courteously inclined and raised eyebrows gazed into the face of him who accosted them as though earnestly seeking within themselves for a suitable response. Meanwhile, quite without any particular object, they put up a hand to their breasts and after a moment proceeded as though to dally with a shirt button that might be concealed beneath the white pinafore. After this they began to talk and sometimes, if they gained sufficient confidence, their first silence might be exchanged for a cheerful loquacity. It was as though they wished to show that, in the very natural and, indeed, most everyday matter of being hoarse, they were not any different from other men. Why they did this they could not themselves have said; and they did not speak of it to each other. Yet they all behaved as though sworn to secrecy by oath; and when a fourth was added to them, he, from the very first, did likewise.

It was just the same, moreover, with the others in the room upstairs who had lost an arm or a leg. They felt no shyness at being seen by strangers with an empty sleeve or a trouser

[1] Published by Martin Secker.

leg dangling loose and empty; indeed some of them vaunted their docked limbs and even went so far as to instil a kind of grizzly veneration in those who had come off more lightly by a display of their sad stumps. Yet the scraping and creaking of the sometimes not very successful appliances with which they had to learn to walk again, caused them acute embarrassment before strangers. At once they came to a stop and tried to disguise the grasp for the lever that enabled them to fix the artificial joint by catching or pulling at their trouser, or by any other apparently trivial movement. They never, either, displayed an unclothed false hand or foot, and at night when they undressed for bed they concealed the arm they had screwed off by hanging the coat over it, or the leg by leaving it carefully in a corner inside the trouser. For they were always afraid of being surprised by outsiders, and would have liked best being always by themselves.

* * *

Among the daily excitements of the War, the great fire of Salonika—which in ordinary times would have provided sensational news for the Press of the world—passed almost unnoticed.

THE GREAT FIRE OF SALONIKA

From *With a Woman's Unit in Serbia, Salonika and Sebastopol*.[1]

By Dr. I. Emslie Hutton

The great fire of Salonika, which began on Saturday, August 18th, must certainly have been one of the most appalling fires of contemporary history. About five o'clock in the afternoon we noticed a thin lick of yellow flame just beyond the bazaar. Half an hour later it seemed to have grown bigger, and we all drew one another's attention to it, but none of us considered it was anything serious, and thought no more about it. The inhabitants must surely have realised the danger, but as they had no fire engines or methods of coping with it, nothing was done. The evening breeze arose and the flames

[1] Published by Williams and Norgate, Ltd.

THE GREAT FIRE OF SALONIKA

licked along eastwards towards the principal parts of the town.

About 7 p.m. Dr. McIlroy and I went into the town and walked up to the city walls; there below us was a belt of leaping, roaring fire that stretched almost from one end of the town to the other, and right across the middle part of it above the rue Ægnatia. This great ferocious monster ate up house after house with lightning speed, for the little evening breeze had developed into a mild Vardar wind, and now all the authorities saw that the situation was as bad as it could be, and that nothing could stop the progress of that roaring furnace. It was unforgettable; all the pictures of hell that were ever painted fall short of it in fearfulness, and its hungry roar, mingled with snarls and hisses and the crash of the falling ruins, was most awe-inspiring. The inhabitants ran about trying to save their possessions and not knowing where to take refuge. The progress of the flames was now so fast that the streets were thronged with the people carrying what they could, and the hamals were making a fortune carrying great loads of household goods for the highest bidder. A huge wardrobe, an enormous and hideous mirror or a piano would come blundering down one of the narrow streets, a hamal peeping out from under it, and it would sometimes meet a sewing-machine or a feather-bed going in the other direction and get jammed. Mothers and children scurried along with as much as they could carry, and bedridden grandmothers or invalids were half-dragged, half-carried along. All was confusion, grief and hopelessness.

We hurried back as soon as possible, for there seemed no reason why the fire should not spread along the line of houses both to our hospital, G.H.Q., and the other offices of the Allies.

By nine o'clock huge fire-balls were being blown right into our hospital and even beyond it, for the wind was still in the same direction, and there was great danger that our tents would catch fire, even if the fire itself did not reach us. Members of the staff, armed with brooms to beat out the flames, perched themselves on the ridge-poles of the high tents and stayed there till the wind changed and there was no more danger. "*Comme ces dames sont pratiques; les seestaires ont merveilleuses,*" said our patients. "*Sont des garçons manqués,*" grunted Danjou, the taciturn old *Médecin Chef* from next door.

Before midnight the entire town was a semicircle of fire, and it seemed as if nothing could escape; mercifully, after midnight the wind suddenly changed, and the flames, instead of licking further eastward, blazed straight southwards to the bay, setting fire to the barques that lay alongside the quay. These barques had been doing excellent work during the progress of the fire, and since the quay was till now untouched they had been able to save the inhabitants and some stores. Now moving out for safety, they spread the fire to other ships, and there was much confusion in the bay for a time. Nevertheless, the change of wind certainly saved the remainder of Salonika, and when daylight broke, though the fire had not stopped, and, indeed, continued to smoulder for days, the danger was over.

On all sides we heard praises of the British lorry-drivers, who worked most strenuously and considerately for all, especially the women and children. Of other Allies it was said that the drivers were not above taking tips and that much stealing went on (this is possible, for all the well-stocked shops were completely looted). It was said, too, that it was revolting to see the Russians lying in the gutters drinking the wine which flowed down from the burst barrels in the store-houses on the quay. Olive Kelso King did splendid work in this fire, and was awarded the Gold Medal for bravery by the Serbian Headquarters for which she was now working.

A few days later we went down to see the town, which was still smouldering and hardly recognisable. All the quayside buildings were completely gutted, and nothing remained of Venizelos Street or the Bazaar but masses of masonry; every shop and hotel had been wiped out, the roads were blocked with smouldering debris, and the whole place was desolation. The Turkish quarter, however, nestled on the hillside as cheerfully as ever, and the old walls and the mosques rose dignified among the desolation, save the beautiful Church of St. Demetrius, which was almost completely destroyed. Many Salonicians were heavily insured with

SUBMARINES IN THE BALTIC

British Insurance Companies, who paid up the full amounts at once, much to the amazement of the inhabitants, who thought it a wonderful and noble act of generosity.

Salonika was soon in working order again, though no attempt was made to rebuild it. The inhabitants went back into the skeletons of their shops, raised tarpaulins and corrugated iron, and carried on as brisk a trade as before. Great fires must have occurred many times there during the previous centuries, and the inhabitants seemed to take it all as a matter of course, and hardly ever alluded to it. There was great discussion as to whether it was caused by enemy incendiarism, and since Salonika was full of spies this would not have been a difficult matter; on the previous day Monastir had been evacuated because of a fire caused by incendiary bombs, and Florina had likewise suffered. Be that as it may, the official opinion seemed to be that it was accidental, and was caused by a careless housewife upsetting some boiling fat on the fire!

* * *

THE exploits of the German U-boats have rather tended to overshadow the splendid work of our own submarines throughout the War. In the days of the Gallipoli expedition, these had worked havoc among the Turkish shipping in the Sea of Marmora. Later a small squadron was posted to the Baltic, where they proceeded to make the seas highly unpleasant for German warships and merchantmen.

SUBMARINES IN THE BALTIC

From *Submarine and Anti-Submarine*.[1]

By SIR HENRY NEWBOLT

Commander Goodhart ran on, at seven and a half knots, till he got within 3000 yards, when he eased to five knots in order to lessen his wake. The wind was slight, from SSE., and there was bright sunlight. The conditions were ideal for

[1] Published by Longmans, Green & Co.

an attack from the southward. All tubes were made ready; the enemy came on at an estimated speed of fifteen knots. At 9.28 the port destroyer passed ahead; four minutes later, Commander Goodhart fired his bow tube at the warship's fore-bridge and began to look out for results.

They came. After one minute he observed a very vivid flash on the water-line at the point of aim. This was immediately followed by a very heavy concussion, and the entire ship was hidden instantly in a huge column of thick grey smoke. Evidently the torpedo had exploded the fore magazine. The sky was filled with debris, and the smaller bits began falling in the water near the submarine. There was no use in spending time on the surface, and in one minute more, E8 was sliding down to 50 feet, where she stayed for eight minutes, to give the rest of the ship ample time to come down. At 9.42 Commander Goodhart rose to 20 feet, and took a survey through his periscope. There was no sign of of the *Prinz Adalbert*. The two destroyers had closed on to the scene of the explosion, but it was not likely that they had been able to find any survivors, for the destruction of the ship had been instantaneous and complete. Commander Goodhart decided not to attack them, because, for all he knew, they were ignorant of his presence; if so, they might very probably imagine the damage to have been done by a mine, and give him future opportunities. The shot had been a long one, about 1300 yards, and this was in the circumstances particularly fortunate; for at a shorter distance, such as 500 or 600 yards, the submarine herself would have felt a tremendous shock from the double explosion.

An hour later he saw four destroyers hovering about the place of the wreck. He turned away, and they made no attempt to follow. At dawn next day he reported by wireless, and then proceeded to his base.

In the meantime E19, Lieut. Commander F. N. Cromie, had arrived. She set to work in earnest upon the German shipping engaged in the service of the naval and military departments of the enemy, towards the western end of the Baltic. Monday, October 11th, was her best day, and the beginning of a downright panic in the Hamburg trade.

SUBMARINES IN THE BALTIC

"8 a.m.," says Lieut.-Commander Cromie, "started to chase merchant shipping." He had good hunting. At 9.40 a.m. he stopped the *Walter Leonhardt*, from Lulea to Hamburg, with iron ore. The crew abandoned ship, and were picked up by a Swedish steamer, considerately stopped for the purpose. A gun-cotton charge then sent the empty vessel to the bottom. By noon, E19 was chasing the *Germania* of Hamburg, signalling her to stop immediately. In spite of the signals and a warning gun-shot, she continued to bolt, and soon ran ashore. Lieut.-Commander Cromie went alongside cautiously to save her crew, but found that they had already abandoned ship. He tried to tow her off, but failed to move her—small wonder, for her cargo consisted of nearly three million kgs. of the finest concentrated iron ore, from Stockholm to Stettin. He left her filling with water, and at 2 gave chase to the *Gutrune*. By 3 he had towed her crew to the Swedish steamer, and started her for the bottom with her 4,500,000 kgs. of iron ore, from Lulea to Hamburg.

The game went forward merrily. At 4.25 he began to chase two more large steamers going south. In twenty minutes he had stopped one—the Swedish boat *Nyland*, with ore for Rotterdam and papers all correct—told her to proceed, and ten minutes later caught the *Direktor Rippenhagen*, with magnetic ore from Stockholm to Nadenheim. While she was sinking he stopped another Swede bound for Newcastle, and gave her the *Direktor's* crew to take care of. An hour later, he proceeded to chase a large steamer, the *Nicomedia*, who tried to make off towards the Swedish coast. A shot across her bows brought her to a more resigned frame of mind. She proved to be a large and extremely well-fitted vessel, carrying six to seven million kgs. of magnetic ore from Lulea to Hamburg. The crew were sent ashore in boats, and E19 proceeded up the west of Gotland. Her cruise was marked by one more incident—a significant one. During the morning of October 12th, Lieut-Commander Cromie stopped the *Nike*, and went alongside to examine her. He found her to be in iron ore from Stockholm to Stettin, under command of Captain Anderson, whose passport from the Liverpool Police proved him to be a Swede. To the Hun, this would have made no difference; but Lieut.-Commander Cromie had British ideas on international law. He sent Lieutenant Mee on board with a prize crew of two men, in the good old style of our ancestors, and ordered them to take the prize into Reval for further investigation. After what we have already said about submarines and war policy, the point needs no pressing. War against trading vessels and non-combatants is possible within the rules, but only in certain circumstances. Even where those circumstances exist, there is no excuse for breaking the rules; and where they do not exist, only a barbarian would hack his way through the net of international law and common humanity. Our Navy has in all circumstances kept both these laws: the German submarines have deliberately and cruelly broken both.

* * *

THE HUNTER HUNTED

From *By Guess and By God.*[1]

By William Guy Carr

Her position was only six miles SSW. of the harbour of Heligoland. As the boat steadied to the proper depth for a diving patrol Horton raised periscope. He watched. The mist was thinning. Through its weak tatters he thought he caught a shape. The fog cleared and showed him an enemy light cruiser about two miles away.

Horton was able to get within 600 yards of her when he recognised her as the light cruiser *Hela*. He told the crew. Nerves tightened, eyes steadied, breathing became a conscious effort. It was a great moment. Our men were still smarting under the loss of H.M.S. *Pathfinder*. And at last the enemy had been found. Here was the chance to even the score.

The crew stood silently at their action stations. Their eyes were glued on the youthful commander crouching with his hands on the handles of the periscope gear. He watched

[1] Published by Hutchinson & Co. (Publishers), Ltd.

the seconds tick off the interval until he should show the periscope for the clipped second needed to fire a torpedo.

The motors stopped. All machinery was silent save for the whirr of the hydroplane wheels or the steering wheel. The tension was great. The atmosphere was charged like a mine. Horton glanced at the clock, the depth gauge, and the compass. "Raise periscope!" Crouching almost to his knees, he raised himself with it, his eye glued to the rubber eye-piece. The moment daylight penetrated the lense he shouted: "Stop periscope!" True to his calculations, the *Hela* was steaming past, oblivious of the menace lurking on her beam.

"Fire one . . . fire two!" The order rang through the compartment like the crack of a revolver. There was a hiss and a muffled roar, followed by a slight shock as the torpedoes left the tubes. Then all waited for the explosion. E9 dived the second the torpedoes left on their death journey. Horton was taking no chances of alarming the enemy before his last moment. As E9 dived, the explosion occurred.

E9 was brought up to periscope depth again. The force of the explosion had stopped the *Hela* dead in her tracks. She took a heavy list to starboard. Horton was studying the success of his attack, when suddenly he was made aware of his own danger. A salvo of shells splattered around the periscope. They came from ships he had not seen. Again E9 dived, but only for a moment.

Evading the attentions of a swarm of mosquito craft, Horton raised periscope again, determined to see the death like a hunter who tracks his kill that he may deliver the last needed shot. But there was no need. The cruiser had gone. All Horton saw was a number of armed trawlers rescuing men on the spot where she had gone down.

Then started forty-eight hours of a living inferno for the crew of the British submarine. A nest of enemy destroyers circled her position and hunted her all day. The water was not deep enough for safety. Several times E9 narrowly escaped ramming. Countless times her hull was brushed by the slowly searching tendrils of sweeps. When darkness came the batteries were dangerously low. All that night E9 and the surface craft played hide-and-seek in deadly earnestness. Time after time the submarine rose to the surface to get her charge under way and was sent into a crash dive by the onrushing rams of the destroyers. Under these conditions the batteries were partly charged.

Next day the weather sided with the enemy. A full gale lashed the shallow waters into a fury of flying foam and breaking wave-tops. The short, steep seas made it impossible for E9 to keep her trim at periscope depth. The bumping made it impossible for her to stay on the bottom. The enemy and the high seas made it seem almost impossible for her to proceed on the surface. In spite of these difficulties, her men managed to bring her back safely to Harwich with word that they had avenged the *Pathfinder*.

.   .   .   .   .

Typical of the work done by the E-boats operating against the ore ships was E19's fruitful career on October 11th. She had proceeded on patrol, and during the forenoon watch, sighted and stopped the *Walter Leonhardt*. To do this she had naturally to come to the surface in what were actually enemy waters. She had to take the chance of being torpedoed by an enemy submarine, and the chance that the innocent-looking merchantman was in reality an armed vessel flying false colours. I mention these possibilities to point out how the crews of submarines belonging to both countries were always on the *qui vive*. They were always under tension; always suffering nervous strain. The *Walter Leonhardt* proved to be bound from Lulea to Hamburg with iron ore. She was legitimate prey. Cromie ordered her crew into the boats. Our men felt about sinking merchant ships as a big-game hunter would feel if he were to turn his rifle on a domestic cow in a barnyard. Attacking warships was a different matter. They were swift of speed and deadly in defence. Hunting them brought a thrill no big-game hunter ever experienced.

From the conning-tower Cromie saw that the weather was growing threatening. Ordering the crew of the ore ship to remain where they were in their lifeboats, he chased off to investigate smoke on the horizon. He found a Swedish vessel, stopped her, and requested that she alter course to pick up the crew of the *Walter Leonhardt*.

Hardly had the huge ore ship settled to the bottom than another ship was sighted. She turned tail the moment she sighted E19 and raced for the beach. Cromie went alongside the stranded vessel and, making fast to her, tried to tow her into sufficient water to sink her. Failing in this, he ordered the crew ashore and damaged the ship to such an extent that salvage would be out of the question. The *Germania* had 3000 tons of ore aboard her.

Just as the men were trying to snatch a bite to eat, E19 stopped the *Gutrune*. Her papers showed her to be bound from Lulea to Hamburg. She was sent to the bottom with 4400 tons of ore. Before sinking her, Cromie placed her crew abroad a Swedish steamer. Within the hour he was hot on the trail of two more large steamers. The first he reached was a Swedish vessel, and as her papers were all correct, she was allowed to proceed. E19 chased after the other, which turned out to be the *Direktor Rippenhagen*, loaded with magnetic ore for Germany. While she was in the process of sinking, he stopped another ship which was bound for Newcastle, England, and put the crew of the *Direktor* aboard. Hardly was this job finished when the *Nicodemia* hove in view. As soon as she sighted the submarine she altered course and headed for the coast of Sweden, hoping to gain the protection of neutral waters. A couple of shots aimed close to her bows made her change her mind, and her crew was forced to watch the cargo of nearly seven thousand tons go crashing downward as the extremely well-appointed ship surrendered to the charges which had been put abroad her. As no other ship was near, E19 towed the crew to shore. Cromie had destroyed more than twenty-two thousand tons of enemy shipping that day, and had made ample provision for the safety of the crews of the destroyed vessels.

* * *

Among the many devices adopted to combat the menace of the U-boats was the Q-boat—an "innocent" merchant ship, simply asking to be torpedoed, but revealing hidden guns at the last possible moment.

U-BOATS

From *The Diary of a U-Boat Commander*.[1]
By "Etienne" (Commander Stephen King-Hall)

Once again Death has stretched forth his bony fingers to catch me by the throat, and only by a chance have I wriggled free.

Yesterday afternoon, at 5 p.m., we sighted a small steamer flying Spanish colours and steering for Cardiff. The weather was choppy, but not too bad, and I decided to exercise the gun's crew, though I did not think there would be much doing, as the Spaniards soon give in.

I opened fire at 6000 metres, and pitched a shell ahead of her and ran up the signal to heave-to. The wretched little craft paid no attention, and continued on her lumbering course. I suspected the presence of an Englishman on her bridge, and determined to hit.

This we did with our sixth shot, and she stopped dead and wallowed in the trough, with clouds of steam pouring out of her engine-room; we had evidently got the engine-room.

As we closed her, it was evident that a tremendous panic was taking place on board. The port sea boat was being launched, but one fall broke and the occupants fell into the water. My navigator begged me to give her another, which I did, and hit her right aft. Two boatloads of gesticulating individuals now appeared from the shelter of her lee side and began pulling wildly away from the ship.

The navigator, whose eyes were dancing with excitement, was very keen to play with them by spraying the water with machine-gun bullets; but it seemed to me to be waste of ammunition, and I would not permit it.

Meanwhile, we had approached to within about four

[1] Published by Hutchinson & Co. (Publishers), Ltd.

hundred metres of her port bow. I was debating whether to accelerate her sinking, when I noticed that a fire had broken out aft, and I became possessed with a childish curisoity to see the fire being put out as she sank. It was a kind of contest between the elements.

As I watched her, I was startled to hear three or four reports from the region of the fire.

" Ammunition ! " shouted the pilot, with wide-open eyes.

In an instant I pressed the diving alarm, as I realised our deadly peril. Fool that I had been, she was a decoy-ship. They must have realised on board that I had seen through their disguise, for as we began to move forward, under the motors, a trap-door near her bows fell down, the White Ensign was broken at the fore, and a 4-inch gun opened fire from the embrasure that was revealed on her side.

We were fortunate in that our conning-tower was already right ahead of the enemy, and as I dropped down into the conning-tower, I saw that as she could not turn, we were safe.

A few shells plunged harmlessly into the water near our stern, and then we were under.

We came up to a periscope depth, and I surveyed her from a position off her stern. She was sinking fast, but I felt so furious at being nearly trapped that I could not resist giving her a torpedo ; detonation was complete, and a mass of wreckage shot into the air as the hull of the ship disappeared. As to the two boats, I left them to make the best course to land that they could.

As they were fifty miles off the shore when I left them and it blew force six a few hours afterwards, I rather think they have joined the list of " Missing."

* * *

Q-BOATS

From *My Mystery Ships*.[1]

By Rear-Admiral Gordon Campbell, V.C., D.S.O.

Having now arranged our normal way of cruising, the next thing was to prepare to meet and engage the enemy. Our

[1] Published by Hodder and Stoughton, Ltd.

object was to entice the submarine to come as close as possible to the ship on the surface with his lids open. How was this to be done? Obviously to encourage him to attack us, and then, by feigning to have abandoned the ship to its fate, induce him to come up. To add to the realism, the "abandon ship" was to be done in a "panic" and confusion, which caused the men who took part in this effort to be referred to as the "panic party."

It must not be imagined for a moment that the average British merchant ship is abandoned, if such becomes necessary, in a panic. We all know of too many heroic cases of ships sinking in war and peace without any trace of it. All the same, there is not too much time to be lost, especially if an impatient enemy is shelling you. The procedure, then, was, as soon as any enemy (even if only periscope) was sighted, the "alarm" was sounded. Different "alarms" were used, denoting whether the submarine was on the port or starboard side: this was done so as to enable any men who were working on the upper deck to proceed to their action station on the offside—if his station was on the bridge, he would come up the "off" ladder. No one was allowed to run to his station (what a disgraceful thing for a man-of-war!); nor was anything in the way of crowding allowed—though this was dealt with by limiting the number of men on deck. The alarm sent all the guns' crews who were not already there to their guns and every man to his station, all the movements taking place unseen and underground, as it were, by the alleyways and trap-hatches; obviously you couldn't have about twenty men running about the deck and disappearing into hen-coops! The men to whom I have referred before as lounging about, etc., remained in the same attitude of disinterestedness.

If a torpedo was fired, the order was given through the voice-pipes—"torpedo missed" or "torpedo hit." In the first case, all went on as before, maintaining the pretence that either we had not seen the "wake" or did not know what it was. In the second case, the ship was abandoned by the "panic party." This order to "abandon ship" might also be given in the event of our being shelled. Now, the "panic party" had to be thoroughly drilled and the whole performance rehearsed. Of course, from time to time we thought of improvements and variations, but the general procedure was as follows: all those men who had been hanging about the upper deck rushed to the boats, men also came tumbling out of the fo'c'sle and up from the stokeholds and engine-rooms; everything was pandemonium, mingled with shouts for help. We did not imagine that the shouts for "help" would be heard by the submarine, especially if she was submerged, but I thought it would add to a more realistic acting of the play than a sort of "dumb" charade. A rush was made for the boats, and one boat was generally let go "with a run," end up. This even happens sometimes in the best-regulated ships. The officer in charge would come to the bridge and swop hats with me, taking my gold-banded hat, and becoming Master. He would be the last to get into the boats, accompanied by a stuffed parrot in its cage. The stuffed parrot was one of our afterthoughts, and we kept it in the saloon in a beautiful green cage. Sailors generally have some pet. Many pets were suggested, but after much discussion in the mess, a parrot won the day. After the boats, which contained about thirty men, and were rigged as a complete ship's company, with a proportion of officers, seamen, firemen, stewards, cooks, etc. had shoved off, a grimy stoker would appear from the stokehold, shouting and yelling, and a boat would go back to fetch him. They would now lay off the ship to see her finish. The ship would now be, to all intents, deserted, but in reality all the guns would be manned, the chief engineer and his party in the boiler-room and engine-rooms, the captain and quarter-master on the bridge, and a signalman ready to break out the White Ensign.

. . . . . .

As soon as the boats were away, the submarine went close to them, only a few yards off; she was obviously going to leave nothing to chance, and it was as well that the crew were carefully dressed to their part with no service flannels. One of the crew in the boats was heard telling another, as the periscope was looking at them: "Don't talk so loud; he'll hear you!"

The submarine now came and inspected the ship at very close range, some ten or fifteen yards—so close that from my look-out at the starboard end of the bridge I could see the whole of his hull under water. The temptation to open fire on the periscope was very great, though obviously not the thing to do, as it would have done no harm. But it looked at the time as if, after getting deliberately torpedoed, we were going to have nothing to show for it, since he appeared to be moving off.

The chief had reported the ship sinking by the stern; still, there was nothing for it but to wait and watch the submarine move slowly past the ship and away ahead. All this time the men on board were lying hidden, feeling the ship getting deeper by the stern—in fact, the men at the after-gun were practically awash—but they all stuck it and never moved a muscle. Each one had a responsibility. Had one man got in a real panic and showed himself, the game would have been up; the scrutiny of the submarine was indeed a severe one. The wireless operator, locked up in his cabin by himself, had to sit still and do nothing; he must have been aching to send out an S.O.S. and have his picture in the illustrated papers next day as "the man who sent out the S.O.S.," but he knew we wanted no one to interfere with our cold-blooded encounter with the enemy.

After the submarine had passed up the starboard side, he crossed our bow and went over towards port; the signalman and I, therefore, did our "belly crawl" and swopped places. At 10.5 a.m. the enemy broke surface about three hundred yards on our port bow, but not in the bearing of any of the guns. Anyhow, things were looking more hopeful, and I was able to tell the men that all was going well. The boats had, by this time, got to our port quarter, and towards them the submarine now proceeded. We heard afterwards that their intention had been to take the "Master" prisoner and also get some provisions. It was only a matter of waiting now, as the submarine was right up, with conning-tower open. It was obvious that she would pass very close to the ship, and we might just as well have all guns bearing, so as to make sure of it. As she came abreast of the ship the captain was seen coming out of the conning-tower. At this moment I gave the order to open fire—at 10.10—twenty-five minutes after we had been torpedoed. The White Ensign fluttered at the masthead, and three 12-pounders, a 6-pounder, the Maxim-guns and rifles all opened fire together. What a shock it must have been for the captain suddenly to see our wheel-house collapse, our sides to fall down, and the hen-coop to splutter forth Maxim shots! But he had not long to think, as the first shot, which was from the 6-pounder, hit him, and I believe the first intimation the submarine crew had that anything was wrong was seeing their captain drop through the conning-tower.

The range was only about one hundred yards, so the submarine never had a chance of escape. It seemed almost brutal to fire at such close range, but we had taken a sporting chance ourselves in decoying him to such an ideal position that one really had no other thought than destruction.

The submarine never seemed to recover from her surprise as she lay on the surface upon our beam, whilst we pumped lead and steel into her. Forty-five shells were fired in all, practically every one being a hit, so that she finally sank with the conning-tower shattered and open, the crew pouring out as hard as they could. About eight men were seen in the water, which was bitterly cold and thick with oil. I ordered the boats to their assistance, and they were just in time to rescue one officer and one man—as the panic party called them, a " sample of each." Thus ended U83. That night we heard his pal calling him up on the wireless and receiving no reply.

* * *

SUBMARINE SURGERY

From *The Diary of a U-Boat Commander*.[1]

By " ETIENNE " (COMMANDER STEPHEN KING-HALL)

Since I wrote the above words this morning, Wiener has taken a decided turn for the worse.

I have been reading the *Medical Handbook* with reference to the remarks on amputation, gangrene, etc., and I have also

[1] Published by Hutchinson & Co. (Publishers), Ltd.

been examining his leg. The poor devil is in great pain, and there is no doubt that mortification has set in, as was indeed inevitable. I have decided that he must have his last chance, and that at 8 p.m. to-night I will endeavour to amputate.

Midnight.

I have done it—only partially successful.

. . . . . .

Last night, in accordance with my decision, I operated on Wiener.

Voigtman assisted me. It was a terrible business, but I think it desirable to record the details whilst they are fresh in my memory, as a Court of Inquiry may be held later on. Voigtman and I spent the whole afternoon in the study of such meagre details on the subject as are available in the *Medical Handbook*. We selected our knives and a saw and sterilized them; we also disinfected our hands.

At 7.45 I dived the boat to sixty metres, at which depth the boat was steady. We had done our best with the wardroom-table, and upon this the patient was placed. I decided to amputate about four inches above the knee, where the flesh still seemed sound. I considered it impracticable to administer an anæsthetic, owing to my absolute inexperience in this matter.

Three men held the patient down, as with a firm incision I began the work. The sawing through the bone was an agonizing procedure, and I needed all my resolution to complete the task. Up to this stage all had gone as well as could be expected, when I suddenly went through the last piece of bone and cut deep into the flesh on the other side. An instantaneous gush of blood took place, and I realised that I had unexpectedly severed the popliteal artery, before Voigtman, who was tying the veins, was ready to deal with it.

I endeavoured to staunch the deadly flow by nipping the vein between my thumb and forefinger, whilst Voigtman hastily tried to tie it. Thinking it was tied, I released it, and, alas! the flow at once started again; once more I seized the vein, and once again Voigtman tried to tie it. Useless—we could not stop the blood. He would undoubtedly have bled to death before our eyes had not Voigtman cauterised the place with an electric soldering-iron which was handy.

Much shaken, I completed the amputation, and we dressed the stump as well as we could.

At the moment of writing he is still alive, but as white as snow; he must have lost litres of blood through that artery.

9 *p.m.*

Wiener died two hours ago. I should say the immediate cause of death was shock and loss of blood. I did my best.

* * *

THROUGH the winter the endless battle of the trenches continued: the most active agent was the artillery, now tuned to a high pitch of efficiency. The novelty of 1914—aeroplanes " spotting " or observing for big guns—was now a commonplace, fire being directed not only against combatant troops, but against inoffensive civilian populations.

SHELLED CITY

From *The Forbidden Zone*.[1]

By MARY BORDEN

The wide, sweet heaven was filling with light: the perfect dome of night was changing into a day. A million silver worlds dissolved from above the earth: the sun was about to rise in stillness: no wind stirred.

A speck appeared in the great immensity. It was an aeroplane travelling high through the mysterious twilight. The sound of the whirring of its engine was lost in the depthless air: like a ghost it flew through the impalpable firmament: it was the only thing that moved in heaven and earth.

The unconscious map lay spread out beneath it: the wide plain, the long, white beach and the sea, lay there exposed to its speeding eye.

On the face of the plain were villages and cities; the dwellings of men who had put their trust in the heavens and had dared to people the earth.

[1] Published by William Heinemann, Ltd.

The aeroplane turned in the sky and began circling over the town.

The town far below was asleep. It lay pillowed on the secure shore; violet shadows leaned against its pale buildings; there was no movement in its streets; no smoke from its chimneys. The ships lay still in the deep, close harbour; their masts rose out of the green water like reeds thickly growing with the great funnels and turrets of warships like strange plants among them. The sea beyond the strong breakwater was smooth as a silver plate; there was no sound anywhere.

The aeroplane descended in slow spirals upon the town, tracing an invisible path through the pearly air. It was as if a messenger from Heaven were descending upon the people of the town who dreamed.

Suddenly a scream burst from the throat of the church tower. For an instant the sky seemed to shiver with the stab of that wail of terror rising from the great stone throat. Surely the town would waken in a panic—and yet, no, nothing stirred. There was no sound or movement in any street and the sky gave back no sign.

The aeroplane continued to descend until it looked from the church tower like a mosquito; then there dropped something from it that flashed through the air, a spark of fire.

Silence had followed the scream.

The aeroplane, superbly poised now in the spotless sky, watched the buildings below it as if waiting for some strange thing to happen; and presently, as if exorcised by the magic eye of that insect, a cluster of houses collapsed, while a roar burst from the wounded earth.

The bombardment had commenced. The big gun hiding in the sand-dunes in Belgium had obeyed the signal.

Still the neat surface of the wide city showed no change, save in that one spot where the houses had fallen. How slow to wake the town was! The daylight brightened, painting the surface of the buildings with pale rose and primrose. The clean, empty streets cut the city into firm blocks of buildings; the pattern of the town spread out on the earth, with its neat edges marked by walls and canals, gleamed like a varnished map.

SHELLED CITY

Then the siren in the church tower screamed again; its wail was followed by a second roar, and a ragged hole yawned in the open square in the middle of the town.

The aeroplane circled smoothly, watching.

And at last signs of terror and bewilderment appeared in the human ant-hill beneath it. Distracted midgets swarmed from the houses; this way and that they scurried, diving into openings in the ground: swift armoured beetles rushed through the streets; white jets of steam rose from the locomotives in the station yard: the harbour throbbed.

Again there was a great noise, and a cloud of debris was flung into the air as from a volcano, and flames leapt after it. A part of the wharf, with a shed on it, reeled drunkenly into the sea with a splash.

The white beach was crawling now with vermin; the human hive swarmed out on to the sands. Their eyes were fixed on the evil flying thing in the sky, and at each explosion they fell on their faces like frantic worshippers.

The aeroplane cavorted, whirling after its tail in an ecstasy of self-gratification. Down among the sand-dunes it could see the tiny black figures of men at the anti-aircraft guns. These were the defenders of the town; they had orders to shoot to death a mosquito floating in boundless heaven. The little clouds that burst in the sunlight were like materialised kisses.

The face of the city had begun to show a curious change. Scars appeared on it like the marks of smallpox, and as these thickened on its trim surface, it seemed as if it were being attacked by an invisible and gigantic beast, who was tearing and gnawing it with claws and teeth. Gashes appeared in its streets, long wounds with ragged edges. Helpless, spread out to the heavens, it grimaced with mutilated features.

Nevertheless, the sun rose, touching the aeroplane with gold, and the aeroplane laughed. It laughed at the convulsed face of the town, at the beach crawling with vermin, at the ant-people swarming through the gates of the city along the white roads; it laughed at the warships moving out of the harbour one by one in stately procession, the mouths of their guns gaping helplessly in their armoured sides. With a last flick of its glittering wings, it darted downward, defiant, dodging the kisses of shrapnel, luring them, teasing them, playing with them: then, its message delivered, its sport over, it flew up and away in the sunshine and disappeared. A speck in the infinite sky, then nothing—and the town was left in convulsions.

* * *

A STRANGE guerilla warfare was being waged in and about German East Africa. Here the German commander, with a few hundred Germans and four thousand native troops, caused the employment of no fewer than 130,000 British and Dominion soldiers, and an expenditure of £70,000,000!

GUERILLA WARFARE
From My Reminiscences of East Africa.[1]
By GENERAL VON LETTOW-VORBECK

So there was nothing for it but to seek to attain our object by means of small detachments, or patrols. To these patrols we afterwards attached great importance. Starting from the Engare-Nairobi, small detachments of eight to ten men, Europeans and Askari, rode round the rear of the enemy's camps, which had been pushed up as far as the Longido, and attacked their communications. They made use of telephones we had captured at Tanga, tapping in on the English telephone-lines; then they waited for large or small hostile detachments or columns of ox-wagons to pass. From their ambush they opened fire on the enemy at thirty yards' range, captured prisoners and booty, and then disappeared again in the boundless desert. Thus, at that time, we captured rifles ammunition, and war material of all kinds. One of these patrols had observed near Erok Mountain that the enemy sent his riding-horses to water at a certain time. Ten of our horsemen at once started out, and, after a two-days' ride through the desert, camped close to the enemy. Six men went back with the horses; the four others each took a saddle, and crept at a distance of a few paces past the enemy's

[1] Published by Hurst and Blackett, Ltd.

sentries, close up to the watering-place, which lay behind the camp. An English soldier was driving the horses, when suddenly two of our men confronted him out of the bush and, covering him with their rifles, ordered " Hands up ! " In his surprise he dropped his clay pipe out of his mouth. At once he was asked : " Where are the missing four horses ? " for our conscientious patrol had noticed that there were only fifty-seven, whereas the day before they had counted sixty-one ! The four needed light treatment and had been left in camp. The leading horse and a few others were quickly saddled, mounted, and off they went at a gallop round the enemy's camp towards the German lines. Even in the captured Englishman, who had to take part in this *safari* on a bare horse, without much comfort, the innate sporting instinct of his nation came out. With great humour he shouted : " I should just like to see my captain's face now ! " and when the animals had arrived safely in the German camp, he remarked : " It was a damned good piece of work."

This capture, increased by a number of other horses and mules we had picked up, enabled us to form a second mounted company. We now had two mounted companies, composed of Askari and Europeans mixed, an organisation which proved successful. They provided us with the means of sweeping the extensive desert north of Kilima Njaro with strong patrols who went out for several days at a time ; they penetrated even as far as the Uganda and Magad Railways, destroyed bridges, surprised guards posted on the railways, mined the permanent way and carried out raids of all kinds on the land communications between the railways and the enemy's camps. In these enterprises our own people did not get off scot-free. One patrol had brilliantly surprised two companies of Indians by rifle-fire, but had then lost their horses, which had been left behind in hiding, by the fire of the enemy ; they had to make their way back across the desert on foot, which took four days, and they had no food. Luckily they found milk and cattle in a Masai kraal, and later on saved themselves from starvation by killing an elephant. But success whetted the spirit of adventure, and the requests to be sent on patrol, mounted or on foot, increased.

The patrols that went out from the Kilima Njaro in a more easterly direction were of a different character. They had to work on foot through the dense bush for days on end. The patrols sent out to destroy the railway were mostly weak: one or two Europeans, two to four Askari, and five to seven carriers. They had to worm their way through the enemy's pickets and were often betrayed by native scouts. In spite of this they mostly reached their objective and were sometimes away for more than a fortnight. For such a small party a bit of game or a small quantity of booty afforded a considerable reserve of rations. But the fatigue and thirst in the burning sun were so great that several men died of thirst, and even Europeans drank urine. It was a bad business when anyone fell ill or was wounded, with the best will in the world it was often impossible to bring him along. To carry a severely wounded man from the Uganda Railway right across the desert to the German camps, as was occasionally done, is a tremendous performance. Even the blacks understood that, and cases did occur in which a wounded Askari, well knowing that he was lost without hope, and a prey to the numerous lions, did not complain when he had to be left in the bush, but of his own accord gave his comrades his rifle and ammunition, so that they at least might be saved.

* * *

The collapse of Russia in 1917 had released a large number or German divisions, which were rapidly transferred to the Western Front. For the first time since Verdun the Germans were now able to assume the offensive. A colossal blow was directed at the British Third and Fifth Armies; the latter, holding a very long front with weak forces, was driven behind the Somme after a desperate defence which inflicted enormous losses on the advancing enemy. In fact, for the first time in the War, the German Army suffered greater casualties than it inflicted.

At the time, the retreat of the Fifth Army was much misunderstood, and the Prime Minister of the day even hinted in the House of Commons that the British troops had not held out as they might have done. The editors only wish that he could have been there to see for himself!

So great was the strain that for a moment it seemed that a complete break through was possible. By superhuman exertion and great devotion the line was held; the Germans had failed in their greatest attack: from that moment—though they did not then know it—they had lost the War.

FIFTH ARMY—RETREAT
From *The Fifth Army*.[1]
By General Sir Hubert Gough, G.C.M.G., K.C.B., K.C.V.O., etc.

Some critics have asked the reason why the Germans were able to hold our attack in the Ypres series of battles in 1917 whilst we on our part were forced to give so much ground in 1918. An elementary consideration of the facts would provide the answer. On July 31st, 1917, we attacked with eight divisions, supported by one division of the Second Army on our right, and two French divisions on our left. After a lapse of weeks further attacks were carried out. This system had been generally adopted by both the French and the Germans, as well as ourselves, in all previous attacks on the Western Front. It enabled the attacking troops to be relieved and spared, but it could not hope for rapid and decisive results. The system evolved and put into force by the Germans in this battle was quite different. The attack was made on four times the front, with more than four times the number of divisions all massed against the part to be attacked and all close up, so that nearly all could move forward almost simultaneously. This ensured an overwhelming force and the maintenance of the battle in full and vigorous activity for days and nights without intermission, which gave the defence no rest, allowed little or no time to bring up fresh divisions, and made the systematic relief of tired ones most difficult.

Then the great extent of front which the Fifth Army was

[1] Published by Hodder and Stoughton, Ltd.

called on to hold only allowed one man per yard of its widely flung line. The situation would at once have been altered immensely in its favour without making any other change in the figures involved in the problem if the front could have been reduced from forty-two miles to, say, twenty-one.

The actual odds (in men) against my Army on the opening of the battle were four to one. It is interesting to note that in no previous assault during the whole of the War had the ratio of attackers to defenders exceeded two to one.

Though as early as February 3rd, during my conference with my Corps Commanders, I had outlined the possibility of an attack by fifty or more German divisions, it remained an uncertainty until the actual day whether this mass would be thrown against the whole of the Fifth Army front, or only against part of it.

At that time, of course, I was unaware of the full magnitude of the coming attack. I knew that it was to be no light blow which the Fifth Army had to meet, but no calculations of any of the Allied Staffs had allowed for such a concentration against us. The Fifth Army Staff alone had foreseen that such an attack was possible.

. . . . . .

The night of March 20th every man in the Fifth Army whose duty allowed him to do so, lay down calmly enough for a night's sleep, but all of us felt perfectly certain that we would be awakened before morning by the roar of battle. And so we were!

. . . . . .

A retreat is not necessarily a defeat. Some of the greatest victories in military history have been based on retreats. The retreat to Moscow and the consequent destruction of Napoleon's army is one example. Wellington conducted many retreats which led to great victories during the Peninsular War—the retreat to the lines of Torres Vedras—the retreat before Salamanca—the retreat from Burgos: these do not complete the list. The retreat from the battlefields of Ligny and Quatre Bras led to the victory of Waterloo.

If the Fifth Army had attempted to hold their ground at

FIFTH ARMY—RETREAT

all costs—if the tactics had not been those of a great rearguard action—the whole Army might have been overwhelmed, in fact almost certainly would have been, in the first two or three days' fighting. There would then have been a gap, not of two or three miles which could be filled somehow—but of forty miles! It does not require a great stretch of imagination to see the disastrous consequences to the Allies if such a position had been created.

The fighting retreat of the Fifth Army was no new operation of war, though perhaps conducted on a greater scale and under conditions of more difficulty and stress than any previous example. Its material effects were vital to the Allied cause. The highest hopes of the Germans, naturally so encouraged by the collapse of Russia, had been staked on this gigantic onslaught. And now the great effort of the German High Command to defeat the British, to cut them off from the French, and to drive them into the sea, had been defeated. The German Army was stopped, it had shot its bolt; the high hopes of a great decisive, and above all a final victory, were dead. From now on, though it still put forth at times a last despairing display of its ancient fierce strength, like the last flickerings of a dying candle, its morale rapidly sank.

The Channel Ports were secure, and though the few divisions of the Fifth Army were shattered, and almost destroyed, Haig had economised his forces, and still had many divisions in hand for the great counter-strokes, when in four months' time the British Army was able to advance on broad fronts, gaining greater victories (if victories and defeats can be measured by captured prisoners and trophies) than it has ever done in its previous history.

Of the results of this battle the Germans themselves have written:

"When a great attack, from which something decisive is expected, fails hopelessly with heavy losses, the cohesion of an army is more shaken than by an unsuccessful defensive battle."

A French officer wrote:

"The morale of the German attacking divisions was very good. They were cheered by their successes at Riga and

Caporetto, buoyed up by hope of victory at a single blow, an end to all their miseries. But if an instant success was not attained, their morale, thus disillusioned, would fall."

As indeed it did!

On March 27th, General Malcolm, commanding the 66th Division, which had just carried out a successful counter-attack and driven back the Germans, making some prisoners, while walking back to his Headquarters met a French officer, who in very evident anxiety inquired of the situation. Malcolm replied: "It is quite good; we have won the War."

He realised the failing energy, the growing weariness of the German troops on his front; he could feel the attack was stayed—the situation saved.

Lord Birkenhead, in his book, *Turning Points of History*, writing of the triumph of the Fifth Army in this battle, says:

"On them fell the brunt of the attack. The armies on his flanks did not hold as firm as they might have done. Gough had neither adequate rear lines of defence nor reserves. Yet with such tenacity and courage did he continue to oppose and muffle the enemy's advance that, after the first terrible fortnight was passed, the front still stood, and Ludendorff's last throw had patently failed. Amiens was saved; so was Paris; so were the Channel Ports. So was France. So was England."

What was the state of these steadfast and heroic men to whom these great results were due? The story, as I have briefly written it, tells something of the heavy casualties, of the dead lying thickly across every mile of the fiercely disputed battlefield, of the wounded and prisoners left behind in the hands of the enemy. Of the survivors, an average of little more than 1000 could still stand to arms in the divisions whose strength on paper should have stood at 10,000 infantry! Some battalions were reduced to 50 men. The staffs, the clerks, the engineers, had all given up their ordinary functions to shoulder a rifle.

· · · · ·

To those who survived I say: Hold up your heads high with pride. History will proclaim the greatness of what you did.

It can be said of no other troops that they did more to win the War. You are the remnants of a gallant band of brothers buffeted by adversity and grievously maligned, yet your spirit is too fine to be damped by such misfortunes: you are the men on whom Britain is based.

To my countrymen from all parts of our wide Empire I say: Read, and think of what it meant to you, this band of men who stood unflinchingly between you and all that defeat meant. And realise that many thousands of the survivors live to-day, passing unnoticed in a civilian crowd; you may meet them day by day, unhonoured and unknown. Acknowledge their valour as and when you can; it is too easy to forget.

To the relatives of the dead I say: Your men died as heroes among heroes. They faced overwhelming odds with a courage beyond the power of words to praise. Battered and bruised, they hung on to the last to enable their comrades to retire, so as to continue the battle—and to save Britain. When the end came they had no regrets, they had done their duty. There is a broad wreath of British dead in that desolate land, which has now become once again a smiling countryside. The rows of crosses mark for ever that scene of their valiant deeds: history at least will give them the great honour they earned. Britain can ill spare such men; they are of the breed which has made her honoured and powerful throughout the world.

* * *

FIFTH ARMY—THE ONSLAUGHT.

From Roads to Glory.[1]

By Richard Aldington

Hanley, Williams, the sergeant, two runners, started for the outpost-line. The trench was drier, the night not so dark, with faint stars mistily gleaming among light clouds. Weather clearing up—just the Boche's luck again. The five men moved along without talking, absorbed partly in a strange anxious preoccupation, partly in keeping upright on the slippery trench. Hanley and Williams, of course, knew the full extent of their

[1] Published by Chatto & Windus.

danger, had faced the ultimate despair, passed beyond revolt or hope. The sergeant still hoped—that he might be wounded and taken prisoner. The two men only knew they were " in for a show." All were dry-mouthed, a little sickish with apprehension, a little awkward in all their movements; the thought of deserting their posts never even occurred to them.

They passed the three Canadian crosses, distinctly outlined on the quiet sky; then the dragon piece of corrugated iron. At the end of the communication trench they found waiting the men from the four posts, under a sergeant. Hanley spoke in low tones—there might be advance patrols lying just outside their wire.

" All your men present, ser'ant ? "

" Yes, sir."

" Right. You know your orders. See that each section joins its own platoon, and then report to your own platoon commander. Don't waste time."

" Very good, sir."

The line of men filed past them in the darkness. For the hundredth time Hanley noticed the curious pathos of fatigue in these silent moving figures—the young bodies somehow tired to age and apathy. When they had gone he took Williams a little aside.

" If I were you, I should see that each of you occupies a separate bay. Get in the first bay yourself, then the runner, then the sergeant. They won't dare try to bolt back past you. Besides—er—there's more chance if you're spread out."

" I was wondering what happens if all three of us are knocked out before the Boche actually gets into the trench, and so no green light is fired ? "

" Oh, we must risk that. Besides, there are similar volunteer parties on every company front."

" I see."

" I took a compass bearing from the fire-step outside Company Headquarters yesterday, so I shan't miss your light. I expect they'll be on us ten minutes later. Perhaps we'll beat off the first two or three attacks.

" Yes. Perhaps."

They were silent. Then Hanley made an effort.

"Well, good-bye, old man. Best of luck."
"Best of luck, good-bye."
They were too shy and English even to shake hands.

. . . . . .

It was past three when Hanley and Parker got back to their own line, and found the whole company standing to in battle positions. Hanley kept his signallers on the first floor of the big dug-out. He sent off to Battalion Headquarters the code message which meant they were in battle positions and all ready. He took a candle and went down to the lower dug-out, where they spent so many nights. It looked barer and damper than ever, empty except for the bare sacking beds, the boxes, the table.

Outside the trench the air was moist and fresh. He took two Verey pistols, one loaded with green, one with red, and laid them on either side of him on the parapet. Hanley was at the extreme left of the bay, with two riflemen to his right. Twenty yards to his left was the communication trench leading to the outpost-line, now blocked with wire and knife-rests, and guarded by a bombing section.

A signaller came up from the dug-out with a message. Hanley went down and read it by the light of a candle. He noticed the bowed back and absorbed look of a signaller tapping out a message on a Fullerphone. The message he had received simply reiterated the order that their positions were to be held at all costs. Hanley felt angry, screwed up the piece of paper and stuffed it in his pocket. Damn them, how many more times did they think that order had to be given? He returned to the trench, and resumed his watch.

. . . . . .

3.50 a.m. One battery of German guns languidly firing on back areas—pretence that all was as usual.

3.52 a.m. Signal rockets all along the German line. Then silence.

3.55 a.m. Two miles to his right a fierce bombardment, stretching over several miles. The battle had begun.

3.57 a.m. Two miles to his left another bombardment. The British artillery on their own front opened up a defensive barrage.

4 a.m. With a terrific crash, which immediately blotted out the roar of the other bombardments, the German artillery on their own front came into action. Hanley half recoiled. He had been in several big bombardments, and thought he had experienced the utmost limit of artillery. But this was more tremendous, more hellish, more appalling than anything he had experienced. The trench of the outpost line was one continuous line of red, crashing trench mortars and shells. The communication trench was plastered with five-nines. Shells were falling all along their own line—he heard the sharp cry of " Stretcher-bearer ! " very faintly from somewhere close at hand.

The confusion and horror of a great battle descended on him. The crash of shells, the roar of the guns, the brilliant flashes, the eerie piercing scream of a wounded man, the rattle of the machine-guns, the Lewis guns, the two riflemen beside him madly working the bolts of their rifles and fumbling as with trembling hands they thrust in a fresh clip of cartridges—all somehow perceived, but thrust aside in his intense watch. A green light went up about half a mile to the left, then another a little nearer. Hanley stared more intently in the direction of Williams' post—and found himself saying over and over again without knowing he was saying it : " O God, help him, O God, help him, O God, help him."

Suddenly two green lights appeared, one fired straight up as a signal—probably Williams—the other almost along the ground, as if fired at somebody—probably the runner, wounded or in a panic. Sergeant dead, no doubt—Williams and his runner dead, too, by now. Hanley fired a green light. Two minutes later the British barrage shortened.

Hanley grasped the Verey pistol loaded with red. Their turn now.

" Stretcher-bearer, stretcher-bearer ! "

Crash ! A shell right on their bay.

Hanley staggered, and felt a fearful pain in his right knee where a shell splinter had hit him. In the faint light of dawn he saw vaguely that one of the riflemen lay huddled on the fire-step, leaving his rifle still on the parapet ; the other man had been blown backwards into the trench, and lay with his feet grimly and ludicrously caught in a torn piece of revetment. His helmet had been knocked from his head.

Faint pops of bombs to his immediate left—they were coming up the communication trench. He peered into the shell-smashed light of dawn, but saw only smoke and the fierce red flash of explosions.

Suddenly, to his left, he saw German helmets coming up the communication trench—they had passed the wire barrier! He looked to his right—a little knot of Germans had got through the wire—a Lewis gun swept them away like flies. He felt the blood running down his leg.

Somebody was standing beside him. A voice, far off, was speaking :

" Bombing attack beaten off, sir."

" Very good, carry on."

" There's only two of us left, sir."

" Carry on."

" Very good, sir."

More Germans on the right ; another, longer row coming up the communication trench. Then suddenly, Germans seemed to spring up in every direction. Hanley fired six shots from his Webley at those in front. He saw others falling hit, or jumping into the trench on either side.

A red light shot up straight in the air. A second later two bombs fell in the bay. A torn, crumpled figure collapsed sideways. The Germans reorganised, while the moppers-up did their job.

* * *

FIFTH ARMY—SAVING THE GUNS

From *Retreat*.[1]

By Charles R. Benstead

Nash reached the guns. His party, a bare score of tired men, silently spread themselves between the first two guns.

Somebody tripped over an obstruction and cursed. A tittering laugh followed, telling of nerves stretched to

[1] Published by Methuen & Co., Ltd.

breaking-point. Nash breathed an oath. After that the darkness became full of heavy sound, of stertorous breathing and suppressed curses, of the clanking of metal against metal, and the plodding of heavy boots in the soft, muddy ground. Inch by inch the howitzers were extracted from their pits.

And then Nash caught the distant purr of engines. The secret was out. "Now," he thought, grimly detached, "for merry hell!"

"Party on to four. Remainder stand by to limber up."

The men bent to the work. Two guns were ready in a trice, and then Nash had the impression of complete unreality. For it did not need the roaring engines of two Thorneycroft lorries to tell the Germans that something was afoot. It merely confirmed their suspicions, and they were ready. Before the two lorries, running in reverse, were half-way to the guns brisk fire was crackling from the German line, directed into the black channel of the valley. A machine-gun joined in, sweeping along. Another followed. And still more. Then patrols pushed out, only to meet stubborn British posts, who refused to budge. Soon, within 100 yards of the labouring gunners, a lively fight was in progress.

Nash knew that he was tearing round and shouting like a man demented, and yet all the while he was saying to himself: "You're getting rattled. You're getting rattled, and you're done for if you do."

The first lorry careered madly past him in reverse. The other lurched to a standstill as Maclachlan sprang out of the murk, shouting.

The sound of the rich Northern accent steadied Nash. He bawled to his sergeant to stand by to limber. The sergeant was already at work.

The firing increased tenfold. Bullets zipped through the fabric of the lorry.

A man was struck in the arm. The sudden pain caused him to cry out, and he stepped back, clutching the wound and gasping. Then, without any warning, he laughed stridently and shouted: "Clicked at last, by God! A Blighty touch all right this time." After that he performed an absurdly clumsy step-dance and then disappeared singing in the darkness. Nash just caught the words: " Highty, tiddle-y-ighty, carry me back to Blighty. . . ."

The first casualty.

Before the two howitzers had been limbered behind the single lorry, three more men had been hit.

" Stand clear. Right away."

It was Maclachlan bawling at the driver above the din. The lorry began to grind forward, protesting against its iniquitous load. Its wheels slipped in the soft ground in spite of their chains.

" Shove behind, you God-forsaken lunatics. Shove behind. You're not a set of statues. Shove—shove——"

The men rallied round, urged on by Nash. The lorry gathered speed. She was off.

Maclachlan stopped just long enough to shout in his ear: " Good-bye, Nash. Don't attempt the fifth. Lorry won't take more than two. Best o' luck."

He set off after the lorry. Somehow Nash retained the impression that Maclachlan's face was strangely twisted.

Next instant an infantry subaltern was crying out with breathless gasps in his ear: " I can't hold 'em much longer. Are you finished ? "

" Finished ! " Nash stared at the fellow and laughed, a mad insane cackle. But he checked himself: " No. For God's sake hang on. We've two more yet. Possibly three."

The subaltern groaned, and started back to his men. Nash saw him crawling up the bank on all fours.

German field-guns now began firing, sending salvos blindly into the valley, though, fortunately, on the far side for the most part. Nash guessed what it meant. Fortunately, too, the swathes of bullets from the German machine-guns were also ill-directed. They passed high, so that it seemed to Nash as if a solid sheet of metal whistled and hissed above his head. He had only to stretch up his hand to touch it. In a detached way he was thankful for the convexity of the hill-side which protected them.

His foot struck against something soft as he made his way to the other lorry, and he stumbled across a body. Even in the darkness the back seemed familiar. Then he saw the sergeant's stripes on the arms. He started to roll the body over, but stopped when he saw the face. He shuddered.

After that something began to beat a queer tattoo in his brain, and the look on his face grew oddly triumphant. There came to him an exaltation that rose above even fear.

He heard men working on No. 6 gun, and shouted to them to leave it and get 4 and 5 out first. Six lumbering shapes blundered by, and the seventh, who carried a hand-spike, just sagged at the knees, and sat down in front of him. He recognised his corporal, the last of his N.C.O.s.

He leapt into No. 4 pit, goading his men on with curses that rose above the uproar. They responded. The gun was tethered behind the lorry.

" Number five," he roared.

Half-way to the pit some cautionary sense warned him that the posts were giving way. He dissolved in indecision. Should he cut and run with the third gun, or risk it and try for another? The firing had stopped, too. It was ominous.

Came the cries of the man who had carried the hand-spike. " Glory be to God! Glory be to God, brother! Glory be . . ."

The dim outline of the dying man held him. He wanted to stop his ears.

But another voice broke across the crying. It said: " Altogether now, lads. He-eave."

" Glory be . . ."

A rattling sound. The dying man gave a convulsive shiver. He was dead.

" Steady, lads. Steady. All together, he-eave."

The voice was more than a tonic to Nash. He wondered which of the men it was. By God, the fellow deserved a D.C.M.! And by God he should have it. Five gun was as good as saved. He'd have six if he had to carry it himself.

Once again Nash forgot himself. He was goading his men in the pit. They had the gun out. It was limbered behind the other. Now for the sixth.

" Come on," he roared, and met the infantry subaltern.

" Get out, man, get out!"

The subaltern waved his arms wildly and blundered on.

Pale-faced infantrymen ducked and fired and fell back across the valley, and the lorry-driver settled matters for Nash by crashing in the gear and lurching off down towards the road.

Nash screwed himself up a further peg.

" Beat it, lads. Leave everything. Make for the road."

A dozen bewildered gunners started off in the wake of the lorry.

Shots rang out. Nash saw the stabs of flame. Two men fell. One said : " Oo-oo-a-ah ! " The other said nothing.

Nash made out the dim silhouettes of German helmets against the sky. He came up to the fallen pair. One did not move. The other lay writhing. Several men stopped, hesitating whether to go on or stay and carry the wounded man.

" Go on," Nash screamed. " Get out."

* * *

FIFTH ARMY—THE FLAME-THROWER

From *Generals Die in Bed*.[1]

By Charles Yale Harrison

Suddenly machine-gun fire opens up. We jump to the parapets.

They are coming again !

They advance in waves, in close formation.

We stand on the firing-step and shoot into the closely packed ranks. Every shot tells. My rifle is hot. On all sides of us machine-guns hammer at the attacking ranks.

They are insane, it seems.

We cannot miss them.

On and on they come.

Above the clatter of the Lewis guns I can hear snatches of song. They are singing.

They are close to us. I fire carefully.

They are close enough to throw grenades.

I see their ranks waver for a moment and then they start to run slowly towards us. Our line is a line of flame. Every gun is in action.

[1] Published by Noel Douglas.

The singing is quite distinct now.

I can see faces clearly.

Each burst of Broadbent's gun cuts a swath in the front ranks of the attacking troops.

They are close to our trenches. Their singing has become a shriek which we hear above the hammering of our rifles and guns.

I am filled with a frenzied hatred for these men. They want to kill me, but I will stay here and shoot at them until I am either shot or stabbed down. I grit my teeth. We are snarling, savage beasts.

Their dead and wounded are piled up about four deep.

They climb over them as they advance.

Suddenly they break and retreat.

We have repulsed them again. Their wounded crawl towards our trenches. We shoot at them.

The shrieking and howling out in front of us sounds like a madhouse in turmoil.

We sink down to the bottom of our trenches exhausted.

It is quiet once more.

Out in front the wounded men still howl. One of them crawls into our trench, and falls near us. Half of his face is shot away.

His breath smells of ether! No wonder they attacked like madmen!

Fry has a flesh wound in his right arm. We dress the wound. It is not serious and we advise him to go back as soon as it is dark.

Out in front the cries of the wounded are worse than ever. We look at each other with drawn, frightened faces.

. . . . . .

The afternoon wears on. We busy ourselves with repairing the trench. We dig it deeper and sandbag our parapets. Behind the German lines we hear them preparing for another attack. We hear voices, commands.

It is nearly dusk.

They begin to shell our trench. They have not got the correct range and the shells fall short in No Man's Land. The shells leap among the bodies of the wounded and dead. The lashing of the bombardment start them shrieking again. It hurls torn limbs and entrails into our trench.

We are lost.

Our ammunition is short.

Fry comes into our bay. His arm is stiff, he cannot move it.

We start to talk of retreating. We work out a plan for falling back.

Anderson begins to pray in a subdued, scared voice:

"O Lord, look down upon me. Search me in Thine infinite pity. . . ."

Broadbent turns on him in disgust.

"For the Lord's sake, Anderson, don't tell God where you are or we'll all get killed. Stop whining."

The shells come closer and closer.

We decide to fall back if the coming counter-attack threatens to be successful.

The fire lifts.

We "stand-to."

We place the Lewis gun on the parapet and begin to sweep the field. Anderson is working the gun. Broadbent supplies him with freshly filled pans of ammunition.

Across the field we see them climbing out of their trenches.

At last our artillery comes to life. Overhead shrapnel hisses over our heads and cracks to fragments in the face of the attacking Germans.

Still they come. The field is full of them. We see their officers out in front of them. Bullets whiz past our heads and smack against the parados in the rear. The firing grows fiercer.

They are about a hundred yards from us. At a given moment they fling themselves down. In that moment their artillery begins to hammer at our trench. They have the range now. The shells scream and whistle and crash into the trenches, on the parapets, behind us, on all sides of us.

We cower down. We cannot face the fire.

The trench begins to cave in.

Sandbags are blown into the air.

The trench is nearly flattened.

The shelling lifts and passes to the rear.

Out in front we hear a maddened howl.

THEY ARE COMING!

We look behind us. They have laid down a barrage to cut us off.

We are doomed.

Anderson jumps from his gun and lies grovelling in the bottom of the shallow trench. I tell Renaud to keep firing his rifle from the corner of the bay. Broadbent takes the gun and I stand by feeding him with what ammunition we have left.

They are close to us now.

They are hurling hand grenades.

Broadbent sweeps his gun, but still they come.

The field in front is smothered with grey smoke.

I hear a long-drawn-out hiss.

Ssss-s-sss!

I look to my right from where the sound comes. A stream of flame is shooting into the trench.

Flammenwerfer! Flame-throwers!

In the front rank of the attackers a man is carrying a square tank strapped to his back. A jet of flame comes from a nozzle which he holds in his hand. There is an odour of chemicals.

Broadbent shrieks in my ear:

"Get that bastard with the flame."

I take my rifle and start to fire. Broadbent sweeps the gun in the direction of the flame-thrower also. Anderson looks nervously in the rear.

"Grenades," I shout to him.

He starts to hurl bombs into the ranks of the storm troops.

Odour of burning flesh. It does not smell unpleasant.

I hear a shriek to my right, but I cannot turn to see who it is.

We continue to fire towards the flame-thrower. Broadbent puts a fresh pan on the gun. He pulls the trigger. The gun spurts flame. He sprays the flame-thrower. A bullet strikes the tank on his back. There is a hissing explosion. The man disappears in a cloud of flame and smoke.

To my right the shrieking becomes louder.

It is Renaud.

He has been hit by the flame-thrower.

Flame sputters on his clothing. Out of one of his eyes tongues of blue flame flicker. His shrieks are unbearable.

He throws himself into the bottom of the trench and rolls around, trying to extinguish the fire. As I look at him his clothing bursts into a sheet of flame. Out of the hissing ball of fire we still hear him screaming.

Broadbent looks at me and then draws his revolver and fires three shots into the flaming head of the recruit.

* * *

FIFTH ARMY—TANK FIGHTS TANK

From " *Everyman At War* "—Sixty Personal Narratives of the War Edited by C. B. Purdom.[1]

By F. Mitchell, M.C.

Suddenly, against our steel wall, a hurricane of hail pattered, and the interior was filled with myriads of sparks and flying splinters. Something rattled against the steel helmet of the driver sitting next to me and my face was stung with minute fragments of steel. The crew flung themselves flat on the floor. The driver ducked his head and drove straight on.

Above the roar of our engine could be heard the staccato rat-tat-tat-tat of machine-guns and another furious jet of bullets sprayed our steel side, the splinters clanging viciously against the engine cover.

The Jerry tank had treated us to a broadside of armour-piercing bullets!

Taking advantage of a dip in the ground, we got beyond range and then, turning, we manœuvred to get the left gunner on to the moving target. Owing to our gas casualties the gunner was working single-handed, and his right eye being too swollen with gas he aimed with the left. In addition, as the ground was heavily scarred with shell-holes we kept going up and down like a ship in a heavy sea, making accurate shooting difficult.

His first shot fell some thirty yards in front and the next went beyond.

[1] Published by J. M. Dent & Sons, Ltd.

Nearing the village of Cachy, I saw to my astonishment that the two female tanks were slowly limping away to the rear. They had both been hit by shells almost immediately on their arrival and had great holes in their sides. As their Lewis guns were useless against the heavy armour-plate of the enemy and their gaping sides no longer afforded them any defence against machine-gun bullets, they had nothing to do but withdraw from action.

We still were lucky enough to dodge the enemy shelling, although the twisting and turning once or twice almost brought us on top of our own trenches.

Whilst we were ranging on the leading German tank, our own infantry were standing in their trenches watching the duel with tense interest, like spectators in the pit of a theatre.

Looking down on one occasion I saw to my horror that we were going straight down into a trench full of men who, huddled together, were yelling at the tops of their voices to attract our attention. A quick-signal to the gears-man seated in the rear of the tank and we turned swiftly, avoiding catastrophe by a second.

Another raking broadside of armour-piercing bullets gave us our first casualty, a bullet passing through the fleshy part of both legs of the Lewis gunner at the rear after piercing the side of the tank!

We had no time to put on more than a temporary dressing and he lay on the floor, bleeding and groaning, whilst the six-pounder boomed over his head and the empty shell cases clattered all round him.

The roar of our engine, the nerve-racking rat-tat-tat of our machine-guns blazing at the Boche infantry, and the thunderous boom of the six-pounders, all bottled up in that narrow space, filled our ears with tumult. Added to this we were half-stifled by the fumes of petrol and cordite.

Again we turned and proceeded at a slower pace; the left gunner, registering carefully, hit the ground right in front of the Jerry tank. I took a risk and stopped the tank for a moment.

The pause was justified; a carefully aimed shot hit the turret of the German tank, bringing it to a standstill. Another roar and yet another white puff at the front of the tank denoted a second hit! Peering with swollen eyes through his narrow slit the elated gunner shouted words of triumph that were drowned by the roaring of the engine.

Then once more with great deliberation he aimed and hit for a third time. Through a loophole I saw the tank heel over to one side and then a door open and out ran the crew. We had knocked the monster out!

Quickly I signed to the machine-gunner, and he poured volley after volley into the retreating figures.

My nearest enemy being now out of action, I turned to look at the other two, who were coming forward slowly. As the German infantry were still advancing, the six-pounder gunner sent round after round of case shot in their direction which, scattering like the charge of a shot-gun, spread havoc in their ranks.

Now, I thought, we shall not last very long. The two great tanks were creeping forward relentlessly; if they both concentrated their fire on us at once we would be finished. We sprinkled the neighbourhood of one of them with a few sighting shells, when to my intense joy and amazement, I saw it go slowly backwards. Its companion did likewise, and in a few minutes they both had disappeared from sight, leaving our tank the sole possessor of the field.

* * *

FIFTH ARMY—RUNNERS
From *War Letters to a Wife*.[1]

By Rowland Feilding

In the course of a battle it is often necessary to send a runner with a message under circumstances which involve almost certain death or wounding, yet never have I seen one of these carefully chosen men waver or hang back. No matter how dangerous the errand—and he well knows what is before him—the runner on duty never wants calling twice. Give him his message, and he will pick up his rifle and be off, often to his death. I have seen so many officers and men go off like

[1] Published by The Medici Society, Ltd., London.

that smilingly to their death in this war, and, looking back, it certainly does seem sometimes as though a special buoyancy of spirit animates those about to die.

* * *

FIFTH ARMY—NOT "ACCORDING TO PLAN"
From *A Fatalist at War*.[1]
By Rudolf Binding
(Translated by I. F. D. Morrow)

There was the corner of a little wood where the English put up a desperate resistance, apparently with a few machine-guns, and finally with only one. When the defence was broken down, out from the lines of our advancing infantry, which I was following, appeared an English general, accompanied by a single officer. He was an extraordinary sight. About thirty-five years old, excellently—one can almost say wonderfully—dressed and equipped, and he looked as if he had just stepped out of a Turkish bath in Jermyn Street. Brushed and shaved, with his short khaki overcoat on his arm, in breeches of the best cut and magnificent high lace-boots, such as only the English bootmakers make to order, he came to meet me easily and without the slightest embarrassment. The sight of all this English cloth and leather made me more conscious than ever of the shortcomings of my own outfit, and I felt an inward temptation to call out to him, " Kindly undress at once," for a desire for an English general's equipment, with tunic, breeches and boots, had arisen in me, shameless and patent.

I said " Good morning," and he came to a stop with his companion. By way of being polite I said with intention : " You have given us a lot of trouble ; you stuck it for a long time." To which he replied : " Trouble ! Why, we have been running for five days and five nights ! " It appeared that when he could no longer get his brigade to stand he had taken charge of a machine-gun himself, to set an example to his retreating men. All his officers except the one with him had been killed or wounded and his brigade hopelessly cut up.

[1] Published by George Allen & Unwin, Ltd.

NOT "ACCORDING TO PLAN"

I asked for his name, to remind me of our meeting, and he gave it. He was General Dawson, an Equerry of the King.

We have now spent two nights in the crater-field of the old Somme battle. No desert of salt is more desolate. Last night we slept in a hole in the crumbly, chalky soil and froze properly. It is impossible to sleep for excitement. Really one would like to be after them day and night and only longs that there shall be no rest until one can feel the first breath of the Atlantic in Amiens. To-morrow we hope to be on a level with Albert where there will be villages again. Here the villages are merely names. Even the ruins are ruined. Yesterday I was looking for Bouchavesnes, which used to be quite a large place. There was nothing but a board nailed to a low post with the inscription in English, " This was Bouchavesnes."

. . . . . .

To-day the advance of our infantry suddenly stopped near Albert. Nobody could understand why. Our airmen had reported no enemy between Albert and Amiens. The enemy's guns were only firing now and again on the very edge of affairs. Our way seemed entirely clear. I jumped into a car with orders to find out what was causing the stoppage in front. Our division was right in front of the advance and could not possibly be tired out. It was quite fresh. When I asked the Brigade commander on the far side of Meaux why there was no movement forward he shrugged his shoulders and said he did not know either; for some reason the division which had been pushed on through Albert on our right flank were not advancing, and he supposed that this was what had caused the check. I turned round at once and took a sharp turn with the car into Albert.

As soon as I got near the town I began to see curious sights. Strange figures, which looked very like soldiers, and certainly showed no sign of advancing, were making their way back out of the town. There were men driving cows before them on a line; others who carried a hen under one arm and a box of notepaper under the other. Men carrying a bottle of wine under their arm and another one open in their hand. Men who had torn a silk drawing-room curtain from its rod and were dragging it to the rear as a useful bit of loot. More men with writing-paper and coloured notebooks. Evidently they had found it desirable to sack a stationer's shop. Men dressed up in comic disguise. Men with top-hats on their heads. Men staggering. Men who could hardly walk.

They were mostly troops from one of the Marine divisions. When I got into the town the streets were running with wine.

* * *

ALBERT, 1918
From *The Challenge of the Dead*.[1]
By Stephen Graham

Oh, Albert, what a place of death thou art now, with thy returned children playing hide-and-seek around the heaps of thy homes. How is it possible to *return* to this place? It is not a return: no one can ever return to the Albert of 1914. These that we see are *revenants* come to look at spectral homes. For Albert is dead. There you can realise that a human home is a living being like the woman who made it. It can prosper or decay. It can go shabby and suffer. It can be wounded or maimed—it can be killed. We mercifully hide our dead in Earth's great bosom—but we leave our dead homes long when they die, in all their horror and terror. There stands a shrunken little house where the tiles have been swept away, the plaster also, and the bare laths of the ceiling are all exposed, but they look like a cap bashed down on the head of a dead man. Yonder lies a recumbent habitation with a welter of grey laths and beams on its burst-out side, like the sun-dried ribs of a dead dromedary. Beyond it stands a wall that is left and then an outraged home with madness fixed in its visage in the moment of death agony. Here is a house with gutted entrails half congealed and terrible to behold. There is a house that died simply of shock. But its neighbour *vis-a-vis* was hit by some striding giant with iron fist. Rows of houses are seen cowering, as if they had had their hands up trying to ward off the dreadful fate which stalked above them. Houses lie killed as it were in the action of flight, veritably in

[1] Published by Ernest Benn, Ltd.

the act of treading on one another's heels in a frenzy to get away. There are houses which are abased, houses which have fallen foremost on their faces, houses which have fallen backwards, bottom over top into confusion and debris behind, houses with their sides torn off as men's sides were torn off in the War, exposing for one instant beating hearts. There are houses where simply the life-breath has gone out—dead, blind, empty and desolate.

One can hardly think of the existence once of rooms, the marriage-bedrooms of sweet human honeymoons, the room where the baby slept a baby's untroubled sleep, the children's room where one thinks of a child's cry in the night or a child's lisped prayer before its mother or the crucifix, the room where the home met, the table round which went food and talk and laughter in a common innocence and ignorance of destiny—all gone now in shapeless ruin.

All the houses were the children of Notre-Dame—the leaning Virgin who hung out from the stricken tower of the mighty masonry of the Cathedral-church, and yearned o'er the city. The miracle of her suspense in air over Albert was a never-ceasing wonder, and the soldiers said the city would never be taken as long as she remained un-shot down from the eminence of the great church.

Alas, Albert had its day of fate and of complete sacrifice ere the War should end—when all should go, yea, Virgin and all, and only Golgotha remain, Golgotha and the Roman soldiers who smote the Master with their spears as He hung from the Cross.

Twilight settles down upon the dead, the twilight of time and misery. The dreadful reality of destruction becomes more intense and real. After all, sunlight and the noonday do not always show us truth. They are in themselves so full of life and happiness that they divert attention from ruins and death unto themselves. Only in the grey light of afternoon and evening, and looking with the empty eye-socket of night-darkness can one easily apprehend what is spread out here— the last landscape of tens of thousands who lie dead. Hamlet must go to the battlements at the time when the ghost walks. The light of day hides the unseen world, or cannot quite hide it. But there is one moment when the ghost of Albert grows into vision majestically before the eyes. You go out through the primeval jungle of dead weeds, the tripartite crowned heads of brown teasles looking like low-lying spectral regalia of the death-kingdom, past dug-outs and deeps and quagmire, past the prostrate ribaldry and obscenity of war's doings with the earth—to the dark-flowing water which nurses its forgotten secrets, flowing on, flowing on. You wait, and whilst mist chills the marrow the ghostly moment of Albert comes once more. Night has more than heralded itself; it is here in a vast-fronted army and comes onward. Demon-eyes look over the ridges, flash angrily, greedily the roar of battle thunder bursts up; the gas-shells cat-calling across the sky fall in showers on the mud; field-guns are advanced to point-blank range—there comes the tide of the war—worn German soldiery of March, 1918, war-worn and yet exultant; the English are driven out, the leaning Virgin falls, and the city is given over to the enemy. Albert is dead; even its soul has died. English soldiers will come back in August, recapture it, but not the city they defended so long, not the city of the little Notre-Dame leaning passionately o'er its life and its defence.

* * *

THE crisis on the Western Front impelled an appeal to America, whose war effort to date had been somewhat disappointing. The response to the appeal was, however, on a colossal scale, and American soldiers crossed the Atlantic (mostly in British vessels) at the rate of 300,000 a month. Their adventures sometimes began long before they reached the battle front!

TORPEDOED
From *Jimmie Higgins*.[1]
By UPTON SINCLAIR

It was the morning of the day they were due in port. Everybody wore life-preservers, and stood at his station; when suddenly came a yell, and a chorus of shouts from the

[1] Published by Hutchinson & Co. (Publishers), Ltd.

side of the ship, and Jimmie rushed to the rail, and saw a white wake coming like a swift fish directly at the vessel. "Torpedo!" was the cry, and men stood rooted to the spot. Far back, where the white streak started, you could see a periscope, moving slowly; there was a volley of cracking sounds, and the water all about it leaped high, and the little sea-terriers rushed towards it, firing, and getting ready their deadly depth-bombs. But of all that Jimmie got only a glimpse; there came a roar like the opening of hell in front of him; he was thrown to the deck, half-stunned, and a huge fragment of the rail of the vessel whirled past his head, smashing into a stateroom behind him.

The ship was in an uproar; people rushing here and there, the members of the crew leaping to get away the boats. Jimmie sat up and stared about him, and the first thing he saw was his friend the "wobbly," lying in a pool of blood, with a great gash in his head.

Suddenly somebody began to sing: "Oh, say, can you see by the dawn's early light——" Jimmie had always hated that song, because jingoes and patrioteers used it as an excuse to bully and humiliate radicals who did not jump to their feet with sufficient alacrity. But now it was wonderful to see the effect of the song; everybody joined and the soldier-boys and working-men and nurses and lady ambulance-drivers, no matter how badly scared, recalled that they were part of an army on the way to war. Some helped the crew to get the boats into the water; others bound up the wounds of the injured, and carried them across the rapidly slanting decks.

The great ship was going down. It was horrible to realise—this mighty structure, this home for two weeks of several thousand people, this moving hotel with its sleeping-berths, its dining-saloons, its kitchens with lunch ready to be eaten, its mighty engines and its cargo of every kind of necessity and comfort for an army—all was about to plunge to the bottom of the sea! Jimmie Higgins had read about the torpedoing of scores of ocean liners, but in all reading he had learned less about the matter than he learned in a few minutes while he climbed half dazed to a stay rope, and watched the lifeboats swing out over the sides and disappear.

"Women first!" was the cry; but the women would not go until the wounded had been taken, and this occasioned delay. Jimmie helped to get his friend the "wobbly," and passed him on to be lowered with a rope. By that time the deck had got such a slant that it was hard to walk on it; the bow was settling, and the stern rearing up in the air. Never could you have realised the size of an ocean-liner, until you saw it rear itself up like a monstrous mountain, preparatory to plunging beneath the waves! "Jump for it!" shouted voices. "They'll pick you up from the other vessels. Jump and swim."

So Jimmie rushed to the rail. He saw a life-boat below, trying to push away, and being beaten against the vessel by the heavy waves. He heard a horrible scream, and saw a man slip between the boat and the side of the liner. People on every side of him were jumping—so many that he could not find a clear spot in the water. But at last he saw one, and climbed upon the rail and took the plunge.

He struck the icy water and sank, and a wave rolled over him. He came up quickly, owing to his life-preserver, and gasped for breath, and was choked by another rushing wave and then pounded on the head by an oar in the hands of a struggling sailor. He managed to get out of the way, and struck out to get clear of the vessel. He knew how to do this, thanks to many "swimmin'-holes"—including the one he had visited with the Candidate. But he had never before swum in such deadly cold as this; it was colder than he had dreamed when he had talked about it with Comrade Meissner! Its icy hands seemed to smite him, to smite the life out of him; he struggled desperately, as one struggles against suffocation.

The waves beat him here and there; and then suddenly he was seized as if by the falls of Niagara, drawn along and drawn under—down, down. He thought it was the end and when again he bobbed up to the surface, his breath was all but gone. The great bulk of the vessel was no longer in sight, and Jimmie was struggling in a whirlpool, along with upset boats and oars, and deck-chairs and miscellaneous wreckage, and scores of people clinging to such objects, or swimming frantically to reach them.

Jimmie was just about ready to roll over and let his face go under, when suddenly there loomed above him on the top of a wave a boat rowed swiftly by sailors. One in the boat flung a rope to him, and he tried to catch it, but missed; the boat plunged towards him, and an arm reached out, and caught him by the collar. It was a strong and comforting arm, and Jimmie abandoned himself to it, and remembered nothing more for a long time.

* * *

On St. George's Day, 1918, the British Navy made an audacious attempt to curb the activities of German submarines by raiding and blocking the harbours of Zeebrugge and Ostend.

ST. GEORGE AND THE DRAGON

From *How we twisted the Dragon's Tail*.[1]

By Percival Hislam

It was about fifteen minutes after the *Vindictive* had taken up her position that a tremendous explosion was heard from the shore end of the Mole—an explosion which caused our men to burst into vigorous cheering. The concrete Mole is not itself continuous, but for a distance of more than a quarter of a mile from the shore takes the form of a great platform erected on trestles. It was part of the scheme to destroy this viaduct early in the operation so as to prevent the arrival of German reinforcements on the Mole, and for this purpose it was decided to expend an old submarine. The little vessel was loaded up with several tons of explosive, and her skeleton crew of six. As she crept towards her objective the Germans sighted her in the glare of the star-shells—splendid help to the submarine!—but they appeared to have a most amusingly mistaken idea of her intentions. They evidently thought she intended to poke her way through the piles of the viaduct into the inner harbour, and as they felt pretty sure of being able to bag her intact, they just let her go on. Swarms of Germans watched her gleefully from the platform above;

[1] Published by Hutchinson & Co. (Publishers), Ltd.

but when the submarine had firmly wedged her nose into the viaduct, the crew slipped over the side into a motor skiff, the captain touched off the fuse, and before the gallant little crew were two hundred yards away the submarine blew up with a terrific explosion that breached a gap a hundred feet long in the viaduct and bade fair to sink the skiff with the debris. The little craft unfortunately lost her propeller in getting away, and the men had to do the best they could for some time with a couple of oars before they were picked up by the boat that had been detailed to assist them, the sadly disillusioned Germans keeping up a heavy fire upon them all the time.

Our men were still busy upon the Mole when presently the outlines of the concrete-laden ships that were to be sunk in the fairway became visible. The *Thetis*, Commander R. S. Sneyd, D.S.O., came first, steaming into a torrent of shell from the batteries ashore. All her crew, save a remnant who remained to steam her in and sink her, had already been taken off by the motor launches, but the remnant spared hands enough to keep her four guns going. It was hers, says the official narrator, to show the road to the *Intrepid* and *Iphigenia*, who followed. She cleared the string of armed barges which defends the channel from the tip of the Mole, but had the ill-fortune to foul one of her propellers upon the net defence which flanks it. The propeller drew in the net and rendered her practically unmanageable; the shore batteries pounded her unremittingly. She bumped into a bank, edged off, and found herself in the channel again, still some hundreds of yards from the mouth of the canal, in a practically sinking condition. As she lay, she signalled invaluable directions to the others, and it was here that her commander blew her up. A motor launch raced alongside and took off her crew. Her losses were five killed and five wounded.

The *Intrepid*, smoking like a volcano and with all her guns blazing, followed; her motor launch had failed to get alongside the harbour, and she had men enough for anything. Straight into the canal she steered, her smoke blowing back into the *Iphigenia's* eyes so that the latter, running a little wild, rammed a dredger with a barge moored beside it. But she got clear through and entered the canal, when a burst in a steam-pipe serving to drive away some of the smoke, Lieut. Stuart Bonham-Carter, in command, took notes of his whereabouts, placed the nose of the ship neatly in the mud of the western bank, ordered his crew away, and blew up his ship by switches in the chart-room. The lieutenant had some exciting experiences before he was picked up later from a Carley float, which, burning a brilliant calcium flare, made an excellent target for the enemy. Lieutenant E. W. Billyard-Leake, commanding the *Iphigenia*, beached her according to arrangements on the eastern side of the canal, blew her up, saw her drop nicely across the fairway, and left her with her engines still going to hold her in position until she should have bedded well down on the bottom.

* * *

The crisis also induced another vital change—unity of command was instituted, with Foch as the first generalissimo.

UNITY OF COMMAND

From *Foch Talks*.[1]

By Commandant Bugnet

" It is not sufficient to issue orders ! It is necessary to see that they are executed ; people must be watched, one must always have them under one's eye. Believe me, if the duties of a commander were merely those of giving orders, it would not be a difficult task. He must ensure that they are carried out. The Commander-in-Chief must exercise supervisory functions. When I commanded the Allied Armies, I always had the means of ensuring this supervision ; I used to send Desticker here, Pagezy there. I kept in touch with the execution of my orders ; they kept me posted. Obviously, when one has subordinates whom one trusts, they can be given liberty of action, but it is always necessary to be certain that orders are carried out. That is the whole secret.

" During the War, I spent my time in travelling from place

[1] Published by Victor Gollancz, Ltd.

to place; I visited the commanders-in-chief, and the general officers commanding Army Corps and even Divisions. When I knew that one of them was in a tight corner, I went back to see him several times in one day. . . .

"You see, the unified command is only a word. It was tried in 1917 under Nivelle, and it did not work. One must know how to lead the Allies—one does not command them. Some must be treated differently from the others. The English are English, the Americans are another matter, and similarly with the Belgians and Italians. I could not deal with the Allied Generals as I did with our own. They also were brave men who were representing the interests of their own country. They saw things in a different light from ourselves. They agreed with reluctance to the unified command; although they loyally accepted the situation, a mere trifle might have upset them and dislocated the whole scheme. I could not give them orders in an imperative manner. One cannot work to a system, especially with them! Anything might have happened It was necessary to hear their views, otherwise they would have kicked. . . . People only carry out orders which they understand perfectly, and decisions which they have made themselves, or which they may have seen made.

"Accordingly, when important decisions were involved, I used to see them, or asked them to see me. We talked and discussed questions between ourselves, and, without seeming to do so, I gradually won them over to my point of view. I provided them with a solution, but I did not force it upon them. They were satisfied. I did my best to convince them. Perhaps it was rather a lengthy process, but we always got there. A talk in the morning, another in the evening, for several days if necessary. And, when I had made them see my point, I left them, but with a written note which we had prepared with Weygand's assistance. I gave it to them without appearing to attach much importance to it. 'This is a summary of my ideas. It agrees with your own in principle. Perhaps you will glance through it; come and see me again and we will go into it together.' A few days later they would adopt this decision, make it their own, and become keen on ensuring its success. If handled differently, they would have strained at their chain, if I had made them too much aware of it!

"That is the method which I adopted with French in 1914, with Diaz in 1917, and with the others in 1918. That is the true spirit of the unified command—not to give orders, but to make suggestions. . . . They look into the question. At first they are surprised, then they move. Do you know, I carried them on my shoulders the whole time. Exactly! We used to meet Haig twice a week. We met half-way, at Mouchy. That is why, in such circumstances, Weygand was so valuable to me. He was patient. He used to return to them, go into the question again, explain my point of view, and persuade them. Is not that the meaning of Inter-Allied command? One talks, one discusses, one persuades, one does not give orders. . . . One says: 'That is what should be done; it is simple; it is only necessary to will it.' That cannot be done on paper: a man is needed! Don't say that it is a difficult problem: it is hardly a problem at all. We have brains, and they are given to us to use."

* * *

FAILING in their tremendous effort to divide the French and British Armies on the Somme, the Germans transferred their offensive to the North. Here, on a smaller scale, their momentary success was equally staggering. Breaking completely through the Portuguese and a British Sector, the enemy advance was only halted with tremendous difficulty. So serious was the position at one time, in fact, that Sir Douglas Haig was impelled to issue his famous message, one of the most dramatic of the War.

BACKS TO THE WALL
From *At G.H.Q.*[1]

By BRIGADIER-GENERAL JOHN CHARTERIS. C.M.G., D.S.O.

The news from the battle is not good. The Germans are making a big effort, and the French are doing nothing. Foch

[1] Published by Cassell & Co., Ltd.

said two days ago that he had at last made up his mind that the big German attack was against the British Army, and that he would send a large French force to take part in the battle, but so far nothing has happened. It looks as if we should have to fight out this battle alone, and we have no reserves. It will decide the War. God grant the decision is not against us! Everything else fades into insignificance. We are paying in blood for the follies of professional politicians. I pray that our payment in the lives of the army may suffice and that the whole nation be not strangled.

D.H. has issued a finely worded appeal[1] to the army to fight to the last, saying that French troops are hurrying to our assistance. I wish they were. It is all so like 1914 when we told the 1st Corps the French were coming, and they did not

---

[1] TO ALL RANKS OF THE BRITISH FORCES IN FRANCE.

Three weeks ago to-day the enemy began his terrific attacks upon us on a fifty-mile front. His objects are to separate us from the French, to take the Channel Ports, and destroy the British Army.

In spite of throwing already 106 divisions into battle, and enduring the most reckless sacrifice of human life, he has as yet made little progress towards his goals.

We owe this to the determined fighting and self-sacrifice of our troops. Words fail me to express the admiration which I feel for the splendid resistance offered by all ranks of our army under most trying circumstances.

Many among us now are tired. To those I would say that Victory belongs to the side which holds out longest. The French Army is moving rapidly and in great force to our support.

There is no other course open to us but to fight it out! Every position must be held to the last man. With our backs to the wall and believing in the justice of our cause, each one of us must fight on to the end. The safety of our Homes and the Freedom of Mankind alike depend upon the conduct of each one of us at this critical moment.

D. M. HAIG,
F.M.

Thursday,
11th April, 1918.

come. Yet then we won alone, and I believe we shall now. All the same I wish D.H. had *not* issued his order. It will immensely hearten the Germans when they hear of it, as they must. I do not think our own men needed it to make them fight it out. If the French are really hurrying to our assistance, they should be here in a few days, almost as soon as the order will reach the front-line troops. If they are not, it may have a really bad effect to raise false hopes in the troops' minds.

Although the position is serious, I do not think this attack can possibly get through. It will outrun its supplies and come to the end of its momentum just as the March attack did. So far there is no sign of a check. Our men are fighting well, but are hopelessly outnumbered, and practically untrained owing to the enormous front we have had to hold all winter, when the divisions should have been training. Our losses are huge, and we are still being steadily pushed back. It is all so sad.

Recriminations are useless. After all, the real judges are those of history, and the army has little cause to fear the verdict.

This northern attack was, of course, a gigantic strategic surprise. Probably it was meant to be the real effort of the Germans, to have followed immediately after the first March attack. The success in the early days then tempted the Germans to develop it, and now they have not enough men left to drive this one through. The Channel Ports are, of course, the vital point to the British Army, and the Germans know it very well. If the French act, there should not be the least possibility of the Germans driving us back to the coast. Even if the French do nothing, I still think the German man-power will be exhausted before the enemy succeeds in driving us back to the coast—but that is not a certainty.

April 14th. The battle is still in full swing, and I see no immediate prospect of relief. I calculate now that the Germans are well past the half-way stage of their whole effort. The slaughter has been enormous. The whole question is now one of man-power. At the Front, both our men and the Germans are utterly exhausted and fall asleep within full view of one another. It has turned bitterly cold to-day with a very high wind.

I managed to get to church this morning. There was quite a big congregation. I wish padres would not always choose "appropriate" hymns. We had "For all the Saints" and "Fight the good Fight." It would be right if we were in the firing-line or in any greater personal danger than from a stray air-bomb.

I had a long interview with D.H. He tells me that Foch has at last ordered French troops to move, and that they will begin to arrive to-day or to-morrow. D.H. asked for eight divisions —four behind the First Army, and four near Albert. He has not a very high opinion of Foch, and thinks he is not really looking ahead—just waiting on events and trusting that our men will stick it out as they did in 1914. It is easy to criticise. If Foch is doing this with the intention of sending in at the right moment a smashing attack by the French on, say, the Aisne or at St. Mihiel, his strategy, if bold, may be perfectly right. If we were a homogeneous army under our own Commander-in-Chief, one could only admire the boldness of the strategy and pray for its success. But we are not a homogeneous army. By all reports the French Army is not yet sufficiently recovered from 1917 to be able to deliver a smashing offensive. The Americans cannot be ready before the autumn. It looks as if Foch were playing for a defensive all this spring and summer and probably autumn, and then give the *coup de grâce* in 1919. If so, it is very unfair to let the British Army take the whole weight of this spring effort unsupported. It shows the difficulty of a generalissimo system with Allied Armies.

The irony of it all is that the Germans, now pretty well exhausted after two big attacks and in two salients, are simply asking for a vigorous counter-attack against one or other of their salients, and we have no troops available. If we had another fifteen divisions, we could easily get a decisive victory. But it will be months before the men can come, however energetic the home authorities may at last be. By all accounts they are now really stirring themselves. Troops are being brought back from Palestine and Egypt, and England is at last being combed for men.

April 18th. The attack is following fairly closely the lines of last month's effort. The Germans are now trying to extend their flank northwards. They attacked Kemmell yesterday, but were driven back, though they made a little ground at Wytschaete; but I think it is now nearly over. We are expecting another attack on the Amiens front in a day or two, but it cannot be anything very big. Probably it is only intended to prevent reinforcements being moved northwards to the new battle area.

There is one very noticeable and encouraging thing. The censor reports that ever since March 21st the whole *tone* of the letters from the troops has improved. All grousing has stopped, and has been replaced by a spirit of great confidence. This is very remarkable, considering what the troops are undergoing: but it was much the same in the early days of each of our big attacks. The grumbling begins when the fighting dies down, and the men have time to think over things.

* * *

THE CREEPING BARRAGE

From *Higher Command*.[1]

By Edlef Köppen

Reisiger looked first at his watch and then at the lists. He knew that gradually the fire of all the batteries along the centre front was being concentrated. Only guns of very heavy calibre were still heavily bombarding the back areas. All the other batteries had combined to form the creeping barrage.

The famous creeping barrage. That curtain of fire and shell-splinters that just then was being put up a short distance ahead of the front-line German trenches, and twenty-eight minutes past five would begin its travels. At 5.28, it would be ten yards ahead; at 5.32, twenty yards ahead of the German position. And after that it would keep steadily advancing towards the enemy. Behind it our infantry would move forward with their rifles at the " ready," and the creeping barrage would move steadily on. Not many would be left alive by that time. Perhaps here and there a wretched creature might

[1] Published by Faber & Faber, Ltd.

have escaped just by chance. The barrage would creep on and scatter him to the four winds. Steadily it would creep ahead, with the German infantry advancing slowly, almost lazily, behind it. The barrage would creep on, stop again for ten minutes at the first enemy trench, then lift thirty yards, in order to give breathing-time to the German infantry, who were now in the first trench amidst their dead foes. Further it would creep, then jump a good thirty yards—then another thirty—and now, finally, another twenty yards till it reached the second enemy position. There it would halt for ten minutes, until the German infantry had got up. Then, on it would go again, past the third and fourth positions; the Germans, of course, being all the time just behind it. It was really just a pleasant stroll, as there was not a single enemy in front of them. By 5.55 the barrage would have advanced beyond the enemy lines, where, of course, there were no more trenches. At 5.57 the barrage would lift some hundred yards, roll on through the villages behind the enemy front, and mop up the Staff, the transport, and ammunition columns.

* * *

THE third German effort was made on the Aisne, where a vastly superior force attacked a weak French and British line. Again the initial progress was rapid, but the advance was finally halted in the Marne valley. At Château Thierry many of the new American levies (arrived in Europe despite the efforts of German submarines!) experienced their baptism of blood and acquitted themselves like men.

CHÂTEAU THIERRY

From *Jimmie Higgins*.[1]

By UPTON SINCLAIR

He did it because he understood that the Germans were coming. He had not seen them; but when the gun fell silent he heard whining sounds in the air, as if from a litter of

[1] Published by Hutchinson & Co. (Publishers), Ltd.

elephantine puppies. Sometimes the twigs of trees fell on him, the dirt in front of him flew up into his face; and always, of course, everywhere about him was that roar of bursting shells which he had come to accept as a natural part of life. And suddenly another man went down, and another—there were only two left, and one of them signalled to Jimmie what to do, and Jimmie did not say a word, he just went to work and learned to run a machine-gun by the method favoured by modern educators—by doing.

Presently the man who was aiming the gun clapped his hand to his forehead and fell backwards. Jimmie was at his side, and the gun was shooting—so what more natural than for Jimmie to move into position and look along the sights? It was a fact that he had never aimed any sort of gun in his life before; but he was apt with machinery, and disposed to meddle into things, as we know. Jimmie looked along the sights, and suddenly it seemed as if the line of distant woods leaped into life, the bushes vomiting grey figures which ran forward and fell down and then leaped up and ran and fell down again. " *Eel vienn!* " hissed the man at Jimmie's side. So Jimmie moved the gun here and there, pointing it wherever he saw the grey figures.

Did he kill any Germans? He was never entirely sure in his own mind; always the idea pursued him that maybe he had been making a fool of himself, shooting bullets into the ground or up into the air—and the poilus at his side thinking he must know all about it, because he was one of those wonderful Americans who had come across the seas to save *la belle France!* The Germans kept falling, but that proved nothing, for that was the method of their advance, anyway, and Jimmie had no time to count and see how many fell and how many got up again. All he knew was that they kept coming—more and more of them, and nearer and nearer, and the Frenchmen muttered curses, and the gun hammered and roared, until the barrel grew so hot that it burned. And then suddenly it stopped dead!

" *Sockray!* " cried the two Frenchmen, and began frantically working to take the gun to pieces; but before they had worked a minute one of them clapped his hand to his side and fell back with a cry, and a second later Jimmie felt a frightful blow on his left arm, and when he tried to lift it and see what was wrong half of it hung loose and blood ran out of his sleeve!

* * *

As if to complete the miseries of Europe, at this time both enemy and Allied countries were ravaged by pestilence—inevitably a by-product of war.

'FLU

From *The Paris Front*.[1]

By MICHEL CORDAY

And all that is going on amid such a novel crisis, under such an unprecedented menace! For the last two months a frightful epidemic, the so-called " influenza," has descended upon France. It has been hovering over Europe since the spring. It was specially violent in Switzerland this last summer. In France, since the beginning of September, it has attacked the troops—herded together as they are, with their poor food, poor accommodation and poor medical attention —at the front as well as in the rear. It is complicated by affections of the lungs or meningitis, often fatal. It is a kind of plague. People have given it an innocent kind of label which is almost amusing. They have even called it " Spanish influenza," since the King of Spain, it appears, has had it. The name suggests the title of a dance, as if it were a kind of fandango. In France words are all-important. An army doctor solemnly remarked to me : " Soldiers are not invalided out for influenza." An official in the Ministry of Education, interviewed as to the expediency of closing the schools, remarked : " Influenza is not mentioned on the official list of diseases for which such a step is authorised."

Later on, this epidemic has been hushed up, censored. At one time even the very name was forbidden in the newspapers. It was not until the middle of October that they mentioned it, since Clemenceau's son-in-law died of it. At present fifty soldiers are dying of it every week in a single

[1] Published by Victor Gollancz, Ltd.

hospital at Sens and 1200 people in Paris. They die in a few days, sometimes in a few hours, of suffocation. Every letter from every part of the country mentions this scourge. In Brittany whole families are being swept away; five hundred soldiers have died in a single depot. Seaports have been especially affected. At Lyons there are not enough hearses to go round. And yet it does not bring peace any nearer than would the death of a sparrow!

At the hospital in Joigny, where my son (who was wounded on September 1st) has been for more than a month, lying between life and death, with relapses and complications, there is a shortage of staff. The Chief Medical Officer was attending his own son, who was down with a severe attack of influenza. His assistant was in bed with pleurisy arising from influenza. The nurses were simply swamped with work. *One man died every hour.* And then, amid this frantic disorganisation, there suddenly appeared a D.A.M.S. He solemnly inspected the rejected linen, insisted on having everything laid out in front of him, noticed a pair of socks, and pronounced that they could still stand a further mending.

* * *

OVER THERE!

From *War Birds*.[1]

DIARY OF AN UNKNOWN AVIATOR

But we've lost a lot of good men. It's only a question of time until we all get it. I'm all shot to pieces. I only hope I can stick it. I don't want to quit. My nerves are all gone and I can't stop. I've lived beyond my time already.

It's not the fear of death that's done it. I'm still not afraid to die. It's this eternal flinching from it that's doing it and has made a coward out of me. Few men live to know what real fear is. It's something that grows on you, day by day, that eats into your constitution and undermines your sanity. I have never been serious about anything in my life, and now I know that I'll never be otherwise again. But my seriousness will be a burlesque, for no one will recognise it. Here I am,

[1] Published by Messrs. John Hamilton, Ltd.

twenty-four years old, I look forty and I feel ninety. I've lost all interest in life beyond the next patrol. No one Hun will ever get me and I'll never fall into a trap, but sooner or later I'll be forced to fight against odds that are too long or perhaps a stray shot from the ground will be lucky and I will have gone in vain. Or my motor will cut out when we are trench strafing or a wing will pull off in a dive. Oh, for a parachute! The Huns are using them now. I haven't a chance, I know, and it's this eternal waiting around that's killing me. I've even lost my taste for licker. It doesn't seem to do me any good now. I guess I'm stale. Last week I actually got frightened in the air and lost my head. Then I found ten Huns and took them all on and I got one of them down out of control. I got my nerve back by that time and came back home and slept like a baby for the first time in two months. What a blessing sleep is! I know now why men go out and take such long chances and pull off such wild stunts. No discipline in the world could make them do what they do of their own accord. I know now what a brave man is. I know now how men laugh at death and welcome it. I know now why Ball went over and sat above a Hun airdrome and dared them to come up and fight with him. It takes a brave man to even experience real fear. A coward couldn't last long enough at the job to get to that stage. What price salvation now?

No date.

War is a horrible thing, a grotesque comedy. And it is so useless. This War won't prove anything. All we'll do when we win is to substitute some sort of dictator for another. In the meantime we have destroyed our best resources. Human life, the most precious thing in the world, has become the cheapest. After we've won this War by drowning the Hun in our own blood, in five years' time the sentimental fools at home will be taking up a collection for these same Huns that are killing us now, and our fool politicians will be cooking up another good war. Why shouldn't they? They have to keep the public stirred up to keep their jobs and they don't have to fight and they can get soft berths for their sons and their friends' sons. To me the most contemptible cur in the world is the man who lets political influence be used to keep him away from the front. For he lets another man die in his place.

The worst thing about this war is that it takes the best. If it lasts long enough the world will be populated by cowards and weaklings and their children. And the whole thing is so useless, so unnecessary, so terrible. Even those that live through it will never be fit for anything else.

* * *

THOUGHT IN WAR-TIME
From *A Junior Outline of History*.[1]
By I. O. Evans

The War was a heavy strain on the nations affected. Most of the younger men were forced to serve in the armies, the rest of the nation being chiefly employed in providing them with weapons, stores, and food. Trade was greatly disorganised; disease, which usually resulted from war, though kept at bay by modern methods of sanitation, showed itself in trench-feet and in great influenza epidemics; famine, another result of war, appeared as a growing shortage of food and as a falling off in its quality.

To encourage their own people and gain the favour of neutral nations, both sides ran a campaign of hate against their foes, who were spoken of as being incredibly wicked and as committing frightful atrocities. This propaganda, with the necessary brutalities of conflict, lowered the character of the common people. *They* had not come into the war for "markets" or for tangled imperialistic schemes—they were fighting to save their country, which they thought was threatened by an unscrupulous foe, and they acted not merely with great heroism, but with unselfish devotion and often with kindness. Yet as the War progressed they became brutalised; prisoners were slaughtered, suspected sympathisers with the enemy were treated very harshly, and profiteers made fortunes out of their country's need.

Except in so far as they helped the War, science, art, and literature were at a standstill. Subjects with military value

[1] Published by Denis Archer, Ltd.

progressed greatly, receiving much more encouragement than in peace; aviation, aerial photography, sanitation, surgery, wireless, the chemistry of high explosives and poison gas. Much war literature became harsh and brutal as well as poorly written, though there still appeared books that well expressed the unselfish patriotism of the common people, or that looked beyond the War to the days of peace.

Amidst the distresses of the War, some people sought consolation in religion. Others, on the other hand, were repelled by churches that seemed to abandon Christian ideals of universal brotherhood and to devote themselves to encouraging slaughter and hate. A few Christians, especially among the Quakers, and a few Socialists, refused to take part in the War; some of these, the conscientious objectors, though imprisoned and maltreated, still held fast to their faith of universal brotherhood.

* * *

In spite of the indignation aroused by such German " atrocities " as the slaughter of prisoners, similar " regrettable incidents " are an inevitable feature of war. The following speech, made by a Warrant Officer to a unit of the Officers' Training Corps, issued to its members and then hurriedly withdrawn, is only typical. In war, mercy, decency, and honour are only sources of weakness. None the less, readers should try to imagine how they would have regarded it had it been reported as made by a German!

NO QUARTER!
From *A Suppressed Speech*.[1]
By Company-Sergeant-Major ——, M.C.

" I wish to speak to you this evening about the spirit of the bayonet. ... I wish to recall something about the first

[1] Published by the No More War Movement. We deem it desirable to withhold the name of its author, who cannot personally be held responsible for so common an outlook.

Expeditionary Force. . . . Those troops knew little or nothing about the bayonet. . . .

At first we had thought that we were going to polish off the old 'boche' in a few days. That was a fine spirit to have, but we found that the 'boches,' who had been preparing for this business for the past forty years, were not to be settled so easily. Then we remembered that all our wars for the past two hundred years had been won by the bayonet. And we intend to win this one with the bayonet too. (Cheers.)

Don't ever forget that the bayonet as a real war-weapon is our invention. When I say our invention I am speaking of the Army Gymnastic Staff. . . . Anybody with any experience of tackling the 'boche' knows that there is something more to be done after you have killed one; you must get it out damned sharp to kill somebody else. It was a good thing to show Tommy how to kill a 'boche' and to get that delightful feeling of putting him out with a bayonet—to feel that he had finished off one of those dirty creatures that we call Germans. But there is something more to be taught. . . . We had to teach the bayonet-fighters that after killing their first man they had got to go forward and kill more, and still more.

The only time the Germans know how to kill a man with a bayonet is when they catch him undefended; of course, that means when he is badly wounded and unable to take care of himself. When we teach you how to use the bayonet we know you will be able to kill a German whatever he has in his hand. . . .

. . . . . .

You've got to get down and hook them out with the bayonet; you will enjoy that, I can assure you. (Laughter.) You will want the bayonet to clear the trench. And it is because I know the value of the bayonet that I want you to forget sympathy.

You should have no sympathy for any damned Germans; I have none, nor has anyone else that I know in France. If at any time you should be sympathetic, let it be to put a square-head out of his misery—you will be doing him and yourself a good turn at the same time. (Laughter.) You will certainly know what it feels like to drive that bayonet home and get it out again; you will feel that you will like to go on killing. You are here to work on that idea and to work damned hard.

· · · · · ·

I have heard of one man accounting for thirteen Germans with his bayonet. I know a case of an N.C.O. in charge of a patrol surprised by Germans. The first thing that the N.C.O. did was to take a flying leap and get his man in the arm, then withdrew and went for the next and got him fairly in the heart When it was over and he came back, his chums asked him if he knew what he had done. He said that he did not, but added that he believed he had killed one man and made the other wish that he had not come out. (Laughter.) Of course, he had gone mad, and he said: 'I felt that I could go on killing.'

That is the spirit to have—to keep on killing. He had cut out sympathy. And I say to you: if you see a wounded German shove him out and have no nonsense about it. We are going to have no sympathy with Germans at any rate.

What is the use of a wounded German, anyway? He goes into hospital and the next thing that happens is that you meet him again in some other part of the line. That's no good to us, is it? So when you see a German laid out, just finish him off. Don't trust him any further than you can see him. Remember that the next thing that will happen if you don't is that he will put a bullet into you or one of your chums while he has the strength to do it. The only time that a German can find pluck to kill with the bayonet is when he comes across one of our own wounded; he will plunge the steel into their hearts as they lie unable to defend themselves. When you see this done, can you have any sympathy for them? No! Ten thousand times no! Kill them, every mother's son of them. Remember that your job is to kill them—that is the only way —exterminate the vile creatures!

Take this game seriously. Remember that there are men in France who are fighting and laying down their lives while, in comparison, we are here in clover, in safety, and are getting our eight hours' sleep each night. They curse a bit, but really they do their work most cheerfully. They know that you are coming out to help them, and when you go we want you to be able to teach them how to murder that vile animal called a German. Then try and experience what it is to have the feeling of the warm blood trickling over your hands. . . .

Get hold of your men; whatever you say, see that it is done. But whatever you do, see that these men are taught to kill. We are going to teach those German curs their manners, and we have to do it and will do it. They don't know them. The more of them we kill the better. If a Frenchman calls you 'comrade' he is a comrade. But when a German says 'Kamerad' you know that he wants to be put out of his agony. (Laughter.)

I remember a corporal saying to me, pointing to some German prisoners close by, "Can I do these blokes in, sir?" I said, "Please yourself." He did. When the corporal came back he said, "I felt something that I have never felt before—and I have been in Dartmoor, too. (Laughter.) I felt what it is like to kill, but it's damned hard to get it out. God! He had a belly like iron." (More laughter.)

I remember once disobeying orders in France. I got permission to go salvaging in High Wood—actually I wanted to go up and see the show. . . . When the show died down I carried on with my salvaging task, and I picked out no less than five German bodies with British bayonets still in them. The bayonets were in their guts! There is an unfortunate tendency with a Britisher to go for a German belly—I suppose that is to let the lager out. (Laughter.) But it shows a lack of direction and withdrawal. When I saw this I thought that there was good food for reflection; I saw that one had not only put the bayonet right in, but he had got the nosecap in as well. (Laughter.) The spirit was there, but skill was not. It is always advisable to avoid the stomach, for you are not likely to get out quickly enough to deal with anyone else who is likely to be coming along.

Now, a closing word. Don't be afraid to die. Go forward, chance your luck, you will come out in the end. Keep your mind employed and you won't think of what might happen."

* * *

MANY of the more experienced soldiers had by now lost their first unthinking patriotism and were becoming increasingly critical not merely of the conduct of the War but of its justification. Usually they kept their opinions to themselves—wisely, in view of the existence of military prison and firing-squad. As alternatives to these the powers that be had more subtle methods of persuasion.

PROTEST OF CONSCIENCE
From *Memoirs of an Infantry Officer*.[1]
By SIEGFRIED SASSOON

" I am making this statement as an act of wilful defiance of military authority because I believe that the War is being deliberately prolonged by those who have the power to end it. I am a soldier, convinced that I am acting on behalf of soldiers. I believe that this War, upon which I entered as a war of defence and liberation, has now become a war of aggression and conquest. I believe that the purposes for which I and my fellow soldiers entered upon this War should have been so clearly stated as to have made it impossible to change them, and that, had this been done, the objects which actuated us would now be attainable by negotiation. I have seen and endured the sufferings of the troops, and I can no longer be a party to prolong these sufferings for ends which I believe to be evil and unjust. I am not protesting against the conduct of the War, but against the political errors and insincerities for which the fighting men are being sacrificed. On behalf of those who are suffering now I make this protest against the deception which is being practised on them; also I believe that I may help to destroy the callous complacency with which the majority of those at home regard the continuance of agonies which they do not share, and which they have not sufficient imagination to realise."

. . . .

In the meantime David sat moody and silent, his face

[1] Published by Faber and Faber, Ltd.

twitching nervously and his fingers twiddling one of his tunic buttons. " Look here, George," he said abruptly, scrutinising the button as though he'd never seen such a thing before, " I've come to tell you that you've got to drop this anti-war business." This was a new idea, for I wasn't yet beyond my sense of relief at seeing him. " But I can't drop it," I exclaimed. " Don't you realise that I'm a man with a message ? I thought you'd come to see me through the court-martial as ' prisoner's friend.' " We then settled down to an earnest discussion about the " political errors and insincerities for which the fighting men were being sacrificed." He did most of the talking, while I disagreed defensively. But even if our conversation could be reported in full I am afraid that the verdict of posterity would be against us. We agreed that the world had gone mad ; but neither of us could see beyond his own experience, and we weren't life-learned enough to share the patient selfless stoicism through which men of maturer age were acquiring anonymous glory. Neither of us had the haziest idea of what the politicians were really up to (though it is possible that the politicians were only feeling their way and trusting in providence and the output of munitions to solve their problems). Nevertheless, we argued as though the secret confabulations of Cabinet Ministers in various countries were as clear as daylight to us, and our assumption was that they were all wrong, while we, who had been in the trenches, were far-seeing and infallible. But when I said that the War ought to be stopped and it was my duty to do my little bit to stop it, David replied that the War was bound to go on till one side or the other collapsed, and the Pacifists were only meddling with what they didn't understand. " At any rate, Thornton Tyrrell's a jolly fine man and knows a bloody sight more about everything than you do," I exclaimed. " Tyrrell's only a doctrinaire," replied David, " though I grant you he's a courageous one." Before I had time to ask what the hell he knew about doctrinaires he continued : " No one except people who've been in the real fighting have any right to interfere about the War, and even they can't get anything done about it. All they can do is to remain loyal to one another. And you know perfectly well that most of the conscientious objectors are nothing but skrimshankers." I retorted that I knew nothing of the sort, and mentioned a young doctor who'd played rugby football for Scotland and was now in prison, although he could have been doing hospital work if he'd wanted to. David then announced that he'd been doing a bit of wire-pulling on my behalf and that I should soon find that my Pacifist M.P. wouldn't do me as much good as I expected. This put my back up. David had no right to come butting in about my private affairs. "If you've really been trying to persuade the authorities not to do anything nasty to me," I remarked, "that's about the hopefullest thing I've heard. Go on doing it and exercise your usual tact and you'll get me two years' hard labour for certain, and with any luck they'll decide to shoot me as a sort of deserter." He looked so aggrieved at this that I relented and suggested that we'd better have some lunch. But David was always an absent-minded eater, and on this occasion he prodded disapprovingly at his food and then bolted it down as if it were medicine.

A couple of hours later we were wandering aimlessly along the shore at Formby, and still jabbering for all we were worth. I refused to accept his well-meaning assertion that no one at the Front would understand my point of view and that they would only say that I'd got cold feet. "And even if they do say that," I argued, "the main point is that by backing out of my statement I shall be betraying my real convictions and the people who are supporting me. Isn't that worse cowardice than being thought cold-footed by officers who refuse to think about anything except the gentlemanly traditions of the regiment? I'm not doing it for fun, am I? Can't you understand that this is the most difficult thing I've ever done in my life? I'm not going to be talked out of it just when I'm forcing them to make a martyr of me." "They won't make a martyr of you," he replied. "How do you know that?" I asked. He said that the colonel at Clitherland had told him to tell me that if I continued to refuse to be 'medically boarded' they would shut me up in a lunatic asylum for the rest of the War. Nothing would induce them to court-martial me. It had all been arranged with some big bug at the War

Office in the last day or two. "Why didn't you tell me before?" I asked. "I kept it as a last resort because I was afraid it might upset you," he replied, tracing a pattern on the sand with his stick. "I wouldn't believe this from anyone but you. Will you swear on the Bible that you're telling the truth?" He swore on an imaginary Bible that nothing would induce them to court-martial me and that I should be treated as insane. "All right then, I'll give way." As soon as the words were out of my mouth I sat down on an old wooden breakwater.

So that was the end of my grand gesture. I ought to have known that the blighters would do me down somehow, I thought, scowling heavily at the sea. It was appropriate that I should behave in a glumly dignified manner, but already I was aware that an enormous load had been lifted from my mind. In the train David was discreetly silent. He got out at Clitherland. "Then I'll tell Orderly Room they can fix up a Board for you to-morrow," he remarked, unable to conceal his elation. "You can tell them anything you bloody well please," I answered ungratefully. But as soon as I was alone I sat back and closed my eyes with a sense of exquisite relief. I was unaware that David had, probably, saved me from being sent to prison by telling me a very successful lie. No doubt I should have done the same for him if our positions had been reversed.

* * *

THE German onslaught had spent its force: with the continuous reinforcing of the American Army the balance of effectives again passed to the favour of the Allies. The moment was ripe for a counter-stroke, and Foch was the last man to miss it. His earliest efforts as a generalissimo were not encouraging: he had but one doctrine—"Attack!" But when the moment of defence had passed and the time of attack did arrive, then Foch was assuredly the right man in the right place.

His counter-stroke on the Marne, although missing its main

objectives, inflicted a definite defeat on the German Army. The battle was remarkable in that French, British, American and Italian troops fought side by side.

THE TURN OF THE TIDE
From *The Kaisers Go : The Generals Remain*.[1]
By Theodor Plivier

It is coming.

He does not dare to raise his head above the edge of the shell-hole, but he feels it coming. He hears it sink gurgling into the hollows of the earth, shovel out again and push on over the level stretches.

Quick-firing guns.

Machine-guns.

And audible amid it all, that heavy lumbering movement and the dull rumbling earth—Tanks. A squadron of oncoming tanks ; one of them must be quite near. Will it pass by ? and if it does pass by . . .

Then what ? and then what ?

Advancing, attacking, retreating, those things are done by sections, platoons, companies. Dying is for each man alone. There lies Number Two of the machine-gun crew. His tunic is open, the shirt beneath it grey and worn. The neck and back of his head are half-buried in the earth. His mouth is open, the teeth are showing. The stubble of the beard will go on growing, the finger-nails too, for a little while. The mouth —where has he seen a mouth like that before ? teeth so bared by the lips. Yes, of course, that was it—when Truda was having her baby—like a woman in childbirth.

But the wide-open mouth of the soldier chatters no longer. The outspread legs are without movement. Number Two is dead ; Number Three is dead also—Karl and the fellow from Hamburg. Karl was firmly convinced that peace was coming at last : " Max, my boy," he would say, " the bloody show is over, I can feel it in my bones. Once we get back to Berlin . . .!" The man from Hamburg had been scooping up water from the

[1] Published by Faber and Faber, Ltd.

shell-hole to cool the envelope of the machine-gun that had become hot with firing. Now he, too, lies with his head in the puddle, the bully-beef tin still in his hand.

The machine-gun stands abandoned on the edge of the shell-hole.

The tuft of grass beside it looks impossibly large.

If only he could see the tank, if he, if very cautiously . . . good God! five of them, eight, in a row! and a second—a third squadron—more tanks than there are heads in all No Man's Land! And on the skyline flights of dark aeroplanes rise over the earth and climb droning into the sky.

The weight of oncoming material is too much. The man sags down on his knees. In mad haste he scoops out two spadefuls of earth from the side of the crater and thrusts his head into the hole. A lump of flesh glued to the wall. And so he waits.

The Americans are landing 300,000 troops a month on the French coast, ten thousand fresh soldiers every day. And tanks, aeroplanes, war material. The Germans have lain now four years in the trenches; the six million sent out have dwindled to two and a half. The casualty lists show 1,600,081 dead.

Gunner Max Müller? Here, Herr Captain!

Blacksmith, 46, Boxhagener Strasse, Berlin.

Married?—Yes, sir!

Children?—Only one, sir!

A clanking.

A rumbling.

The earth trembling.

The man cannot stop himself—he withdraws his head from the hole; he looks upward, and sees the tank. He sees it above him, over his head. The tank makes a clumsy cradling movement against the arc of the sky, hovers for a moment, its prow in the air.

Gunner Müller feebly raises a hand as if to ward it off. The great belly rocking downwards upon him—the livid, striped steel armour, the double rows of rivets, the caterpillars dripping earth—all these are etched on the retina of his eyes as on photographic plates. The tank weighs three to four tons, sixty to eighty hundredweight. The human body may withstand a pressure of six hundredweight; with seven the breath goes out of it; eight and the bones crack; eighty . . .

The lips draw back. The teeth are bared. Max Müller's face has the same expression as the dead Number Two; the same anguished mouth as a woman's in childbirth.

The tank slides smoothly down into the crater.

Two dead Numbers and one living, it irons them out flat. Then it lifts itself up again to the level ground and rolls on in line with the rest of the squadron, clanking and firing, against the retreating German Front.

* * *

YANKS AND LIMEYS
From *God have Mercy on Us!* [1]
By William T. Scanlon

Another column of foot soldiers came moving in from the road on the left. They travelled along the left side of our road. I got a good look at them after a while and saw that they were English soldiers.

It was the first time that we had ever marched down the same road with the English to battle. Usually our experience with English troops was in some railroad yard. They would be pulled up on one track and we on the next track, both in box-cars. Then the wisecracks would begin. We would yell:

" Would you have a bit of tea ? "

Then we'd get rougher: " Go on, you damned English; you don't know how to fight ! "

Then the English would yell: " Ah, you come over now, when it's all over ! " and, " Why didn't you come four years ago ? "

Then we would remind them how we knocked hell out of them during the Revolution. We would keep it up, as long as they were in sight. Usually the English soldiers would try to be a little sociable at first, but not us. Our vocabulary of coarse words was never put to such a task as when we met the Limeys. Three, four, and more dimensional cuss words were the rule.

[1] Published by Noel Douglas.

But the English soldiers, trudging along the other side of the road, in the Forest of Villers-Cotterets that evening were not met with any wisecracks. It seemed good to have them along.

* * *

DEATH IN THE FOREST
From *Higher Command*.[1]
By Edlef Köppen

So far they had been steadily moving downhill. Now the ground began to slope gently upwards. They were approaching a birch-wood. Mere saplings, about nine feet high. The silvery trunks gleamed softly in the sunshine.

All of a sudden Boll stopped dead, and gripped Reisiger's arm.

"Well, what's up, Boll?"

"Pardon me, sir, but I don't think that wood is quite right. The leaves are not green—they're lilac."

Lilac-coloured leaves? Reisiger pulled up with a jerk. It looked very strange indeed. Yes, those leaves were lilac: anyhow, not the natural colour of birch foliage. There was not a trace of green about them.

"Boll, do you think that it's gas?"

"Yes, sir, gas," replied Boll, with a nod.

They approached nearer to the wood. Gas? reflected Reisiger. Certainly none of these batteries could have fired on it.

"Boll, did you hear any enemy batteries firing this morning? I think that the wood can only have been gassed by the enemy."

They advanced a few paces further. The wood looked ghastly. Presently they could see that even the silvery trunks had been sprayed with a pinkish lilac slimy fluid, and there were little shallow craters in the freshly turned soil. Yes, the enemy must have fired without being heard.

He looked at his map. They had got to get through here. The only question was: what was the best way of getting into the open again and up to the former German trenches?

[1] Published by Faber and Faber, Ltd.

"It's not so bad, Boll. The whole birch-grove is, at most, less than a mile across. We shall do it in ten minutes. So let us put our gas-masks on and plunge in."

No sooner said than done. It was not easy for them, however, to decide how to manage it. One thing was certain, they had to get through it as quickly as possible, even if it meant running full speed. But how could they do it with gas-masks on? Equally obvious was the danger of stumbling against any trees or touching any leaves. The only thing to do was to keep their hands in their trouser-pockets, make themselves as slim and small as possible, and then it would be all right.

They entered the birch-wood, but could see nothing around them but the gassed trees, with their lilac leaves and the red patches on their white trunks.

Perhaps they would have done better to have gone dead slow. Or, better still, just crawl along. The whole business was horribly uncanny. The wood looked as if it had been plunged into an enormous glass retort full of oil.

Resiger looked up. He couldn't help standing still for a moment, The wood had been outraged, he felt. These birches were only three years old—perhaps five at most. They had nothing, absolutely nothing, to do with the War. They had declared neither for the Germans nor the French. They neither hated nor killed. They just stood there and came into leaf and blossomed in spring, shed their leaves in the autumn and shivered uncomplainingly until the following spring. There was no fuss about them! They were probably devoid of any instinct, save the craving for sunshine.

And look at them now. These poor little birch trees had been polluted by the greatest brutes on the earth—to wit, men. This wood was a victim of man's mad caprice. And yet it died uncomplainingly and with a resignation that its murderers were incapable of. True, there was a breath of wind, and the tree-tops still fluttered a little. But their branches were already limp and drooping, and their leaves were falling continually. And within another twenty-four hours there would be nothing left but barren trunks : all just because man would have it so.

It was childish to go on dreaming like this. Boll was

DEATH IN THE FOREST

several paces ahead of him. He turned round and stood still. He was obviously trying to say something as his gas-mask had become dilated. Resiger couldn't understand a word, but he nodded in reply and followed him. The two trunks of their masks knocked against one another.

"What are you saying, Boll?"

Boll squinted through his big goggles at the trees.

"This is bloody awful, sir."

"Yes, Boll, I only wish we were out of it."

They proceeded very cautiously on their way, with Boll leading. At length, just ahead of them, the wood got thinner. They could see brownish sand-drifts, and overhead, patches of blue sky.

Reisiger followed close behind on Boll's heels.

"Hurry up, Boll. We'll be out of this beastly place presently!"

Boll sprinted ahead. Suddenly, Reisiger noticed a branch of one of the birches protruding right across their track. Yes—but did Boll see it!

"Boll!"

Just then the branch ripped open the corporal's gas-mask behind the goggle, down the whole length of the cheek. The india-rubber yawned wide like a gaping wound. Boll put up his hand to the rent and rushed out, followed by Reisiger. Three strides more and they were in the open.

"Boll!"

Boll spread his arms wide apart. Was he welcoming the freedom of the open air, after this danger?

But he sank slowly to his knees: very slowly—gracefully, in fact. Reisiger sprang towards him.

"Boll, what's up?"

The white in Boll's eyes had suddenly turned a deep red, and his mouth was covered with white pustules.

"Boll! Boll!"

Reisiger shook him. If he would only say something. But there was no means of getting him to speak.

From a kneeling position Boll was slowly slipping backwards, slipping, slipping, till his head touched the ground behind his heels.

There must be someone at hand. He knew very well that there were hundreds of thousands of infantrymen close by. And, of course, stretcher-bearers with oxygen breathing apparatus and special antidotes for gas-poisoning. But could he leave Boll here alone so long? Or must he just try once more to. . . .

" Boll, shall I get a doctor ? "

Reisiger was kneeling beside him all this time, looking at the red patch in his eyes. A strangely complicated complaint, he thought to himself. What about feeling his pulse?

" Boll, please let me feel your pulse."

He gripped Boll's hand, but let it drop much quicker than he had picked it up. It was no longer a hand. There was no life left in it.

" Well, I must go ahead alone. Poor old Boll! " he said aloud, and then went on.

* * *

AFTER a lull, there followed weeks of ceaseless battle. The German " victories " of the Spring had really been their greatest defeats, for by this time the German soldier had begun to realise that the War could not be won by fighting. The enormous casualties sustained in the recent offensives had further reduced the power of resistance of the German Army. Consequently, when the Allied onslaughts fell like hammer blows along the length of the line, the German front cracked for the first time in the War.

THE BLACK DAY OF THE GERMAN ARMY

From *My War Memories*, 1914–1918.[1]

By GENERAL LUDENDORFF

August 8th was the black day of the German Army in the history of this War. This was the worst experience that I had to go through, except for the events that, from September

[1] Published by Hutchinson & Co. (Publishers), Ltd.

BLACK DAY OF GERMAN ARMY

15th onwards, took place on the Bulgarian Front and sealed the fate of the Quadruple Alliance.

· · · · · ·

Early on August 8th, in a dense fog, rendered still thicker by artificial means, the English, mainly with Australian and Canadian divisions, and the French attacked between Albert and Moreuil with strong squadrons of tanks, but otherwise in no great superiority. Between the Somme and the Luce they penetrated deep into our positions. The divisions in line at that point allowed themselves to be completely overwhelmed. Divisional staffs were surprised in their headquarters by enemy tanks. The breach very soon extended across the Luce stream; the troops that were still gallantly resisting at Moreuil were rolled up. To the northward the Somme imposed a halt. Our troops in action north of the river had successfully parried a similar assault. The exhausted divisions that had been relieved a few days earlier and were now resting in the region south-west of Peronne, were immediately warned and set in motion by the commander of the Second Army. At the same time he brought forward into the breach all other available troops. The Rupprecht Army Group dispatched reserves thither by train. The Eighteenth Army threw its own reserves directly into the battle from the south-east, and pushed other forces forward in the region north-west of Roye. On an order from me, the Ninth Army too, although itself in danger, had to contribute. Days, of course, elapsed before the troops from more distant areas could reach the spot. For their conveyance the most extensive use was made of motor lorries.

By the early hours of the forenoon of August 8th I had already gained a complete impression of the situation. It was a very gloomy one. I immediately dispatched a General Staff officer to the battle-field, in order to obtain an idea of the condition of the troops.

· · · · · ·

The losses of the Second Army had been very heavy. Heavy demands had also been made on its reserves to fill up the gaps. The infantry of some divisions had had to go into action straight off the lorries, whilst their artillery had been sent to some other part of the line. Units were badly mixed up. It could be foreseen that a number of additional divisions would become necessary in order to strengthen the Second Army, even if the enemy continued the offensive, and that was not certain. Besides, our losses in prisoners had been so heavy that G.H.Q. was again faced with the necessity of breaking up more divisions to form reserves. Our reserves dwindled. The losses of the enemy, on the other hand, had been extraordinarily small. The balance of numbers had moved heavily against us; it was bound to become increasingly unfavourable as more American troops came in. There was no hope of materially improving our position by a counter-attack. Our only course, therefore, was to hold on.

We had to resign ourselves now to the prospect of a continuation of the enemy's offensive. Their success had been too easily gained. Their wireless was jubilant, and announced —and with truth—that the morale of the German Army was no longer what it had been. The enemy had also captured many documents of inestimable value to them. The Entente must have gained a clear idea of our difficulty in finding reserves, a further reason why they should pursue the offensive without respite.

The report of the Staff Officer I had sent to the battle-field as to the condition of those divisions which had met the first shock of the attack on the 8th, perturbed me deeply. I summoned divisional commanders and officers from the line to Avesnes to discuss events with them in detail. I was told of deeds of glorious valour, but also of behaviour which, I openly confess, I should not have thought possible in the German Army; whole bodies of our men had surrendered to single troopers, or isolated squadrons. Retiring troops, meeting a fresh division going bravely into action, had shouted out things like "Blackleg," and "You're prolonging the War," expressions that were to be heard again later. The officers in many places had lost their influence and allowed themselves to be swept along with the rest. At a meeting of Prince Max's War Cabinet in October, Secretary Scheidemann called my attention to a Divisional Report on the occurrences of August 8th, which contained similar unhappy stories. I was not acquainted with this report, but was able to verify it from my own knowledge. A battalion commander from the front, who came out with a draft from home shortly before August 8th, attributed this to the spirit of insubordination and the atmosphere which the men brought back with them from home. Everything I had feared, and of which I had so often given warning, had here, in one place, become a reality. Our war machine was no longer efficient. Our fighting power had suffered, even though the great majority of divisions still fought heroically.

The 8th of August put the decline of that fighting power beyond all doubt, and in such a situation as regards reserves, I had no hope of finding a strategic expedient whereby to turn the situation to our advantage. On the contrary, I became convinced that we were now without that safe foundation for the plans of G.H.Q., on which I had hitherto been able to build, at least so far as this is possible in war. Leadership now assumed, as I then stated, the character of an irresponsible game of chance, a thing I have always considered fatal. The fate of the German people was, for me, too high a stake. The war must be ended.

* * *

ONCE the tide had turned, it flowed with resistless force. Hitherto Allied attacks had been confined to one or at most two sectors, which meant that the German reserves could be switched to meet the danger. Now, during the last three months of the War, our blows fell on the German line in a continuous sequence, the scene of battle ever changing. The German resistance was not that of two years earlier; the enemy soldiers, their bodies undermined by the rigours impelled by the blockade, their spirits by the ever-increasing certainty that they had lost the War, recoiled in dismay before each hammer blow. As Horace Walpole had remarked over a century and a half before, it was necessary for Englishmen to read their newspapers carefully every morning, lest some new victory should be missed.

THE LAST HUNDRED DAYS
From *A Last Diary of the Great Warr*.[1]
By "SAML. PEPYS, JUNR."

August 11th, 1918 (*Lord's Day*). The battle in France continues and grows these 2 days gone, with great advantage to us in all parts. By the river of Somme our line of battle carried so far as our army and the French reach their old stations allmost, where they did stand this time was 2 yeares, before the great battles about the Somme. And yesterday, yet another French army (Humbert's), engaging the German, they win back Montdidier and chase the enemy 10 kilometers beyond this towne. The prisoners now reckoned to be near 30 thousand, and cannon taken 2 or 3 hundred. Which, and the enemy bereft of all hope of taking Amiens, nor even so much as playing upon it with his great guns, do mightily chear men's hearts.

. . . . . .

August 26th. No news come out of France since Saturday but of our 2 armies ousting the enemy from one place and another, to a width of 30 miles, and 17,000 prisoners gathered these 4 days. But what is most wonderfull is so many names of places taken with the greatest pains and bloodshed 2 yeares since in battles about the Somme, such as Thiepval, Contalmaison, Grandcourt, and Moocow Farm; but now we do leap over them in a bound. I with Mr. Sills, and to play at golph in his club, where we met with a certain major, his friend, that come lately out of France; and another joining us, Mr. McDougall, out of Fifeshire, we did make a 4-some. I plaid with Major Shirborne to my partner, with great satisfaction both in his skill and discourse. He told me, having a good inkling of it from certain great generalls, that the

[1] Published by John Lane, The Bodley Head, Ltd.

campane in France is yet no more than begun ; that Foch will unfold his design by steps, so as presently the whole line of battle shall blaze from the sea to the Vosges mountains ; that the proof is indeed seen of late that the Emperour's armies do buckle; that, albeit some companies and regiments be stout men and do fight with heat, yet many do show themselves soft in surrendering, whereby the number of them taken in the present battles do surpass our own of killed and wounded ; that by many signs is known of great disorders upon the enemy's side, the soldiers unruly, the generalls at oddes. In fine, that it were no astonishment to him if he should see the whole in flight come Michælmas. Which I was glad to hear.

. . . . . .

August 30th. Blessed be God! Bapaume is again fallen to our army (companies out of New Zealand), and Noyon to the French. And such a tale as is now made of villages gained (Haig's reckoning of 30 in one day), and our great booty of prisoners, cannons, and other matters, our reading of news sheets of mornings grows to be the greatest joy imaginable.

. . . . . .

September 4th. Haig do report the fortrice of Quéant fallen to us, with many other places, so as the enemy withdraws his whole line of his battle some miles betwixt the Scarpe and Somme rivers. It is a plain thing, I believe, that the army did on Monday gain the greatest of victories, the prisoners of that day reckoned above 10 thousand. By which, and Haig lately reporting the tale of August takings to be 57 thousand, and other 4 thousand taken in Peronne, the sum is made above 71,000 since our present attaque begun to-morrow will be 4 weeks. This day a-golphing with Mr. Sills some houres, and home with great fatigue of body, and, what is worse, the heel come off 1 of my boots.

. . . . . .

September 14th. Up, and to find a report come from Gen. Pershing of their winning a brave victory in Loraine. Of which the manner is that, the Amerikans assaulting the enemy on his 2 flanks, and the French doing the like about his middle part, above 13,000 Germans and Austrians be cut off ere they may get away ; whereby the towne of St. Mihiel delivered out of the Emperour's hand, he holding it these 4 yeares. Which is indeed the best possible answer to William and his generalls, who did mock the Amerikans' armies, yet now their own power is humbled before them.

· · · · · ·

September 28*th*. Blessed be God ! the Boulgars did yesterday dispatch one with a flag of truce to Generall d'Esperey, and to pray a truce of 48 houres, whiles they send an embassage to treat with us. Moreover, did also, it seems, give our ministers here to know that their mind is to have peace. And from all sides come the most splendid newes of triumph in the warr. The 1st and best, of Sir D. Haig bravely assaulting Hindenbourg's fortifications along 12 miles this side Cambrai, and breaks through many parts ; Bourlon wood reconquered and passed ; Flesquieres and many other places taken, and the prisoners 5 or 6 thousand ; Amerikans helping us one side. In Champain, in a great battle, Genll. Goureaud shoves the enemy 5 miles, and has 10 thousand prisoners these 2 days, he says. By the Meuse, Pershing's 1st army has 4 or 5 towns of the enemy, above 100 guns, and 8 thousand men taken alive in the battle. So, in sum, it is brought to a bill of 24,000 Germans caged since Thursday, above what all our armies kill. And our force enters the Boulgars' town of Strumnitza. A great grief it is to me that I am myself made a prisoner in such an houre, and no hearing what is talked of in the towne.

· · · · · ·

October 10*th*. Our army yesterday in Cambrai ; our reward, I believe, of Tuesday's battle. As to which, by Marshall Haig's dispatch come this morning, it is the greatest of victories won in the war allmost ; 10,000 prisoners and above 100 guns taken, and now the enemy do withdraw his whole force in that region. He says all Hindenbourg's works 'twixt Arras and Cambrai be now broaken, and our armies to fight wholly eastward thereof, and since our first attaquing it, August 21st, our prisoners above 110,000 and cannons taken 1200. God be praised for it. But as to Cambrai, they say it is a ruine of a city; and from all parts a sad relation is made how the Germans do sack and lay waste such places as they yield up; which do make men's hearts very stubborn to have no peace with them but they make good their devastation. To Trafalgar Square, and to see the model that is made of a village wrecked in warr, which is done with ruines of houses, a windmill, and other matters, and the end of it to move men's hearts to lending their money for feeding our guns. A great croude in the square, but more, I thought, for seeing the sight and to hear the musique than to bring money. However, it give me the good thought that, the warr indeed ending, it is an end of my getting 5 per centum with so good safety. So home, and reckoning what I am worth with my banque, and having, I believe, above 1000*l* for carrying me to Xtmas, I resolve to put 300*l* to the warr bonds. So writ the banque to do it. It is all over the towne this afternoon that German William hath abdicated himself, but I doubt he will do it, bating he be pushed further.

. . . . . .

October 31*st*. The news of the warr do continue most brave. The Austrian army is, it seems, wholly routed, and to flee with disorder, and their prisoners grown to 33 thousand. So their suing to have a truce without delay is no wonder. Likewise, on the Tigris, the Turke again cacht by Genll. Marshall, and beaten out of his posts that he holds, and a thousand prisoners counted. Only it do trouble me these 4 days gone Haig do report no progress of his armies. As to which, in discourse with Genll. Pirpleton, he told me what he hears of the major, his son, of great floods made by the Germans about Valenciennes, to show how their cunning do outwit us. He do confess his hope to be shrunk of Foch making an end of them in one stroak, but his fear is the enemy will yet withdraw his force whole out of France, so to withstand us on his own ground, it may be a yeare or two. Which I was sorry to hear. However, in the midst of our discourse, come one in great joy with the newes of the Turke suing for peace; which is true, it seems, and presently confirmed by Sir G. Cave to the

Commons; the truce allready signed, by which (among other things) the streights laid open to our fleet, and all forts surrendered that do guard Stamboul. So our reward is gained of all our labour in fighting the Turke these 4 yeares, and our men's lives lost in it. God be praised for such great mercy.

* * *

ADVANCE!
From *A Generation Missing*.[1]
By Carroll Carstairs

Zero hour was at 5.20 and promptly at that minute all the guns crowding the area behind let out a prolonged blast. Those were moments when to the ear all was noise, while the mind took on a silence of another sort—the complete absence of familiar sound.

I struggled out of a very deep dug-out, up the steps crowded with the men of my company, and into the early morning air—and then all alone I stood a witness of this ever awe-inspiring, this tremendous and transfixing thing called battle. It was still dark enough for the shells to flash with a certain splendour all along the Boche line, forging the horizon into a savage furnace (there is an incendiary shell that bursts into a crowd of great sparks that is very 4th-of-Julyish, and must terrify the enemy).

The morning light appeared, faint and pallid against these flaming particles, but day transformed them into a multitude of geysers spouting smoke and dirt. Bourlon Wood, on high ground, from which there was excellent observation, entirely disappeared behind our artillery smoke screen.

And while I watched—four hours or more—there passed me by a parade no other may see. Battalion after battalion in battle order moved, with no martial tread, no swinging up the Champs-Élysées or down Fifth Avenue or up the Mall, but rather with bowed heads and the patient step of choirboys, along the little valley at my feet. But dauntlessly, relentlessly they moved as any stream, while battalion after battalion disappeared over the ridge to melt into the wide ocean of battle,

[1] Published by William Heinemann, Ltd.

to give the finishing punch, to carry our lines forward to their final objectives.

Soon the backwash of their advance drifted by in the stretcher cases and walking wounded and prisoners. Some of the men of the company who had gathered about me greeted good-humouredly their enemies the Germans, treating them like children, rather inferior children, but still children who did not know any better.

"Hello, Jerry! Got a souvenir?"

"Have a drink, Jerry."

The Germans drank and said "Gute."

The Englishman laughed delightedly and said triumphantly: "I told you he'd say 'gut.'"

On top of this, we were suddenly changed from spectators to participants, as an order arrived from the company to "mop up" an enemy strong point that had held out all day. It was with very different feelings and in complete silence that we moved off now that we were to take part in the show. We advanced along the communication trench, glad of any slight halt or delay that counted just that many minutes of comparative safety. We had almost reached our jumping-off position when a command came to about turn. The party of the enemy had surrendered. The officer in command gave himself up, smoking a cigar, wearing white gloves and carrying a stick.

2

For a minute we were out of it—not far out—bivouacked in that part of the Somme which had felt the ebb and flow of battle throughout so great a part of the War. It presented a dismal prospect.

The battalion had come through with few casualties. One officer had a terrible experience. With a section (about seven men) he had been detailed to work up a trench. He encountered a small party of the enemy, who surrendered. He could not spare a man as escort and so told his prisoners to find their own way back into the British lines. After the Germans had gone around a traverse in the trench one of them whipped out a concealed hand grenade and threw it at his captors. The bomb hit the top of the parapet and exploded without doing any damage, but it might have " done in " the lot. Naturally incensed at this duplicity, the British took no more prisoners. The officer himself killed seven Germans in cold blood who tried to surrender. Some squealed like pigs. But what else could he do ? He had the lives of his own men to consider and could not run the risk of further treachery. That German who threw the bomb, instead of killing any English, was responsible for the death of some thirty-odd of his own countrymen—war is certainly hell !

* * *

BREAK THROUGH

From *The Cavalry Went Through*.[1]

By Bernard Newman

A strong wind from the east howled through the night, to our great glee, for our one apprehension was that the noise of the tanks might perhaps be heard as they neared the line. In our front trenches were assembled the troops allotted to the first assault—good, honest, county regiments. A mile in the rear was gathered the host of tanks. And in the support trenches were quiet groups of men who had a look of solid pride in their eye. These were the men of the shock divisions, who would bear the heat of the final assault, and behind them, horses pawing the ground impatiently, and men gazing eagerly to the east.

Capewell walked with me along the Armentières-Lille road. Staff officers in duplicate, so to speak, we were to follow up the waves of the attack, reporting to H.Q. periodically. Beside us marched orderlies with carrier pigeons. Not till we reached La Chapelle d'Armentières was it necessary to take to the communication trenches : everything was so still. I was more excited than I ought to have been. I should have considered what the coming battle would mean to England : instead, I thought of what it would mean to Duncan. Was he right in selecting this ground, after all ? It was almost flat ; so many waterways, too. Could the tanks negotiate them ?

[1] Published by Victor Gollancz, Ltd.

But Capewell was of the imperturbable kind. I remember his conversation as we passed between the ghosts of what had been houses. Had I noticed that we were fighting in Dumas's country, he said. Remember the executioner of Bethune? And the exciting events near Lens in *Twenty Years After?* And was it not in the Lys at Armentières—within a mile of where we stood—that Milady was forcibly deprived of her sinister existence? Really good literary talk Capewell produced, but as a listener I responded feebly to his efforts. I could see those faces peering into the unknown; I could hear watches ticking; I could hear hearts beating; mine own louder than any.

Here and there we crossed lines of broad white ribbon—paths that were to lead the tanks to the attack before the dawn. Yes, before the dawn. At dawn itself, of course, there is a general " stand-to " by all combatants. But in that hour before the dawn man's vitality is at its lowest—unless he is prepared: the enemy was not. The moon had set. Only the occasional glare of the Verey lights illumined the scene. I looked at my watch every few minutes. Not a gun spoke. I strained my ears in the darkness. Only in the gusty intervals did I think I heard a faint rattle. Would the German sentries hear it? Or, if they did, would they think anything of it? Surely not. But what would they think of the tanks when they saw them? Remember that only a few hundred living Germans had ever seen a tank! Ten minutes to go. What would happen before nightfall? Fancy being here all these months and never realising that the Three Musketeers used to gallop around these very spots. Eight minutes. Will the tanks really be able to negotiate the waterways? Poor old Milady! I wouldn't have objected to her so much if she hadn't killed little Madame Bonacieux. Six minutes. Where are those tanks? They mustn't be late. Could they get across Douai–Lille Canal? The executioner of Bethune killed Milady in the Douai–Lille Canal—no, dammit, in the Lys. Four min. —they're coming! Listen! What a racket! Get ready! Watch yourselves as they cross our lines! Can hardly see them—great monsters in the darkness. Half an hour to dawn —two minutes to zero. A clatter-clatter-clatter. A whistle!

And a hundred thousand men sprang from their trenches and followed in the paths of their iron pilots.

Capewell and I separated: it would not do for us both to be killed. I was with a battalion of the Koylies. The men marched with a grim stolidity that was comforting. Through a tangled, trodden path of wire we plodded: the enemy machine-guns and rifles opened, but we were a poor target. With only a few dozen casualties, we reached the German trenches. Here the attack was simple but systematic. The leading company and two tanks remained behind to mop up the line: the rest leap-frogged and pressed on. In fifteen minutes the German first line was ours on a front of twenty miles. The scared and incredulous faces of the prisoners made me happy. This was surprise!

Desultory action in front. The tanks did all the work—the company I was with had so far fired no shot. Now a grey dawn was breaking. We seemed to be surrounded by tanks—there were eight on the battalion front of a quarter of a mile. These stolid Yorkshire faces expanded into grins as they saw how great their success was going to be.

By this time the din was infernal. From north, south, east and west thousands of guns were vomiting smoke, steel and, noise. All along our front, from the Somme to the sea, every gun we could raise was pounding forth: from behind us our supporting artillery spat metal at the trench lines in front of us. Flights of German shells passed over our heads. (What a mess if two shells met in mid-air! said the Company Commander.) Now, follow the tanks.

But now the country opens. We are getting beyond the region of trench medleys. The whippet tanks speed along at a merry pace: the troops break into a jog-trot. Yes, we are moving. A big effort, boys. Another mile, I think. A hush from behind. Our fire on the German line has ceased. We are due there. Now only the heavies support us, for the moment. But, could we have been transported to the rear, what sights we might have seen. Guns limbering up and galloping forward: men working feverishly, filling in trenches that they might pass over. And behind—not far behind—

horses impatiently pawing the ground, and eager eyes straining to the east.

The third German line—the last of the solidly prepared defences—lay along the little ridge of Premesques. I waited while it was stormed—mine seemed a coward's part to-day. There was a slight halt while the division formed for the attack. The tanks—reduced in numbers, but still formidable —lumbered forward. A mighty yell from lusty throats and the infantry followed.

Here the enemy was better prepared, of course ; here his reserve regiment was lying. But nothing could stop the impetus of the attack. Men fell, but others pressed on. There was confusion for a few minutes ; then a red flare. The ridge was ours. I sent off my first pigeon.

Only occasional sniping delayed our advance. We were clear of the main fortified lines : we had passed the first lines of defenders. Our next fight would not be an attack but the repulsion of a counter-attack. Were we in a position to meet it ? I almost doubted it. This battalion was barely two hundred strong now—not that casualties had been unduly heavy, but companies and platoons had been detached continuously to mop up dug-outs and gun-pits. Halt ! There is a general stocktaking all along the line. And, too, we are waiting.

Waiting for five minutes, waiting for ten minutes. These honest Yorkshiremen have made the biggest advance of the War. Yet it is not enough. Remember Duncan's maxim, " The second attack should be stronger than the first." So we sit, waiting.

Look—look ! over to the crest of the ridge behind us. Men in khaki—hundreds of them ! Advancing at the double, too ! I got ready to send off my second pigeon. For five shock divisions—the finest men a far-flung Empire could raise—were about to charge the last German posts and let the cavalry through.

On they ran. The Koylies cheered like schoolboys as they passed through them. Yes, these were men. Not a falter in a stride. The third brigade of Guards—told to capture Lomme. You could count Lomme already in their hands.

War seems unreal. These houses have roofs.

* * *

DOUGHBOYS IN ACTION

From *God have Mercy on Us!*[1]

By William T. Scanlon

The man I shot in the leg was lying at least five feet in back of the first man. I had thought he was right behind him. He must have been one of the ammunition carriers, as I saw two cans beside him. He heard us coming and sat up. When he turned his head and saw me he looked wild-eyed. I was hoping he would not reach for any weapon, as I didn't care to kill him now. He tried to put his hands up and at the same time point to his wounded leg.

I hollered, "No, no!" and motioned to him to keep his hands down. I didn't want him sticking his hands up. The Germans up ahead might see him and get wise that we were advancing.

He had the wounded leg partly bared and it was bleeding. I remembered that I had an extra paper-covered first-aid packet in my blouse pocket. I pulled it out, partly tore it open and handed it over to him, making a rolling motion with my hand. The wild look on his face changed and I guess he tried to thank me.

In order not to expose myself in the gully I had knelt down and stretched in order to give him the packet. I was about to straighten up when I noticed a startled look come into the wounded man's eyes. He was staring above me. I turned my head to the left and at the same time a rifle cracked over my head. A German with a rifle fell forward over some bushes. Young had picked him off just in time. The German had been waiting for me to get up. He sure had me dead to rights. No doubt he was the machine-gun's fourth man—the one that had got away.

I didn't know how to operate the machine-gun so it was no use trying to take it along.

The firing on the right got heavy. It sounded like a pitched battle. I started over toward Murphy and was just in time to

[1] Published by Noel Douglas.

see his group get tangled up with a bunch of Germans who were hiding behind some brush in a small hollow. The Germans were surprised, but were showing fight.

Murphy's men were in a general mix-up. They were fighting in all directions and in all manners. Some were wrestling on the ground without any weapons. Others were standing apart clashing bayonets. The nearest German to me was wrestling with one of our men. They had locked bayonets high in the air. One was trying to push the other down. They were standing close together and I didn't know what else to do, so I gave the German a stiff jab in the hip with my bayonet and he fell.

The next fellows were sparring at one another. I jabbed that German in the leg and he was through. The leg was the best place and it wasn't so messy. I saw one fellow drive a bayonet through a German, but before he could get it out another German ran him through. A short jab and a quick withdrawal is the best.

The next German had one of our men in a bad fix. Our man had fallen and was now grasping the German's bayonet with both hands trying to keep it from going into him. The bayonet was piercing the gas-mask bag on his chest. I yelled and rushed for the German. He saw me coming and swept his bayonet free from the fellow's grasp and swung straight for my head. I ducked low, but I must have thrown my rifle up because he struck my bayonet, knocking it to one side. From my crouching position I socked the rifle butt into his groin. It lifted him off his feet and he sank to the ground in a heap. It took all the wind out of me and I slipped down myself. The man that had been grasping the bayonet must have fainted. He was lying back rather dead-looking—his now fingerless, bleeding hands limp at his sides.

I could see some of our men trying to help out another fellow. They kept fiddling around trying to get at the front of the German with their bayonets. I yelled at them, " Jab him in the leg!" One of them did, and the German was through.

These Germans were wearing square packs on their backs, and it was no use trying to stick them through the packs as it would be hard getting the bayonet out again. If you hit them over the head you were likely to bust your rifle.

I spotted Murphy and he was bloody, but I didn't think it was his blood, judging from the way he was dancing around. Spud and a German were going to it. The only trouble was, there was a tree between them. Spud was having a hard time trying to get at the German, who always kept on the other side of the tree. I slipped over and jabbed the German in the leg and he tumbled over backwards. Spud came around the tree, and he was mad.

"What the hell did you do that for? I'd 'a' got him!"

* * *

BULGARIA was the first of Germany's allies to collapse. Then, advancing across the scriptural plain of Armageddon, Allenby administered the *coup de grâce* to the Turkish armies in Palestine.

ARMAGEDDON
From *With Our Army in Palestine*.[1]
By ANTONY BLUETT

The main difficulties were to concentrate unseen a large force of infantry in the plain of Sharon, and to bring the remainder of the cavalry from the Jordan Valley without observation by the enemy. The vast olive-groves round about Ludd and Jaffa comfortably concealed the infantry, whose movements were carried out at night and with the utmost caution, but the transport of the cavalry was a tougher problem, for the Turks were very much on the alert in the Jordan Valley, and did in fact expect the attack to be made in this direction.

Considerable guile was therefore necessary, into which entered a little innocent fun. It was a general and strictly enforced rule that no lights should be shown after dusk, on account of bombing raids, yet during the last weeks of August long lines of bivouac fires twinkled nightly in the Jordan Valley; and the authorities seemed to be singularly blind to this flagrant disobedience of orders. During the day, at stated hours, groups of men riding aged and infirm horses were

[1] Published by Andrew Melrose, Ltd.

strung out at fifty-yard intervals, engaged in the gentle pastime of dragging sacks and branches along the roads; they made so much dust that it might easily have been caused by, say, a cavalry division going to water. Also, thousands of tiny tents sprang up round the bivouac areas, in front of which were equally diminutive soldiers in squads and companies, whose function it was to stand rigidly to attention all day long, and who treated the frequent bombing raids with utter contempt. A careful observer would have noticed a certain woodenness about them, but enemy airmen were profoundly impressed by this large concentration of troops.

Meanwhile, every night, brigade after brigade of British cavalry left the Jordan Valley on their fifty-mile ride across country to the friendly shelter of the orange groves of Jaffa and Sarona, and the men left behind complained bitterly of the increase of work in having to light so many extra bivouac fires! The whole concentration was carried out without the Turks being any the wiser, and by the middle of September thirty-five thousand infantry were ready to pour forth from their hiding-places, with four divisions of mounted troops to follow hard upon their heels; it was scarcely possible to move in the coast sector without falling over a battery of artillery, and tucked away round Richon and Duran were thousands of transport camels of every shade and breed.

At dusk on the night of September 18th the orange groves began to erupt, and for eight hours horse and foot in orderly columns marched silently forward, the infantry to their battle positions and the cavalry to the beach between Arsuf and Jaffa, there to wait till the breach had been made. At half-past four the next morning the shattering roar of artillery proclaimed that the offensive had begun, and at dawn the infantry attacked the Turkish positions, swept over those nearest the coast at the first onslaught, and then swung eastwards. One after another from Et Tireh to Jiljulieh, strongholds upon which months of labour had been expended fell before the irresistible *élan* of our men, though the Turks fought magnificently to hold their line. By noon the whole of the coastal sector was in our hands, and the plain of Sharon lay open to the cavalry, who had started on their historic ride north soon after our first attack.

In the meantime the infantry, driving before them the demoralised remnants of the Turkish Eighth Army, captured Tul Keram, Turkish G.H.Q., together with a host of prisoners, and then continued east to help the Welsh and Irish divisions in their assault on Nablus. The Turks here had no information of the *débâcle* on their right, for the R.A.F. had started out at dawn and had destroyed every means of communication, except the roads, between the two armies. They, therefore, fought with the utmost determination, and aided by their well-chosen and well-fortified positions, held off our attacks all that day and the next, though the Irishmen, by extraordinary exertions, crumpled up one flank. Then the last message ever sent from the north informed them that the British cavalry had overrun the whole country in their rear, so far as they knew the only line of retreat left open to them was eastward across the Jordan, and this loophole, too, was soon to be closed. Panic reigned; the roads leading east were black with long columns of guns and transport and men mingled in hopeless confusion, fleeing with no thought of anything but their own safety; a routed, utterly demoralised rabble.

Nablus was occupied without difficulty on the 21st, but the infantry, who had been scrambling about the hills of Samaria for three days, could not run fast enough to catch the Turks, who were making their way through the Wadi Farah towards the Jisr ed Damieh ford. Half-way through the wadi the road has on one side a deep, gloomy gorge, while on the other stretch gaunt hills terrible in their desolation and stony barrenness. The whole aspect of the place is sinister and forbidding in the extreme, and one can imagine the panic-stricken Turks hurrying through yet a little faster, eager to sight the yellow waters of the Jordan. But they never reached the goal, for the Royal Air Force found the column half-way through the gorge. Relays of machines joined in the attack, first dropping bombs and then flying low and spraying the column with bullets. In five minutes the road eastwards was blocked, and driven by the slow but remorseless advance of our infantry far in the rear, with impassable hills on the one hand, and a precipice on the other, the column was caught in a trap.

A part of it tried to escape, before being driven into the

gorge, by a road leading to the north, but were bombed back again into the shambles. Mad with terror, some of the Turks tried to scramble up the steep hills, others made an attempt to descend into the deep gorge; anywhere to escape from the awful hail of bombs and bullets. For four hours the slaughter continued, and when " Cease Fire " was ordered, the road for nine miles was literally a vast charnel-house. Guns, limbers, commissariat wagons, field-kitchens, every conceivable form of vehicle, including a private barouche, lay heaped together in monstrous confusion; and when night fell ragged, half-starved Bedouins descended upon the stricken valley, stealing from pile to pile of debris in search of loot, nor could the rifles of the Guards deter them from the ghoulish task. It took an entire division three weeks to clear the roads and bury the dead.

. . . . . .

The column advancing on Nazareth had met with equal, though not quite bloodless, success. Arriving at dawn they, too, found the town asleep, and clattered through the streets in search of Liman von Sanders. He was warned in the very nick of time, however, and the cavalry had an interesting back view of a swiftly disappearing car in which sat Liman von Sanders in his pyjamas, followed at a respectful distance by some of his staff not so discreetly clad. Undisturbed by the defection of their chief, the Germans resisted stoutly for a time, both in the streets of Nazareth and in the hills north of the town, but, ultimately, all were gathered in and sent across the ancient battle-field of Armageddon to join the rest at Afule.

The aerodromes at Jenin were captured, or, to be more exact, rendered useless by our aircraft, who had hovered over them ever since the beginning of the battle, dropping an " egg " whenever enemy machines attempted to come out. When the cavalry arrived, practically all they had to do was to tie up the hordes of men who were only too anxious to surrender.

In five days the combined forces had smashed up two Turkish armies and had taken forty thousand prisoners.

I cannot do better than to end this chapter by giving in full

General Allenby's letter to the troops thanking them for this remarkable achievement:

"I desire to convey to all ranks and all arms of the Force under my command, my admiration and thanks for the great deeds of the past week, and my appreciation of their gallantry and determination, which have resulted in the total destruction of the Seventh and Eighth Turkish Armies opposed to us. Such a complete victory has seldom been known in all the history of war."

* * *

IN spite of the severe buffetings it had received, the German Army was still a formidable fighting organisation. Defeated, it was by no means destroyed, and it might easily have retired to the line of the Meuse or the German frontier, for the advance of the Allies was slow because of the lack of mobile formations. Two factors, however, determined that the War should not be continued into 1919—first, the collapse of Germany's allies, for Bulgaria, Turkey, and Austria, in turn, capitulated after suffering overwhelming defeats in the field; second, the German spirit, undermined by the four years' blockade-impelled shortage of food and the insidious propaganda of the Allies, collapsed.

The first note of revolution was sounded by the German Navy—ordered, as a last desperate measure, to go to sea and die fighting.

MUTINY

From *The Kaiser's Coolies*.[1]

By THEODOR PLIVIER

The funnels vomit sparks.
Shadow-like, a ship passes.
Another. The fleet is moving.
A cry rends the air—one man shrieks. Hundreds of throats echo the sound. Rage and desperation! The upper deck of *Thüringen* is black with men. At the moment the other

[1] Published by Faber and Faber, Ltd.

MUTINY

anchor falls, a couple of men have let it go. The cable rattles through the hawse-pipe and the ship is moored again. Now the stokers have acted. They put out the fires. The columns of smoke cease, white steam pours from the funnels.

The mass of the men begin to act.

They storm the casements, into the forward battery, make the anchor fast, close the doors of the petty officers' mess below and batten down the hatches. They cut the lines and falls, not a boat can be lowered. Officers coming down from the bridge are pelted with buckets, boots, boiler scales, anything that comes in handy. Arms. Fists. The picture of the " Victor of Jutland " is torn in pieces. Lamps are broken, rifles and ammunition served out. Shells for the secondary armament put ready.

The casemates echo.

" We must have peace."

" We must have freedom."

The aristocrats! The cut-throats! The Imperial Navy! Down with them all! A searchlight. Morse signals.

S.M.S. *Helgoland* replies :

" Comrades, on with the good work! We're doing the same."

Thüringen remains in Schillig Roads.

Helgoland remains in Schillig Roads.

The fleet, the battle cruisers and battle squadrons sail. In the white beams of the searchlights the commanding officers have succeeded in dispersing the men who gathered on deck, and in getting the anchors weighed. One last appeal is made by the officers to the disciplined minds of the men on whose credulity they impose. " No, we are not going to attack England. We are only out to cover the mine-sweepers. There are ninety submarines outside. They don't know the way in. We must fetch them."

The fleet stretches out in line ahead.

At slow speed ! The stokers keep the pressure low.

Twelve or fourteen miles out is all that is necessary to cover mine-sweeping and bring submarines home. As they leave the Jade the wind rises. The mist disperses, some watery stars appear. The ships roll heavily in the waves. An alteration of course! The weather side changes. The men below in the casemates notice it.

Course, north-west!

Towards England!

Orders that do not originate on the bridge. "Out of your hammocks! Into the forward battery! All men forward."

A man stands on the chain-locker.

"Course, north-west! An attack! The navigator has got charts of the English east coast on his table. The paint for the funnels is ready on the running bridge." "They've deceived us as they always have! Four and a half years of war! Now it's all over. Their careers have gone to hell: their glorious idle existence. They are frightened of the future and want to commit suicide." "This advance is suicidal! And we're to be in it."

"We're to get killed."

The ship rolls in the swell.

Five hundred men are gathered in the forward battery round the chain locker. Mutiny means death. Round one of the 6-inch guns a group has gathered, trying to quiet their anxiety by singing: "I want to go back home . . ."

A speech, a second, a third.

Now the commander comes along.

"Now only one at a time, please; two at the most. . . . I am a South German, eighteen years afloat. My life is very precious to me. . . . Somebody threw something at me. That's bad . . . Comrades, comrades."

"Liar."

"At him, at him!"

Lamp bulbs are shattered.

The forward battery is plunged in darkness.

Stamping of feet! Rush of many bodies!

"Damned cowards, stop that singing." "Stokers, where are the stokers? To the stoke-holds! Draw the fires! Out with the searchlights!"

"Lights out."

"Draw the fires."

For a minute the searchlights illumine the men pouring from the armoured decks and the masses thronged about the

MUTINY

decks. Then the beams wander skywards and are extinguished. A wireless from the Commander-in-Chief: " Advance to be carried out at all costs." Reply: " Advance will not be carried out."

A siren howls.

Between decks. Passages to the boiler rooms. Clusters of sailors. Cursing chief engineers. Lumps of coal are hurled at the latter. Petty officers defend the sentries.

Wheels! Handles! Weights!

Fires are drawn.

Furnace doors torn open!

The alarm bell! Telephone!

A last attempt by the staff.

" Clear for action! Action stations! "

The ruse doesn't work. In the stokeholds the steam rises like an enormous wild jungle. In the light of the furnace doors a struggling mass of bodies. Engineers, warrant officers are overcome by the mass of men.

The last boiler fails.

The ship stops.

. . . . . .

Down with the ensign.

A pair of arms wave a swab in the air, a dirty swab used to wash the decks, old and frayed with the sweat of innumerable coolies sentenced to extra work.

" The swab—tie it on! "

" Ready . . . all of you. Up with it! "

The swab rises in the air; hangs up there, at the gaff; at which, during four and half years of war and from the very foundation of the navy, the symbol of the Empire has flown.

And on board the other ships, the flags go down: swabs, coal sacks, red flags, go up.

Five thousand officers, sworn to defend the flag. At drunken orgies, with glasses filled with champagne in their hands they have numberless times repeated their oath to risk their life for Emperor and flag.

Five thousand admirals, captains, officers.

Only three of them defend their flag.

In S.M.S. *König*, the captain, the commander and the

adjutant, a sub-lieutenant of twenty. Pistol in hand, the three stand on the quarter-deck, deserted by all the others. A sailor falls to their fire. Then they are overwhelmed by a rush of men, a grey wave. Blows of rifle butts, shots! Bodies! Arms! Legs! Captain and commander wounded.

The adjutant dead.

The Emperor's flag sinks.

The red flag ascends.

All the other ships fall without a struggle.

The shore establishments fall without a struggle.

The Admiralty in Berlin—Secretary of State, admirals, captains, commanders, hundreds of officers armed with swords, pistols, hand grenades, machine-guns; supported by a loyal, full-strength company of Jäger, this fortress capitulates to a warrant officer and six men.

And the supreme War Lord, William II, Imperator, Rex?

After his flight across the frontier in a motor car, his Adjutant, Lieutenant-Colonel Niemann, asks him why he did not seek death at the head of his troops.

He answers:

"The day of heroic gestures is past."

* * *

THE last week of the War was one of scurried sensations. Once Germany revealed herself to the world as hopelessly defeated, however, her doom approached with hurricane swiftness. It is advisable, in order to avoid judgment based on surface considerations only, to examine the fundamental causes of the final collapse.

SURRENDER

From *A History of the World War*.[1]

By B. H. LIDDELL HART

What caused that astonishingly sudden collapse and surrender of Germany which, as by a miracle, so it seemed, lifted the nightmare load of war from Europe? To arrive at a

[1] Published by Faber and Faber, Ltd.

SURRENDER

satisfactory answer it is not sufficient to analyse the hectic weeks of negotiation and military success which preceded November 11th. Even in the military sphere we need to go back to August 8th, the day which filled the German command with the conviction of defeat, and to July 18th, which witnessed the visible turning of the tide. And if we go back thence we must go back further, to March 21st, for the decline of Germany's military power is not explicable without reference to the consummation of that military effort, and consumption of her military resources, in the great series of offensives which opened in the spring of 1918.

We ought, however, to go back further still. Indeed, if the historian of the future has to select one day as decisive for the outcome of the World War he will probably choose August 2nd, 1914—before the War, for England, had yet begun—when Mr. Winston Churchill, at 1.25 a.m., sent the order to mobilise the British Navy. That Navy was to win no Trafalgar, but it was to do more than any other factor towards winning the War for the Allies. For the Navy was the instrument of the blockade, and as the fog of war disperses in the clearer light of these post-war years that blockade is seen to assume larger and larger proportions, to be more and more clearly the decisive agency in the struggle. Like those "jackets" which used to be applied in American gaols to refractory prisoners, as it was progressively tightened so did it first cramp the prisoner's movements and then stifle his breathing, while the tighter it became and the longer it continued the less became the prisoner's power of resistance and the more demoralising the sense of constriction.

Helplessness induces hopelessness, and history attests that loss of hope and not loss of lives is what decides the issue of war. No historian would underrate the direct effect of the semi-starvation of the German people in causing the final collapse of the " home-front." But leaving aside the question of how far the revolution caused the military defeat, instead of *vice versa*, the intangible all-pervading factor of the blockade intrudes into every consideration of the military situation.

This, during the last year of the War, is studded with "ifs." If Germany, instead of throwing all her military resources into a series of tremendous offensives in 1918, had stayed on the defensive in the West, while consolidating her gains in the East, could she have averted defeat? Militarily, there seems little doubt that she could. In the light of the experience of 1915, when the Allies had 145 divisions in the West to Germany's 100, and when the German trench systems were a frail and shallow bulwark compared with those of 1918, it is difficult to see that the Allies could have breached it, even if they had waited until the inflowing tide of American manpower had restored to them the relative numerical superiority that they had enjoyed in 1915.

And if so, in face of the accumulating cost of vain assaults, would they not eventually have inclined towards a compromise peace. A peace, peradventure, which, in return for the relinquishment of Belgium and Northern France, might have conceded to Germany part or the whole of her gains in the East. Yet as we ask the question, and militarily find an optimistic answer difficult, the factor of the command of the sea comes to mind. For it was the stranglehold of the British Navy which, in default of a serious peace move, constrained Germany to carry out that *felo de se* offensive of 1918. She was dogged by the spectre of slow enfeeblement ending in eventual collapse.

Perhaps if she had adopted such a war policy of defence in the West, offence in the East, after the Marne in 1914, or even, after 1915, continued the policy which she had that year temporarily adopted, the prospect might have been brighter and the story different. For, on the one hand, she could have consumated unquestionably the dream of " Mittel-Europa," and on the other, the blockade was still a loose grip, and could hardly have been drawn effectively tight so long as the United States remained outside the conflict. But in 1918 the best chance had passed.

Another big " if," often mooted, is the question whether even in the autumn of 1918 Germany could have avoided capitulation. Would the fighting front have collapsed if the War had gone on after November 11th? Was capitulation inevitable, or could the German armies have made good their retreat and stood firm on their own frontiers? German opinion largely says " yes " to the latter question, and blames the surrender on the " home front." Many open-minded and diligent students of the War among the Allies are inclined to agree that it was possible from a military point of view. But again the naval aspect intervenes. Even if the German armies, and the German people, roused to a supreme effort in visible defence of their own soil, had managed to hold the Allies at bay, the end could only have been postponed. The most that history is likely to concede is that they might have held on long enough, tightening their belts, for the Allies, already weary, to sicken of the effort, and thus concede more favourable terms than those of Versailles.

• • • • • •

Rather does the record of the last " hundred days," when thoroughly sifted, confirm the immemorial lesson of history —that the true aim in war is the mind of the enemy command and Government, not the bodies of their troops, that the balance between victory and defeat turns on mental impressions and only indirectly on physical blows. That in war, as Napoleon said and Foch endorsed, " it is the man, not men, who counts."

The reiteration of this great truth is to be found in the War's last phase. Great as was the stimulus and visible success of the tide-turning battle on the Marne in July, Ludendorff was still planning and preparing fresh offensives thereafter. If he was chagrined, he does not appear to have been so disillusioned as he had been after his own outwardly successful attack on the Lys in April.

But the Fourth Army surprise attack before Amiens on August 8th was a dislocating moral blow. Prince Max put August 8th in its true light psychologically when he defined it as " the turning point." Even so, to develop the conviction of failure into the conviction of hopelessness required to compel surrender, something more was needed. It came not from the Western Front, but from a despised " side-show "— Salonika, long condemned by Allied military opinion and scornfully ridiculed by the Germans as their " largest internment camp." With Bulgaria's collapse the back gate to

Austria, as well as to Turkey, and through Austria to Germany, lay ajar.

The immediate issue of the War was decided on September 29th, decided in the mind of the German Command. Ludendorff and his associates had then "cracked," and the sound went echoing backwards until it had resounded throughout the whole of Germany. Nothing could catch it or stop it. The Command might recover its nerve, the actual military position might improve, but the moral impression, as ever in war, was decisive.

Yet, let us once again emphasise that the fundamental causes of the decision are more various than the acts which immediately produced it.

The truth is that no one cause was, or could be, decisive. The Western Front, the Balkan Front, the tank, the blockade and propaganda have all been claimed as the cause of victory. All claims are justified, none is wholly right, although the blockade ranks first and began first. In this warfare between nations victory is a cumulative effect, to which all weapons—military, economic and psychological—contribute. Victory comes, and can only come, through the utilization and combination of all the resources existing in a modern nation, and the dividend of success depends on the way in which these manifold activities are co-ordinated.

It is even more futile to ask which country won the War. France did not win the War, but unless she had held the fort while the forces of Britain were preparing and those of America still a dream the release of civilization from this nightmare of militarism would have been impossible. Britain did not win the War, but without her command of the sea, her financial support, and her army, to take over the main burden of the struggle from 1916 onwards, defeat would have been inevitable. The United States did not win the War, but without their economic aid to ease the strain, without the arrival of their troops to turn the numerical balance, and, above all, without the moral tonic which their coming gave, victory would have been impossible. And let us not forget how many times Russia had sacrificed herself to save her Allies; preparing the way for their ultimate victory as surely as for her own downfall. Finally, whatever be the verdict of history on her policy, unstinted tribute is due to the incomparable endurance and skill with which Germany more than held her own for four years against superior numbers, an epic of military and human achievement.

* * *

In the grey hours of the morning of November 11th, 1918, courageous German officers met Marshal Foch and his staff in a clearing in the Forest of Rethondes, near Compiègne; it was agreed that an Armistice should be signed, hostilities to be terminated at 11 a.m. on that day.

ARMISTICE

From *The Memoirs of Marshal Foch*.[1]

(Translated by Colonel T. Bentley Mott)

Places were now taken at the conference table.

Marshal Foch asked the German delegates the purpose of their visit.

Herr Erzberger replied that the German delegation had come to receive the proposals of the Allied Powers looking to an armistice on land, on sea and in the air, on all the fronts and in the colonies.

Marshal Foch replied that he had no proposals to make.

Count Oberndorff asked the Marshal in what form he desired that they should express themselves. He did not stand on form; he was ready to say that the German delegation asked the conditions of the armistice.

Marshal Foch replied that he had no conditions to offer.

Herr Erzberger read the text of President Wilson's last note, stating that Marshal Foch is authorised to make known the armistice conditions.

Marshal Foch replied that he was authorised to make these known if the German delegates asked for an armistice.

"Do you ask for an armistice? If you do, I can inform you of the conditions subject to which it can be obtained."

[1] Published by William Heinemann, Ltd.

Herr Erzberger and Count Oberndorff declared that they asked for an armistice.

Marshal Foch then announced that the armistice conditions would be read; as the text was rather long, only the principal paragraphs would be read for the present; later on the complete text would be communicated to the plenipotentiaries.

General Weygand read the principal clauses of the armistice conditions (text agreed upon at Versailles on November 4th).

The reading terminated, and Herr Erzberger requested that military operations be immediately suspended. He gave as a reason the disorganisation and lack of discipline which reigned in the German Army, and the spirit of revolution that was spreading through Germany as a consequence of the people's sufferings. He described the difficulties which he and his fellow delegates had encountered in passing through the German Armies and in crossing their lines, where even the order to cease fire was executed only after considerable trouble. All these circumstances led him to fear that Germany might soon fall into the grip of Bolshevism, and once Central Europe was invaded by this scourge, Western Europe, he said, would find the greatest difficulty in escaping it. Nothing but the cessation of Allied attacks would make it possible to re-establish discipline in the German Army and, through the restoration of order, save the country.

I immediately answered: "At the moment when negotiations for the signing of an armistice are just being opened, it is impossible to stop military operations until the German delegation has accepted and signed the conditions which are the very consequence of those operations. As for the situation described by Herr Erzberger as existing among the German troops and the danger he fears of Bolshevism spreading in Germany, the one is the usual disease prevailing in beaten armies, the other is symptomatic of a nation completely worn out by war. Western Europe will find means of defending itself against the danger."

When I had finished my statement regarding the impossibility of my acquiescence to the verbal request of Herr Erzberger, General von Winterfeldt asked to be heard. He

ARMISTICE

had a special mission to fulfil on behalf of the German Supreme Command and the German Government.

He read the following statement, prepared in advance:

"The Armistice terms which have just been brought to our knowledge require careful examination by us. As it is our intention to come to a decision, this examination will be made as promptly as possible. Nevertheless, it will require a certain amount of time, especially as it will be necessary to consult our Government and the military Supreme Command.

"During this time the struggle between our Armies will continue and it will result, both among soldiers and civilians, in numerous victims who will die in vain at the last minute, and who might be preserved to their families.

"Therefore, the German Government and the German Supreme Command have the honour to revert to the proposal made by them in their wireless message of the day before yesterday, viz. that Marshal Foch be kind enough to consent to an immediate suspension of hostilities on the entire front, to begin to-day at a certain fixed hour, the very simple details of which could be decided upon without loss of time."

To this Marshal Foch replied:

"I am the Commander-in-Chief of the Allied Armies and representative of the Allied Governments. These Governments have decided upon their terms. Hostilities cannot cease before the signing of the Armistice. I am likewise desirous of reaching a conclusion and therefore I shall help you as far as is possible toward this end. But hostilities cannot cease before the signing of the Armistice."

. . . . . .

General Order.

"Officers, non-commissioned officers and soldiers of the Allied Armies:

"After resolutely repulsing the enemy for months, you confidently attacked him with an untiring energy.

"You have won the greatest battle in History and rescued the most sacred of all causes, the Liberty of the World.

"You have full right to be proud, for you have crowned your standards with immortal glory and won the gratitude of posterity.

"F. Foch,
"Marshal of France,
"Commander-in-Chief of the Allied Armies."

* * *

The whole world, relieved from unbearable tension with such dramatic suddenness, went mad. In London memories of Mafeking were overshadowed in the furious and riotous rejoicing.

ARMISTICE NIGHT

From *The Crater of Mars*.[1]

By Ferdinand Tuohy

Such an outburst of spontaneous enthusiasm marked Armistice Day, November 11th, as made up for all Germany's shouting during the War. The joy-making has gone on ever since, day after day, night after night, and to-day, as these lines are being written, six days after the signing of the Armistice, the festive rejoicings have reached their climax. The beflagged and brightly lit streets of London are congested with a dense, cheering crowd, bands are playing, processions forming, all the premonitory symptoms of a final "joy night" on the tapis.

It has been a very wonderful week—a week in which every class of the community has formed up, as it were, in one delirious ring-a-ring-o'-roses. Gorgeously gowned women in silks and satins have linked up in the street revelry with Australian private soldiers, and stern and be-decorated generals have tripped the light fantastic down Piccadilly arm in arm with shell-girls and bus conductresses. It has been a veritable apotheosis of democracy.

To understand what has occurred one must first picture the London war-types who have participated in the revelry—as hectic a pageant of humanity as ever a revue producer could conceive. Stately, khaki-bloused Australians and New

[1] Published by William Heinemann, Ltd.

ARMISTICE NIGHT

Zealanders; land girls in smock, field-boots and breeches; convalescent wounded in bright blue uniforms and garish red ties; pretty girl drivers of the Army Service Corps; munitionettes, special constables, naval officers and men of the Grand Fleet; French and Belgian poilus; quaintly capped American seamen; tall, determined "Yanks"; Canadians, cavalry, V.A.D. girls in dark-blue or grey; red-tabbed and gold-laced staff officers; Tube girls and bus conductresses in trim and dainty uniforms; "Waacs" in khaki, some wearing service chevrons and even wound stripes; "Wrens" dressed like naval officers and ratings; "Penguins" and "Wrafs."

One could go on indefinitely, enumerating this amazing London potpourri of the times. No carnival ever equalled it in life or colour.

This past week it has been as if all had crowded on to the stage at the end of the last act and had proceeded to go mad. Dancing, cheering, frolicking, waving flags, letting off fireworks, operating on every manner of instrument from trumpet to squeaker, banging drums, blowing horns and sirens, ringing bells and whirling round nerve-racking rattles—all this in the sober, sedate West End, hour after hour, day after day, night after night.

The ball was started rolling at 11 a.m. on the 11th, when the guns of the anti-aircraft defences thundered the great news east and west, south and north. Instantly London, as one man and woman, rose from its desk and proceeded to forget that such a thing as work existed. Out into the streets surged hundreds of thousands. Flags appeared as if by magic on every house and office. People in the street, complete strangers, cheered one another as they made their way towards the West End—for all roads led to the time-honoured celebrating region of Piccadilly, Regent Street and the Strand. Here, towards two o'clock, the scene baffled description. Not an inch of pavement or roadway could be seen. Simply one vast, multi-coloured human throng, all cheering, screaming, yelling. Every motor car, taxi or lorry or bus that passed was commandeered by hundreds who clambered up, men, women and children, old and young, and proceeded to set off on a triumphant, cheering joy-ride.

One counted as many as twenty on a taxi-cab and thirty on a private car. Girls sat astride the bonnet, others hung perilously on to the mudguards. All cheered and went on cheering. The speed of the "joy chariots" averaged perhaps a quarter of a mile an hour through the continuous sea of humanity. Sometimes an army lorry would come by, completely smothered by clinging forms, not even the wheels visible.

In the midst of it all, while the Kaiser was sneaking into Holland, appeared the King and Queen, joy-riding through the dense mass like everyone else. Their Majesties will live to be very old before they ever hear such cheers again as on that Monday afternoon in the Strand.

. . . . . .

One night a rush was made for the Mall, where 400 German guns were lined up. Dozens were trundled out and through the West End, officers superintending operations from the limbers. In Trafalgar Square a huge bonfire was made of captured guns, hoardings, chairs, anything to hand. And when the fire brigade arrived the Australians calmly cut the hose-pipes and proceeded to dance madly round the flames, mounting fifty feet high. The Australians and American troops and the shell-girls have been the moving, careering spirits of the revelry, during which, of course, all traffic has been completely at a standstill.

Pickpockets have had a record week, second only to the hawkers and street vendors selling the flags and favours of all nations and picture postcards of the Kaiser behind prison bars. Paper hats have also had a great vogue—a strange phase of London's delirium, in fact, has been the riot and interchange of headgear. Pretty girls paraded wearing shrapnel helmets and officers countered by donning dainty toques and bonnets. An atmosphere of perfect good-humour has pervaded all; the the police having had nothing to do save stand about and receive the plaudits of the multitude. Someone very high up must have said: "Let them carry on. They deserve it!" For all restrictions as known under Dora have been thrown to the winds. People have fairly done things that a week before would have earned them six months' imprisonment.

. . . .

In the hotels and restaurants the scenes have been just as unrestrained. Not a seat has been available the whole week, while the obtaining of food has been a farce. People didn't go to the restaurants to dine this week. They went to revel. The orchestras largely controlled operations. They played every popular tune from the " Marseillaise " to " Auld Lang Syne " over and over again, the diners shouting in chorus at the tops of their voices. Proceedings would be punctuated by cheers for war celebrities such as Wilson, Lloyd George, Foch, Haig and Clemenceau, and by groans and hisses for the Kaiser and the Crown Prince and Ludendorff. Or people would make speeches, inarticulate vapourings drowned in applause. A toast to the Czechoslovaks would produce a tremendous outburst of enthusiasm, though half the assembly had but the vaguest notion who the Czechoslovaks were. Pretty women and gallant officers mounted tables and, standing amid their dinners, waved champagne bottles on high and called for cheers for anybody, anything. And the response would be defeaning. To wave a Belgian, or a British or a French or American flag was to bring down the house.

After the hors-d'œuvres, dancing usually broke out, and soon the whole room at the Savoy or Romano's or the Carlton would be fox-trotting and prancing up and down, in and out of the tables ; no such person as a stranger in the room, all welded together by the wonderful occasion. Men who normally would have been madly jealous of handing their wives over to others, strangers, promptly gripped hold of the stranger's wife. Sedate uncles and aunts donned paper caps and blew tin whistles.

Every now and then the room would resound to the National Anthem and the " Marseillaise," this latter a long way the most popular. Few knew the words, but all shouted the intoxicating air. And meanwhile champagne corks popped, and diners danced with the staff, and more speeches were made, and more cheers for favourites would be called for and thundered forth. Sometimes the guests waited on themselves, going even down to the kitchen. At many restaurants giant " bowls " were made of every conceivable wine and liquor, and ladled around like soup to all and sundry.

Any celebrity of social life, such as a politician or an actress, would be hoisted bodily on to the table and forced to address the room. One attractive young actress astonished people on such an occasion by solemnly declaiming:

"I'm going to give you an entirely new toast. England! We've done more and said less than anybody else!"

* * *

For many months the Allies had dangled President Wilson's famous Fourteen Points before Germany as an incentive to peace. When, beaten to her knees, Germany demanded an Armistice, she fondly imagined that it would be on the basis of these Fourteen Points. She had completely misjudged the temper of her enemies—particularly of France.

THE FOURTEEN POINTS

By President Wilson

I. Open covenants of peace, openly arrived at, after which there shall be no private international understandings of any kind, but diplomacy shall proceed always frankly and in public view.

II. Absolute freedom of navigation upon the seas, outside territorial waters, alike in peace and in war, except as the seas may be closed in whole or in part by international action for the enforcement of international covenants.

III. The removal, so far as possible, of all economic barriers, and the establishment of an equality of trade conditions among all the nations consenting to the peace and associating themselves for its maintenance.

IV. Adequate guarantees given and taken that national armaments will be reduced to the lowest point consistent with domestic safety.

V. A free, open-minded and absolutely impartial adjustment of all colonial claims based upon a strict observance of the principle that in determining all such questions of sovereignty the interests of the populations concerned must have equal weight with the equitable claims of the Government whose title is to be determined.

VI. The evacuation of all Russian territory and such a settlement of all questions affecting Russia as will secure the best and freest co-operation of the other nations of the world in obtaining for her an unhampered and unembarrassed opportunity for the independent determination of her own political development and national policy, and assure her of a sincere welcome into the society of free nations under institutions of her own choosing, and more than a welcome, assistance also of every kind that she may need and may herself desire. The treatment accorded Russia by her sister nations in the months to come will be the acid test of their goodwill, of their comprehension of her needs as distinguished from their own interests, and of their intelligent and unselfish sympathy.

VII. Belgium, the whole world will agree, must be evacuated and restored without any attempt to limit the sovereignty which she enjoys in common with all other free nations. No other single act will serve to restore confidence among the nations in the laws which they have themselves set and determined for the government of their relations with one another. Without this healing act the whole structure and validity of international law is forever impaired.

VIII. All French territory should be freed, and the invaded portions restored, and the wrong done to France by Prussia in 1871, in the matter of Alsace-Lorraine, which has unsettled the peace of the world for nearly fifty years, should be righted in order that peace may once more be made secure in the interest of all.

IX. A readjustment of the frontiers of Italy should be effected along clearly recognisable lines of nationality.

X. The peoples of Austro-Hungary, whose place among the nations we wish to see safeguarded and assured, should be accorded the first opportunity of autonomous development.

XI. Roumania, Serbia and Montenegro should be evacuated; occupied territories restored; Serbia accorded free and secure access to the sea; and the relations of the several Balkan States to one another determined by friendly counsel along historically established lines of allegiance and nationality; and international guarantees of the political and economic independence and territorial integrity of the several Balkan States should be entered into.

XII. The Turkish portions of the present Ottoman Empire should be assured a secure sovereignty, but the other nationalities which are now under Turkish rule should be assured an undoubted security of life and an absolutely unmolested opportunity of autonomous development, and the Dardanelles should be permanently opened as a free passage to the ships and commerce of all nations under international guarantees.

XIII. An independent Polish state should be erected which should include the territories inhabited by indisputably Polish populations, which should be assured a free and secure access to the sea, and whose political and economic independence and territorial integrity should be guaranteed by international covenant.

XIV. A general association of nations must be formed under specific covenants for the purpose of affording mutual guarantees of political independence and territorial integrity to great and small states alike.

* * *

THE PEACE TERMS

From *A Junior Outline of History*.[1]

By I. O. EVANS

The Conference that settled the terms of peace was very much in the hands of the leaders of France, Britain, Italy and America. The United States President, Woodrow Wilson (1856–1924), was an idealist, who, even during the War, had advocated a peace that would be fair to all and lead to a lasting world brotherhood. His famous " Fourteen Points " included " the freedom of the seas," free commerce, open agreements to take the place of secret diplomacy, reduction of armaments, and " a general association of all nations " in a world council. These aims appealed to reasonable people of both sides, and it was hoped that they might be made the basis of the peace.

[1] Published by Denis Archer, Ltd.

THE PEACE TERMS

Unfortunately other members of the Council were thinking not of world peace, but only of gains for their own nations and of revenge on their defeated enemies. The final terms of peace, as signed on June 28th, 1918, at Versailles (where in 1871 the King of Prussia had been made German Emperor) were merciless. Germany was to restore Alsace-Lorraine to France and large regions to Poland, to lose other valuable home areas and all its colonies, to surrender its navy, to reduce its land armaments, to have its chief waterways internationalised, and to pay impossibly huge sums by way of " reparations."

The treaty with Austria (September 10th) broke up the Austro-Hungarian Empire altogether. Parts of its territory were given to Italy, Roumania, and Poland, others formed the new republics of Czechoslovakia and Jugoslavia. Austria was separated from Hungary and was not allowed to unite with Germany, even though both nations desired it. Bulgaria gave up territory to Roumania, Serbia, and Greece. Turkey lost to Greece almost all its European possessions, except for a small region round Constantinople and the Straits leading to the Black Sea were internationalised; its dominion in Asia was confined to Asia Minor, the Italians getting a number of its islands, the British " mandates " over Mesopotamia and Palestine, and the French over Syria.

These harsh terms naturally led to further wars and civil trouble. The Greeks, who had been given the coast of Smyrna, invaded Turkish territory, only to be repulsed with great slaughter and driven out of Asia Minor altogether. The newly formed Poland made war on Bolshevist Russia, seized territory in Lithuania, and suffered from financial trouble and civil war. The Italians seized the Port of Fiume, on the Adriatic, from Jugoslavia. When the Germans, helpless to refuse the peace terms, were unable to make the huge payments demanded, the French occupied their chief industrial region, the Ruhr Valley, destroying its commerce and tyrannising over its people. Wherever the peace terms had placed districts under the rule of unsympathetic states, great hardships were inflicted on their inhabitants.

* * *

From all parts of the world statesmen gathered in Paris to wrangle out terms of the Peace Treaties. The man-in-the-street was dazed and bewildered at the medley of ethical and national claims forcefully presented, and some of his uncomprehending dizziness was communicated to the principals in the piece.

PERSONALITIES OF THE PEACE CONFERENCE
From *Grandeur and Misery of Victory*.[1]
By Georges Clemenceau

I waited. At last a providential hand draws back the curtain of the somewhat vulgar golds and faded silks of the Quai d'Orsay. And here is Lloyd George, fresh and pink, coming forward with a bright, two-fisted smile, and gesticulations now and then so violent that one day President Wilson had to interpost between us with outstretched arms, saying pleasantly: "Well, well! I have never come across two such unreasonable men!" which allowed us to end the angry scene in laughter.

And here is Mr. Arthur Balfour, the most cultured, the most gracious, the most courteous of adamantine men. Mr. Bonar Law, the prince of balance, who would have been a first-class Frenchman had he not been wholly British. Lord Robert Cecil, a Christian who believes and is fain to live his belief, with a smile like a Chinese dragon to express a stubborn mind, banged, barred and bolted against arguments. Lord Milner, a brilliant intellect crowned with high culture that culminates in a discreet sentimentality. Extreme gentleness and extreme firmness. A poet in his moments. The man who, in an official report on a night journey from London to Versailles at one of our most trying moments, paused to speak of the loveliness of the moonlight and the young spring grass.

Later there comes on the scene President Woodrow Wilson, armoured in his "fourteen points," symbolised in as many pointed wisdom teeth that never let themselves be turned

[1] Published by George G. Harrap & Co., Ltd.

THE PEACE CONFERENCE

aside from their duty. Edward House, "Colonel House," a super-civilised person escaped from the wilds of Texas, who sees everything, who understands everything, and, while never doing anything but what he sees fit, knows how to gain the ear and the respect of everybody. A good American, very nearly as good a Frenchman, a sifting, pondering mind—above all, the traditional gentleman. I should be most ungrateful if I could forget the eminent services that this man, one of the best types of the true American, rendered the cause of a civilised peace. Were it only for picking out this good auxiliary, Mr. Wilson would deserve the gratitude of the friends of humanity.

Doubtless he had too much confidence in all the talky-talk and super-talky-talk of his "League of Nations." But what could he do with an assembly of talkers to whom he saw himself obliged to refuse all executive power? Excess of confidence in words can only lead to disappointments.

I must furthermore mention our excellent General Bliss, an independent mind who had well-anchored personal opinions and never budged from them. Also an admiral physician who returned an everlasting *no* to whatever he was asked, and never attempted a word of explaining. And Mr. Hoover, to-day President of the United States, who was conspicuous for the stiffness of the man whose nerves are at the end of their tether; Signor Orlando, all things to all men, very Italian, seconded by Baron Sonnino, possessed of a formidable irony, who never let go once he had got his teeth in anything; M. Hymans, a Belgian, politely incisive.

And then comes one of the best of them all, Benes, the man of resuscitated Czecho-Slovakia, who won general esteem and confidence by the high rectitude of his speech and by his lofty intellect. Venizelos, the veritable son of Ulysses and Calypso, imbued, as was meet and proper, with ancient Hellenic guile. Paderewski, great harmonious soul, making his overflowing heart sing his dream. And there are many others whom I ought to name, not to mention the ineffable group of malcontents—Robert Lansing, Keynes, etc.

How many more as well—Wellington Koo, like a young Chinese cat, Parisian of speech and dress, absorbed in the pleasure of patting and pawing the mouse, even if it was reserved for the Japanese. His inexhaustible flow of eloquence used to irritate Baron Matsui, a massive chunk of Japanese mentality, who spoke little, but did not shrink from speaking out. Amiable Prince Saionji, impetuous once, to-day quietly ironical, an old comrade of mine at the lectures of our law professor, Emile Accolas. Count Makino, understanding and reserved.

In the first rank I ought to have placed Mr. Hughes, the noble delegate from Australia, with whom we had to talk through an electrophone, getting in return symphonies of good sense. Doherty, the delegate from Canada, good-looking, but with an expression of limited intelligence. The delegate from New Zealand, Massey, who takes his place in the first rank for the loftiness of his sentiments and the eloquent kindliness of his broad speech. It was a stock joke to ask him how old he was when he gave up being a cannibal, to which he would answer: " Anyway, I had mine cooked, but you eat yours raw." Smuts of South Africa, with his forced smile, who made the mistake of leaving papers about in which he vented his spleen against the French. And then, flitting round this nosegay of minds in flower, those constellations of faces for consultation, which lit up and died down at the questions of those who had brought them there to endow them with omniscience.

Then, moving about in the heart of this crowd with an amiable smile, the real master of ceremonies, Maurice Hankey, secretary of the British delegation, dragging along after him a huge leather satchel, overflowing with papers. His superior qualities of order, of loyalty, and of impeccable discipline conferred upon him the function, if not the title, of universal keeper of the documentation of the Treaty. At anyone's demand the great leather bag was brought forward, and the papers required were instantly produced.

. . . . . .

To be quite candid, there was no serious opposition to the harshest clauses of the Armistice except among our British allies, who were applying themselves heartily to the task of

THE PEACE CONFERENCE

sparing Germany—fearing nothing so much as that the balance of power might too markedly swing over to the advantages of her " ally," France. In his book, *The World Crisis*, Mr. Winston Churchill, who is very far from being our enemy, relates how he dined with Mr. Lloyd George on the evening of the Armistice, and how the conversation turned on the sole topic of the best way of helping Germany. At such a moment perhaps it might have been more natural to think first and foremost of succouring France, so cruelly ravaged by the German soldiers.

On my return from India, as I was passing through London on my way to Oxford to receive an honorary degree, Mr. Lloyd George asked me to come and see him at the House of Commons. His first words were to ask me if I had anything to say to him.

" Yes, indeed ! " I replied. " I have to tell you that from the very day after the Armistice I found you an enemy to France."

" Well," he rejoined, "*was it not always our traditional policy?*"

In conformity with this view, Mr. Lloyd George and Field-Marshal Sir Douglas Haig had sought to mitigate the terms imposed on Germany. But throughout all discussions the French point of view was upheld. It was upon just this divergence of views that the Germans had speculated when they declared war on us. But they grossly miscalculated the British mentality when they had actually believed, like the simple barbarians that they were, that, with Belgium violated, Great Britain would look on without raising a hand.

Great Britain has not ceased to be an island defended by the waves, which is why she believes herself obliged to multiply causes of dissension among the peoples of the Continent, so as to secure peace for her own conquests. This policy brought her many a day of triumph, in opposition to us.

The new men on the other side of the Channel have not yet perceived that since those days there have been many changes. They were fully aware, however, that the invasion of Belgium meant that they were directly menaced in their most vital parts by a Germany that was declaring that *her future was on the water.* They decided to save England with our assistance, at the risk of freeing France at the same time. They gallantly fulfilled their part, and we treasure up for them a gratitude they mistrust, through fear that we may make it an excuse for securing those future advantages which still haunt the dreams of some of our warlike civilians. Our fate seems to be settled, for an invading America has taken it into her head to pay us visits the aims of which are commercial, and Great Britain may yet suffer more from this than the insight of her latter-day politicians yet allow them to suppose. How many notes of interrogation attend the mere statement of the first problems of the peace !

* * *

WHILE politicians wrangled, the soldiers remembered that they were really civilians, and clamoured to return home to an England " fit for heroes to live in."

DEMOBILISATION

From *War Letters to a Wife.*[1]

By ROWLAND FEILDING

The raging desire still continues to be demobilised quickly. Nevertheless, I feel pretty sure that, for many, there will be pathetic disillusionment.

In the trenches the troops have had plenty of time for thought, and, as *Happy Days* said the other day, there has grown up in their minds a heavenly picture of an England which does not exist, and never did exist, and never will exist so long as men are human.

After all, there was a good deal to be said in favour of the old trench life. There were none of the mean haunting fears of poverty there, and the next meal—if you were alive to take it—was as certain as the rising sun. The rations were the same for the " haves " and the " have nots," and the shells fell, without favour, upon both.

[1] Published by The Medici Society, Ltd.

In a life where no money passes the ownership of money counts for nothing. Rich and poor alike stand solely upon their individual merits, without discrimination. You can have no idea, till you have tried it, how much pleasanter life is under such circumstances.

In spite—or partly perhaps because of the gloominess of the surroundings, there was an atmosphere of selflessness and a spirit of camaraderie the like of which has probably not been seen in the world before—at least on so grand a scale. Such is the influence of the shells!

The life was a curious blend of discipline and good-fellowship; wherein men were easily pleased; where there was no gossip; where even a shell when it had just missed you produced a sort of exultation;—a life in the course of which you actually got used to the taste of chloride of lime in tea.

In short, there was no humbug in the trenches, and that is why—with all their disadvantages—the better kind of men who have lived in them will look back upon them hereafter with something like affection.

* * *

Meanwhile an Allied Army of Occupation had advanced into the Rhine valley. The British contingent, stationed about Cologne and Bonn, saw for the first time the misery in Germany caused by the blockade, and few felt the anticipated thrill of victory.

THE HERO'S HOME-COMING

From *A Passionate Prodigality*.[1]

By Guy Chapman

We were melting fast. In two months we should be down to cadre strength. We should be dispersed into an unfriendly hungry world, Smith back at business, Whitehead sailing for Port Elizabeth, Gwinnell going east, Uncle in Chelsea. A commission for the employment of ex-service officers and

[1] Published by Ivor Nicholson & Watson, Ltd.

men under the leadership of Sir Henry Lucy arrived at divisional headquarters. Smith, Blake and I went to hear what they were offering. I, alone of the three, needed advice and help. An elderly bilious person attended to my questions, after he had explained pathetically that this was the first holiday he had taken for four years. " How old are you ? " he asked. " Twenty-eight ! Oh, you're far too old. I'm sorry. I can do nothing. Good morning." Disconsolately, I rejoined Smith and Blake outside. " My old sod," said Blake harshly, " told me that military distinction was a quite useless recommendation for civil life. Then I told him that I'd got a better job in London than he was ever likely to get; but that if he was going to hand out this kind of stuff to my subalterns, the sooner he cut his holiday short the better."

We stopped in the market square. It was the day of condemnation for our horses. They were to be examined by the A.D.V.S., and those which he cast were to be sold to the Belgians. Knowing the manner in which the natives treat their animals we were as angry at this as at every other scheme which a vile administration was putting into practice. Hallam met me with a gap-toothed grin more distended than ever. " It's all right, sir. She's going home. Aren't you, my beauty ? " Ginger took her congratulations coldly. She was quite aware of her value. Home too was the sentence for Polly and the quartermaster's Bob. Something had been saved.

Quartermasters' hair turned grey during these days. Each battalion was required to hand in the full equipment laid down, neither more nor less. And every battalion had in the past years jettisoned what it considered unnecessary and doubled its necessities. It came to a matter of bargaining. " Who'll take two telescopes and twenty bomb buckets for half a limber and four bill-hooks ? " asked A. " I don't want telescopes ; I'm two over establishment now. But I'll let you have a whole limber for eight Lewis gun magazines and a couple of wire-breakers," B. would reply. A spare pair of mules lay on Keeble's conscience. He decided to lose them. They were ridden out six miles at midnight and left beyond a wood, through which the abductors fled. At 5 a.m. they were braying outside the stables. The ruse was repeated. Back they came. In the end the Babes in the Wood were surrendered to the Veterinary section as two strays.

The whole of our world was crumbling. Presently we could not find a rugger fifteen; not even a soccer eleven. There were no drums to beat Retreat. Grooms, to mind the few horses we had left, became a problem, as did cooks, signallers, pioneers. Our civilisation was being torn in pieces before our eyes. England was said to be a country fit only for profiteers to live in. Many of us were growing bitter. We had no longer the desire to go back. It was an island we did not know. Isn't there a fairy tale about two countries held together by a hair, and when that broke, they fled apart? England had vanished over the horizon of the mind. I did not want to see it. In February, we were offered the opportunity of volunteering for the Army of Occupation. We debated the prospects. We were by now too fast wedged in our narrow life, and the country viewed from our rut was not propitious. Eight of us elected to go up. On March 1st, we shook hands with Smith, with Whitehead, with George Knappett, who was to take over from me, with R.S.M. Armour. They stood on the steps of the mess and grinned, English fashion. We grinned back. It was the end.

With two hundred unreleasable boys, we marched down to Charleroi and boarded the familiar horse-trucks. We journeyed all through that night, past Huy, Namur, Liege. I woke from a fogged sleep. The train was standing still. I drew back the door and peered out. There was a damp platform and the name "Herbestahl," the frontier station of Germany. Beyond, a dark, grey morning, windless with a hint of drizzle, colourless trees and hedges, and no sound but the steam from the engine. The train jerked into movement. We passed over into Germany. No trumpets sounded.

* * *

AND the peasants of France and Flanders returned to their shattered homes and blasted fields, appalled at the sight of destruction before them. But what Man had destroyed, Man could replace—and in his task he was aided by the healing hands of Nature and Time.

RECOVERY

From *The Silence of Colonel Bramble*.[1]
By ANDRÉ MAUROIS

The three friends passed slowly across the silent plains, which only a few months before had been the formidable battle-field of the Somme. As far as the eye could see, there were low, undulating hillocks covered with thick, coarse grass, groups of mutilated tree-trunks marking the place of the famous wood, and millions of poppies made these dead fields glow with a warm and coppery light. A few tenacious rose-trees, with lovely fading roses, had remained alive in this wilderness, beneath which slept the dead. Here and there posts, bearing painted notices, like those on a station platform, recalled villages unknown yesterday, but now ranking with those of Marathon or Rivoli: Contalmaison, Martinpuich, Thiepval.

"I hope," said Aurelle, looking at the innumerable little crosses, here grouped together as in cemeteries, there isolated, "that this ground will be consecrated to the dead who won it, and that this country will be kept as an immense rustic cemetery, where children may come to learn the story of heroes."

"What an idea!" said the doctor. "No doubt the graves will be respected; but they will have good crops all round them in two years' time. The land is too rich to remain widowed; look at that superb lot of cornflowers on those half-healed scars."

And truly, a little further on, some of the villages seemed, like convalescents, to be tasting the joy of life once more.

[1] Published by John Lane, The Bodley Head, Ltd.

RECOVERY

Shop windows crowded with English goods in many-coloured packets brightened up the ruined houses. As they passed through a straggling village of Spanish aspect the doctor resumed:

"Yes, this is a marvellous land. Every nation in Europe has conquered it in turn; it has defeated its conqueror every time."

"If we go a little out of the way," said Parker, "we could visit the battlefield of Crécy; it would interest me. I hope you are not annoyed with us, Aurelle, for having beaten Philippe de Valois? Your military history is too glorious for you to have any resentment for events which took place so long ago."

"My oldest resentments do not last six hundred years," said Aurelle. "Crécy was an honourably contested match; we can shake hands over it."

The chauffeur was told to turn to the west, and they arrived on the site of Crécy by the same lower road taken by Philippe's army.

"The English," said Parker, "were drawn up on the hill facing us, their right towards Crécy, their left at Vadicourt, that little village you see down there. They were about thirty thousand; there were a hundred thousand French. The latter appeared about three o'clock in the afternoon, and immediately there was a violent thunderstorm."

"I observe," said the doctor, "that the heavens thought it funny to water an offensive even in those days."

· · · · · · ·

Heavy black clouds were showing up against the brilliant sunshine: a storm was coming over the hill. By the valley of Renaud's clerks, they climbed up on to the summit and Parker looked for the tower from which Edward had watched the battle.

"I thought," he said, "that it had been made into a mill, but I don't see one on the horizon."

Aurelle, noticing a few old peasants, helped by children, cutting corn in the next field, went up to them and asked them where the tower was.

"The tower? There is no tower in these parts," one of them said, " nor mill either."

"Perhaps we are wrong," said the major. "Ask him if this is really where the battle was."

"The battle?" replied the old man. "What battle?"

And the people of Crécy turned back to their work, binding into neat sheaves the corn of this invincible land.

* * *

To-day memories are unsteady and fleeting, but the soldier of 1914–1918, returning to the scenes of combat, forgets the pastoral peace about him in poignant recollection. There is no place so provocative of thought as a battlefield.

MEMORIES

From *The Wet Flanders Plain*.[1]

By Henry Williamson

The wraith of the War, glimmering with this inner vision, bears me to the wide and shattered country of the Somme, to every broken wood and trench and sunken lane, among the broad, straggling belts of rusty wire smashed and twisted in the chalky loam, while the ruddy clouds of brick-dust hang over the shelled villages by day, and at night the eastern horizon roars and bubbles with light.

And everywhere in these desolate places I see the faces and figures of enslaved men, the marching columns pearl-hued with chalky dust on the sweat of their heavy drab clothes; the files of carrying parties laden and staggering in the flickering moonlight of gun-fire; the "waves" of assaulting troops lying silent and pale on the tape-lines of the jumping-off places.

Again I crouch with them while the steel glacier rushing by just overhead scrapes away every syllable, every fragment of a message bawled into my ear; while my mind begins to stare fixedly into the bitter dark of imminent death, and my limbs tremble and stiffen as in an icicle; while the gaping, smoking

[1] Published by Faber and Faber, Ltd.

parapet above the rim of my helmet spurts and lashes with machine-gun bullets.

Until, in the flame and the rolling smoke, I see men arising and walking forward; and I go forward with them, in a glassy delirium wherein some seem to pause, with bowed heads, and sink carefully to their knees, and roll slowly over, and lie still. Others roll and roll, and scream and grip my legs in uttermost fear, and I have to struggle to break away, while the dust and earth on my tunic changes from grey to red.

And I go on with aching feet, up and down across ground like a huge ruined honeycomb, and my wave melts away, and the second wave comes up, and also melts away, and then the third wave merges into the ruins of the first and second, and after a while the fourth blunders into the remnants of the others, and we begin to run forward to catch up with the barrage, gasping and sweating, in bunches, anyhow, every bit of the months of drill and rehearsal forgotten, for who could have imagined that the "Big Push" was going to be this?

We come to wire that is uncut, and beyond we see grey coal-scuttle helmets bobbing about, and the vapour of overheated machine-guns wafting away in the fountainous black smoke of howitzer shells; and the loud crackling of machine-guns changes to a screeching as of steam being blown off by a hundred engines; and soon no one is left standing.

An hour later our guns are "back on the first objective," and the brigade, with all its hopes and beliefs, has found its grave on those northern slopes of the Somme Battlefield.

A year drifts by, and I am standing on a duck-board by a flooded and foul beke in the Salient, listening in the flare-pallid rainy darkness to the cries of tens of thousands of wounded men lost in morasses of Third Ypres. To seek them is to drown with them . . . the living are still toiling on, homeless and without horizons, doing dreadful things under heaven that none want to do, through the long, wet days and the longer nights, the weeks, the months, of a bare, sodden winter out of doors.

The survivors are worn out; some of them, tested beyond

human dereliction, put the muzzles of their rifles in their mouths, in the darkness of the terrible nights of the Passchendaele morasses, and pull the trigger.

Those at home, sitting in arm-chairs and talking proudly of Patriotism and Heroism, will never realise the bitter contempt and scorn the soldiers have for these and other abstractions; the soldiers feel they have been betrayed by the high-sounding phrases that heralded the War, for they know that the enemy soldiers are the same men as themselves, suffering and disillusioned in exactly the same way.

And in the stupendous roar and light-blast of the final barrage that broke the Hindenburg Line I see only one thing, which grows radiant before my eyes until it fills all my world: the sight of a Saxon boy half crushed under a shattered tank, moaning, " Mutter, Mutter, Mutter," out of ghastly grey lips. A British soldier, wounded in the leg, and sitting nearby, hears the words, and dragging himself to the dying boy, takes his cold hand and says: " All right, son, it's all right. Mother's here with you."

The bells cease, and the power goes from me, and I descend again to the world of the living; and if in some foolish confiding moment I try to explain why I want to re-live those old days, to tear the Truth out of the past so that all men shall see plainly, perhaps someone will say to me, " Oh, the War! A tragedy—best forgotten. No use dragging in the skeleton of the feast!" or, " There always will be war: it's deep in human nature." They may say as a friendly hint, " Don't talk about the War before my boy, old chap, if you don't mind I don't want him unsettled: you know what youngsters are—very impressionable. And after all there is such a thing as loyalty to one's country, you know."

Sometimes it seems even more hopeless, as when I hear a few hundred school-children, marched to the local picture palace for patriotic purposes, cheering and booing at a film which only faintly suggests reality, called " The Somme," frantically cheering the " British heroes " in their immaculate uniforms, and booing the " German cowards " who always seem to be hurrying away from the heroic British (O wraiths of the 18th Division at Thiepval!). They booed even when one poor lad in grey, who went forth to fetch water for a dying comrade, was knocked over by a shell.

The children, I know, are but mirrors of the mental attitudes of their parents, of their school and religious teachers, but surely, after the bitter waste and agony of the Lost Generation, it is time that these people should begin to know " what they do."

* * *

THE COST OF ARMAGEDDON

From *The World's Almanac* for 1933

In dead soldiers (of all nations)	9,998,771
Seriously wounded	6,295,512
Otherwise wounded	14,002,039
Prisoners and missing	5,983,600
Civilian refugees, victims of pogroms and massacres	Not counted
Total direct costs, net	£38,340,254,547
Capitalised value of human life:	
Soldiers	£6,903,554,790
Civilians	£6,903,554,790
Property losses:	
On land	£6,164,609,053
Shipping and cargo	£1,399,176,955
Loss of production	£9,259,259,259
War relief	£205,761,317
Loss to neutrals	£360,082,305
Total indirect costs	£31,195,998,469
Grand total	£69,536,253,016

Indeed a " grand " total!

* * *

TWENTY YEARS AFTER

From *The Yarn of a Yeoman*.[1]

By S. F. Hatton

Has anyone noticed the most pathetic sight in London? I will tell you what it is. Go on a bright spring morning and watch that glorious military spectacle of pomp and splendour the Changing of the Guard. Outside the Palace Square you will see visitors from all nations, French and Belgian officers thrilled with the "snap" and precision of our crack corps; clear-skinned, bright-eyed American girls laughing and joking of "Pop" and "Mama" with square-shouldered Cyruses and Hirams; swarthy Indian and Persian students gazing stolidly through the railings with that impassivity so characteristic of the Oriental; and best sight of all, fine, bonny, curly-haired young babies, with the steel-blue eyes and the flaxen locks of the real Saxon, held high on their nurses' shoulders as they clap their hands in rhythm to the music and chuckle with delight at the sight of the "Solgers."

But you have missed someone. Look again. There, on the fringe of the crowd, is a pale, white face, lined with worry and pinched with want. A shabby cap or greasy bowler half shields his dull hopeless eyes that glance furtively around as if half-apologising for their presence "in such a goodly company." A threadbare suit with ragged sleeves and trouser-legs completes the picture. The air is chilly yet he boasts no great-coat, but has his muffler wrapped high around his neck; you would scarcely notice that he wears no collar.

Now that you look more closely at the crowd about you, you see many just such another, and you wonder, perchance, what fascination that picturesque ceremony can have for such a "poor fellow," thin, weedy and wan. Has he no work to do that he can thus idle away his time on the precious hours of this perfect morning, even as you are doing? If he has not, he should be off looking for it. But wait, his moment is to come. The ceremony is over and with slow step the band

[1] Published by Hutchinson & Co. (Publishers), Ltd.

leading the Old Guard marches out of the Palace gates. A few more paces, and " rah, rah, rah " on the drums, the band breaks into quick step and to the tune of " Colonel Bogey " off goes the Guard on the march back to the barracks. As you stand to watch the departing troops—why, bless my heart and soul, look at that " little fellow " you noticed just now—there he goes down the broad walk with dozens of his brothers around him. Did you see him square his shoulders, fling back his head; did you see that back straighten up and that step become more firm? Why, even his arms are swinging now with something of a swagger—well up to the front and back to the rear. There he goes, his eyes are no longer dull, but hold a light of joy as for a brief moment he unconsciously throws himself back to the past, when he, too, wore the King's uniform and was the honoured servant of the nation. And as he marches he feels around him a little of the old spirit of comradeship and cheerful endeavour of those thousands of " good fellows " who lie in foreign fields, and who went to their death with a song and a jest, that you and I—and he—might live in freedom, peace and happiness in " England's green and pleasant land."

He asked you for bread, but you gave him a stone.

LIST OF AUTHORS

Aldington, Richard, 253, 345
Alverdes, Paul, 317
Austin, F. Britten, 200

Barbusse, Henri, 100
Beaverbrook, Rt. Hon. Lord, 178
Benedict XV, His Holiness Pope, 139
Benstead, Charles R., 349
Binding, Rudolf, 245, 265, 360
Black, Donald, 287, 300
Blaker, Richard, 189, 193
Bluett, Anthony, 412
Blunden, Edmund, 227
Borden, Mary, 335
Botcharsky, Sophie, 131
Brandenfels, Freiherr Treusch von Buttlar, 81
Brussilov, Gen. A. A., 62, 260
Bugnet, Commander, 206, 369
Burrage, A. M., 247, 292

Campbell, Rear-Admiral Gordon, V.C., D.S.O., 329
Carossa, Hans, 218, 231
Carr, William Guy, 324
Carstairs, Carroll, 99, 270, 404
Chapman, Guy, 441
Charteris, Brig.-Gen. John, 371
Churchill, Rt. Hon. Winston S., C.H., M.P., 40, 50, 177, 199, 209
Clapham, H. S., 88
Clemenceau, Georges, 436
Cohen-Portheim, Paul, 307
Corday, Michel, 378
Crile, George W., 33
Crozier, Brig.-Gen. F. P., C.B., C.M.G., D.S.O., 303

Dorling, Capt. Taprell, D.S.O., R.N., 67
Doyle, Arthur Conan, 64
Dunsany, Lord, 250
Durnford, Hugh, 310

Edmonds, Charles, 275
" Etienne," 328, 333
Evans, A. J., 311
Evans, I. O., 381, 434
Ewart, Wilfrid, 59
" Ex-Private X," 247, 292

Falkenhayn, Gen. Erich von, 145
Feilding, Rowland, 219, 359, 440
Foch, Marshal, 425
Frankau, Gilbert, 96, 108

Gibbs, Sir Philip, 206
Gordon, Jan and Cora, 127
Gough, Gen. Sir Hubert, G.C.M.G., K.C.B., K.C.V.O., etc., 268, 341
Graham, John W., M.A., 240
Graham, Stephen, 21, 237, 362
Graves, Robert, 92, 104
Griffith, Ll. Wyn, 141, 182
Grinnell-Milne, Duncan, 55, 315

Hanbury-Sparrow, Lt.-Col. A. A., 272
Hankey, Donald, 36, 45
Harrison, Charles Yale, 353
Hatton, S. F., 450
Hay, Ian, 37, 58
Hemingway, Ernest, 170
Herbert, A. P., 75, 301

LIST OF AUTHORS

Hislam, Percival, 367
Hodson, James Lansdale, 214, 299
Hutton, Dr. I. Emslie, 129, 318

Johnston, Sir Harry, 118

King-Hall, Commander Stephen, 328, 333
Köppen, Edlef, 375, 393
Krupskaya, Nadezhda, K., 257

Lettow-Vorbeck, Gen. von, 338
Liddell Hart, B. H., 420
Ludendorff, Gen., 396

MacGill, Patrick, 216, 262
McKenna, Marthe, 28
Mackenzie, Compton, 77
MacMillan, Capt. Norman, M.C., A.F.C., 279
Manning, F., 185
Markovits, Rodion, 164
Masefield, John, 70, 80
Massey, W. T., 284
Maurois, Andre, 444
Mitchell, F., M.C., 357
Montague, C. E., 234
Morgan, J. H., 106
Morse, John, 52
Mottram, R. H., 136

Newbolt, Sir Henry, 321
Newman, Bernard, 406
Nicolai, Col. W., 110, 256
Northcliffe, Lord, 94

O'Duffy, Eimar, 157
Osburn, Arthur, 29, 304

Pankhurst, E. Sylvia, 86
Peel, Mrs. C. S., O.B.E., 84
Pétain, Marshal, 148, 151
Pier, Florida, 131
Plivier, Theodor, 390, 416

Pocock, Roger, 242
Ponsonby, Rt. Hon. Arthur, 39, 289
"Private 19022," 185

Raymond, Ernest, 72
Reed, John, 134
Remarque, Erich Maria, 168, 249
Renn, Ludwig, 24
Richards, Private Frank, 125
Rogerson, Sidney, 192, 226

"Saml. Pepys, Junr.," 400
Sassoon, Siegfried, 386
Scanlon, William T., 392, 410
Severn, Mark, 143
Sinclair, Upton, 364, 376
Sleath, Frederick, 196

"Taffrail," 67
Thomson, Basil, 112
Tilsley, W. V., 221
Tomlinson, H. M., 42, 203
Tuohy, Ferdinand, 121, 295, 428

Watson, Capt. W. H. L., 47, 281
Wells, H. G., 65, 123
Williamson, Henry, 212, 446
Wilson, President, 432

Yeats-Brown, Francis, 154

Zweig, Arnold, 114

Commanding Officer of H.M.S. *Ardent*, 175

Company Sergeant Major ——, M.C., 382

"The Diary of an Unknown Aviator," 379

Navigating Officer of H.M.S. *Broke*, 173

World's Almanac, 1933, 449